THE
CONTINUING
BATTLE

THE
CONTINUING
BATTLE

MEMOIRS OF A EUROPEAN   1936–1966

PAUL-HENRI SPAAK

TRANSLATED FROM THE FRENCH BY HENRY FOX

LITTLE, BROWN AND COMPANY · BOSTON · TORONTO

This is a version, slightly abridged by the author, of the work which first
appeared in French under the title *Combats Inachevés*.

The translation was begun by Ray Steding, whose death prevented him
from completing more than a quarter of the work.

Contents

PART ONE

The Policy of Independence
1936–40

I Become Foreign Minister

On 13 June 1936 I became Foreign Minister, somewhat surprised and a little afraid of my new responsibilities. I knew the extent both of my task and my ignorance and I have to admit that I knew little about the problems with which I would have to deal. I had not met any of my foreign colleagues and even most of my own diplomats were strangers to me. There was thus a danger that I might be very isolated in my post. Luckily, I could rely on the support of two outstanding aides at the Ministry – M. van Langenhove, the Secretary-General, and Baron van Zuylen, the Head of the Political Department.

During my first conversations with them I was amazed to find my advisers rather ill-disposed towards France, for I had arrived at the Ministry with all the solemn declarations of the past still ringing in my ears. I was convinced that France was our greatest friend and Paris our wisest counsellor. It was several years before I came to understand the attitude of my colleagues, if not to share it completely.

The intellect of the French can be powerful. Their logic can transform an international meeting and their language is unsurpassed as a vehicle for argument. However, the French are so often apt to be haughty and disdainful in their conduct of diplomacy. Due to their self-confidence, they are less than tolerant of their partners who lack their own elegant facility. I have known foreign ministers of France who could be the kindest, most charming and understanding of men: Delbos, Blum, Pinay and Robert Schuman, to name but a few, were admirable colleagues. But there were others who were condescending, absolutely convinced as they were that the representative of a small country – or a great one for that matter – could not possibly have the wisdom or experience of the spokesman for France, the head of the Quai d' Orsay.

The Quai is a great institution. I have known many worthy French diplomats, and the best of them were sometimes the most difficult. But one thing is certain: it is easier to get a sympathetic hearing at the British Foreign Office (and even more so at the American State Department) than at the Quai d'Orsay. At the Foreign Office you are more likely to be given a friendly reception and not be left with the impression that you are merely being tolerated. I remember Bech, for so long the Premier and Foreign Minister of Luxembourg, saying to me in Geneva when I was just a novice: 'To be well thought of in Paris one must love France and France alone.' I have always loved France, and I still do. But I confess that I have loved other countries as well. Sometimes I have had the impression that this is the one thing the Quai d'Orsay cannot forgive.

The mistrust between Belgium and France stems from soon after the First World War. Clemenceau had little time for Hymans, the Belgian Foreign Minister, and behaved most unfairly towards him during the preliminary discussions on the Versailles Treaty. France gave no support to Belgium's claims, and King Albert had to make a dramatic trip to Paris to uphold her interests. Whether or not these Belgian claims were reasonable I do not know, but our negotiators believed they could count on support from Paris. Those involved realized how greatly our hopes had been thwarted.

I am generally considered to be the minister responsible for the so-called 'independent line' that Belgium followed in international affairs between 1936 and 1940. Many people think this policy differed fundamentally from the line the country had previously followed. This is not so. Obviously, as Foreign Minister for most of this period, I can hardly deny my responsibility for this policy, and indeed why should I do so? It is true that the policy failed: it did not save Belgium from war. However, I still believe it was the only possible course. It was the only way to maintain national unity and ensure the country's survival. I have read many books on the last war and am more than ever convinced that if Belgium had pursued a different policy, if for example she had ranged herself alongside France and Britain from the start of hostilities, the course of events would not have been fundamentally different. Belgian leaders would, however, have had to account for their decision. There can be no doubt we would have been beaten in the first phase of the war, just as we were in May 1940. We would have borne a very heavy responsibility and, justifiably, our countrymen would never have forgiven us. It was our right and our duty to try in every honest way to save Belgium the terrible ordeal of a war that would at best mean the destruction of our little country, and at worst – and this is in fact what happened – its destruction and its occupation. We knew from experience what dangers occupation might mean for a country like Belgium. Not to try in every way to avoid this peril would have been inexcusable.

Historically, I think it is clear that the policy of non-alignment that I spelled out in 1936 did not represent a fundamental change in Belgian policy. My original contribution was to express with force and realism ideas outlined by my predecessors. It is perhaps also to my credit that I drew the logical conclusions from my ideas and acted accordingly.

The Franco-British Declaration of 23 April 1937

To give our theoretical position concrete shape, we clearly required fresh guarantees of respect for our neutrality from France and Britain, and of course, also from Germany. We were convinced that Belgium's independence was in the best interests of all concerned and it was therefore our aim to seek such guarantees. To safeguard our independence the more effectively we were resolved to refrain from any commitment to third parties.

A series of protracted negotiations began, lasting several months. There would be no point in trying to recall all the ups and downs of these talks. However, on 23 April 1937 a joint Franco-British note was presented in Brussels in the form of a unilateral declaration. The two governments began by noting that the provisions of the Locarno Treaty were no longer effectively in force and went on to say that pending the conclusion of a new general agreement it would be right to meet certain Belgian requests and, more especially – in view of Belgium's geographical position – to define that country's international status more precisely. The two governments took note of the Belgian Government's express intentions, in particular:

1 That it was Belgium's resolve, repeatedly and publicly affirmed:
   a to defend, by all the means at its disposal, the country's frontiers against any attempt at aggression or invasion and to prevent Belgian territory being used with a view to an aggression against another state, as a corridor or as a base for military operations by land, sea or air;
   b to organize, in an effective manner, Belgium's defences to this end;

2 That Belgium had reaffirmed both its loyalty to the League of Nations Treaty and its desire to meet its obligations under that Treaty.

'Taking note of the above intentions and assurances, the Governments of the French Republic and the United Kingdom therefore:

'Declare that they consider Belgium to be henceforth free of all its obligations in regard to the above two Powers resulting for that Power from the Treaty of Locarno and the arrangements agreed in London on 19 March 1936;

'And declare, moreover, that they are willing to honour the pledges of aid to Belgium implicit in the above instruments.'

This declaration was an undeniable diplomatic success. Our views had thus been officially accepted by our best friends. I was able sincerely to thank my colleagues who had advised me so ably, and expressed my satisfaction in a speech in Parliament.

So far as I can recollect, at the time no one dissented from this view of the Anglo-French declaration. Nevertheless, it contained a sentence which subsequently gave rise to a grave difference of views between the King and his Government.

To be more exact, the statement took note of our resolve to defend our frontiers, but it also said that we had pledged ourselves to 'prevent Belgian territory being used with a view to an aggression against another state, as a corridor or as a base for military operations by land, sea or air'.

When, on 28 May 1940, it became clear that the Belgian Army, with its back to the sea, was unable to carry on the struggle and had no choice but to surrender, the King took the view that we had honoured our pledge, fulfilled all our obligations and were now free to cease hostilities. The Government, on the other hand, believed that it was essential if we were to implement our obligations, to prevent our occupied territory from being used as a base for possible attacks against France and Britain and that it was therefore necessary to continue the struggle from abroad and to mobilize such resources as remained at our disposal.

France and Britain had made their views clear to us; what was now needed was a statement from Germany. This was essential in order to maintain the necessary balance in our foreign policy however much we might doubt the value of any promise given by Hitler.

I made no secret of my intention to seek such German assurances. This is what I said to the House: 'The Government knows full well that it will only have implemented its task fully when agreement has been reached on a formula to which Germany feels able to subscribe.'

We were greatly helped in this task by the Belgian Ambassador in Berlin, Vicomte Davignon, a highly competent, astute and well informed diplomat. The ambassador, who was wholly in favour of our policy, loyally carried out his instructions and thus contributed greatly to the success of our negotiations.

On 13 October 1937, Germany, in her turn, made a unilateral declaration. After a preamble which expressed very much the same views as the Franco-British statement, Baron von Neurath, on behalf of the German Government, went on to say:

> 'The Reich Government declares that the inviolability and integrity of Belgium are of benefit to all the Western Powers. It therefore reaffirms its resolve on no account to infringe this inviolability and integrity and to respect Belgium's territory except – it goes without saying – in the event of Belgium assisting a military action directed against Germany in an armed conflict in which the latter might be involved.'

I took note of this declaration and considered that I had completed this part of my task. Everything humanly possible had been done to improve Belgium's chances of avoiding being dragged into a war in which her own interests were not directly involved.

The following year, in my capacity as Premier, I made it my business to persuade Parliament to vote a large sum of money to strengthen our country's defences. In view of this twin effort – diplomatic and military – which we then accomplished, I feel entitled to claim that I did everything possible at that time to safeguard Belgium's security. It was beyond my powers to prevent the events which were soon to shake Europe and the world.

The final months of 1937 and the year 1938 were a very busy time for me. On 15 May 1938 I became Premier and remained in office until 9 February 1939, when I was overthrown. At no time was our foreign policy called into question.

I was out of office for eight [*sic:* H. F.] months, but the day Germany attacked Poland a Government of National Union was formed, with M. Pierlot as Premier. I was reappointed Foreign Minister. It seemed only natural that in the hard times that lay ahead, when our policy of in-dependence was bound to be put to a hard test, I should assume responsibility for the conduct of our foreign affairs. One of the most stirring chapters of my political career was about to begin. No doubt I made more than one mistake during that time, and the fact that I was lucky enough to avoid even grosser blunders was due more to luck than to judgement.

I shall try to describe these developments without mincing words, exactly as they happened or, at least, as I saw them. And why, in fact, having come through the test with honour, should I not do so? I shall try to be as objective as one can be in giving an account of a tragic time, a time one needs to have experienced at first hand if one is to appreciate the circumstances which governed the actions of those involved.

3

A King and a Premier

If the events that I shall now describe are to be understood, I must say something about two men who helped to shape them: Hubert Pierlot, the Premier, and King Leopold III.

As I write, I have before me a very fine portrait of Pierlot. The artist has captured all the melancholy and reserved nature of his subject, a man who was serious to the point of severity and honest almost to a fault. He was a tireless worker, a devout Christian and an exemplary public servant, devoted to his family and his country. He was a fine man, but he was never popular. Indeed, he never tried to be. In our political circles, people used to say jocularly: 'I would rather have a favour refused by Broqueville than have it granted by Pierlot.' Pierlot may not have known the fleeting pleasures a politician may derive from the fickle support of the mass. On the other hand, he did experience that rarer satisfaction of being loved and respected by his collaborators, by those who knew his work at first hand and knew what was in his mind. His faults: first, too great a love of detail. He was profoundly shocked when I once said that of any one hundred decisions, ninety-five were unimportant and should be taken quickly so as to give one time to concentrate on the important ones. He replied that we should pay as much attention to little things as to big ones. Moreover, some people found him lacking in warmth, especially those who preferred a ready handshake and an easy compliment to a sincere expression of esteem. Finally, there was a certain inflexibility in his way of thinking that made compromise difficult. During a discussion I would often try to bring together different points of view, emphasizing what each speaker had in common. He, on the other hand, would seek out any divergencies with an obstinacy I found obsessive. He was determined we should understand each other completely and that no possible doubts should persist after a meeting.

For a man who loved order, he was thrown into a most unlikely adventure, in which he was forced to take sides against his King and to do things he found hateful. He did them without complaint, but not without suffering; he did them with the sole intention of carrying out what he believed was his duty as a citizen, a parliamentarian and a premier. It was this sense of duty that always guided him. The more difficult this duty was and the more he was driven to go against his inclinations, the more he devoted himself to the task. His determination was all the more striking for being silent.

It is for historians to recognize and praise such qualities. The contemporaries of such an exceptional man cannot judge him fairly. Pierlot has had more than his share of injustice and ingratitude. After the war he was rejected by his political allies, who had forgotten his great services to his country. His own kind turned against him full of hatred when honesty compelled him to tell the truth about the events of 1940. I lived through historic hours at his side. With him I undertook the heaviest responsibilities. His presence alone was a source of comfort, a reassuring element of certainty. At his side I may have made mistakes, but I am sure I can have done nothing to trouble the most sensitive of consciences.

Pierlot was a Catholic, a conservative, a monarchist by tradition. I was an agnostic, a socialist and a monarchist for reasons of common-sense. We understood one another, listened to one another and relied on one another. In all we endured together, my affectionate respect for him never failed even for a moment. Would another man have been a better wartime leader, would he perhaps even have avoided the conflict with the King? I think not. Relations between the two men were certainly not easy. It was a meeting of two strong wills; Pierlot's respectful deference was sometimes little more than icy. When a question of principle was involved he would concede nothing. His advice was frequently given without consideration for the man to whom it was addressed. But this was only an error of style and not fundamental. What was fundamental, as will be seen, was our sudden discovery during the war that two policies existed where we had thought there was just one, two conflicting notions of duty that could not be reconciled. It is my belief that if Belgium's Premier had been less intransigent, the conflict with the King in 1940 might well have been avoided. In 1945, however, our country would not have found itself in the camp of the victors. The credit for this must go principally to Pierlot.

I have no qualms about how future generations will see him. Historians will tell about his country's debt to him, and their tributes will be all the more fulsome because his contemporaries understood him so little. I never had any lasting difference with Pierlot, and have never had to revise my opinion of him.

King Leopold is, of course, a rather different case. My feelings towards him have varied. At the beginning of my career as a minister I liked him sincerely; I was as devoted to him as a minister can possibly be to his King. I was in sympathy with him in his official position, but I also appreciated how lonely he was as a man. When events came between us I was very upset. It was a terrible political ordeal for me, and a source of personal sadness.

The King was a hard-working and thoughtful man. He took an active interest in foreign affairs and played an undeniable part in shaping Belgium's independent policy; to some extent he even helped to put it into practice. He frequently wrote to me offering suggestions, and we met often. Our conversations were friendly and wide-ranging. We shared the same hopes, the same desire to avoid war. We were, significantly, of the same generation, and almost the same age. This made dealings with him easier for me than for some of his older ministers. Whenever I reported to the King on some important question he would listen attentively, but never reacted immediately. He would always ask me to come back the next day or the day after. This would have been fine had it not been for his advisers. I think it is here Leopold made his greatest mistake.

Under our Constitution it is the ministers who are the King's advisers. It is in them he is meant to confide, with them that he is meant to discuss any problems that arise. If he goes elsewhere for his advice, to unknown men accountable to nobody, then the whole regime is compromised. This, in fact, is what happened.

Even before the war I sometimes had the impression, despite the confidence the King reposed in me, that I was not the only person to discuss certain matters with him. I sometimes felt others – men I did not know – had intervened and advised him what to say to me. I now know that this was so. General van Overstraeten's memoirs are very revealing in this respect. It seems that de Man, my former Socialist colleague, played a role that nothing could justify as the King's adviser in the crucial days before the Army's surrender, and that Count Capelle also made more of his position as counsellor to the King than was legitimate.

It is hard to be a king. Relations between a monarch and those one must call his subjects are damned from the start. Even in a democracy like Belgium's, the King is treated with a deference that is bound to affect his judgement unless he is a man who understands his fellows well and who also has something of a sense of humour. The dangers become even greater if he accepts as personal the tokens of respect addressed to the office itself. These unnatural relationships tend to foster a distinctive ambience around the King. He is surrounded by people who serve him and are close to him in his day-to-day life. It is easy for them to acquire a hold on him, and if he is careless cliques will quickly form. He must keep clear of intrigue and squabbles.

A king's adviser must have great qualities, among them good judgement, a total lack of personal ambition and complete objectivity. Leopold I, Leopold II and King Albert had excellent advisers. Leopold III did not. Count Capelle was more of a courtier than an adviser. General van Overstraeten, although a most intelligent man, was too bound up in himself, too convinced of his own worth and judgement, and too contemptuous of other people's. His whole training made it difficult for him to appreciate certain problems. As for de Man, when he made a mistake it was a bad one, and he was all the more dangerous because his arguments were forcefully expressed and his intellectual brilliance beyond question. How tragic it was that in 1940 the King did not choose to follow the advice of his ministers! He would then have returned in 1945 in triumph, like the

Queen of the Netherlands, the King of Norway and the Grand Duchess of Luxembourg. He would have been able to arbitrate between the parties and to have acted as an elder statesman whose advice was valued.

In surrendering, the King's intentions were good. He had Belgium's interests at heart and thought that in this way they would be protected. He was the victim of the article in our Constitution that made him Commander-in-Chief of our armed forces. Surrounded and advised by soldiers, he could not understand that his function as Head of State took precedence over that of Supreme Commander. He could not see that the fight had to go on, that because we were beaten in Belgium we would not have to abandon the struggle everywhere. He could not appreciate that, having appealed to France and Britain for protection, we could not abandon them before the war was over. We tried to break down his obstinacy, but he was a stubborn man. Even when events had proved him wrong he persisted in his mistakes. A little flexibility would have been his salvation. One reason for his obstinacy was his conviction that he could see things more clearly than his ministers, and that he could see further. He believed that while he represented continuity and spoke for the future, we politicians, embroiled in our petty wrangles, were incapable of appreciating the real interests of the country. This sense of superiority prompted him to reject our advice. The fact that Catholic, Liberal and Socialist ministers were unanimous in their views was not enough to make him budge. Standing alone against us he felt himself every inch a king.

But are these traits of character enough in themselves to explain what happened? I think there was another, more decisive, influence on Leopold's behaviour – the teaching of his father, one might almost say his father's example. The real story of King Albert's part in the First World War has yet to be told. For the full details we must wait for the personal papers of Count de Brocqueville to be published. But from what we now know it seems certain that if King Albert had found himself in the same position as his son, he would have reacted in like fashion.

4

The Phoney War

The first eight months of the war were eventful for us Belgians. Circumstances changed so fast that our nerves were continually on edge, and time and again we were faced with the most difficult decisions. Having proclaimed our neutrality, we intended to observe it meticulously in order not to offer Germany any pretext. I say Germany, because it was obviously Germany we feared. That was where the danger lay.

The Government had to be discreet, particularly as the public, while wanting peace, made no secret of their sympathies. Press comment on the war caused us much worry. Our Ambassador in Berlin was warning us continually to be on our guard. The situation resulted in friction between successive governments and certain sections of the population, but this diminished as the situation became more alarming and our country appeared increasingly threatened by war. The added danger made us appreciate the need for caution. On two occasions between 1 September 1939 and 10 May 1940 we thought Germany was about to invade. Each time we were warned by our Ambassador in Berlin, who had been informed by his Military Attaché, Colonel Goethals. The colonel was in close contact with his Dutch counterpart, who got *his* information from the most reliable of sources, a high-ranking assistant to Admiral Canaris. This may sound difficult to believe, but it is nevertheless true. It seems utterly incredible that the intelligence services of Hitler's Germany, that most abominable of police states, should be run by people who gave information to the enemy. Whatever administrative inefficiencies one might find in a democracy, nothing like this has ever been seen. For several months this one man, known to us at the Foreign Ministry as 'Sheep', kept the Dutch and ourselves regularly informed about the plans being made to invade our countries.

At the beginning of November he passed on some disturbing information to the Dutch Government. Queen Wilhelmina wrote to King Leopold asking him to join her in an attempt to 'prevent, or at least make more difficult, certain evil schemes' by addressing to the Chancellor of the Reich, the King of England and the President of France a message tendering the good offices of the Netherlands and Belgium in any negotiations. I had no faith in this move. I could see it would be useless, even dangerous. We would be doing something for which we were totally unprepared. The King thought differently. In his memoirs, General van Overstraeten reports that Leopold said to him: 'It seems inconceivable to me that we should not associate ourselves with a Dutch initiative. If we do not make common cause with the Netherlands we shall be destroyed one by one. This is a matter between sovereigns. I see no reason why we should not go to The Hague to discuss it with the Queen.'

'A matter between soverigns.' If I had realized that this was how Leopold saw the meeting I would have had an inkling of his future policies.

I gave way to the King's arguments and his wishes. I set out with him and General van Overstraeten for The Hague. The short trip left me sad and anxious. I well remember my pessimistic discussions with my Dutch counterpart, van Kleffens.

The two sovereigns and the two ministers finally agreed on the wording of an appeal to the belligerents. General van Overstraeten has since claimed that the final version was largely his own. He alleges that he and the King amended the version van Kleffens and I had prepared. This I am ready to accept, the more so since, as I had foreseen, the *démarche* had absolutely no effect. Nevertheless, it was with some surprise that I learned that the King's military adviser had taken it on himself to correct my diplomatic notes.

I returned to Brussels in the early evening of 7 November. On reaching the Ministry I learned that the news was not good. The German press had unleashed a campaign against

Holland and Belgium. We knew from experience that such attempts to prepare public opinion often had sinister sequels. I decided to send for the German Ambassador at once.

Herr von Bülow-Schwante was the man who was to declare war on Belgium on behalf of Hitler's Germany. In spite of that I do not think too badly of him. In fairness, I have to admit that he never tried to deceive me. He never offered me empty assurances that his country would not attack mine. On the contrary, he gave me frequent warnings.

Later that evening he came to my office. I explained why I had gone to The Hague, and told him the gist of our public appeal to the belligerents. As a result of the information reaching us from Germany, I had earlier asked for a telephone call to our Ambassador in Berlin. When it came I left the little table at which we had been sitting and took the call at my big desk. The Vicomte Davignon reassured me at once. He told me the newspaper campaign was losing some of its earlier virulence and added: 'It will all be over by tomorrow.'

I had asked the Ambassador to remain in the room with me. When I rejoined him at our table, I told him the news Davignon had just given me. As I repeated the words: 'It will all be over by tomorrow,' the ambassador seized my arm and said, his voice thick with emotion: 'So it's tomorrow.' He had evidently misunderstood me. His spontaneous reaction, and the apparently genuine emotion which went with it, allow me to forgive him much.

But what a lesson for me! What a warning! The Ambassador clearly had no illusions about the fate in store for my country. The only thing he did not know was the exact date of the invasion.

The false alarm in January 1940 was a much more serious affair. Serious because at the beginning of that winter Hitler, I believe, had wanted to invade Holland and Belgium. Serious also because of other incidents to which it led. Our anxiety was mainly due to the news reaching us from Italy. Princess Marie-José, Count Ciano and the Papal Nuncio had warned us many times. Ciano had previously alerted us in November about the preparations that were being made to move against us. In January he was both more definite and more pessimistic. He was convinced an attack was imminent. It was in this tense situation that a German aeroplane made a forced landing in the Province of Limburg on 10 January.

There were any number of extraordinary incidents during the war. Several important decisions were based on insufficient evidence, sometimes on completely false information. Fate often plays a decisive role in history, and this case of a German airman forced to land in Belgium is an instance in point. The officer was carrying vitally important documents, in fact, the plans for the German attack in the West. For the most frivolous reasons he was late in setting out on his mission, and to make up for lost time he thought he would fly instead of going by train. He lost himself in the mist, confusing the Rhine with the Meuse, and bad weather forced him to land in Belgium. The repercussions were immense. When Hitler learned that his plans for an invasion had fallen into Belgian hands, and had doubtless been passed on to the French and the British, he abandoned them. Instead, he adopted another plan, drawn up by Guderian and Model, which he had hitherto rejected. This second plan involved crossing the Ardennes, which were reputed to be impassable for an army, and making a major onslaught on the French front at Sedan. Since the discarded plan had relied on a flanking movement through Holland and Belgium, if the German airman had not landed in Belgium the war would have developed according to the predictions of the French General Staff, with consequences that we shall never know. It seems that the pleasures and indiscretions of one man may have changed the course of history.

In his memoirs, General van Overstraeten tells us hour by hour what happened that day. Early in the evening he was told of the nature of the documents found on the German officer. The wretched man had tried to destroy them by throwing them into a stove at the guard post where he had been taken. A Belgian gendarme had retrieved them only partially burnt.

One regrettable fact emerges from the General's account. The incident led him, and unfortunately the King as well, to take a number of important steps without informing the Government. The most extraordinary of these, and the most dangerous, nearly resulted in Belgium being drawn into the war. This was the strange mission of the British Admiral Sir Roger Keyes, a personal friend of King Albert.

At the beginning of 1940 the British Government had accredited Keyes to King Leopold, a good idea in principle but one which was to have disastrous consequences. Keyes was at the King's side during the eighteen-day campaign. His activities in fact proved disastrous. I do not for a moment doubt his complete devotion to the Belgian Royal Family and I am sure he was a valiant sailor. But events were to show that he had not the slightest notion of diplomacy, nor the slightest understanding of our constitutional law. His deference to the King and his naval background made him quite unable to comprehend the complexity and gravity of the political affairs in which he meddled. His actions were thoroughly clumsy and his advice odious. Loyalty alone does not qualify one to play a leading role in historic events.

In his account of what happened on 10 January, van Overstraeten reports that he informed the King of the nature of the captured documents:

'His Majesty has been informed that verbal instructions to the guaranteeing powers have been sent to our Ambassadors in Paris and London. The request for a guarantee for the security of Belgium and the Congo is still under discussion. M. Spaak has said he considers it inadvisable to raise the question, and His Majesty is thinking of recourse to the good offices of Sir Roger Keyes.'

General van Overstraeten does not think it necessary to comment further. He has nothing to say about the King's decision to entrust a British Admiral with a vitally important diplomatic mission, undertaken against the advice of his Foreign Minister, and therefore without Government approval. He finds such a procedure quite normal. It did not occur to him to warn the King either of the risk he was running or the responsibility he was taking upon himself. When I had earlier discussed with the King whether we should seek guarantees from France and Britain in the event of our being drawn into the war on their side, I advised him against making such an approach. I was sure it would be difficult to keep it secret, and it would therefore be dangerous because Hitler would be furnished with a pretext, if not a justification, for attacking Belgium. I have never understood how the King, who until then had been so cautious, could allow himself to be tempted into undertaking such a risky diplomatic manoeuvre. We now know that on 13 January the King charged Keyes with finding out what protection the British could offer Belgium. This he did entirely on his own initiative, without informing either the Prime Minister or the Foreign Minister. The instructions to the Admiral were communicated through General van Overstraeten. It seems they were never put in writing. This, too, was unwise for it inevitably led to misunderstanding.

Even today what followed is unclear. Keyes went to Arras on 13 January. From there he telephoned London and spoke not to the Prime Minister nor the Foreign Secretary, although the matter clearly concerned them both, but to Churchill, who was then First Lord of the Admiralty. We still do not know how Keyes viewed his task, or how he approached Churchill. Nor do we know how Keyes interpreted Churchill's reply, or pretended to interpret it. The fact remains that on 15 January Keyes returned to Brussels with a reply from the British Government. The Belgian Government was still completely ignorant of what was going on. The King must have read the reply with dismay. It began: 'His Majesty's Government are ready to accept the Belgian Government's invitation to the British forces to enter Belgian territory. His Majesty's Government has reason to believe the French Government are adopting the same attitude.'

The British Government had assumed that the King had decided to abandon Belgium's neutrality and, appealing for British assistance, had asked for British troops to be sent to Belgium immediately. This was a terrible shock for the King. Too late he realized how unwise he had been and what a diplomatic confusion he had unwittingly caused. On 15 January he had another conversation with Keyes. Van Overstraeten was again present, although in what capacity it is hard to see. The three actors in this extraordinary drama counted the cost of what they had done. They decided to ask Keyes himself to reply to the note from his own Government, another irregular procedure, to say the least. He set to work and produced a draft telegram containing some strange phrases: 'The King thinks it preferable to negotiate directly without involving the Government. He would consider a simple promise from the Prime Minister adequate.' This was followed by a justification of Belgian policy and of the King's conduct which was neither lucid nor well phrased.

The King and van Overstraeten thought the wording excellent. They asked the Admiral to pass this new message on to the British Government. But the complications were only just beginning. The French had been alerted by the British, and they, too, had reacted. That afternoon I received a telegram from our Ambassador in Paris. It told of a conversation he had just had with Daladier. I read with amazement:

> 'Although French intelligence does not confirm Belgian information about the immediate urgency of the situation, the French High Command has taken steps to assist Belgium. M. Daladier adds that in the circumstances the French Army cannot remain on stand-by too long and the Belgian Government should make known before 8 p.m. whether French troops should move into Belgium.'

I had no idea what it was all about, or to what information the French message referred. At that time I knew nothing of the approach Keyes had made to London, or of how the British Government had responded. I saw myself the victim of a political manoeuvre, with an ultimatum to back it up. I immediately informed the Premier and the Minister of Defence. We decided to speak to the King. He received us at Laeken Palace, in the centre of Brussels. When we told him of what Daladier had said, I fancied he was not as surprised as we had been. But he said nothing about the Admiral's activities. In our innocence, we had not the slightest suspicion of what had happened. We decided that our policy should remain unchanged: we would not enter the war unless we were attacked. This decision I telephoned to Paris. The other members of the Government, who were as astonished as ourselves, endorsed our action at a hastily summoned Cabinet.

Very early the next morning the phone rang. It was the

King calling from the Palace. He wanted to see me at once. I found him tense but determined to be charming, as charming as he could be when he wanted something. I was far from immune to this charm. Speaking quietly, he admitted everything to me – the instructions he had given Keyes, the British reply and the misunderstanding. He was fully aware of his own difficult situation, for which he was himself responsible, and he appreciated that the Government's position was even more embarrassing. He was rightly afraid that the whole story would leak out and that he would be accused of having assumed responsibility for setting aside our neutrality before an attack had been made. He dreaded the consequences of his mistake.

He asked me to help him and to maintain the strictest secrecy, for he was visibly afraid of the legitimate reaction of the Premier. Feeling for him as I did, I promised to help, even though this conflicted with my loyalty to M. Pierlot. I resolved to conceal the truth until the matter could be smoothed over. I knew I would have to obtain from Keyes a signed declaration to the effect that the King had never asked for British or French troops to enter Belgium, and explaining that he had confined himself to a general inquiry about possible guarantees. I was convinced this had been the King's real intention, and I promised to do what I could.

I got in touch immediately with Baron de Cartier, our Ambassador in London, and told him what had happened. I asked him to agree with Keyes on the text of a letter which would cover the King. The Admiral was a loyal man and Cartier had no trouble in convincing him. The letter was written and the King's mind set at rest. I wonder, however, if Keyes resented my intervention. I think he did, and I assume this is why he displayed such a marked aversion to me during the eighteen-day campaign.

This incident showed clearly that the King was pursuing a policy of his own, a dangerous thing to do in the circumstances. I now admit that I did not protest energetically enough at the time. I thought he had learned his lesson, but in fact he had not.

Admiral Keyes's mission was not the only result of the January scare. Another was the resignation of the Chief of Staff, General van den Bergen. And the false alarm was also responsible for the first serious split between the King and his Government.

There can be no doubt that we all thought an invasion was imminent. General van Overstraeten, writing of his visit to Army Headquarters on 13 January, says:

'Clearly, everyone was convinced there would be an invasion soon. In the confusion, various steps were suggested: put our troops on a general alert; evacuate the airfields; ask the broadcasting services to put out a warning; keep the Air Force chiefs posted on the lines of the German advance. General van den Bergen later claimed that he had suggested opening the frontier to our allies, although in the hubbub I heard nothing of this. It was in any case a matter for the Government, not for the General Staff.'

Where did General van Overstraeten acquire this new-found respect for ministerial authority, I wonder? It is strange, too, that he had not heard of General van den Bergen's suggestion of opening the frontiers, something of far more significance than certain other matters he could remember perfectly. Could it have been that General van Overstraeten sometimes shrank from his responsibilities? Whatever really went on at Army Headquarters that day, there is no doubt that on the night of 13–14 January van den Bergen gave the order to open the border with France. On 27 January he was asked to resign. His decision could have had grave consequences. The border with France was left undefended for forty-eight hours.

The whole truth about this episode has yet to be told. General van den Bergen has never publicly given his version of these events. All we know is that, when questioned by the Minister of Defence, he claimed that the order had been given in the presence of General van Overstraeten without the latter demurring. Van Overstraeten's defence against this charge is not impressive. He points out that the order was given after he had left headquarters. But although the decision was indeed put into effect late at night, there is nothing to suggest that it was not taken earlier that evening. The incident does at least show the situation at Army Headquarters at that time. The Chief of Staff felt justified in taking a crucial decision merely on the basis of the tacit approval of the King's military adviser. No reference was made to the King himself, and the attitude of the Minister of Defence or others in the Government was not considered. General van den Bergen's mistake is perhaps understandable when one considers the scope of van Overstraeten's military and diplomatic activities that January, and his closeness to the King.

I remember the night of 13–14 January very clearly. I spent a good part of it at Laeken with the Premier and General Denis. We were sure Germany would invade the next day. That evening Army Headquarters had received a telegram from our military attaché in Berlin which asked:

'Were there any military documents in the German aeroplane? Well-meaning informant of doubtful value claims it was carrying plans from Berlin to Cologne for an attack on the western front. He says that since these have fallen into Belgian hands, the attack will now take place tomorrow to forestall counter-measures! I have many reservations about this information, which I do not consider reliable, but feel you should pass it on. I suggest you verify it as far as possible.'

For security reasons the Embassy in Berlin had not been told of the documents we had acquired in such a strange way, and this, of course, gave the telegram added importance. An immediate attack on us seemed inevitable. The King was kind enough to tell us about the military preparations that had been made. They seemed to meet the case. Late that night, feeling we had done everything humanly possible, we finally went off to bed. I slept very soundly. When I woke up a few hours later, I cautiously opened first one eye, then the other. I sat up, amazed to find Belgium was not at war. I heaved a deep sigh of relief. It was to be one of the last.

The papers found in the aircraft had been handed over to General van Overstraeten, and it was he who decided what steps were called for. We learned that he had given the French and British only a summary of the contents. The

Premier and I should not approve. We thought the French and British should be fully briefed as it seemed increasingly likely they would soon be our allies. We took the opportunity to raise with the King the whole question of relations between our military leaders and the French and British commanders. We thought it essential to establish the closest cooperation.

To this day I still cannot understand why the King was so reticent about what had already been done. The extent of the contact that existed has been revealed in the memoirs of General Gamelin, the French Commander-in-Chief at the time. The question was of vital concern. It would have been dangerous to ask the French and British for assistance without giving them a chance to explain how they proposed to collaborate with the Belgian Army should their help be needed.

When, in 1940, we were on the point of defeat we were severely reproached on this point by Reynaud, the French Premier. In May of that year I met him in Paris and he was sharp almost to the point of rudeness, complaining bitterly about our alleged opposition to full cooperation with the French Army. I was forced to conclude that he had been misinformed, for his reproaches were unjustified, as General Gamelin's memoirs confirm. Gamelin states that from November 1939 the French Commander-in-Chief was in close contact with the Belgian military authorities. In a series of notes, Gamelin made recommendations, to which we replied verbally. A dialogue was thus begun. I was not aware of this dialogue until later and that is why, after the scare about a January invasion and supported by the Premier, I insisted on an exchange of military intelligence.

In February and again in March 1940, General van Overstraeten asked General Delvoie, our military attaché in Paris, to get in touch with Gamelin and to pass on to him two documents. The first was a review of French suggestions concerning operations in Holland and Belgium. The second raised questions of a technical nature about the movement of French and British troops in Belgium, should they be called in. Gamelin replied in writing. He confirmed that, to begin with, he intended to advance in one bound to a line from the Meuse to Namur and Louvain, preceded by cavalry and armoured divisions. The left flank would push forward as far as possible to the north-east of Antwerp to link up with the Dutch. 'It is not possible to give a definite commitment about a French and British intervention on the Albert Canal and the Meuse. Although one would like to help Belgium resist, the bulk of the force will only be moved across the Meuse-Namur-Louvain line if this can be done in time and the force moved in good order. The decision will be taken in the light of the effect of the first British advance.'

For once, the King passed on this reply, presumably because we had been responsible for the approach to Gamelin. General van Overstraeten describes how we were informed: 'They [the ministers] listened with great satisfaction. Even though allied assistance meant that the very heart of Belgium would be turned into a battlefield, they were delighted to hear that they would not be held responsible.' The palpable ill-will of this remark shows once again the mentality of the King's advisers. We were most certainly not delighted to learn that Belgium would become a battlefield. That we already knew. Yet we were pleased that Gamelin had been given a chance to study our plans, and to ask for clarification where necessary. In fact, there had been no questions and we thus had every reason to think that all was as it should be. Contact had been established. We felt we had done all we could to ensure effective military cooperation with the French and British without compromising ourselves politically.

5

'Me First'

And so, from incident to incident, from false alarm to false alarm, we moved steadily nearer to war. We now knew that war was a certainty. The brutal aggression against Norway at the beginning of April would in any case have opened our eyes and dispelled any remaining illusions.

The days of 9 and 10 May I remember very vividly. Alarming news had been reaching Brussels for several days. Across the frontier, the German troops seemed to be massing in greater numbers every day. Our Ambassador in Berlin was sending us discreet warnings. On the afternoon of 9 May we received another piece of worrying news. A member of the German Embassy in Brussels had called on a Belgian friend, a diplomat, to say goodbye. He had scarcely bothered to conceal the reasons for his departure.

It was with a heavy heart that I dined with the Bulgarian Minister. While we were playing bridge after the meal, the phone rang. It is not too much to say that at that moment I knew intuitively that the worst had happened. A servant told me my private secretary was wanted on the phone. When he returned I knew my fears had been confirmed. He said they were waiting for us at the Foreign Ministry. We took leave of our hosts, and returned to the office. The Chief of Staff had sent word that a strange, unidentifiable noise could be heard the whole length of the frontier with Germany. No one could be sure, but it sounded like columns on the move. The invasion was imminent.

So began the last night of the phoney war. The Premier, the Defence Minister, the King's private secretary, the Prosecutor General and my top civil servants gathered in my office. We remained in constant touch with The Hague and Luxembourg, where our anxieties were shared. In the middle of the night we learned that the sky over Holland was full of planes. Since no other military incident had been reported, we assumed it must be a heavy raid on England. By 3 a.m. our fears had subsided. Nothing had happened in Belgium. From the Hague we learned that van Kleffens had gone home to get some sleep. In Luxembourg they were playing down some of the more alarming reports circulating during the night.

The atmosphere in my office became more relaxed. We smiled at each other, happy that once again we had escaped unscathed. Someone risked a joke. We laughed at our fears. Then, in the clear sky of the spring morning, the German planes arrived. The anti-aircraft guns opened up and the windows shook. It was all over. Our hopes collapsed. Our efforts had been in vain.

The Premier seized the phone and spoke to Army Head-quarters. When he returned he was pale. He said: 'They've captured Eben Emael.' The fort was our strongest armed position, the key to our deployment on the Albert Canal. Our defences had been shattered before war had even been officially declared. Without losing a moment we decided to appeal to France and Britain. There was no need to consult the King or our colleagues. We had discussed the various contingencies often enough for everyone to know what to do.

We had arranged direct telephone links with our Embassies in Paris and London and were able to get in touch immediately with our ambassadors and to instruct them to deliver notes to the Quai d'Orsay and the Foreign Office appealing to our protectors. The notes had been drawn up some months before. To support our efforts in Paris and London and leave nothing to chance, I decided to call on M. Bargeton, the French Ambassador, and Sir Lancelot Oliphant. By then it was about 5 a.m. Sir Lancelot was waiting for me. On the stairs behind him I noticed his wife in a dressing gown – the only time it has fallen to me to see a British Ambassador's wife in that state.

Once the appeal had been sent I went with Pierlot and General Denis to see the King. We found him calm, self-controlled and ready to approve everything we had done. We would have liked him to accompany us to the Houses of Parliament, as his father had done when war was declared in 1914. Since he had decided to waste no time in going to his headquarters at the Fortress of Breendonck, between Brussels and Antwerp, he did not take up our suggestion. We regretfully deferred to his wishes. We thought the King's appearance in Parliament would have been valuable; it would have been an encouraging demonstration of national unity.

When we parted we were certainly shaken by events, but we left full of confidence in one another. When I returned to the Foreign Ministry I found the German Ambassador waiting to see me. I sat at my desk and drew up my statement to him. M. van Langenhove, the Secretary-General of the Ministry, was with me when the Ambassador was shown in.

The Ambassador was wearing formal dress; his manner was grave. He took from his pocket a piece of paper. Before he was able to read it, I shouted 'No, me first!', and without pausing for breath I read out to him the statement I had prepared, my voice trembling with emotion and indignation: 'The German Army has just attacked our country. This is the second time in twenty-five years that Germany has criminally and without provocation attacked neutral Belgium. The present aggression is, if anything, more vile than that in 1914. No ultimatum, no note, no protest has reached the Belgian Government. The attack itself was our first warning that Germany intended to violate the agreement signed on 13 October 1937 and readily renewed at the beginning of the war. Germany's aggression is without any shred of justification. It will condemn her in the eyes of the world, and in the eyes of history the German Reich will bear the burden of responsibility. Belgium is determined to defend herself. Her cause, the cause of justice, cannot be defeated.'

The Ambassador was still standing in the doorway. He began to read the note he had been charged with delivering: 'The German Government has instructed me to convey to you the following message. In order to forestall the planned invasion of Belgium, Holland and Luxembourg by Britain and France, a move clearly directed against Germany, the Government of the Reich has no alternative but to uphold the neutrality of these three countries by force of arms. To this effect, the German Reich has put into the field an armed force of such strength that resistance to it would be futile. The Government of the Reich guarantees the European and colonial territories of Belgium and its ruling dynasty on condition that no resistance is offered.'

At that moment I literally tore the paper from his hands and said: 'I'll spare you the rest.' I read on myself: 'Should any resistance be offered, Belgium risks destruction and the loss of her independence. It is therefore in Belgium's interests that an appeal be made to the population and the Army to cease all resistance, and that instructions be given to the authorities to get in touch with the German High Command.'

I said to the Ambassador: 'You'll find your answer in the statement I have read to you.' He bowed and left. I was to meet him again some ten years later during a visit to Germany. We did not reminisce.

That afternoon I went to the Chamber of Deputies. I realized I had unintentionally coined a phrase that would be remembered. I told the deputies what had just happened, and, without realizing the effect the words would produce, I explained how I came to shout 'Me first' at the German Ambassador. The words were greeted with a great roar of applause. In the Senate I was given a standing ovation the moment I mounted the rostrum, and it began afresh when I repeated the words I had used.

'Me first!': the words sprang quite naturally from my indignation and my emotion. They have since been repeated to me dozens of times by well-wishers wanting to show their admiration or friendship.

At the end of the day I went home completely exhausted. It was a beautiful spring evening, warm and sunny. An evening when it should have been good to be alive. British soldiers were crossing Brussels in clouds of dust to the accompaniment of applause. Their quick arrival seemed to bode well. The King and the Government were in apparent agreement. Parliament had reacted to the war with a surge of patriotism. Our protectors had answered our call without a moment's hesitation. This, however, was the last of the good news. Our ordeal was to be far worse than we had foreseen.

6

A Tragic Misunderstanding

I do not intend to recount the history of the eighteen-day campaign. It has already been done several times. There will be controversy about the way the war was conducted in this first phase for a long time. The Government of which I was a member in 1940 never managed to establish satisfactory relations with the Army. The fact that under our Constitution the King was Commander-in-Chief of the armed forces did not help matters. Successive kings and ministers have disagreed about how to interpret this role. Conflicts thus resulted between King Albert and de Brocqueville in the First World War and King Leopold and Hubert Pierlot in the Second. The two Kings argued that Article 68 of the Constitution gave the King a special position *vis-à-vis* the Army. In time of war this meant that for certain acts he was not accountable to the Government. The Government had always maintained that in military matters, as in others, there were no exceptions to the binding custom that the King could act only with the consent of his ministers.

The dispute was never satisfactorily resolved. Both de Brocqueville in 1914 and Pierlot in 1940 were forced to compromise, and I think they were right to comply. This explains why we were not kept informed of the progress of the eighteen-day campaign, let alone consulted. On a number of occasions Pierlot and I had unpleasant arguments on the subject with the King.

Only twice did I have an opportunity for personal contact with the Army during the campaign of May 1940. On 16 May I visited the King at his headquarters at Breendonck, and on 21 May I met General Weygand at Ypres. Both occasions were unhappy and left me profoundly disturbed. Both meetings were occasioned by the long discussions we were having with the King about future policy.

I have already said that when I left the King on 10 May in the small hours I had the impression we were completely at one. The terrible ordeal that the dispute with the King would cause me began only on 16 May. I had spent the previous night at the Ministry of Defence with Army officers who had explained the military situation to me. At about 4 a.m. I decided to go to bed, and left in the company of the Premier. Outside, in the street, Pierlot turned to me and said: 'I am very worried about the way things are going. I saw the King yesterday and we talked about it. There were some very dangerous ideas in the air. I'd like you to come with me to headquarters this afternoon.' Although he added nothing more, I was struck by his seriousness and his obvious anxiety.

Early in the afternoon Pierlot, General Denis and I travelled to Breendonck. The King made the military situation plain to us. It was bad. On the Belgian front the German offensive was limited, but the breakthrough at Sedan was being exploited to the full, and the Germans were advancing at a terrifying speed.

One must admit that van Overstraeten and the King showed considerable insight. They were sure the Germans would ignore Paris and push on to the coast. They were to be proved right. The threat of a German wedge being driven between the French forces and the Belgian and British armies was already apparent.

The King and Pierlot resumed their discussions of the day before, discussions which had left the Premier most anxious. Pierlot insisted that the retreat, which now seemed inevitable, should be towards the south so that contact with the French could be maintained or re-established. To my complete amazement the King favoured a retreat towards the north, hinting at withdrawal to a stronghold in the Zeebrugge area.

The Premier attacked this suggestion with all the vehemence he could muster. He stressed that 'if the Belgian Army allows itself to be pushed back to the sea, then surrender is inevitable, a surrender which would not only put our troops out of the reckoning, but separate its fate completely from that of the allied armies. This would be the worst thing that could happen.'

The King did not seem in the least impressed by this argument, even though General Denis and I backed up Pierlot as strongly as we could. We thought it would be better to try and escape the German advance by retreating to the west, thence to the south and into France if necessary. Even if the entire Army could not be saved in this way, we thought it vital that at least some of our troops should escape. Our ideas about strategy did not seem to please the King. He made every kind of objection which, although perhaps technically well-founded, showed his extreme reluctance to leave Belgian soil whatever the circumstances.

During our discussion the King asked me what had become of the Queen of the Netherlands. When I told him she had just arrived in England he said, to my utter amazement: 'I wonder if she has done the right thing.' I was anxious to convince the King that in no circumstances should he allow himself to be taken prisoner. It was vital that he should be free to continue the struggle, even if we were beaten in Belgium. Clearly, the King was undecided. When we left him, no decision had been reached one way or the other. Neither side would give way. In the next ten days our differences were to become increasingly obvious.

In the next room we met the Army Chief of Staff and some of his aides, and we discussed the situation with them. General Michiels himself was calm, and seemed to have kept his head, but some of the others made a much less favourable impression. General Nuyten, in particular, was most pessimistic, claiming that the war was well and truly lost. He said this with so much unconcern, or seeming unconcern, that we had a sharp exchange of words with him. We returned to Brussels very worried men.

It was not until 21 May that I had a further opportunity to discuss the military situation with the King. That day we learned by chance that he had arranged to meet General Weygand, who had replaced General Gamelin as Supreme Allied Commander. The Premier had to insist that we be allowed to go to Ypres, their meeting place. At first the King was against the idea, but finally he agreed.

Pierlot, General Denis and I spent some humiliating hours at Ypres. The King would not allow any of us, not even General Denis, his Minister of Defence, to be present at his meeting with Weygand. His intention of ignoring the Government in military matters was again clearly demonstrated, even when, as in this case, they were bound to have a bearing on the fate of the nation. Thus we waited outside while the important council of war was held.

There are two very different versions of what transpired, one van Overstraeten's, the other Weygand's. One need only read their respective memoirs to appreciate their complete disagreement about what the Belgian Army should have done. Weygand's plan was quite definite. He suggested that the Belgian forces retreat to the west, as far as the Yser if necessary. In this way they would remain in contact with the British. Weygand says of van Overstraeten's contribution:

> 'He apologized with a polite smile for differing so completely. As far as he was concerned the Belgian Army should not retreat to the west. In his view it would be better to leave the left flank of the Army where it was, on the Terneuzen Canal, and to fall back with the right, deploying it in a vast arc, with the sea behind. When van Overstraeten had finished, I told the King that this plan would inevitably result in the separation of the Belgian Army from the allied forces. For my part I could never support a strategy that would result in such a split, as all our efforts should be directed towards maintaining coordinated action. The King did not commit himself. He told me he would think about it.'

General Weygand's account is clear. It corresponds to what he told us during a brief conversation immediately after he had left the King.

General van Overstraeten's account is rather different. His description of Weygand's position agrees with Weygand's own, but he challenges the Supreme Commander's account of his own ideas.

> 'During a second meeting he [Weygand] told the ministers of the objections I had raised to an immediate retreat to the Yser. Pierlot claimed I had some hidden design to separate the Belgian from the allied forces, to deploy the Army in a semi-circle with its base on the coast, and to

have it supplied via Dunkirk and Ostend. I maintain that such a scheme, totally inept and contrary to all the rules of strategy, was never envisaged or discussed by me or in my presence, at Ypres or elsewhere. Moreover, the orders given during the battle of Lys show that contact with the British Expeditionary Force remained my first concern. General Weygand spoke out against any such idea and, with a pencil in his hand, took the trouble of demonstrating its absurdity to the ministers. General Weygand, with whom I went over these events again in 1950, told me that at a luncheon with our Ambassador to France M. Spaak had informed him that he still had in his possession the piece of paper with the sketch.'

It is clear that General van Overstraeten has either made a mistake, or has suffered a lapse of memory. The scheme he calls 'totally inept and contrary to all the rules of strategy' is, according to General Weygand, the one that he put forward. When van Overstraeten claims he never envisaged such a scheme or heard it discussed, he is losing sight of the fact that the King had expounded the idea to Pierlot on 15 May, and again the following day before Pierlot, General Denis and myself. No one can believe that the King's military adviser was in no way responsible for the suggestion, or that it was simply the fruit of the King's own thinking. Finally, and this I remember clearly, General Weygand's sketch was intended to show the absurdity of a movement that would leave the Army with the sea behind it. But Weygand said he wanted us to oppose van Overstraeten's proposal. I can still see him tracing with a firm hand an oblique line representing the Belgian coast, then a semi-circle showing the limits of the Army's retreat, as suggested by van Overstraeten. Weygand then added three arrows pointing south to show the direction of an offensive he was planning with, he hoped, the support of Belgian troops.

General van Overstraeten backs up his claims, which are in clear contradiction to the recollections of Weygand, the Premier and myself, by referring to orders given during the battle of Lys. These, he says show that contact with the British Expeditionary Force remained his prime concern. In fact they show only one thing: that van Overstraeten's plans, advanced by him on 21 May, were fortunately not put into effect in the days that followed. The King had told Weygand that he would 'think about it'. This was certainly in character. The result of his ponderings was a compromise between the two suggestions. The Army would not withdraw into a redoubt, but nor would it fall back on the Yser. It would fight on the Lys. What was behind this compromise? Was it the outcome of the King's conversation with Lord Gort after Weygand's departure, or was it the result of ministerial protests and entreaties?

After Weygand had left we were shown into the King's presence. The conversation was a painful one. We were totally dissatisfied with the way we had been treated. We had been strengthened in our views about what should be done by the knowledge that they were shared by the Supreme Allied Commander himself. The King later told van Overstraeten in confidence that we had been very harsh and unjust to him. He went so far as to write to us to complain about our conduct and our reproaches. I remember that as I was telling him what I thought, he pushed a map across the table towards me and exclaimed: 'You tell me what you would do in my place!'

To pursue the war after Belgium's defeat would necessitate remaining in contact with France and thus retreating towards the French border and attempting to get at least some of our troops across. However, withdrawal into a final redoubt, isolating ourselves, would imply that we considered that the capitulation of the Army marked the end of the war for us. The end would be all the more symbolic in that the King, the Head of State, would be offering up his person as a prisoner.

The King's stand in the event of the Army's surrender was also discussed, our disagreements becoming more and more heated and passionate as we went on. It is always difficult to report on and to sum up an argument one has bitterly opposed. Nevertheless, I think I am being fair to the King when I say that he never accepted, even after Belgium's entry into the war, that we were now allied with France and Britain. His view was that our foreign ties were relevant only in so far as our country must be defended as well as possible and for as long as possible. Once that task was accomplished, we would again be masters of our own destiny. I must add that the King was sure the allies had lost the war irretrievably. His accuracy in predicting the outcome of the first days of battle had given him added confidence in his own judgement. He was convinced France would soon be beaten, and again he was right. But he was wrong in thinking that once isolated, Britain would make peace. His perspicacity enabled him to predict the immediate future, but he was unable to see beyond the next two months. His decision to remain in Belgium with his troops and his people can thus be readily understood.

We in the Government thought very differently. We maintained that since we had of our own free will appealed to France and Britain – after all, we could have conducted our defence alone – we were now, for better or worse, committed to their cause. We were now allies *de facto* if not *de jure*. We further thought that, in return for the protection our allies had offered and given us, we were now obliged not only to defend our own frontiers and territory, but also to prevent Belgium being used as a base to attack France and Britain, and that we therefore had a legal, political and moral obligation to continue the war. We were still well placed: our youngsters had been evacuated to France, our gold was in safe keeping and we had all the wealth of our colony. Despite the military disaster we had suffered, we still believed in ultimate victory. We were fully aware how vital it would be for Belgium to be in the camp of the victors.

For these reasons we asked the King, indeed begged him, at first with feeling and respect, later with all the strength we could command, not to allow himself to be taken prisoner. We implored him to leave for France or England as soon as it became clear that further armed resistance was useless. He would thus remain Head of State even if his role as Commander-in-Chief was temporarily in abeyance.

There would be little point in recalling our subsequent discussions with the King in minute detail. They continued almost daily until 25 May. At his request four ministers had remained in Belgium: Pierlot, General Denis, the Minister of the Interior and myself. Our other Government colleagues had already withdrawn to France. We followed the Army's retreat. Between 18 and 20 May we were at St Denis and on the 21st at Ypres. We obstinately reiterated our arguments, always with the same lack of success, but without any definite decision being taken either way. After the Ypres meeting we stayed at the Governor's residence at Bruges, virtually isolated, and ignored by Army Headquarters.

By a miracle, we had kept in touch with Gutt, a colleague who was in London on official business. The telephone link between Bruges and London was still open, and he kept us in touch with British opinion. He made it clear that the Belgian disaster, which looked as if it might mean the destruction of the British Expeditionary Force, had not weakened the British will to fight. He added that he was sure the war would continue and that we should not despair. His words of comfort strengthened us in our determination.

By then we were preparing for our escape from Belgium. We still hoped the King would come with us, but whether we left with or without him, British help would be essential. Since the airfields were out of action, we would go by sea. Gutt had no difficulty securing help from the British Government. Plans were made to pick us up at Ostend, and then, when this became impossible, at Dunkirk.

On the evening of 24 May, disturbed by the continuing lack of news, we got in touch with Army Headquarters. We were told the Germans were at Balgeroeck, ten kilometres from Bruges. The reply was given in a curt and off-hand manner, making it clear that the Army had other things to do than to worry about us. We decided on a last meeting with the King. We had some difficulty locating him, and nobody wanted to help. Although we were still bearing all the responsibilities of government, the military were clearly making no effort to keep us informed or to find out what we thought.

Pierlot later described the evening:

'The King had changed his headquarters, but I managed to discover his latest phone number. The duty officer was evasive, saying he did not know if he was authorized to

44

reveal where the King was staying. We had to search through the phone book to discover that the number I had been given was that of Wijnendaele Castle.'

That was how the King's ministers kept in touch with their sovereign during those crucial days.

Wijnendaele Castle, 25 May 1940. The words seem like the stage directions for a tragedy, and that is what it turned out to be. The 25th was a poignantly beautiful day. Throughout this period of the war the sun never stopped shining. It was a marvellous spring that year, and the fields of Flanders, with their herds of lazy cows, gave one a sense of complete tranquillity and of quiet contentment. With nature so insensitive to human anxieties and misfortunes, I shared the anger of the romantic poets.

We left Bruges at dawn and travelled at first along deserted roads. Later we passed some troops who were resting, a regiment of Ardennes Chasseurs. They seemed in good spirits despite the difficult time they had been having. Finally we arrived at Wijnendaele. The château was an imposing building set in a fine park but the windows let in very little light and the place was steeped in an air of melancholy that the beautiful sky and the sunlight could not overcome.

The King received us after a brief wait. There was a lack of cordiality from the start. Since he remained standing, we, of course, could not sit down. A political discussion that starts on those terms is likely to be difficult and fruitless. After a few minutes I asked the King if it would not be better to relax a little and sit down. He agreed and took a seat. It was my only success that day.

For more than an hour we went back and forth over the same arguments we had used in previous discussions. But this time there was something new – the King's mind seemed irrevocably made up. He refused to leave the Army after the surrender; he had decided to remain a prisoner in Belgium.

There are several more or less full accounts of this meeting at Wijnendaele. Those of Pierlot and myself differ from those of the King's side. My own recollection of the essential points is still very clear and agrees completely with that of Pierlot. Nevertheless, I appreciate that we were all under physical and mental strain and that we must be extremely careful in our judgements. In the circumstances, our words did not always convey quite what we meant.

The discussion was intensely dramatic. We observed none of the rules of protocol and deference that so often forced one to temper one's views. The King and ourselves spoke as man to man. For our part, we made our points with all the passion, and at times the fury, we could muster. The King, completely isolated, argued with dignity, feeling and not a little stubbornness.

It was here at Wijnendaele that I nearly committed the worst blunder of my political life. I have already said how attached I was to the King. I could see he was on the point of making a fatal mistake. He was about to do a dangerous thing, and at the moment of decision he was so terribly alone in his distress that I was tempted to stay at his side. My words must have betrayed my feelings, and one glance at the faces of Pierlot and General Denis was enough to make me realize the error I was about to make. I owe a lot to that glance. What would have become of me if I had remained with the King I would rather not contemplate.

I do not want to repeat in detail everything that was said at Wijnendaele. I have already summarized the views of the opposing sides. But I must stress that at no time did we ministers ask the King to abandon the Army before the end of hostilities. This charge has often been levelled at us, and we have always resented it. The Premier repeatedly stated that he was ready to stay in Belgium with the King until the latter's task as Commander-in-Chief had been ended by defeat. In exchange, he asked that the King promise that then, and only then, he would attempt to reach either France or Britain. It was this promise that the King refused to give at Wijnendaele.

The King had no clear idea of what being a prisoner would mean, and he seemed uncertain about his future. We believed he had not considered all the implications of his decision, and he gave off the cuff answers to our questions. This, in fact, was the most disconcerting aspect of our last meeting.

A Tragic Misunderstanding

When we left the King at the end of our tragic conversation we were in despair, but absolutely convinced we had done all that duty demanded.

Luckily for everyone, some of our worst fears were not to be realized. It was not long before the King understood that he would be unable to take part in politics in occupied Belgium. On the advice of three legal experts, he made the surrender a purely military act, and offered himself as a prisoner. In this way he avoided the worst mistakes at which he had hinted in our last conversation.

The historian will no doubt find much to praise in Leopold's intentions. He will try to understand the King's motives and acknowledge his sacrifice for the sake of what he considered military honour. He will recognize Leopold's wish to help and comfort the Belgian people by his presence, but he will, I think, be forced to admit that the King's action was unconstitutional. By pursuing an unjustified personal policy, the sovereign compounded a military defeat with a constitutional crisis. He involved Belgium in a venture so risky that it threatened to destroy everything, even the monarchy itself.

Even now, the attitude we ministers adopted still seems entirely justifiable to me. We were right to leave the King and to pit our policy against his. In the ensuing weeks we made mistakes, but until then our understanding of events had been consistently better than the King's. Despite the handicaps imposed by his behaviour, we managed to safeguard the future.

7

A Time of Errors

From Wijnendaele we left for Dunkirk. When we arrived, the town was under bombardment and there were fires burning everywhere. We boarded a waiting British ship and a few hours later we were in England.

I do not propose to give a complete account of what happened after 25 May any more than I did of the eighteen-day campaign. Pierlot has given his account in a series of articles published in 1947 in the Brussels evening paper, *Le Soir*. I have given mine in a very detailed speech to the Chamber of Deputies on 24 and 25 July 1945. I shall therefore confine myself to a few incidents which throw some light on the drama we were to live through in France.

We stayed in England only a short while. We flew to Paris on the 26th and lost no time in meeting our colleagues to explain the situation. We needed the reassurance of their approval and they gave it unreservedly and unanimously. The surrender of the Belgian Army, although inevitable and militarily justifiable, was nevertheless a great shock.

The French Premier, Paul Reynaud, whom I later came to esteem and respect during our common struggle for a united Europe, treated us cruelly. He had worries enough of his own, and also certain reservations about us that I have already mentioned. He spared us nothing.

On 27 May, late in the afternoon, he sent for Pierlot and General Denis and received them in the presence of Marshal Pétain and General Weygand. Pierlot still did not know about the surrender. When Reynaud asked him what news he had, he explained the situation to the best of his knowledge, without ruling out all hope of some improvement. Reynaud let him speak for a while before brutally interrupting him to say that King Leopold had that day sent an official to the German High Command. Reynaud rounded off his statement with a virulent attack on the Belgian Army that was both excessive and unfair. France was far from blameless for the military disaster of 1940. Pierlot and General Denis could not let the attack go unchallenged and at one point the meeting looked like ending in uproar. Things quietened down when Pierlot announced that the Belgian Government wished to continue the struggle.

That night I was awakened at about two o'clock. Pierlot told me that Reynaud wanted to see us at once. Together we went to his private residence. Reynaud said that he would be announcing the Belgian surrender on the radio in a few hours' time, as he was obliged to do – I have not forgotten his words – in terms which might well compromise the safety of tens of thousands of our compatriots who had taken refuge in France.

What could we do? Our army had been defeated; we were separated from the Head of State and at odds with him; we were in a foreign country whose Premier treated us as guilty men. Our situation was an unenviable one. At moments like this Pierlot managed to remain calm and dignified. Quietly but firmly he put the record straight. He made the position of the Belgian Government clear. He reaffirmed our wish to continue the war with all the means at our disposal but ruled out all the more extreme suggestions that had been made. Some of these were as extravagant as they were ill-considered, including, as they did, a proclamation of the King's dethronement and the adoption by Belgium of the French Constitution.

Reynaud has never been forgiven in Belgium for the speech he made a few hours later. I listened to it at our Embassy, crying as I had not cried since childhood. I felt an extraordinary sense of collective shame. The misfortunes of my country, of all the Belgian people, touched me to the quick.

On 29 May Pierlot, too, made a broadcast. We had written his speech, which was also to cause much controversy, together. No criticism should be levelled at the Premier. Even allowing for differences in the interpretation of some of the words he used, he was doing no more than to repeat faithfully what we had been told at Wijnendaele.

He had to set out our position. Such a speech could only be of value if it explained without ambiguity that we had definitely broken with the King and wished to continue the war. It was also necessary to make it quite clear that the Government was assuming all executive powers. Amid so much confusion this was not an easy thing to convey. The military, he said, would henceforth owe allegiance to the Government alone and were released from their oath of allegiance to the King.

Being directly involved and the co-author of the statement, I am perhaps insufficiently detached to judge the usefulness of what we did in those few hours. It seems to me, however, that we had no choice in the matter. We had to set out our policy unequivocally. We must await the judgement of future historians, who will have all the evidence at their disposal. I have no fears about their verdict.

The Belgian Government did not make any serious mistakes before France asked for an armistice, but I cannot and would not want to hide subsequent errors. For several weeks after the French defeat we thought the war was over. We believed ourselves completely beaten and bereft of authority to pursue the struggle. This story of faint-heartedness I must now tell.

At Poitiers, about 15 June, the Cabinet discussed whether, with France beaten, we should follow the example of the French Government. We did not then know of its plans – whether it would remain in France or, as some of us hoped, move to North Africa.

Our Cabinet had always been unanimous, united in its determination. But at Poitiers differences became evident for the first time and agreement on what decisions to take harder.

The British Government had offered us an aircraft with eighteen seats – not enough for all of us. It was supposed to take off for England very shortly. We refused their offer for a very good reason. It seemed dangerous to split up the Government, with one party of ministers going to London and another staying in France. There was a severe risk that the two groups might take up different, perhaps incompatible, attitudes. Not all the ministers could leave

France. The Defence Minister was responsible for what was left of the Army, and the Minister of the Interior and several other ministers for the refugees, who were eking out a precarious existence. If we decided to split up, should the Premier stay or go to London? In addition to these political considerations, there was another, more sentimental one. As one minister put it, we had stuck together, living side by side and sharing our ordeal. Solidarity was our last trump card, and if we split up we would be throwing it away. We found the idea moving – and convincing. We refused the British Government's offer, and thus threw in our lot with the French. With the benefit of hindsight I admit it would probably have been better if one of us had left for England. This was, in fact, the solution we adopted two months later.

On 18 June we arrived in Bordeaux, where the French authorities had already installed themselves. We were assigned lodgings in a modest house in the Rue Blanc-du-Trouille.* One can guess at our enemies' jokes at our expense when they found out.

The Government departments were no longer organized. Most of our civil servants had left us at Poitiers to return to Belgium. They could not remain with us on what was beginning to look rather too much like a headlong flight. With the few who were left we held our meetings in a room which was a jumble of ill-assorted furniture. It had not been dusted for months. Some of us had to sit on packing cases. The disorder without was beginning to lead to intellectual confusion within.

The French Government was most off-hand with us. After its own misfortunes, those of others counted for little. Only with great difficulty were we able to learn about what was going on. I remember having to wait several hours outside the room of Charles-Roux, the Secretary-General of the Ministry of Foreign Affairs. The way in which I was ultimately received left me with no illusions about the extent of our decline.

However, it was a conversation with M. Baudouin, the Foreign Minister in Marshal Pétain's newly-formed government, that helped us make up our minds. He told us that

* The name means 'white with fear' (Translator's note).

France had made approaches with a view to obtaining an armistice and about the Franco-British discussions a few days before. He assured us: 'The British understand our position, and they approve. But they can't say so publicly.'

This statement weighed heavily on us, casting doubt on Britain's will to win. It did not, however, resolve our problems since Baudouin had not told us what attitude his Government would ultimately adopt. He did not rule out the possibility of a move to North Africa. We insisted we should be allowed to take part in any such move, and this was agreed. We also made a wasted journey to the Spanish frontier, having been told that everyone was leaving. No one told us the plan had been cancelled. The only advantage I derived from the trip was three days of motoring through magnificent country and a chance to get to know the road to Perpignan. This was to prove useful a few weeks later.

We left the Rue Blanc-du-Trouille, which was really most uncomfortable. Instead, we took refuge – the only word for it – on the *Baudouinville*, a Belgian steamer anchored in the Gironde Estuary. On board we resumed our endless debate. Should we attempt to reach England or not? We were divided. The Premier, Gutt, Janson and myself thought that, on balance, we should. Others felt we ought to remain in France. The discussions were long and often heated. Our side almost carried the day. Just when our arguments were beginning to tell, a heavy German air raid forced us to disperse. The next day we met again. For once, sleeping on a problem had not helped. When the Premier put it to the vote, he was supported only by Gutt and myself. We were in the minority, and we made the mistake of giving way.

We had an excuse. With the King absent, there was no one to try and reconcile our differences. It would have been senseless to provoke a Cabinet crisis. The little legality and authority we still had would have totally disappeared. We therefore accepted the will of the majority. If the three of us had not allowed ourselves the luxury of legalism, but had left for England, we would have spared ourselves the difficulties of the days ahead. We would not have jeopardized what had been saved. In the next few weeks we were to come close to disaster.

After the French defeat and the armistice, our morale was

very low. The collapse had come as a complete surprise. We had never for a moment imagined France would be put out of the war so quickly, and our plan had always been to fall back on France if Belgium were defeated. When the Government had left Ostend because of the bombing, the ministers had made their way to Le Havre, the seat of the Belgian Government during the First World War. By force of tradition we had thought of installing ourselves there once again.

We had a terrible time in France. We stopped only for a few days in Paris, Poitiers, Bordeaux and Sauveterre. With each move we lost a little more of our confidence and our resources. When we arrived in Vichy we were still ministers in name, but we no longer had any authority, and what remained of our functions was derisory.

At Sauveterre we had to take our most difficult decisions. We met in a café, virtually cut off from news from the outside world, except occasionally from London. We had completely lost contact with our embassies abroad. The terrible confusion about us did not help matters.

Worse was to come. The first of our compatriots to arrive from occupied Belgium did not hide the fact that the overwhelming majority of the population approved of the King's attitude and that our unpopularity was total. In this atmosphere of military defeat and political and moral opprobrium, we had to resolve the problems posed by the French authorities.

The first of these was what to do with the remnants of the Belgian Army. Could we disengage ourselves from France? What would be the fate of our soldiers and the young evacuees if we did? The second problem: how to repatriate the enormous number of refugees without dealing directly with the Germans. A third question was far more important still: were we to continue to take decisions in the name of Belgium?

As long as France and Britain had stood together in the war we had no doubts. The mandate we had been given by the nation seemed clear enough. But as soon as France and Britain parted company, we found ourselves in a situation we had never envisaged. We were uncertain what to do, and we were divided. If we had been with the King and in touch with Parliament and the mood of the country, adequate answers would probably have been found fairly quickly. But we were isolated, and knew we had been repudiated. We had no resources, were discredited at home and scarcely recognized in France. To pursue the war seemed beyond our powers. We were, I must admit, utterly discouraged and at a loss what to do.

We tried to keep in touch with the French Government, and to get in touch again with the King in Belgium. We made our feelings known in Brussels. Pierlot wrote a letter to Frédéricq, the King's private secretary; it arrived on 28 June. It said:

'We believe that two things must be done urgently: (1) negotiate with the Germans for the return of the Belgian military personnel and civilians in France; (2) negotiate with the Germans the terms of an armistice or a convention for Belgium. On this last point, being unfamiliar with the situation, we are not prepared to act without knowing the King's views. If the King thinks it advisable and possible to form a new government, we are of course ready to tender our resignation.'

On 4 July Frédéricq sent a verbal reply through Vicomte Berryer, who had also taken the Premier's message. 'The King's position has not changed. He abstains from all political action. He is receiving no politicians. The Red Cross is undertaking the repatriation of Belgian civilians.' In his personal capacity, Frédéricq added that he did not think the return to Belgium of Pierlot and his associates(!) was advisable at that moment.

After the war, when the debate about the Royal Family was to set Belgian against Belgian, this letter and the reply to it became a source of heated argument.

The King's supporters have claimed that Leopold saved Belgium on this occasion. Count Capelle, in his book, which bears the significant title *In the Service of the King*, has this to say:

'His [the King's] silence must be seen as expressing disapproval of our proposals [those of the ministers]. Although a prisoner of the Germans, he refused to be overawed by their temporary triumph and refused to consider the game lost. The King's silence was in fact a positive act since by it he made it clear that he was not prepared to deal with the ministers alone.'

Some have gone even further. They have claimed that the answer we had been given represented an implied order, or at least a suggestion, to go to England. How I wish this had been true. There would then have been no problem of the monarchy. But interpretations of this sort are not consistent with the facts. They are attempts to plead a cause.

All the documents since published show clearly that these were not the King's feelings. In spite of our appeals, he gave us no hint that he approved of our flight to England and our decision to continue the war. If the King had really felt the way some of his supporters claim, it would have been easy for him to let us know. He could have done so through Vicomte Berryer, on whose discretion he could rely entirely. At all events, we did not interpret what we took to be the King's reply in this sense.

Pierlot has said in one of his articles:

'Information that reached us immediately after Berryer's mission and which was later confirmed, suggested that the King wanted no more contact with the Government, even indirectly. In his eyes, the Government had ceased to exist, and there was no question of further dealings except, perhaps, to ask, at the appropriate time, for a formal signature for the handing over of power.'

Thus the King refused to give us his views as we had requested. He refused to take up any position, preferring to let us get by as best we could. This was all we needed to fill our cup of bitterness to overflowing. But it matters little what the King really meant by keeping silent. The fact is that his silence saved us from making a very bad mistake

Pierlot's letter shows that we were in two minds about what to do. We had taken no decision. If, during those days of confusion, the King had sent word that we should resign, we would have done so. Officially, Belgium would then have ceased to be at war and our country's history would have been very different. By refusing to speak, the

King put the ball firmly in our court; we had to face our responsibilities alone. Deliberately or otherwise, we were given a chance to pull ourselves together.

In fact, little by little, Pierlot, Gutt and myself were beginning to realize that our game was not yet up, and that one hope was left – Britain. We realized it was on Britain we had to gamble. Every day as we sat down for lunch I would say: 'Gentlemen, I trust you realize we have won this war. England has not given in, and Russia has not been conquered. Remember Napoleon.' As a joke, it was not a great success. But our change of heart was also helped by the news from London, and by words of encouragement that reached us from some of the best elements in occupied Belgium.

Our Ambassador in London and de Vleeschauwer, the Minister for the Colonies, whom we had dispatched to Lisbon and London to look after the Congo, had both sent word that there was no question of a British surrender. Isolated on their island, the British were fiercely determined. By the middle of July, they had persuaded us to leave France. By the beginning of August, after Churchill had curtly rejected Hitler's peace proposals, we were convinced that even if the situation was not good, there was hope of improvement. From then on it was our duty to put at the service of the common cause all that remained of our resources.

A minority of our countrymen had taken heart at the same time. Our supporters, people in whom we had confidence, were surprised by our inaction. This decided us. There were, to be sure, obstacles enough to overcome. Some of our colleagues were very much against this adventure. They dwelt on the risks involved, of which there was no lack. Pierlot, finding himself unable to persuade all the ministers to follow his lead, was afraid the Government would be split, as it had been at Poitiers and Bordeaux, and that the legality that was our last strength, our *raison d'être*, would disappear. The French Government was also against our departure, and the Spanish Government showed no willingness to grant us transit visas. We were thus beset by a series of political, emotional and material difficulties.

After a meeting that Pierlot, Gutt and I had with de

Vleeschauwer at the Spanish frontier, Gutt, with the Premier's full consent, left for London. Pierlot and I returned to Vichy to sort things out finally with the other ministers. After some difficulties in talking matters over with them, we agreed that Pierlot and I should join Gutt and de Vleeschauwer in London. The four of us would comprise the Government. To avoid any misunderstanding, the ministers remaining in France would tender their resignation. This is what was in fact done.

Recalling the period after the French armistice and before we left Vichy, Pierlot has written:

'Few of our compatriots are well qualified to hold against us our decision of 18 June to stay in France rather than take the Government to London at once and continue the war at Britain's side. But I have not been slow to admit this decision was an error. The Government's line from the beginning of the war to the liberation was otherwise consistent; the decision taken at Bordeaux was a momentary but undeniable aberration. The head of the Government must accept responsibility. It was lucky that among our country's misfortunes we were able to redress this mistake during the Battle of Britain, when friendship was still highly prized – that is, before Britain's fortunes turned. For this I thank Providence.'

Having quoted this confession of errors, let me pay tribute to Hubert Pierlot, who throughout this period of misfortune behaved with such dignity. He had been hurt and his most cherished convictions assaulted, but in the end it was he who showed us where our duty lay. With quiet courage, he agreed to what turned out to be a great adventure. There was nothing in his character which predisposed him to undertake it. I can still hear him talking about his native Ardennes, telling me how attached he was to the land where he had been born and raised: 'How I should like to die at home surrounded by my children and the things I know best,' he once said to me.

Gutt was a tireless traveller. He knew the world and liked England. He was more adaptable, less home-loving, more adventurous, and perhaps also more convinced of ultimate success. For him the decision to leave was easier, but he must be praised for the ardour with which he defended his convictions and the unfailing loyalty he showed his two companions, both then and later. As for me, at forty-one I still believed in the future, and in miracles.

We left Vichy, where we had spent such miserable weeks, on 24 August. Our party consisted of the Premier, his wife, his seven children, his principal private secretary, a governess and myself. The journey to England was to be long and difficult.

8

The Story of an Escape

Our adventure was about to begin. I think I might best describe it as 'the story of an escape'.

Having left Vichy in the early morning of 24 August, we passed through Perpignan the same evening. A few miles beyond the town we were stopped by French gendarmes who, after checking our identity papers, asked us to turn back. The Préfet of the Département, they said, was waiting for us. We were met by a gentleman whose name and appearance I no longer remember, but whose words have stuck in my mind: 'The French Government,' he said, 'will not permit you to cross the frontier unless you first give a written undertaking not to go to Britain for the duration of the war.'

We were flabbergasted. While we were at Vichy, no one had ever suggested anything of the sort to us. M. Pierlot and I retired to a corner of the office, where we had a lively discussion. What passed between us does more honour to the Premier than to myself, but I nevertheless propose to give a faithful account of it. At any rate, our discussion will give the reader some idea of the sort of man I was dealing with.

My advice was that we should sign and then carry on as if nothing had happened. I believed that too much was at stake for us to take any unnecessary risks. Morally, the Vichy Government had no claim on us, I said, since it was trying to extort a promise from us under duress. Such a promise could not be considered binding. It was unthinkable, I added, that we should allow our efforts to fail at the very outset.

M. Pierlot, on the other hand, believed that a promise, even one given in such unusual circumstances, must be honoured. It would be inconceivable, he declared, that he should give a pledge knowing he had no intention of keeping it. He was just as anxious as I was to reach the free world, but to him his moral scruples were the overriding consideration.

I was stunned. The Premier requested the Préfet to telephone M. Marquet, the Vichy Minister of the Interior, and the official did as he was asked. In a matter of minutes the minister was on the line. Never in my life have I heard a minister treated the way M. Pierlot treated M. Marquet that day. Our difficult plight may have made it hard for M. Pierlot to impose his authority, but the moral effect of his words was possibly all the greater for this. M. Pierlot gave the minister a piece of his mind. He reminded him that we had entered France of our own free will as friends and allies and that it was unthinkable that we should be prevented from leaving by the imposition of unacceptable conditions. M. Pierlot invoked all the highest moral principles and finest sentiments known to mankind. I listened full of admiration but rather sceptical about the final outcome. But I was wrong: M. Pierlot won the day. His anger may have frightened the man at the other end of the line or, who can say, it may even have touched his heart. Whatever the truth of the matter, M. Marquet gave way and we received permission to continue our journey without having to promise not to go to Britain.

We breathed a deep sigh of relief: the first obstacle had been overcome. We went back to our car and soon our convoy was on its way again. We arrived at the Spanish frontier in the middle of the night. There we came up against another snag. Mme Pierlot, her children and their governess, as well as M. Pierlot's principal private secretary, Roger Taymans, had their passports in order. The Premier and myself, however, had failed to obtain Spanish visas in Vichy. Despite this, the Belgian Ambassador in Madrid, the Comte de Romrée, advised us to leave, adding that he thought he could deal with the matter at his end. He therefore sent a member of his staff, M. Quérin, to the frontier. The Spanish Government, however, could not agree among themselves what should be done with us. Beigbeder, the Foreign Minister, was in favour of allowing us into the country, but Serrano Suñer wanted to keep us out.

An interminable discussion began at the frontier post, the feeble lamp of which was the only light to pierce the darkness all around us. The Spaniards did not know what to do. They were impressed by M. Quérin's heated arguments and may also have been moved by the presence of the Premier's seven children. On the other hand, they were terrified at the thought of having to take so heavy a responsibility upon themselves.

In the end, however, miraculously the police officer in charge decided that we should be allowed to cross the frontier, though only on condition that we should be arrested at La Junquera, the first village on the Spanish side. Before we could go any further, he said, he would first have to obtain instructions from Madrid. We gratefully accepted this compromise and put up in the village inn, one of those modest Spanish hostelries where you are as comfortable as you make yourself.

We spent several days in the place. Our ambassador in Madrid did his utmost to obtain transit visas for us, but his efforts were foiled by a mixture of indifference and ill will on the part of the Spanish authorities.

One evening the police chief who had allowed us to enter Spain came to see us. He was clearly embarrassed at having to execute the instructions he had received: 'You will have to leave La Junquera and go back to France,' he said. 'I took a great deal upon myself when I allowed you to cross into Spain and my career is in danger. Please do as I ask.' M. Pierlot refused bluntly. He realized that if we returned to France we should never get out again. However, in the end we decided we could not turn a deaf ear to our policeman's pleas. We simply could not ignore the request of one who had been so kind to us. It was now our turn to suggest a compromise. We said we would leave La Junquera without, however, crossing the French frontier. In other words, we would stay in the no-man's-land between the two customs posts. Our suggestion was accepted and we settled down in the middle of the road at the foot of a statue put up to the greater glory of General Franco. It must have been a strange sight indeed to see the Belgian Prime Minister, his wife and seven children, and the Foreign Minister, too, seeking shelter from the hot sun by moving round and round the statue so as to remain in the shade so generously provided by the Caudillo. We ate the food I had had the foresight to bring along, slept in our cars, and used the water from a nearby fountain for drinking and washing. Throughout this whole episode our morale remained high. I read to the children and played with them. We stayed there for three days, and no one complained even once throughout the whole of this time. Our little band attracted the attention of passers-by, and those among them who realized what was going on were rightly indignant. I do not know whether this came to the ears of the Spanish Government or whether they finally gave way to the arguments of our ambassador. At any rate, after three days we were allowed to proceed to Gerona, where we were to be arrested.

It was now clear to the Premier and myself that sooner or later we might have to escape from Spain. In order to gain some freedom of movement, we decided to separate from those members of our party whose passports were in order, and Mme Pierlot, her children and their governess, as well as M. Taymans, left us.

The Premier and I stayed together for several weeks. We read, wrote, learned English and played cards. I believe this was the first time in his life that M. Pierlot indulged in such a pastime. I taught him how to play piquet and took several thousand points off him. During this time I got to know him, and the better I knew him the more I liked him. Gradually, affection mingled with my respect and esteem for the Premier.

It was at this point that we made up our minds to make our way to Britain as soon as possible. We left Gerona for Barcelona under police guard. At the Barcelona police headquarters we were asked to give our personal details. I can still hear the Premier say that his name was 'Pierlot, Hubert' and, with an air of solemnity, that his occupation was 'Belgian Prime Minister'. I could not help smiling sardonically as the thought crossed my mind how strange this title sounded in our present surroundings. This, however, did not prevent me, when it was my turn to be questioned, from saying that I was 'Minister of Foreign Affairs'. Nothing is easier than to follow a good example.

We were taken to a hotel – one of the better ones in

Barcelona – and received permission to go out during the day, though never without a police escort. Luckily for us, the Spaniards made one mistake: they allowed us to get in touch with M. Jottard, the Belgian Consul. This proved our salvation. M. Jottard was one of those unpretentious people whose modesty hides a quiet courage. Without a moment's hesitation and without giving a thought to the risks he was letting himself in for, he immediately went to work to help us the moment we mentioned we might one day wish to escape from Spain. Without his assistance, we should never have succeeded. And since we were clearly on a winning streak, M. Jottard was able to enlist the help of another of our compatriots, a M. Hubert, who became the brains of the whole operation. We held a council of war every day at the consulate, with our policemen awaiting our return down below in the street. We considered various methods of escape – all more or less risky. Finally, we decided on the simplest one of all: we would travel by car. Another fellow Belgian, a M. Henning, agreed to drive us. I was immediately won over by the simplicity of his scheme; 'I shall stick to the main roads without the slightest attempt to hide. If anyone asks us for a lift, we shall take him along even if he is a policeman.' I was reassured by M. Henning's air of calm confidence.

Thanks to M. Hubert, we got hold of a van and had a secret compartment, just large enough for two people, installed behind the driver's seat. A Spanish workman whom we could trust did the job for us. We had succeeded in gaining the confidence of our guards. One Saturday afternoon they told us they wanted to go to a football match but could not do so unless we first promised not to run away. Not only did we give them the required pledge but even let them have a little money to help them enjoy themselves. In this way we established a relationship built on mutual trust which was to stand us in good stead a few weeks later.

Although we had taken the necessary practical steps, we were doubtful whether we should make good our escape, for the chances of success were very slender indeed. We had to cross Spain from Barcelona to the Portuguese frontier, traversing several mountain chains on the way – in all, a journey of at least fifteen hours. There was every chance of our escape being discovered and the frontier posts being alerted before we managed to get out of the country. Once arrested, our position would be anything but enviable.

In the event, it was Himmler who forced our hand. It came to our knowledge that he was to visit Franco and we were not slow to realize the danger of the situation. There was a good chance that this time we might really be imprisoned or even handed over to the Germans. Nothing was impossible in those days and there was nothing for it but to take our chance without losing any more time.

In the early afternoon of 18 October – it was a Saturday and our policemen had left us to go to a football match – we set out on our journey. We made a point of leaving our luggage in the hotel in a prominent position and first went to M. Jottard, the Belgian Consul. The other members of the conspiracy were already there and we discussed the last few details of our scheme. It was about four o'clock when, having made sure we were not being watched and with trembling hearts, we slipped into the secret compartment in the van. We set off with M. Henning at the wheel.

Almost immediately M. Pierlot took out his rosary and, having made sure I had no objection, began to say his prayers. Not only did I readily agree but I remember that I myself, in my heart of hearts, called upon all the gods and prophets that I could think of, including Mohammed, Confucius and Buddha. I took the view that if I was going to take out an insurance policy at all I might as well have maximum cover.

As it happened, luck was on our side and our dash for freedom succeeded. However, we owed this happy outcome to a number of lucky coincidences.

It was not till Sunday lunchtime that our guards realized we were not there. At first they thought we had gone to Mass and decided to wait a little longer. At about two o'clock they began to get worried and went to see M. Jottard at the Consulate. The Consul feigned utter surprise and said he shared their concern. At that point they decided to give the alarm. Again, our luck held: the head of police happened to be at the bull ring, and refused to attend to the matter until after the *corrida*. Precious hours went by and as it turned out, this was exactly what we needed, for our journey to the Portuguese border, instead of taking fifteen hours as we had thought, took more than twenty-four hours – twenty-four hours during which M. Henning never left the driver's seat.

A football match, a bull fight, the negligence of our poorly paid police guards, the incredible energy of our compatriot, M. Henning, not to forget the loyal devotion and courage of a number of others – all this we needed to get away from Spain and escape the Germans.

At the Spanish-Portuguese border we were in a state of great trepidation. Customs officers opened the van and searched the heap of old tyres we were carrying in the back. Having failed to discover our hiding place, they allowed the van to proceed. M. Pierlot lightly touched my hand. For him, this was an unusual gesture of friendship to make, and it moved me greatly. At last, we thought, we were safe.

However, hardly had our van covered a few hundred yards when it stopped again and we heard footsteps. Was our game up? We did not move an inch. Heavy beads of sweat ran down my face and I had pins and needles in my legs. The Premier remained motionless, as if he were lying in wait during a shoot in his native Ardennes. We looked at one another full of fear and neither of us said a word. Then the van moved off again. In our anxiety, we had forgotten that there was also a Portuguese frontier post to pass. As we left our hiding place a few miles further down the road, stiff after being cooped up for so long, we were dazzled by the bright sunlight after the many hours we had spent in total darkness.

We had the necessary money to telephone Lisbon and, using code language, informed the Belgian Minister of our arrival in Portugal. He told us Mme Pierlot was on her way to meet us and before very long she appeared. After our first joyful greetings were over I asked her: 'Are you not surprised to see us?' 'Not at all,' she replied. 'This morning, at Mass I came upon a passage in my missal which begins with the words "The captives shall be delivered." So, you see, I knew you were coming.'

How marvellous, and how simple and genuine! In later years, reflecting on the strength such a profound faith can give a person, I often regretted being unable to share it.

We did not stay long in Lisbon. The Portuguese Government seemed anxious we should not prolong our visit and we, for our part, were keen to get to Britain.

On 24 October we left for London in a British flying boat. The same evening we touched down at Bournemouth. How green England seemed after the parched Spanish countryside, how welcoming and pleasant on that autumn evening! We made the journey to London by car. By the time we got there night had fallen, and the darkness was pierced from time to time by the powerful beams of searchlights. An air raid was in progress. Two bombs burst not far from our car. M. Pierlot has described what happened. He says he watched my reactions with some curiosity since this was my first direct encounter with war. I said to him: 'I am glad we have made it.' He smiled at me and again, the second time within the space of a few days, we shook hands.

A new chapter in our lives was about to begin.

PART TWO

London

9

In London

For four years – four very important years – I lived in Britain. They were a period of transition in my life. From advocating a policy of neutrality towards other countries I passed to one of positive cooperation. From introspection I turned to the broader horizons offered by exciting new forms of international collaboration.

My ideas changed and I became a different person. When they told me in England that only bullfighters wore a broad-brimmed hat like mine, I abandoned it. This simplification in dress corresponded to a more simple style of conduct, of thinking, even of talking. From then on I made fewer gestures. I acquired more sobriety, reserve, restraint.

All those who lived through this period alongside the British were strongly affected by the experience. No one could remain indifferent to their strength, courage and tenacity. It was a wonderful thing to be with them in their isolation and to share their ordeal. They were so calm in their darkest hours, so modest when things were going well.

I have often said jokingly: 'I like the English because they prefer animals to people, because they don't stare at lovers kissing and because they know they are citizens of a great empire.' I like them for their combination of discretion and greatness. I like their weekends, the host not worrying about his guests and everyone doing as he pleases. I like their restful conversation. Above all, I like the respect they show for others, surely the highest and only acceptable form of egotism.

I like the English countryside, so clean and neat – the peaceful landscape of a country spared by war for many centuries. I like the picturesque old houses, the narrow country lanes, the great spreads of field and meadow saved from monotony by the occasional old tree, and the abundant flowers that brighten the scene from spring to autumn with their changing colours.

At the end of 1940, all this was not clear to me. I did not speak English and sometimes felt very alone. But little by little I won through, and I now admire the English with the force of a love and a friendship that have ripened slowly. In public life I have learned from them that firmness of character is often more important than a sparkling wit.

I am still grateful to them for welcoming me after the long weeks I had spent wandering the roads of Belgium and France. I was confused, discouraged and overwhelmed by defeat. I thank them for restoring my confidence and hope. From the day I set foot on English soil I never again doubted final victory. I knew I would see my country again, free and independent. I knew that life as it should be lived would begin again. I knew we would escape the Nazi horror and shame.

Those years in Britain can never be forgotten. If, later, I sometimes found the British slow, hesitant, unwilling to make the most of their opportunities, if sometimes I even spoke out against them, it was more in sorrow than in anger. It was never, never, a sign of ingratitude.

My first official contact with the British was at Geneva in 1936. That year, Van Zeeland was President of the League of Nations Assembly. He introduced me to Anthony Eden. We went to see Eden in his hotel suite overlooking the lake. There was a marvellous view of the mountains from the window.

We were given a very friendly welcome, but we talked of the weather and the countryside and discussed a few general topics only in the vaguest terms. Afterwards I could not hide my surprise and disappointment from the President. Was this really how great international questions were handled? Van Zeeland reassured me: 'That's what the English are like. If after three or four years you've won their confidence, then they will begin to talk seriously to you.' He was right. It took me several years to win Mr Eden's confidence and, I believe, his friendship as well.

I was to see more of him in 1940. He always welcomed me at the Foreign Office with the same mixture of kindness and distinction. His manner impressed me a great deal. I envied his impeccable waistcoats, forever denied to a man of substantial build like myself. I also liked his open mind. Our conversations were, in the language of official communiqués, 'cordial'.

One day in 1943 Eden invited me to lunch. I accepted, expecting to find myself dining with colleagues from other governments in exile in London. When I arrived I found him alone. We lunched *tête à tête*. Confidence had been established.

I have taken part in several conferences together with Mr Eden. Most of the time we were in agreement without needing to consult. He is a man whose judgement and thinking I unfailingly respect.

I was very sorry when his career was interrupted by illness. It so happened that I was in London very soon after his resignation, and I wanted to bid him farewell. It was a melancholy occasion at Chequers, where he was staying, made worse by the first chill of winter. We chatted, exchanged reminiscences and went over the years since our first meeting. We recalled the difficulties we had gone through together and the hopes we had shared. When I left him he was standing in the doorway, very straight and still, a fine looking man whose face was marked by illness and sadness. I have never forgotten the gesture of farewell with which he sent me on my way.

A few days after our arrival in 1940 we lunched at the Belgian Embassy with Mr Churchill. Churchill had detested our policy of independence before the war and had not hidden his feelings. He had certainly not found our wavering in France any more to his liking. However, this did not prevent him giving us a courteous welcome. It is perilous to attempt to describe a man about whom everything has been said, but I must do so for all that.

When journalists ask me – they are rather fond of putting this type of question – who is the man in my life whom I have most admired, I answer without a moment's hesitation: 'Churchill.' I feel this way because Churchill's contribution was decisive to the outcome of the war, because every free human being owes him a personal debt of gratitude.

General de Gaulle has said: 'Once I am gone, everything

will collapse in ruins.' What a terrible confession of lone-liness! Churchill's achievement was that he was greater, stronger, more indispensable and yet a faithful interpreter of the will of his people and, for a number of years, of all men fighting for freedom.

He was the embodiment of that quality which all truly great statesmen must possess: he did not dominate and tyrannize his fellow men, but was the spokesman of their common hopes and, at a crucial stage in history, acted as a catalyst of the energies and best qualities of his nation. He did not impose himself on his people in order to become their leader – he embodied their virtues.

During the war he radiated strength. His mere presence bred confidence. And whenever he made a speech – although he never sought to conceal the all too frequent perils of the situation – this feeling of confidence became even stronger. His voice, his words the way he bore himself, the way he dressed – his siren suit and ten-gallon hat, his bow tie – the gestures he used, particularly his V-sign, his cigar, all these things went into the making of a personality whose presence made a quite extraordinary impact – moving and reassuring at the same time.

Those who had the privilege of meeting him at close quarters will never forget his eyes. There was often a twinkle in them, ironical, with a dash of mischief. But when he dealt with a major issue or happened to mention one of his enemies, a hard glint would suddenly come into his eyes. One realized right away that here was a man that one would rather have on one's side than against one.

He was great because he was a real man, with all his passions, his weaknesses, his fondness of the good things in life, his love of beauty, his ambitions and his hates. Those who look down on their fellow men, who are excessively proud of their intellect and too sure of their judgement, only experience a partial and fickle glory. To govern men well, one must understand and love them despite all their inadequacies; one must live amongst them and live as they do. True greatness is the sum total of all these simple virtues, virtues which Churchill posssessed in the highest degree.

At our embassy luncheon, Churchill made a characteristic remark. When M. Pierlot turned to him and said – in a manner just as typical of himself: 'I am glad to hear, Prime Minister, that the British pilots are trying to bomb military targets only,' Churchill replied in his rugged French, with his inimitable accent and a smile which somewhat softened the brutality of his reply: 'For the moment we are still short of ammunition. Work before pleasure.'

M. Pierlot was too serious a man to understand and appreciate such humour.

I got to know Churchill better after the war. In Brussels and Strasbourg, like Churchill, I attended the unforgettable meetings in support of a united Europe, of which he had become a champion. He was a member of the European Consultative Assembly when I was its President. In 1950, when some Dutch conservatives opposed my re-election because of my attitude over the question of the Belgian monarchy, it was thanks to a speech by Churchill that I was spared a humiliating defeat. I am sure he did not approve all my actions in this connection, but in 1940 he had been too firmly opposed to Leopold's policy not to understand the importance to us of this issue and the passions it had aroused.

I am also indebted to Churchill for a very important political lesson. When one considers that he was rejected by the British electorate even before the war was over, I think that no politician, whoever he may be, whatever he has done, has the right to complain. In his greatness Churchill has taught me many things, but in this defeat at the polls he also taught me something about wisdom in times of defeat – something about wisdom, but nothing about taking defeat lying down. One only had to hear him speak of that cruel shock, and the revenge he would wreak, to know the two sentiments should never be confused.

I met him a number of times after that. Whenever possible I went to pay him my respects and show him my friendship. I saw the old lion when he was tired, but I never saw him without being moved. To the very end I tried to show that, like so many others, I had not forgotten what we owed him.

As soon as we arrived in London in 1940 we got down to work. The task we faced was not easy. We had to establish ourselves with the British Government as well as the Belgian expatriate colony. Everyone had to be convinced that the four of us – Pierlot, Gutt, deVleeschauwer and I – were the embodiment of Belgium's constitutional legality, and that we therefore had the incontestable right to be heard, and even obeyed.

First, we had to make our view of the war quite clear and thus put at ease any who might have doubts about following us. We had to restate the truth about our Army's efforts in the eighteen-day campaign. We wanted to define the King's position and our attitude towards him. On 22 November 1940, a month after my arrival in London, I drew up a memorandum for our diplomats, defining our stand *vis-à-vis* the King, the Government, Belgium and the Congo. The position of the King was our primary concern. We decided to make every effort to sort things out and were convinced of the need to avoid, if possible, the likely dangerous post-war consequences of the conflict with Leopold. All four of us were monarchists, albeit for different reasons, and we thought that a constitutional crisis following the liberation could have grave repercussions in Belgium. We thus resolved not to make political capital out of our disagreement with the King, but to adopt the formula of a 'regrettable misunderstanding', which Cardinal van Roey had used in a pastoral letter shortly after the surrender.

Throughout the war we repeatedly proclaimed our loyalty to the King, underlining the firmness of the royal prisoner in abstaining from all political action, thus symbolizing passive resistance to the enemy. We explained at length that there was no inconsistency between what the King was doing in Belgium and what the Government was doing in Britain. They were two aspects of the same policy.

Cut off from the King, who ignored us and rejected our overtures, we were far from sure that our official propaganda represented the true state of affairs. But we preferred not to look at reality too closely. We let ourselves be guided entirely by what we believed was a *raison d'état*. After the war, when the quarrel we had tried to avoid broke out, our opponents attempted to make political capital out of what we had said at this time. They thought they could cause us embarrassment by quoting our own arguments back at us. This was neither fair nor clever.

It is difficult to understand why the King did not seize the opportunity we had offered him. With our agreement, even assistance, he could have re-established himself by appearing to favour our presence in Britain. He did not choose to do so. Why, I do not know, but I still regret it.

On 10 May 1941, the first anniversary of the invasion, I spoke to the Belgian people over the BBC. I restated our position and told them: 'Rally around our imprisoned King. He personifies our martyred land. Keep faith with him, as we here are doing.'

It was very wrong to portray these words later as signifying repentance. They were the considered and calculated expression of a policy which, had it won acceptance, would have allowed us to avoid many a tragedy.

The Benelux Plan

We were quite busy in London. Governing several tens of thousands of Belgians presented the same problems as governing nine million, but, on the other hand, we were freed from certain peace-time chores. There were no sittings of Parliament, no Party meetings. This gave us time to consider the main problems in greater depth. As soon as military victory seemed certain, we began to think about the future.

I have found some of the notes written in those war years and can trace back to them the ideas which were to inspire me after the victory. Re-reading years later what one has written about oneself or about events is often a painful experience. One is surprised at oneself and saddened to have misjudged things so often. However, one is also pleased at one's insight when one has not been proved too wrong. My wartime predictions about the future have been largely justified. In a note written in 1941 to Miss Irene Ward, the Conservative MP, a note which, I believe, reached the Foreign Office, I said:

'Allow me to end with a few thoughts about the future. The events of the last twenty months in Europe have shown that its countries must unite. They have been shown to be dependent on each other for their security. After the war Europe will be glad to unite behind Britain's victorious leadership, providing that (1) Britain remains strong, (2) Britain concerns herself with Europe. It will not be sufficient for Britain to establish, and try to maintain, a balance of power to offset a hegemony in Europe. She must herself assume the responsibilities born of her supremacy.

'If Britain fails to recognize her duty to Europe, if she

does not pursue a continental policy which makes her a strong leader of Europe, she must expect to be rapidly deprived of the fruits of her present efforts. Europe will organize against her, and I dare say that Germany, despite her defeat, will be the leader. The ideal solution would, of course, be a world organization, or failing this an organization embracing all Europe. But ideals are rarely compatible with political reality. After the war it will be essential to try and construct something solid, but to do this it may be necessary to sacrifice some of the more grandiose features of such an organization.

'Naturally, the security and prosperity of Western Europe is Belgium's main preoccupation. The countries of Western Europe have their own peculiarities, but there are no territorial disputes which divide them. On the contrary, they share political, legal and moral standards as well as a broadly similar standard of living. They possess all that is necessary for close cooperation. A united or federated Western Europe must be the nucleus of post-war policy and reconstruction, and it is on this that Britain must lean.'

By 1942, my thinking had become more specific.

'There can be no political solution without an economic solution, and vice versa. In the world of tomorrow, especially the Europe of tomorrow and, more particularly, the small countries of Europe, the problems of security and prosperity will be inseparable. The formula 'United in war, but isolated in peace' did not apply yesterday and it will be completely inapplicable tomorrow. We must reconcile the rebirth of nationalism with an internationalism which will be essential. This can be done, and I believe we shall have to go a long way in this direction. The principles of national sovereignty will have to be modified not only where the small countries are concerned but also in regard to the great ones. If we try to cling to old formulae we shall achieve nothing worthwhile. The experience of the League of Nations demonstrates this point. Its rule of unanimity, its deference to national sovereignty, was one of the principal reasons for its failure. Tomorrow there will be international, regional,

European or world organizations, it does not matter which. But they are doomed to failure from the outset if their participants do not accept that the body must be superior to its individual members. No system is without its disadvantages. Order always involves some restriction of liberty. We must make our choice and, above all, having made it, accept the consequences.'

Thus, in the middle of the war, long before the hour of decision had struck, I was thinking of the future, dreaming of a united or federated Europe. I wanted to see Britain leading a movement which would champion this idea. I refused to make a distinction between military alliances and economic agreements. I pleaded strongly against the absolute sovereignty of States, and for supra-nationalism, ideas for which I was to go on fighting for the next twenty years.

During my stay in Britain I had the opportunity, in laying the foundation of the Benelux plan, to participate in setting the first major example of European economic collaboration.

On 11 June 1941 I received the following letter from Gutt:

'My dear Spaak,

I have just received some routine papers which have arrived in the bag from America. Among them there is a record of a conversation I had over there with a M. Vandenbroek. He is the real leader of the Dutch delegation to the tin cartel. This cartel consisted essentially of Vandenbroek, Lyttleton, a top British civil servant, and myself. The negotiations were very tough, and because of this very fact they resulted in a fair measure of friendship and confidence between us. Vandenbroek is not a civil servant. He is an industrialist, but has a good deal of influence in Government circles. Basically, what he said was this: "If we all take back to our respective countries the same ideas with which we left them, the economic war between Belgium and Holland will start up again. There is only one way of ending once and for all the "war" over cauliflowers and sulphuric acid, and that is to create a complete customs union between our two countries. But if you suggest such a thing only two weeks after our return, all our industrialists will protest, and so will your farmers. We must go back to Holland and Belgium with the union already made."

'This of course, sounds very interesting, and from what I know of Belgium, it would, on the whole, be favourably received. How would the British react? If we did anything of the sort, could other countries invoke their commercial agreements with us, notably the most favoured nation clause? These are questions I cannot answer, but I thought it worth reporting this conversation to you so that you can act on it as you see fit.'

11 June 1941. I will not go so far as to say this was the day Benelux was born, but it was certainly the day the good seed was sown in my own mind. The notion of a customs union between Holland, Belgium and Luxembourg was a bold one. It meant giving a new dimension to the relations between our three countries, shedding established traditions and upsetting important economic interests.

Vandenbroek's advice was excellent: 'Create an economic union at once, while the war is still on. If you wait for the liberation and your return to your respective countries, you will never do it.' I am sure he was right. Isolated as we were, and sheltered from the pressure groups which oppose revolutionary ideas of this sort, it still took us more than two years to give our idea concrete shape.

My colleague, M. Van Kleffens, the Dutch Foreign Minister – precise, prudent, opposed to romantic flights of fancy – at first did not appear to be enthusiastic. He favoured a military alliance which would encompass the principal countries of Western Europe. He was hostile to anything which might, even superficially, weaken the Netherlands' ties with Britain. In this respect, he was a resolute champion of a strong Dutch tradition.

The turning point in the long negotiations was the provisional monetary agreement, considered so vital by our financial experts. On 21 October 1943 we fixed the official exchange rate between the Dutch guilder and the Belgian franc. Having thus begun to resolve our economic problems, we were ready to take a much more important step.

On 5 September 1944, a few days after our return to Belgium, we issued a communiqué announcing that a customs union would be set up to include the Belgium-Luxembourg Economic Union and the Netherlands.

'This will be a temporary arrangement, intended to promote the restoration of economic activity and to create conditions which would favour the establishment of a more lasting union later on. It follows the monetary convention concluded by the three countries on 21 December 1943. The agreement, signed by the Ministers of Foreign Affairs and Finance of the three countries, provides for a customs union and will eliminate the levying of duties between Belgium, the Netherlands and Luxembourg. There will be joint arrangements governing the entry of goods from other countries, conceived along liberal lines. All essential commodities, materials and equipment for restoring production will be temporarily exempt from duty. These supplies will account for the bulk of the imports during the period of the agreement.'

Some technical details followed, and the communiqué finished thus: 'The agreement will take effect provisionally as soon as the governments are once more installed in their liberated countries.' Clearly, we were not lacking in optimism or boldness.

In the first months after returning to our respective countries, our decisions came up against strong opposition. Many of our civil servants viewed our London agreement with slightly contemptuous scepticism. They tended to claim that the common tariff proved for in the agreement would be difficult to put into effect, that we had behaved like amateurs, barely aware of the real problems, and that we should now allow experts to reopen the issues we had settled. In fact, we were marking time. We let ourselves be impressed by the objections of the technicians. Contrary to our hopes, the London agreement was not implemented after the liberation of our countries. We had to wait until April 1946 before we could make any real progress. At that time I called on the Dutch Government, then presided over by Mr Schermerhorn. Our meeting was decisive.

Schermerhorn asked me frankly if I still remained a supporter of the London agreements. I said I did. Since he, too, reaffirmed that he stood by the 1944 treaty unconditionally, we decided not to hesitate as we had been doing in the months before. We called in our civil servants and told them that in the next six months the technical problems must all be solved so that the customs union could come into effect. They at once protested and attempted to show that what we wanted them to do was impossible since we had grossly underestimated the difficulties involved. They raised every conceivable objection. Mr Schermerhorn and I stood our ground. We did not give an inch and just went on reiterating our instructions. Six months later the difficulties had been overcome. On 14 March 1947 a supplementary protocol to the customs union convention was signed at The Hague. These events helped me to crystallize my ideas about the relationship that should exist between a minister and his experts. Ministers who do not know how to deal with a problem tend to set up a committee. The experts, left without directives, discuss endlessly, produce objection after objection, stubbornly defend their respective points of view, and end up by confusing the whole issue. They are often completely negative. But they are not to blame. The guilty party is the minister who is trying to dodge his responsibilities. But when, on the other hand, a minister is courageous enough to make a decision and then turns to his experts to discover how his political decision can be implemented in practice, they will apply all their technical knowledge, all their intelligence and imagination to find a solution. That is how technicians should be used. And that is how I was later to use them many times.

On 1 July 1947 I spoke in Parliament in favour of a motion recommending acceptance of the treaty. I remember only the last sentence of my speech: 'I believe that this agreement between Belgium, Luxembourg and the Netherlands is good for our country and an example to the world.'

The example was to be followed by others!

Early Attempts to Promote European Unity

If my diplomatic endeavour in 1942 was based on the idea of a general European understanding, in the next three years it was devoted to the organization of Western Europe under British leadership.

On re-reading my notes dating back to this period, some of which were addressed to the British Foreign Office, I wonder if my insistence did not strike the British as excessive. I now feel that I was occasionally importunate. However, this may to some extent be unavoidable if one wants to arouse interest in a problem, and particularly if one wants people to stray from a well-trodden path and to take the risks inseparable from any innovation. Patience, I have learned, is a great diplomatic virtue, but too often it is an alibi as well.

Then, suddenly, my efforts seemed to have been rewarded. On 13 July 1944, Mr Eden asked to see me at the Foreign Office. According to the notes I made immediately after my interview, here is what he said:

'You may have been somewhat surprised that I have not given a more definite answer to your various suggestions regarding the organization of Western Europe after the war. You may well have thought that I was not responding enthusiastically, and that I was perhaps not even interested. Of course, this is not so. I thought it better to allow talks on the general organization of the world to get under way before beginning a discussion about the organization of Western Europe. I have acted in this way principally because the President of the United States and Mr Cordell Hull might have been embarrassed if attempts to organize Europe had begun without them. The isolationist element, which is still important in America, might well have taken the attempts to organize Europe as an excuse for claiming that Europe had no need of the USA. Moreover, I have always tried to be very careful with the Americans. They are sometimes a little difficult to deal with. They are averse to taking the initiative, but, on the other hand, they do not like things to be done without them.

'I can now drop my reserve, as discussions are about to begin in Washington between the Americans, the Russians and the British. The aim of these talks will be to draw up a plan for a world organization to guarantee peace. I intend to send Cadogan to Washington to represent us.

'Without being certain of what will happen, I think something will emerge from these talks. As the world organization must be backed up by regional groupings, the time is approaching when talks between Britain, Belgium, Holland, Norway and France could be of use.

'The idea of a Western European organization has been approved by the Russians. Stalin and I discussed the matter when I went to Moscow in 1941, and not only did the Russians raise no objection to the idea, they went so far as to say that it would have their support. Stalin made it clear that the Soviet Government would back any British attempt along these lines.' (Mr Eden then had the relevant file brought in and read to me an account he had made of the discussion he had had on this point during his meeting with Stalin.)

'Eden told me that the British civil service was working on certain proposals to be put before us. He summed up what he had in mind when he said we should join together, but without Germany, in a kind of Locarno Pact.

'I told him how pleased I was to hear this, and also how glad I was that he had finally been able to break his silence; I said I understood very well that his position was delicate, that there were different interests to be considered, but that I was glad to learn what was in his mind. I said that in the circumstances, and given the likely state of opinion in my own country and Holland, it would probably not be difficult to agree on political

83

and military formulae which would give us security; that although I was persuaded of the necessity for a world organization, I also believed firmly that there was an equal need for regional organizations of the sort he envisaged, and that it was necessary to go beyond the point that had been reached at Locarno, in the sense that the political commitment should be more definite and the military organization more comprehensive.

'To make things clear, I told him how our talks with Holland about military matters had progressed and that the Dutch and the Belgians were inclined to accept a close union with Britain and their other neighbours. Naturally, I profited from the occasion to return to my cherished idea – monetary and economic cooperation. I elaborated certain ideas I had suggested previously about the need to combine our interests.

'Mr Eden asked me to think further about the points we had discussed, and suggested that any ideas or proposals we might wish to submit could be passed on to him informally in a memorandum.'

On that day, for the first time, post-war problems had been approached in what seemed to me the right way. Several months later, at the end of 1944, on returning to London for a few days, I had the opportunity to meet Eden again to discuss the same subject. He then told me that, following his talks with the Russians and the Americans, he had come to the conclusion that Stalin was anxious to create a buffer zone between Germany and the Soviet Union, more or less independent and capable of absorbing the impact of any new German aggression. Stalin would therefore raise no objection if Britain were to provide herself with a similar zone and were to agree with Belgium, Holland, Luxembourg, Norway and possibly France on erecting a barrier against a sudden German attack, which was always a possibility. Eden added that he had every reason to think that the Americans shared the Russians' feelings on the matter.

Not having had enough time to examine the problem, Eden asked me to put to him some of my ideas in writing as a basis for discussion. He said he would like to make a start very soon. The next day I handed to Sir Alexander Cadogan, the Permanent Under-Secretary at the Foreign Office, a memorandum for which M. van Langenhove was mainly responsible. It was entitled 'Suggestions for British-Belgian cooperation within the framework of a regional agreement for Western Europe', and covered military, political and economic affairs.

This important document was in many ways a precursor of the kind of negotiation that was to lead to the setting up, in 1949, of the Atlantic Alliance. It reflected my ambitions and showed how far I thought it possible to go in reaching an understanding with Britain.

I discussed the main points of this memorandum at a meeting with Sir Alexander Cadogan. His reaction was understanding, sympathetic but non-commital. No answer could be given to me before Eden himself had taken a stand and the War Cabinet had expressed its opinion. Such a reply was inevitable, and I had no choice but to accept it.

My efforts thus made no immediate impact. A few months later Churchill's Government was defeated, and Labour came to power. Ernest Bevin became Foreign Secretary, and I had to begin all over again. I started from the same principles, but put less emphasis on economics, since the Labour Party was more insular than the Conservatives, and Bevin less disposed than Eden to take on European commitments. At the end of 1945 I again offered close military cooperation to Britain. I suggested this should be brought about in the following stages:

1 Creation of one or more mixed commissions which would examine the technical problems of coordinating the work of the British and Belgian Armies and Air Forces and submit relevant proposals to the two Governments.
2 Extension of the military arrangements to France, the Netherlands and Luxembourg.
3 Coordination of these arrangements with the provisions of the UN Charter.
4 A Belgian offer of a treaty of friendship with the USSR, similar to the Anglo-Soviet and Franco-Soviet treaties.

Bevin signified his agreement in principle with these

suggestions, but thought that nothing could be finalized before the UN Charter had come into force. So, once again, it was necessary to wait.

In the meantime I tried to discover what was in the minds of the Soviets. We were most anxious at that time to do nothing that might displease the Russians. On 8 February 1946 I met Vyshinsky, the head of the Soviet delegation to the first UN Assembly, then meeting in London, over which I presided. I said to him:

'I am not calling on you as the President of the Assembly but as the Foreign Minister of Belgium, interested in examining the relations between our two countries. I am grateful to you for receiving me and giving me the opportunity to explain to you the main features of Belgian foreign policy.

'We have been invaded twice, and the main objective of our policy is to avoid war. We think the best way of doing this is to maintain unity between the main members of the wartime Alliance. I think the small Powers must do all they can to help preserve this alliance, and avoid doing anything liable to make friendship between the Great Powers more difficult. I am therefore opposed in principle to the idea of a Western bloc in the sense of a political alliance directed against Russia. Nevertheless, I am bound to tell you that for a country like mine there are questions that can be dealt with only in a regional context. Take, for example, the military problem. Belgium can today no longer guarantee her security with her own resources; she must of necessity become part of a wider organization. To me, this does not seem to be contrary to the UN Charter, which allows for regional agreements and special arrangements.

'Belgium is also obliged to try and extend its range of economic activity. This is why we have already formed an economic union with Luxembourg and Holland, and why we must attempt to include other neighbouring countries in this economic union. There is strong support in Belgium for a similar agreement with France, for example.'

At this point Vyshinsky interrupted me to say: 'You are right, we are strongly opposed to a Western bloc. Certain people would like to incorporate Poland, Czechoslovakia, France and other Western countries, including Germany if need be, in an anti-Soviet alliance. We are, of course, utterly hostile to such a policy.'

I replied that although I did not know of such plans, Belgium would certainly not agree to be a party to them and, moreover, I thought we in Belgium should help build bridges between East and West. I said I had been wondering how we could help in this respect and that I had considered the possibility of a Soviet-Belgian friendship pact on the lines of the Anglo-Soviet agreement. Such a gesture, I suggested, might make a good impression and help clear up certain misunderstandings.

Vyshinsky replied that what I had said seemed interesting and could be of benefit to both our countries. He said he would inform Molotov. We discussed the matter no further.

There was no sequel to this conversation. Eight years later, in the Kremlin, when Bulganin and Khrushchev took me to task for allegedly having frequently expressed anti-Soviet sentiments, I recalled my conversation with Vyshinsky. They seemed very surprised. The next day they admitted to me that they had checked their files and verified my account and that there was nothing to find fault with. Their comment was: 'Let's forget all that, it is never too late for a good deed!' But events do not happen at the pleasure of ministers and diplomatists. It is difficult to make up for lost time, and missed opportunities do not come again.

After 1945, relations between the Russians and their Western allies began to deteriorate. Regional groupings first conceived as part of a comprehensive agreement for the whole of Europe little by little changed into antagonistic blocs – and this we deplored. In 1948 the measure we had seen as a move to protect us from Germany was in fact turned against the Soviet Union. In 1954, Germany, the original object of our fears, became our partner in the Western European Union and the Atlantic Alliance.

It is certainly bad policy to allow problems to drag on. I have found that out many times. But perhaps, in this case, it was for the best, for from an organization that was merely an idle dream there sprang one which was effective because it was based on a realistic concept.

Franco-Belgian Relations

In my eagerness to achieve an alliance with Britain I did not lose sight of the fact that a proper balance in Belgian policy also depends on France.

During the war years France's situation had been strange. Although Britain had broken off diplomatic relations with the Pétain Government, she still considered it the legal government of France. The US had maintained its links with Vichy. Roosevelt was not hostile to Pétain, and his relations with de Gaulle were always difficult. The two men did not get on at all. My sympathies were with the Free French. I had foreseen that de Gaulle would head the first government of a liberated France, and I did all I could to convince the British of this. I did not hesitate to ask the Belgian Government to make its position in this matter absolutely clear.

As early as 3 October 1941, Pierlot wrote to de Gaulle:

'The Belgian Government has decided to recognize you as the leader of all the free French who, in the United Kingdom and throughout the world, have rallied to you to fight under your leadership for the Allied cause, to defeat Hitler's Germany and restore their national independence. I have pleasure in notifying you of this decision of the Belgian Government and in informing you that we are prepared to join with you in establishing and pursuing the fullest cooperation against the common enemy.'

This decision had been made easier for us by the fact that on leaving Vichy we had instructed our Ambassador to France to inform the Government that his mission was at an end and he was returning to Belgium. We had not broken off diplomatic relations, properly speaking; we had merely decided not to keep them up.

In May 1942 we agreed to the designation of a representative from the French National Committee to the Belgian Government. My private secretary was assigned to represent us *vis-à-vis* the Free French.

In the spring of 1943, after de Gaulle had installed himself in Algiers, we recognized the National Liberation Committee as 'the body qualified to conduct the French war effort within the framework of allied cooperation as well as to administer all French interests'. A new bridge had thus been crossed, and I sent Count de Romrée, one of our best diplomatists, to Algiers to represent us.

Finally, when in March 1944, the Committee transformed itself into the French Provisional Government, I indicated our intention of offering official recognition, and this was accorded in June. The Belgian Government was one of the first to do so, despite the hesitations of the British and their counsels of prudence. To underline the importance of this step I appointed Count de Romrée Ambassador to the Provisional Government.

Thus, throughout these years we had, as far as possible, given diplomatic expression to our wish to support the efforts of General de Gaulle. He embodied our hopes of seeing France rise again to take her rightful place in Europe and the world. We considered this essential.

But relations between France and Belgium are never easy. There is always a gap between the fine speeches which are customarily exchanged and reality. All my correspondence with de Romrée when he was in Algeria and I in London in 1944 shows how eager I was for trusting collaboration. On 13 April 1944, after having explained why negotiations for a customs union between France and Belgium seemed premature, I indicated those economic, political and military subjects which could be the subject of discussion and on which we could try to build an agreement. My proposals were very similar to those I was also making to the British at the same time. They were generally well received, although it was clear that the French authorities were more concerned with immediate problems than with those of the future.

Our talks yielded few results. After the liberation, France was much more interested in her relations with the

USSR than in the idea of organizing Western Europe. General de Gaulle's trip to Moscow illustrated this point. We had to wait until mid-1947 before there was a change.

On 8 June 1947 I spent an afternoon with M. Bidault. I received him at the Château d'Ardenne. He had made the journey from Paris in the greatest secrecy. We talked for several hours. What he had to say seemed very interesting. Immediately afterwards I drafted a memorandum on what had taken place. Here is an extract:

> 'Bidault made no secret of his belief that agreement with the Soviet Union was impossible. He stressed that this statement of his should be considered the more important as he had hitherto sincerely tried to move closer to Russia. He told me frankly that he considered he had failed; that one could have no confidence in the Soviet leaders, that they were narrow-minded, set in their intentions and untrustworthy. Everything he said made it clear that he had decided on a change of policy and would now rely much more on the Anglo-Saxons, above all, the Americans.'

Bidault was, from this moment on, mentally prepared to accept the Marshall Plan and the treaties of Brussels and Washington.

The years 1947 and 1948 were the turning point in post-war international politics. Henceforth our activity was to be very different from what we had hoped only a few years before.

During my years in Britain I learned a great deal. I was involved in varied and important negotiations. I made the acquaintance of the most important men on both sides of the Atlantic, men who were to remain important when peace returned. My political horizons were greatly widened. The responsibilities I undertook together with my colleagues made me more prudent and mature. Little by little, I acquired the qualities of a good foreign minister. But I thought my career, if not at an end, was about to suffer an eclipse. I felt it was improbable that it could continue uninterrupted in a liberated Belgium since I would have to account for my actions before the war and, even more so, during the war.

I was ready for these new battles. They never came. Contrary to my expectations, I remained in the Government and, before leaving in 1949, became Prime Minister again in 1947.

However, we were not received with much enthusiasm in Belgium. We returned to Brussels a few days after its liberation. The reception was hardly equal to our dreams during our years abroad. We disembarked on a deserted aerodrome from planes which had been put at our disposal by the British Government. Nobody had been warned of our arrival. The cars which took us into town were preceded by a jeep. One of our colleagues stood in it, shouting to the few citizens we passed: 'Here is your Government.' I must confess that this produced no reaction at all, neither hostility nor enthusiasm, just total indifference. We arrived in the Rue de la Loi, where at least the joy of being reunited with my family awaited me. A few friends presented themselves in ragged array. Among the first was Achille van Acker, who was later to play such an important part. Certainly we were all pleased to see one another. But it was hard to make contact. In spite of our reassuring words from London, they were a little frightened of us. There was a fear that we had returned as judges, ignorant of what had happened under the occupation and anxious to dominate. Nothing could have been further from our minds. In the weeks that followed, the impossibility of finding another Prime Minister had to be proved beyond all doubt before Pierlot, completely against his inclinations, was persuaded to accept and to keep his post.

Soon after our return we decided to lay a wreath on the tomb of the unknown soldier. I still have sad memories of the ceremony. A few ministers, surrounded by a handful of aides and flanked by policemen, walked from the Rue de la Loi to the memorial. The passers-by looked on, silent, astonished, wondering who we were and what on earth we were doing. I no longer knew if I was celebrating victory or, surrounded as we were, being marched off to the High Court. A few hours later we were plunged again into the debates and intrigues of domestic politics. Things had not changed.

PART THREE

The United Nations

13

The World Organization

During the autumn of 1944 we learnt officially that the United States, Great Britain, the USSR and China were meeting at Dumbarton Oaks to draft the charter of a new League of Nations.

This attempt was in line both with my own wishes and those of the Belgian Government. I had mentioned this again and again in my papers on post-war problems. To this day, despite the disappointments with the UN, despite its inadequacies, it is my considered belief that we must remain loyal to it and, accepting it with all its faults, seek to improve it. If one day we succeed in creating a world organization with sufficient authority to legislate in the field of international law and, above all, to enforce respect for that law, relations between peoples will be raised to a higher level. World peace will have been safeguarded beyond all doubt. At present this is still a dream, though not an idle one. Great scientific experiments fail untold times before they succeed. Why, then, should great human experiments succeed from the very start? It is by repeating those experiments, by studying the reasons for their failure, that we shall finally discover the formula for success. We shall have to go about this task with patience.

At the beginning of 1944, having earlier declared that we must allow ourselves to be hypnotized no longer by the 'mirage of universality', I set out the conditions which, to my way of thinking, any future member countries would have to meet before being admitted to the new organization. I said they must have democratic institutions; be ready to join an international armed force; renounce any territorial claims; agree to a minimum of social legislation; surrender the right to manipulate their currencies, and, finally, agree to the abolition of the rule of unanimity, i.e. they must be prepared to respect the will of the majority in international relations.

The discussions between the Great Powers did not take this line. Unfortunately, contrary to what I believed to be right, the concept of universality set the tone. In the event, admission to membership, although subject to certain rules of procedure, was made extremely easy. In fact, it finally became a mere formality. I remain convinced that, far from being helpful, this eventually became one source of the UN's weakness.

Haunted by the experience of the League of Nations and mindful of the fact that the rule of unanimity was one of the basic causes of its failure, the representatives of the Great Powers accorded the right of veto to the permanent members of the Security Council. While this was a step in the right direction, the result was far from ideal, as the future was soon to show.

14

San Francisco –
Roosevelt and Truman

The San Francisco conference, during the course of which the UN was established, opened towards the end of April 1945. The war had not yet ended either in Germany or Japan. The urgency with which the problem was tackled was both symptomatic and welcome. It reflected the impatience of a world which had not yet wakened from its nightmare.

Leaving Brussels on 11 April, I stopped for the night in London, from where I was to fly to the United States. I spent the night at the Dorchester. The following morning I read in the paper that had been slipped under my door the news of President Roosevelt's death. A great war leader had passed away before the day of victory. Thus it was not to be Roosevelt who would welcome us at San Francisco and guide us along the paths of peace. His cruel death bore the tragic stamp of a destiny unfulfilled. It brought home to us how the unknown can so often determine events. So much that happens frustrates our reasoning, still more our hopes.

I was genuinely moved, though perhaps not as deeply as I might have been. I hesitate to admit it but I was disappointed in President Roosevelt. I am aware of his place in history, his incomparable ability, displayed on many occasions, the vital part he played both in his own country and internationally. However, the dealings I had with him in 1941 left me with an unfortunate impression which I have never been able to forget.

I first met him during my first visit to the United States, at a time when that country had not yet entered the war. I had crossed the Atlantic to attend a conference of the International Labour Organization and had taken the opportunity to request a meeting with the President. My intention was to explain to him the food situation in Belgium, which was worrying us.

It was my first visit to the White House, my first glimpse of the famous oval room, which I entered after passing through noisy offices crowded with journalists, secretaries and aides. The peace which reigned in this room, with its unusual shape and its great bay windows looking out on the gardens, made a striking contrast with the noise and bustle outside. I entered with some awe, but prepared to be charmed. I saw Roosevelt as the author of the New Deal, the generous democrat, a man whose economic and social achievements I admired, whose speeches I had read, who had, in a manner of speaking, been my guide and mentor in the pre-war years. I hoped to be able to make it clear to him how much I admired him.

In fact, I was not at all well received. At that time, Belgium's stock abroad did not stand particularly high. The President was cold and matter-of-fact in what he had to say. I explained to him the food situation in occupied Belgium and exerted all my powers of persuasion to interest him in the fate of my compatriots. He listened to me impassively. When I had ended my plea, he declared coldly, without betraying the slightest sign of human warmth or compassion, that nothing could be done. This unfeeling answer was accompanied by comments which angered me, and this anger was all the harder to contain as I was forced to hide it. He declared that the trials through which Belgium was passing were not so tragic, that Germany had gone through much the same experience after the First World War and had yet produced a generation that was physically fit: the proof of this could be seen in the way the Germans were now fighting.

I was dumbfounded, and so was M. Theunis, who was with me. It was he – his English was very much better than mine – who replied rather pointedly, but to no effect. There was no common ground between us, no meeting of minds. I left the room which I had entered so confidently, so ready to show my admiration, in a mood of sadness and disappointment.

I was to see President Roosevelt only once more. He

was giving an official reception for the conference delegates. We filed past him one by one. He shook each of us by both hands affectionately, smiled, and had a few friendly words for everyone. He treated each delegate as a guest of honour, as a very dear friend whom he was glad to see again after a long absence. This artificial display of affection was almost more painful to bear than his cruel indifference of a few days before. To me, President Roosevelt remains a great man with whom I was unable to enter into spiritual communion. My memory of him is tinged with frustration.

I arrived in Washington two or three days after Roosevelt's funeral, and was received by President Truman. I was one of the first foreign visitors to meet the new President. The impression he made on me was altogether different from that of his predecessor. As I entered the presidential study once again, I was undoubtedly less over-awed than on the first occasion. This time, according to what I had been told, I was not about to be admitted into the presence of a great man. In fact, I was wholly captivated by the new President. He did not try to impress me; on the contrary, with touching sincerity he spoke to me of his anxiety about the responsibilities which he had just under-taken, and made no attempt to hide his feeling of not being altogether ready for the part he was expected to play. At the same time, however, he declared with calm but moving firmness that he was determined to do his duty.

Each time I met President Truman I was struck by his modesty, which went hand in hand with a resolve to do what had to be done without ostentation, but also without fear. He lacked Roosevelt's brilliance, Roosevelt's charm, which worked with certain people. Truman may have dis-appointed the intellectuals with whom he came into contact, but I believe he was a very great President of the United States. Admittedly, he had excellent assistants at the State Department in General Marshall and Dean Acheson. This, however, in no way detracts from his merit – on the contrary. Surely one's choice of advisers and helpers is the best possible proof of sound judgement. Great kings have always had great ministers.

Truman has been much criticized. Like all politicians, he was to experience injustice and ingratitude. But with the passage of time, when the facts come to be seen in their true perspective, I am sure his work will receive due credit. It was Truman who put an end to the war with Japan by taking one of the gravest decisions ever taken by man. It was he who saved Europe through the Marshall Plan. It was he who transformed the USA's traditional foreign policy by signing the North Atlantic Treaty. It was he who put a halt to the expansion of communism by applying in Greece what came to be known as the Truman Doctrine. It was he who saved the United Nations by enforcing – and enforcing boldly – the principle of collective security in Korea. It was he who launched the concept of aid to the underdeveloped countries, and it was he who effectively maintained the rights of the civil power and thus made a vital contribution to the maintenance of democratic government. Through the Fair Deal, Truman continued the pursuit of social justice begun by his predecessor, and applied himself courageously to the problem of racial equality.

There is another thing about him I like: his simplicity. For example, this is what he says in his *Diary*: 'Today Bessie and Margaret are leaving Washington and I feel terribly lonely.

There may be those who will think such an admission naïve, but I consider it revealing. To me, it proves once again that to govern one's fellow men well one must be as they are, one must share their feelings, their anxieties, their simple pleasures.

Finally, I admire him because he is a fighter. What a splendid campaign he fought for his re-election in 1948! Everybody – all the embassies, which are by no means always well-informed – believed his chances to be nil. All the press was against him. There was one man in the United States, however, who knew that he could still win, and that man was the President himself – that was enough to give him victory. He proved a first-rate judge, not only of the ups and downs of political life but also of the state of mind of his fellow Americans. Nor am I in the least surprised by this. Many is the time when, walking or driving down the 'Main Street' of one of America's larger provincial towns, I would remark full of amazement to whoever happened to be with me: 'Just look at that man over there! He is the spitting image of President Truman.'

Truman is a typical product of his country – both down to earth and generous, an idealist and a realist. He is proud of his country's wealth and greatness, but is not in the least grasping. He is one of those who believe that power brings with it more duties than rights. Less brilliant than either Roosevelt or Kennedy, less famous in his own lifetime than Eisenhower, his place in history, I am sure, will be no less illustrious than theirs.

I arrived in San Francisco two or three days before the opening of the conference. The preliminary discussions began immediately. They were to reveal, to the dismay of most delegates, the first serious rift between the Russians and the Anglo-Americans.

A meeting of the delegation on the morning of 27 April had to decide who was to represent Poland at the conference. The Soviet Foreign Minister, Molotov, urged that an invitation be sent immediately to the Government about to be set up in Lublin. Eden and Stettinius, the American Secretary of State, replied that it had been decided at Yalta that a Polish government of national union would be established in which the Poles who had spent the war in the USSR and those who had spent it in London would be equally represented. Poland should not be invited to the conference until such time as that step had been taken.

A lively discussion ensued. To those who, like myself, still believed in good faith and understanding among the great allies, the violence of the discussion came as a genuine surprise. These were not friends who were locked in debate; this was a confrontation of adversaries. Molotov was particularly aggressive. He turned arrogantly to the representatives of Czechoslovakia and France and asked for their support. The Czech Foreign Minister, Masaryk, an attractive figure, loyal and well-meaning, at this point set out on his road to Calvary. After some hesitation, he rallied to the Soviet point of view. Bidault, who was making his debut in international affairs, was dumbfounded by the appeal made to him and lapsed into an embarrassed silence.

We delegates of the medium and small powers exchanged anxious glances, suddenly aware that the world was destined to become a place far removed from that of our dreams. It was a dramatic moment.

At this point I made my first attempt to act as mediator. I was to make many more such efforts in the years that followed. Concerned, above all, to maintain accord among the Great Powers and anxious not to take sides or do anything to inflict a humiliating defeat on either side, I proposed that the debate be adjourned until the 'inviting nations' had found a solution. This may not have been a brilliant suggestion but the time gained allowed tempers to cool. My proposals were adopted unanimously, with only Molotov abstaining. He wanted to bring the matter before the Excutive Committee of the conference.

The first plenary session ended that afternoon. The agenda comprised fifty-six carefully prepared speeches, read with varying degrees of skill from the rostrum. It was a severe test and also the beginning of that open diplomacy of which the UN was to become the main – and noisy – venue. True, I am opposed to secret diplomacy, which is in any case impossible now that indiscretion has become not only the custom but almost the rule, but I confess that open diplomacy of the kind that is being practised nowadays is not to my liking. I believe it to be ineffective. Those who are involved are forced to pay more attention to the repercussions of their actions in the outside world than to the goal they are seeking to achieve. They are bent on asserting themselves rather than trying to convince others of the rightness of their cause. They give far more thought to public opinion at home than to the problems which call for a solution. Moreover, once a speaker has taken a clear-cut position publicly, it is difficult for him to modify it. In such a situation, how can agreement be reached?

However, I made the best of the opportunity to explain my principal ideas: the need to be realistic, not to strive for ideal solutions but to advance step by step; to waive the rule of unanimity in certain cases in order to make effective decisions possible, and I spoke of the need to establish a force capable of ensuring respect for international law. Finally, I made a plea for economic and social cooperation.

As happens all too often in such circumstances, procedural difficulties slowed down our main work. After the Polish episode, we had the Argentinian incident. The heads of delegation had met on 30 April under the chairmanship of Mr Stettinius, and had recommended that the representatives of the Argentine be invited to join the conference forthwith. Molotov opposed this in full session. He was looking for a chance to avenge himself for the setback he had suffered over the Polish affair. He declared that to allow delegates from the Argentine to attend the conference, representing as they did a country with a fascist government, having earlier refused this privilege to the delegates of Poland, could not but harm the prestige of the conference. He was strongly opposed by several Latin American delegates. To the surprise of many, I spoke in support of the Soviet view. I was anxious to be consistent with myself. Having called for agreement among the Great Powers to help solve the Polish problem, it was my belief that the same method should be applied in the case of the Argentine. I thought this impartial approach essential if the experiment that was just beginning was to succeed. It was also my aim to show that, far from being hostile to the USSR, I was, on the contrary, ready to support any reasonable proposal that it might make. I therefore voted with Mr Molotov in favour of a motion for the adjournment of the session. We were defeated by twenty-eight votes to seven.

My part in the affair gave rise to much comment. It was seen as evidence of a measure of independence, of a clear desire for reconciliation and a reasoned refusal to oppose the USSR on each and every issue.

The *New York Herald Tribune* noted the following day:

'M. Paul-Henri Spaak is regarded by all as a most important force at this conference. Belgian Foreign Minister before the war, during his years of exile and after the liberation of his country, Paul-Henri Spaak seems today to be one of those rare politicians who bridge the gulf between Europe's troubled past and her still uncertain future. He is one of the first European Socialists to have grasped the importance of the national element in contemporary European life. Far from being sectarian, he has nothing in common with the outdated anti-clericalism of the Belgian Socialist Party. He has no doctrinal sympathy whatever for Soviet Communism, nor with the semi-totalitarian regime in the Argentine. His chief aim is to consolidate democracy in Western Europe, and this cannot be done except through the closest possible cooperation between Britain and France. On the other hand, he believes that Western Europe must on no account appear to be under orders to oppose Soviet Russia, directly or indirectly.'

I admit that in quoting these few lines I may have given way to that vanity of which no man is wholly free, but my aim is also – and this is my excuse – to establish that even then there were those who were aware of my dream for Europe and my anxiety to make it come true without coming into conflict with the USSR.

My stay in San Francisco was to end forty-eight hours later. I received a cable announcing the freeing of King Leopold III by American troops. My presence in Belgium was required.

15

The First Assembly
in London and New York:
A Difficult Election

The charter having been signed, it was decided to hold a meeting of the Preparatory Committee in London to decide where the Organization would have its seat. There was talk of my becoming head of the Organization. The British advised me against accepting and assured me that I would be their choice as president of the first assembly. I therefore stood down in favour of the delegate from Colombia, Señor Zuleta Angel, who filled the post with great distinction.

A sub-committee presented a report which recommended that the seat of the Organization be established in the United States, although I pleaded in favour of Europe. After putting forward a number of arguments on behalf of the Old World, I declared that it would be wrong to concentrate the majority of international organizations in one part of the world. The World Bank, the Monetary Fund and the civil aviation organization were either already established, or about to be established, in America. I argued that it would be wise to maintain a balance. I went on to urge – and this was my principal argument – that the Organization should not be based in the territory of a permanent member of the Security Council. I quoted the apt remark of my compatriot M. Bourquin:

'The state in which the Organization has its permanent seat has a certain advantage over the other members of the Organization. Its relations with the latter, relations established between the leaders of the host country and the officials of the Organization, as well as the impact of

105

the local press, are bound to have a considerable influence. In the case of a second-rate Power this may be of slight consequence. However, the situation is altogether different with a great Power, not only because the influence brought to bear on the collective work of the member countries is necessarily very much greater, but also because the entire system of cooperation is based on a balance between the Great Powers, and that balance would then be threatened.'

In conclusion, I declared that if the permanent seat of the Organization were established on the soil of one of the five Great Powers, that Power, or at least its Foreign Ministry, would soon have cause for regret in view of the trouble which might arise as a result of possible conflicts between the policies of the host country and those of the Organization.

After twenty years of experience I can find no fault with these arguments. Nevertheless, I was defeated, although only by a narrow margin. After Adlai Stevenson had said a few words on behalf of the US delegation, of which he was the leader, stressing that it would be a great honour for his country to welcome the UN and announcing his intention to abstain in the ballot, the amendment calling for the establishment of the Organization's seat in Europe was defeated by twenty-five votes to twenty-three. The Russians and all the communist countries voted for the United States. I wonder if they have ever regretted their decision.

The first part of the General Assembly's first session was due to begin in London on 10 January 1946. I left Brussels on the 8th, convinced that I would be elected chairman without difficulty since the British had chosen me as their candidate and there appeared to be no opposition.

I went back to my old office in Eaton Square. There, on the 9th, in the early afternoon, I received Noel-Baker, a member of the Attlee Government. He seemed embarrassed and had a disagreeable surprise for me. He said he felt bound to tell me that my election as chairman was impossible. The Great Powers, he declared, had discussed the question among themselves, and the Russians had strongly opposed my candidacy. The Americans were anxious not to clash with the Russians over such an issue and the British did not think it wise that the atmosphere should be troubled at the very outset of a session that was bound to be of great importance.

I was disappointed. True, I would have understood very well if the choice of the Assembly had fallen on another candidate, but the Belgian press had reported that my election was certain and my failure was bound to come as an unpleasant surprise. What could I do? Nothing, apart from accepting my defeat with good grace and putting on a brave face. This I was ready to do.

The session began on 10 January, Señor Zuleta Angel presiding. The first item on the agenda was the designation of a chairman. Gromyko immediately signalled that he wished to speak, and he put forward the name of Trygve Lie, the Norwegian Foreign Minister. He paid tribute, quite rightly, to the fine qualities of the Norwegian people and their Minister. Trygve Lie was supported by the delegates of Poland, the Ukraine and Denmark. No one rose to propose any other name. The whole affair seemed as good as over. Manuilsky, the Ukrainian delegate, who was to reveal himself as a remarkably skilful operator, called on the chairman to declare Trygve Lie elected by acclamation. No rules of procedure had yet been laid down and everything had to be improvized as we went along. At this point a certain hesitation became apparent at the chairman's table and on the floor of the hall. Finally, the President declared that since this was a matter of an appointment, it would be right to take a vote by secret ballot, despite the fact that only one name had been put forward. However, not wishing to impose his views, he would put his proposal to a vote. Voting was by show of hands; fifteen delegates were in favour of a secret ballot, nine in favour of a vote by acclamation, and there were twenty-seven abstentions. These figures reflected the confusion which reigned in the Assembly, and possibly also the reluctance of certain delegates to take a public stand against a Soviet motion.

Señor Zuleta Angel had rendered me, deliberately I believe, a great service. The vote was taken immediately. The circumstances were rather strange as far as I was concerned, since at this point my name had not even been mentioned and I had thus not been officially put forward as a candidate. My chances therefore seemed minute.

I was seated in the first row of delegates, facing the table behind which the scrutineers were sitting. I noticed immediately that there were two small heaps of voting slips which grew slowly and remained more or less equal in size. I followed the proceedings anxiously. At this moment the Bolivian delegate turned towards me and whispered in my ear: 'You have nothing to worry about; Latin America is voting for you.'

Nothing had indicated that there would be this support for my candidacy, nor did I have time to ask myself what was behind it. The President rose from his seat and announced in a grave voice which seemed strangely solemn: 'For M. Spaak, twenty-eight votes; for M. Trygve Lie, twenty-three votes.' I had been elected by a narrow majority, to the surprise of all.

I took my place in the Chairman's seat and thanked Zuleta Angel most sincerely for all he had done. Not having prepared a speech, I confined myself to declaring open the first part of the first General Assembly of the United Nations. The following day, feeling calmer, I made my formal speech of thanks. It contained all the usual banalities and is best forgotten.

My next four weeks in London were full of interest. The work was exciting both from the technical and the political point of view. Our task was to draw up the rules which were to ensure the Assembly continued existence. In the presence of so many different nations with such a variety of traditions it was not easy to devise and propose rules acceptable to all.

In the chair, I learned a great deal, above all that one must always be courteous, that one must always appear interested in whatever suggestions may be submitted, even if one thinks them ridiculous and absurd, and that one must always be patient in the extreme. One must be discreet in one's conduct and abandon any idea of showmanship. Wit and humour – these are qualities most difficult to display at an international gathering. One incident taught me that lesson. The speakers who followed one another at the rostrum were long-winded and I therefore decided to allot fifteen minutes to each. After I had announced my decision, the delegate from San Salvador spoke for at least half an hour. Before calling upon the next speaker, I declared: 'I should like to remind delegates that I have limited speakers to a quarter of an hour each, and by this I do not mean a Latin American quarter of an hour.' My remark was not particularly funny, but neither was it malicious. Nevertheless, these few words, which were intended as a good-natured joke, started a veritable tumult. The delegate from Chile warned me that he would not allow his country to be insulted. I apologized forthwith, declaring that my intentions had been good, and succeeded in calming the Assembly. Privately, I made up my mind that from now on I would be trite rather than brilliant, an ambition which is none too difficult to achieve.

At the close of the first part of the proceedings on 14 February, it was decided to resume the session in New York towards the end of the year, which would enable me to carry on as Chairman. I thus remained Chairman during the second part of the first session, from 23 October to 15 December 1946. The rules of procedure having been agreed in London, the life of the Assembly now followed a settled course. However, the atmosphere in which we worked fell far short of our hopes. Understanding between the Russians and the Anglo-Saxons was anything but good. We were witnessing the beginning of the cold war. I have never understood the Soviet Union's motives in all this. The behaviour of its representatives was intolerable. They opposed everything, contesting the most innocent proposals and putting the most far-fetched interpretations on the rulings given. In this way they ensured their regular defeat by massive majorities in the General Committee, the Security Council and the Assembly. They seemed surprised by this – hurt and angry. They owed it to their crude tactics. I have never seen a fund of sympathy and opportunity for influence dissipated so quickly. If they had so desired, if they had behaved reasonably, they could very easily have played an important role and counteracted American influence during those first few years, when the memory of their part in the war was still fresh. For reasons unknown to me to this day, they chose a very different course, systematically opposing everything and bent on isolating themselves, content with the unconditional support of the communist countries of Eastern Europe.

Molotov, Vyshinsky, the Deputy Foreign Minister, and Gromyko, Soviet representative on the UN Security Council, made life hard for me. The meetings of the General Committee went on for hours on end owing to constant Soviet obstruction. I stood up to it untiringly, remaining at my post as long as necessary to solve whatever problems arose. The Russians applied their obstructive tactics as assiduously where major issues were concerned as on the most trivial occasions. They never agreed to anything, neither the agenda, nor the time of a meeting nor disarmament proposals. They were at all times utterly negative and, once they had taken up a position, nothing would persuade them to change their minds. They repeated exactly the same arguments time and again without even attempting to answer such objections as might have been raised. They turned down all offers of help or support, and were even more difficult with delegates who tried to meet them halfway than with those who stood up to them.

Molotov and Gromyko practised these tactics with imperturbable calm, without ever losing their temper's or raising their voices, but also without ever smiling or relaxing. As for Vyshinsky, he could keep up an amazing flow of words.

The meetings were often stormy and the exchanges devoid of courtesy. On one occasion, Mr Fraser, representing New Zealand, said to Gromyko: 'I am going to make you take back that lie if I have to smash in your face.' Mr Gromyko did not bat an eyelid. Another time Vyshinsky said to General Romulo, the Philippine chief delegate: 'Empty vessels make the most noise.' He obstinately refused to take back these words despite my appeals.

In those troubled days the chairmanship was no rest cure. The USSR – and I am speaking of the USSR at the time of Stalin – was largely responsible for the partial failure of the UN. When the question of the veto came up at San Francisco, the USA and Britain had promised, in order to gain the support of doubtful and opposing member-states, that they would make use of their right of veto only in cases of absolute necessity. They kept their word, as did France and China. The USSR, on the other hand, not only used its right but in fact abused it. It had recourse to the veto dozens of times in the Security Council, thus rendering the latter's debates both exhausting and fruitless, and preventing the UN from doing its work.

The USSR also made use of the General Assembly as a platform for political propaganda. Vyshinsky's speeches had nothing in common with the language of traditional diplomacy. He was not out to obtain specific results, and his speeches bristled with accusations, imprecations, and often with oaths. Although no great orator, he was forceful, but his speeches were much too long and he would go over the same arguments again and again. The speed with which he spoke was the despair of the interpreters. His arguments were often very weak and reminded one of the sort of speech one may hear at a mass rally. He was more concerned with impressing the like-minded than those opposed to him. For all that, his verve made an impact which was all the more striking as he was addressing an audience which was cool and correct.

The Americans were poor at this type of oratory. I cannot recall a single true debater among the members of their delegation at that time. The vehemence of Senator Connally was artificial, and Senator Austin's amiable manner made little impact compared with the Soviet pronouncements. Only later did Cabot Lodge, and above all Adlai Stevenson, succeed in gaining a true hold on the Assembly.

Some delegates, however, did manage to stand up to the Soviet spokesmen. I am thinking, for instance, of Sir Hartley Shawcross, who, in the absence of Bevin, headed the British delegation. He provided a striking contrast to Vyshinsky. He was as coldly incisive as the other was immoderate in his language. The logic of his arguments was impeccable, his irony redoubtable and his sangfroid imperturbable. To see the two locked in battle was a stirring experience. It was like watching a well-bred British greyhound fighting a powerful, rugged, and sometimes cruel Russian bear. Observing the two of them from the chairman's seat was a sight to remember.

Another star performer in the Assembly at that time was

Mrs Pandit, the Indian delegate. She was a very beautiful woman, with regular features and a face lit up by great black eyes which reflected her eager spirit and the ardour of her convictions. Her English was impeccable, with an accent as pure as Sir Hartley's. Always elegant, her gestures at the speaker's rostrum were infinitely graceful. I could see only her back, but I am bound to admit that I often paid more attention to her figure than to her arguments. When it was her turn to speak, the delegates would leave the lobbies where they had sought refuge from the many boring speeches and returned to their seats in haste, like ants drawn by sweet honey. It was all they could do to hold back their murmurs of admiration. It is sometimes said that in politics to be a woman is a handicap, but having seen Mrs Pandit's success in New York I believe that provided the lady concerned is attractive it can in fact be an advantage.

The chief problem before the General Assembly was disarmament. The Russians made the running by putting down a motion in three parts: it called for a general reduction in armaments, for a ban on the production and use of atomic energy for military purposes, and for the Security Council to assume responsibility for the application of both these principles. Thus began a debate which continues to this day, a debate which, after more than twenty years, has borne little fruit.

I certainly do not wish to appear sceptical. I am fully aware of the importance of the problem and am convinced that in the long run world peace can only be safeguarded by general disarmament. However, as time has passed I have become more certain that such action must be gradual; the task must be tackled stage by stage and we must needs be content with only partial success. I do not believe that in the world's present state spectacular results are within our reach. We are losing valuable time in seeking such triumphs while neglecting efforts which, though more modest, could be beneficial for all that.

In 1946 each delegation expounded its position at length in the Assembly. All were agreed on the goal but none would agree on the means. Ever since then the problem of control has been the chief stumbling block.

A sub-commission was set up and I was made its chairman. At its meetings, I witnessed some fascinating debates between Vyshinsky and Sir Hartley Shawcross. What struck me above all, apart from the virtuosity of the two opponents and their amazing powers of oratory, was the different way in which each argued and approached the problems under discussion. I became convinced that they had extreme difficulty in understanding one another, even assuming that they were both of equally good faith. The fact that they mistrusted each other did not help matters.

Finally we succeeded in drafting a declaration which set out the principles for a general reduction of armaments. It was adopted unanimously. I do not propose to reproduce it here, to summarize it or to enlarge upon it. It contains all the principles, all the ideas which were to be discussed in later years. Though, in a sense, it is still topical, it has at the same time become utterly outdated.

16

The Greek Question

The second session of the United Nations General Assembly opened at Lake Success on 16 September 1947.

Mr Trygve Lie, who had become Secretary-General of the UN, was kind enough to ask me if I would be prepared to serve as chairman yet again. He thought that if I agreed my candidacy might well receive unanimous support. I turned the offer down, for I believed that the vote would not be unanimous and that it would be in the best interests of the UN if someone else were asked to take on the chairmanship. Moreover, Belgium was then a member of the Security Council. She had also been elected to the Economic and Social Council, but I had surrendered this privilege to the Netherlands. Enough honour had been bestowed on my country; to provoke jealousy would have been pointless. Lastly, I had just become Premier once again, and was thus unable to absent myself from Belgium for the whole of the session.

Señor Aranha, the Brazilian delegate, was elected chairman. It was a good thing that a representative from Latin America should hold the post.

This second session was to witness a heated debate on Greek affairs. Greece was in the throes of a civil war. The Greek Communists were supported by the USSR, which was dreaming of access to the Mediterranean through the help of friendly governments in Greece and, above all, in Bulgaria and Yugoslavia. The Greek Government had submitted a complaint to the Security Council and the latter had instructed a commission to investigate the situation on Greece's borders and to report back. The Greeks maintained that the Communist rebels would withdraw into Yugoslavia each time they were on the point of being encircled, and that they were receiving constant aid and support from their neighbours, which enabled them to regroup and prepare for new offensive operations in safety.

Belgium was a member of this commission of inquiry. She was represented by General Delvoye, formerly Military Attaché in Paris. I had given him complete discretion in making his reports on the situation. These were the circumstances in which I spoke in the subsequent debate. In supporting the position of the Greek Government, I set forth two important principles, which I had occasion to cite repeatedly thereafter. The Communist delegates, making no attempt to adhere to the problem before us, openly raised the question of Greece's internal affairs. They attacked the Government of that country at length – a striking example of their wish to use the UN as a rostrum for political propaganda. I declared that Paragraph Seven of Article Two of the Charter prohibited such pronouncements, adding that it was highly dangerous for the UN to infringe this vital rule. An unfortunate precedent was being established. Subsequently, several member countries were to rue that day.

I also pleaded earnestly for the right of governments to seek aid from their friends in the event of a rebellion supported from abroad. At that time the situation in a number of European countries was worrying. The Communist Parties in these countries spoke for a minority only but they were active thanks to the support they were receiving from the USSR, and were therefore potentially dangerous. We took the events in Rumania, Bulgaria, Hungary and Poland as a serious warning.

As regards the Greek affair, the facts were plain. The findings of the commission of inquiry were clear. It was proved that Yugoslavia had aided the rebels. All the tricks and all the rhetorical flights of Bebler, the Yugoslav delegate, supported by Vyshinsky, could not cancel out the facts. The two were pleading a hopeless cause so far as the uncommitted delegates were concerned. A resolution which took note of the commission's conclusions was passed by a massive majority. Albania, Bulgaria and Yugoslavia were found to have been giving aid and comfort to the guerrillas fighting the Greek Government. These three countries were called upon to do nothing calculated to assist or support the guerrillas. The resolution went on to list a number of measures to be taken. Had these been implemented, the conflict would have been settled. In practice, however, the governments so charged deliberately ignored the UN, which had no means of forcing them to comply.

US intervention in Greece was needed before the insurrection was defeated, but the civil war was long and cruel. Considerable damage was caused to property, but worse still, many thousands of children were snatched from their parents and taken abroad. They were never to be restored to their families.

Several years later, when travelling in Greece, I was to come upon traces of this tragedy. With desperation in her voice, an old woman in a remote mountain village beseeched me to do something to ensure the return of her son. This vain hope had been kept alive by her immense love.

17

Fear

Paris, 1948. The UN met at the Palais de Chaillot, a decision taken for propaganda reasons. The point was to give the Organization publicity in Europe. The experiment was never repeated. It turned out very expensive, and there was no purpose in advertising the international disunity revealed in our discussions.

Like the two earlier sessions and the many others that were to follow, I do not believe this session made a particular impact on the world. However, for me it was a great occasion since it was there that I delivered the most important speech of my career.

In the general debate, Vyshinsky had spoken at even greater length, and in even more violent terms, than usual. He brusquely criticized the UN itself. None of its organs was spared – not the Security Council, the Assembly nor the Secretariat, nor even the Economic and Social Council. He condemned the Marshall Plan and had the temerity to say that it had 'aggravated the economic situation in the countries involved'. His speech was an apologia for Soviet policies which, he claimed, were 'logically and consistently designed to expand and strengthen international cooperation'. These policies followed inevitably from the very nature of the Soviet State, he declared.

Having thus begged the entire question, Vyshinsky did not feel there was any need to explain the USSR's failures to observe the Charter, since nothing his country ever did could be anything but perfect. His attack was directed particularly against the countries of Western Europe which had just signed the Brussels Treaty, and against the United States which, he said, was plotting a new war. His arguments were uncompromising and over-simplified. When the USSR concluded an alliance with one of the East European countries or Finland, it was to safeguard peace. When other countries entered into alliances, it was in preparation for another war. In all this, he made no attempt to support or explain his assertions, and this allowed him to proclaim them all the more forcefully. He followed this up with a long list of wrongs, which included a random mixture of quotations, taken out of context from statements by American speakers and from diverse publications. It all amounted to a severe and unjust indictment. It was difficult to decide whether his feelings were genuine and his fears real, or if he was merely making a speech for propaganda purposes, since the arguments which one might conceivably have taken seriously were mixed up with childish nonsense.

Having listened to Vyshinsky, I was convinced that a reply was called for. It was unthinkable that Western Europe and the United States should allow such accusations to pass without a rebuttal. Bevin took on the task, but it seemed that his speech had been drafted before he had heard Vyshinsky. There was much that was admirable in what Bevin had to say. He was firm, understanding, constructive, but in view of the time factor he was unable to deliver the resounding reply which I thought was called for. I decided that it was up to me to undertake the task. Vyshinsky had spoken on 25 September, I replied on the 28th.

Although I did not write out my speech, I prepared it carefully. For three days I lived with it in all my waking hours – while shaving, in the bath, walking – and even in my dreams. I have never liked writing my speeches. Before finally shaping them I must feel in touch with my audience. Much depends on the way my words are received, whether I sense that my listeners are with or against me. But it would be wrong to think that my speeches are improvised merely because they have not been drafted in writing. On the contrary, I believe it takes longer to prepare a speech in this way than to write it down. First, it is essential to work out a careful scheme. The ideas must be expounded in logical sequence; they must follow one another in a natural order. That is the only way to ensure one does not forget at least part of one's argument. However, all this work is in vain without a reaction from the audience, an indication of its agreement or disapproval. If they remain indifferent, all is lost. If they respond, all may be won.

On 28 September 1948 I felt I was in for a good day. The feeling came to me the moment I mounted the rostrum at the Palais de Chaillot to face a hall and galleries filled with people. As always, the intense stage fright which grips me at such moments evaporated directly I had spoken my first words. This happened all the more quickly as I immediately observed that the great majority of the audience were on my side, ready to be convinced, ready to support me. From the outset the Assembly was attentive. I had the feeling that my listeners were tense, that they were expecting something to happen.

I have often re-read this speech, made eighteen years ago, and I have just glanced through it yet again. I think it was a good speech, but its success, the explosion of enthusiasm in the Assembly, the undeniable stir which it caused in the world outside – all these were due to the circumstances in which it was delivered. It was a timely speech and successful because it was sincere. The audience was glad to hear its simple, direct language, free from all artifice and the traditional hypocrisy of diplomacy. It was successful, furthermore, because of the courage which I was thought to have shown – representing as I did a nation as small as Belgium – in standing up to the representative of one as powerful as the USSR. The commentators waxed lyrical and spoke of a contest between David and Goliath.

Was I being brave or merely presumptuous in speaking as I did on that day? I shall not try to answer this question. The greatest feats of bravery depend on a certain insensitivity to possible danger, and if a speaker is sincere people are apt to overlook his presumption. I was sincere, and I thought at the time there was no point in worrying about the perils that might lie ahead.

Without mincing my words, I immediately took Vyshinsky to task:

'Mr Vyshinsky's speech [I said] can only be understood in one of two ways. Either it was a propaganda exercise or he sincerely meant what he said. In either case it calls for an answer. If it was a propaganda exercise, then others are equally entitled to use this rostrum for counter-propaganda. If it was sincere, it showed a complete lack of awareness of what the people of Western Europe are thinking and what they want. These mistakes must be put right so that the USSR can base its policy on a correct assessment of what is happening and what people are thinking in this part of the world.'

I went on to paint a picture which contrasted the values and ideals of the Communist and the free world.

'The free countries stand for liberal democracy, that is to say they believe with all their hearts in the need to build a society based on freedom of thought, freedom of the press, freedom of assembly and freedom of association. We want free elections, a government responsible to the people, respect for the dignity of the individual and a state which serves the individual, and not the contrary. Least of all do we want the individual to be at the beck and call of a party. Our form of government has immense advantages. It makes possible unrestricted economic and social progress. It rejects intolerance, the use of force and the use of violence. It puts its faith in the good sense and wisdom of the individual. I admit that ours is without any doubt the most difficult form of government to operate and I also admit that it presents certain difficulties, perhaps even certain dangers. In our part of the world freedom of thought and of the press brings with it the freedom to think and to write even that which may be wrong. But in our view it would be a mistake to combat error by reliance on the police, on the courts, on the power to send people into exile and worse. We believe that the right way to counter false propaganda is to put out propaganda based on truth.'

In recalling these great principles I was doing nothing original, and the reader may find all this rather trite. But these words were spoken during the aftermath of a war in which millions of men and women had sacrificed their lives in order that Nazism, fascism and all totalitarian regimes might be wiped from the face of the earth. My audience was ready to respond when I reminded them of the hopes and reasons which had inspired this sacrifice.

I went on to refute – which was easy – the accusation of bellicosity which Vyshinsky had levelled at the countries of Western Europe, with what was perhaps the boldest passage in my speech, a passage which made a great impression because it reflected the innermost feelings of the many people who were reluctant to express their thoughts openly. Turning to the Soviet delegation, I declared that there was no point in looking for complicated explanations of Western actions. They were, I said, the result of fear – fear of the USSR, fear of its Government, fear of its policies.

The word fear made a sensational impact because it was so unusual in that forum and because it was so blunt. I thought it wise to make it clear that the fear of which I spoke did not stem from cowardice, nor was it to be likened to the fear of a craven politician asking for another chance; rather it was the fear of one faced with a future which could bring possible horror, tragedy and heavy responsibilities.

My next task was to explain the reasons for this fear, and this gave me an opportunity to indict Soviet policies:

'Do you know why we are afraid? We are afraid because you often speak of imperialism. And what is the definition of imperialism? What do people mean by imperialism these days? An imperialist country is generally a Great Power bent on conquering foreign territory and seeking to spread its influence throughout the world. And what are the facts of recent history? There is only one Great Power which emerged from the war having acquired foreign territory, and that Great Power is the USSR. It was during the war, and thanks to the war, that you were able to annex the Baltic countries. It was during the war, and thanks to the war, that you were able to lay hands on a part of Finland. It was during the war, and thanks to the war, that you seized a piece of Poland. And it is thanks to your brazen and clever policies that you have become all-powerful in Warsaw, Prague, Belgrade, Bucharest and Sofia. It is thanks to this policy that you occupy Vienna and Berlin, cities which you do not appear willing to leave. It is thanks to your policy that you now feel able to claim a share in the control of the

Ruhr. Your empire stretches from the Black Sea to the Baltic and the Mediterranean. Now you want to advance to the banks of the Rhine and you ask us why we are worried. The fact of the matter is that your foreign policy is now more audacious and ambitious than that of the Tsars themselves.'

No one had ever spoken to the Russians in this way at the United Nations. No one had ever confronted Vyshinsky so directly. Sensing that the great majority of the delegates, now freed from their burden of fear, were behind me, I pressed on.

Vyshinsky, I said, had criticized the United Nations. But who was really responsible for its partial failure if not those who had misused the right of veto, those who had made themselves champions of the outdated and reactionary doctrine of absolute national sovereignty, those who were refusing to cooperate with the UN whenever its recommendations ran counter to their wishes?

In explaining why our fear was justified, I went on to deal with an even more delicate subject. I declared:

'We are worried, finally, because in every country represented here you are maintaining a fifth column compared with which Hitler's fifth column was a troop of boy scouts! There is no part of the world and no government, be it in Europe, Africa or Asia, which has not had to cope with problems and difficulties you have done your best to foment. That is your way of cooperating with the governments here represented, governments with which you should be collaborating for the benefit of peace! In every one of our countries there is at this time a group of people who not only champion and defend your foreign policy (which would not in itself be a tragedy), but who also never miss a chance of weakening the country in which they live – politically, morally and socially.'

I had reached the climax of my indictment. Experience had taught me that if one wants to make a good speech one must know when to change one's tone. After the strong language I had used, it was time for some words of reconciliation; after the clenched fist, it was time for the outstretched hand.

I therefore held out to the Soviets an offer of an honourable compromise designed to produce a relaxation in the general tension. I said that countries like my own might feel able to abandon the idea of a revision of the Charter and abolition of the right of veto – proposals which they had put forward repeatedly and which seemed to irritate the Russians greatly – if the latter, for their part, would promise to cooperate in putting the Charter into effect not only in the letter but – more importantly – in the spirit. The Soviet Union must cease its systematic opposition to the admission of new members; it must no longer bar from the UN family countries entitled to become its members, and, once a recommendation had been adopted, the Soviet Union must show itself ready to cooperate in its implementation. The United Nations, I said, needed the USSR if it was to succeed in its work and it did not want the USSR to sabotage its efforts.

It only remained for me to appeal, in my peroration, for universal concord. I called upon the Soviet Union to respond in a like spirit to the sacrifice that others were ready to make.

'The United Nations must make a fresh start by trying to understand and draw closer to one another. If they join hands in such an endeavour, the flame which was kindled at San Francisco will again burn bright and clear. It is not yet too late, but it is high time.'

Agency reports said the speech had been repeatedly interrupted by applause and that its closing passages had given rise to an ovation lasting more than five minutes.

How is this to be explained today? Although it is difficult to judge one's own actions objectively, in my view the speech, or at least certain parts of it, was good because it suited the atmosphere prevailing at the time. Its success can only be explained by the fact that it reflected a mood which was widespread at the time and which, until then, no one had had the courage to put into words. In those days people were really afraid of the Russians. My speech came as a sort of spiritual release.

I was congratulated on all sides. There were a great many official messages, but what touched me even more were those I received from dozens of ordinary people unknown to me – from France, Belgium, Switzerland and other countries. Having heard my speech on the radio, they wrote to thank and encourage me.

In Brussels I was received in triumph. My party organized a mass rally which proved a great success. Long before the doors of the hall – one of the biggest in the Belgian capital – were opened, all the seats were taken, and there were hundreds of people thronging the entrances. I was acclaimed as never before or since. It was a strange and moving experience to be the spokesman for a vast multitude, expressing its desire for peace and security as it would wish it expressed.

18

The Suez Crisis

The year 1956 was dominated by two grave developments: the Suez crisis and the Soviet intervention in Hungary. Some observers thought we were on the brink of a third world war, although I was never quite as pessimistic as that. I was alive to the difficulties and dangers of the situation but convinced that the USSR and the USA would not go to war over Suez, and that the West, however much sympathy it might feel for the Hungarian rising, and however great its indignation at the Soviet intervention, would not go beyond expressing its feelings.

I played only a modest part in the Suez affair, a part arising out of Belgium's membership in 1956 of both the Security Council and NATO. I was anxious lest dangerous divisions should appear among our allies. It is not my intention to go over the events of this long and delicate episode. All I wish to do here is to describe my own reactions and relate certain incidents in which I was personally involved.

In the summer of 1956 I was visiting the Congo and it was there I heard of the nationalization of the International Suez Canal Company. Some days later, events seemed to be taking a dangerous turn, and I thought it wise to return to Belgium.

In my study a message awaited me from Selwyn Lloyd, the British Foreign Secretary, in which he explained why Belgium had not been invited to take part in the Canal Users' Conference in London, called to devise a solution to the problem created by nationalization. The reasons he gave were perfectly valid since the criteria adopted to limit the number of participants excluded such countries as Belgium, Canada and South Africa – countries which the British Foreign Secretary would have been happy to invite to London. He assured me of his intention to remain in

close contact with the Belgian Government with regard to
the very serious situation brought about by the Egyptian
Government. I accepted his decision most readily for my
initial reaction was against such a conference. I felt it
would result in excessive concessions to Nasser. I replied
to Selwyn Lloyd in a personal letter, dated 21 August. Our
relations were excellent and I was thus able to write quite
candidly:

'On my return from the Congo, where I spent some weeks,
I found the message that you were good enough to send
me, explaining why Belgium has not been invited to the
London conference. Allow me to thank you sincerely. I
am very touched by the trouble you have taken in writing to me. I quite understand the reasons that have led
you to adopt certain criteria and I accept, too, that it was
therefore impossible for you to include Belgium among
the participating countries. However, I should like to take
this opportunity to inform you of the grave view I take
of developments in Egypt, which call for a policy of
absolute firmness from the Western Powers.

'I do not wish to hide from you that I am haunted by
the memory of the mistakes made during the early years
of the Nazi regime, mistakes which cost us so dearly.
Nasser's action goes far beyond the question of the Canal.
We must stand up to these tactics and, if they are to be
halted at all, they must be halted before worse befalls.

'Far be it from me to deny the importance of ensuring
that the Suez Canal Company is indemnified, and, above
all, that the Canal is placed under an international administration; however, I believe the psychological and political aspects of the matter to be far more important.

'If Nasser's coup is allowed to go unpunished, the
prestige of this new dictator will grow vastly, and so will
his ambitions and his audacity. The entire situation in
North, and even in Central Africa, may be affected to our
detriment.

'I must admit I am a little dubious about the conference
itself. It is very unlikely that unanimity will be achieved.
Nasser will surely receive considerable support for his
intransigent attitude from the sizeable minority which is

bound to emerge, and I believe it will prove very difficult to put the majority's decisions into effect.

'Will not France and Great Britain once again find themselves in the same position they were in following nationalization? Nasser, moreover, will have been granted time to enlist the support of certain quarters.

'Since it has been decided – and with good reason – not to have recourse to the United Nations, would it not have been better to negotiate directly with Egypt? I think it would.

'I should like to add that I regret that no one has thought of calling a meeting of the NATO Ministerial Council. The "Three Wise Men" are now in the process of devising ways and means of lending added vitality to our Alliance. Is it not strange, even a little disappointing, that at a time of grave political crisis nothing has been done to reaffirm within the Alliance the West's identity of views, so necessary at the present time?

'The London conference has not yet ended. I hope the West will stand firm on the key issues. We cannot allow ourselves to lose face any more than the other side. If this were unhappily to occur I am convinced it would be only the first of many abdications and defeats as a result of which we should be faced with an increasingly critical situation.

'I have every confidence in your wisdom and firmness, and today these two qualities are synonymous.'

My sentiments were clearly reflected in this letter, above all my horror and fear of all dictators. I am convinced that to understand what happened in Egypt in 1956 one must bear in mind that men like Guy Mollet, the French Prime Minister, Christian Pineau, the Foreign Minister, and Anthony Eden were obsessed with the need to avoid making the mistakes in the Middle East which we made in Europe during the early stages of the Nazi regime. I remember Pineau saying: 'If we had gone to war with Germany in 1935 when the Germans reoccupied the Rhineland, we should have been blamed for the loss of the few thousand lives this would have cost, and possibly condemned by a section of public opinion. However, we would have prevented the Second World War and saved many millions of lives.'

This view was shared by many in Europe who had held positions of responsibility before the Second World War. Foster Dulles, who entered political life later, was a stranger to such notions.

I had misgivings, too, about a possible break-up of NATO as a result of the differences between the British and the French on the one hand and the Americans on the other. This seemed to me the most serious risk of all.

From the outset of the Suez crisis, there were thus two issues on my mind: the need to be firm with Nasser, and the need to help maintain unity among the Nato allies. Selwyn Lloyd adopted one of my suggestions and brought the issue before the NATO Permanent Council. The result, though none too happy, was at least helpful inasmuch as it revealed the true state of affairs.

I wrote about this to the Belgian Ambassador in Washington, Baron Silvercruys:

'Here, in Europe, it is difficult to obtain an accurate picture of US policy, and the American Ambassador in Brussels does not seem able to explain it to me. He appears to be without either instructions or information. American policy gives the impression of being very hesitant and much more timid than that of the British and French, despite the communist view of it. What made a particularly bad impression was the American delegate's total silence at the last NATO meeting. He did not even re-affirm the American attitude as outlined at the London conference, and his sullen silence seemed almost to hint at a disavowal of that stand. This silence was all the more inexplicable as Mr Dulles himself had firmly insisted some time ago that the policies of NATO should be strengthened. How can one explain his present refusal, made at the very first opportunity of an exchange of information and views? Let the Americans be in no doubt: if the British and French fail in Egypt, we shall blame this on the lack of US support. A severe blow will have been dealt to NATO and, by the same token, the Russians will have won a victory and will gain indirectly what until now they have been unable to obtain by direct action.'

I was also anxious to make it clear that Nasser, by nationalizing the Suez Canal Company, had violated the Treaty of 29 October 1888. This seemed to me to be the crux of the matter. If the nationalization of the Canal were an act of domestic policy, this might be a matter for regret but would not give us the right to intervene. If, on the other hand, Nasser had violated a treaty – as I was convinced he had – we should not only be justified in protesting, but would be duty bound to act in order to prevent a dangerous precedent from being established.

In a letter to Baron van den Bosch, the Belgian Ambassador in Cairo, I analysed the legal issues involved. My views, I said, might best be summed up as follows: the 1888 Treaty established the freedom of navigation in the Canal, while the International Company provided the signatories with a guarantee that this freedom would remain in force until 1968. This view, I pointed out, was opposed to that of the Egyptians but, on the other hand, it was also not entirely in line with the attitude of the eighteen Powers represented at the London Conference. I stressed that a distinction must be made between the legal position obtaining up to the expiry of the Suez Canal concession, due in 1968, and the position thereafter.

While maintaining a firm attitude on the essence of the problem, I had devised a legal formula which could have served as the basis for a compromise. A provisional solution could have been worked out to cover the period from 1955 to 1968, since my thesis recognized that from that date Egypt could legally nationalize the Company.

I made these points at meetings in London with Eden and Selwyn Lloyd. Strangely enough, I was not in direct contact at that time with Guy Mollet and Christian Pineau, although both were old political and personal friends of mine. Pineau had always been friendly towards me before becoming Foreign Minister, and was so again afterwards. However, during his tenure of office he kept his distance; I never knew why. Am I unduly suspicious in thinking that the influence of the Quai d'Orsay was responsible?

I would not go so far as to claim that the British gave unreserved support to my legal arguments and the conclusions they implied. Nevertheless, they did not object to my presenting them before the Security Council. Immediately after my speech, Selwyn Lloyd sent me a message scribbled on a piece of paper: 'Thank you, and congratulations on your splendid speech.' I took it he agreed with me.

In my address to the Security Council I was much more outspoken than in my letter to our Ambassador in Cairo. I developed my views at some length, and this is not the place to reproduce them in full. My arguments were solid, even though they failed to convince all the members of my audience.

I have since read two studies of the legal points raised by the nationalization of the Canal – one by Georges Scelle and the other by Roger Pinto. Their conclusions agreed with mine.

In my speech I did my best – regardless of my feelings about Nasser and my detestation of his methods – to outline a compromise. I proposed that the legal aspects of the matter be submitted to the International Court, subject, however, to two conditions: first, the two parties must solemnly undertake to abide by the Court's ruling; second, agreed maintenance operations must continue until such time as the Court had given its ruling. This was much too reasonable to be accepted by Egypt, which sought a political triumph!

The Security Council failed to find a solution to the problem and a few weeks later the French and the British launched their military operation against Egypt.

Before speaking in the Security Council, I met Foster Dulles. As usual, the Secretary of State was frank with me. Over the years we had had numerous dealings based on mutual trust – first when I was Foreign Minister and later as Secretary-General of NATO. Admired by some, Foster Dulles was fiercely criticized by others. Although personal feelings had little or no bearing on his relations with others, to me he behaved differently. I always had the impression that behind his mask of a puritanical, committed idealist who was often brusque, there was a sympathetic mind and a generous soul.

At a time when many in positions of responsibility were apt to hesitate and falter, Foster Dulles knew what he wanted. His sureness of purpose was a comfort to those working with him. No doubt, it is dangerous for any individual to believe he has been entrusted with a mission. To divide the world arbitrarily into absolute good and absolute evil in politics – this attitude takes the form 'the West versus Communism' – does not help one deal with life's practical problems. Yet this is precisely what Dulles did. This simple outlook gave him confidence and peace of mind in making grave decisions. He was strong because his was not a complex mentality.

His hostility to Communism, his conviction that one had to fight it everywhere and at all times, was without the shadow of a doubt the bedrock of his policies. I am loath to pronounce an overall judgement on these policies, but from my particular vantage point I am bound to say that in general I approve of his actions. He was loyal to the United Nations, a convinced champion of the Atlantic Alliance and European unity. In fact, with regard to this latter issue, I found Foster Dulles more farseeing and courageous than many a European. For an American it was no mean feat for him to take this attitude. He was well aware that a united Europe would be a redoubtable business competitor of the United States, a fact of which the Department of Commerce reminded him from time to time. He accepted this risk with his eyes wide open because he saw in a united Europe a worthy political partner. This was what he sought.

Leaving aside his manner, which was at times abrupt, his vision of the world was not without grandeur. He was big enough to realize that minor sacrifices are essential for the sake of a grand design. He did not deal with the problems that came his way on a day-to-day basis, changing his outlook according to circumstances, but was governed by his faith and ideals. The result may not always have been perfect, but at least he never did anything mean or petty.

At our first meeting after I returned to office in 1954 he promised me his complete support in my efforts to promote European integration. He was as good as his word. During the crises over the European Defence Community and

131

German entry into NATO, and later in connection with the negotiations on the establishment of the Common Market, Dulles always gave me encouragement and support.

Subsequently, in NATO, he backed my efforts for more effective political consultation. He viewed my proposals kindly even when they made life difficult for him. In Copenhagen, during a NATO meeting, he received me for a talk on current problems, and I can still hear him say: 'You are asking a lot; you always want more and more. What a difficult man you are!' Then, after a brief silence, he continued with a friendly smile: 'Carry on.'

During the Berlin crisis in 1958, he was quite remarkable. The Soviet demands had produced an atmosphere of grave disquiet within NATO, an atmosphere reflected in the uncertain tone of the statements made by some of the ministers. After a speech by Foster Dulles, everything returned to normal. His calm, the impression of power emanating from him, the sincerity of his words and the firmness of his views restored the confidence of the entire Alliance. He spoke like a truly great statesman faced with an historic occasion.

On the morning of 5 October 1956 I found Foster Dulles worried and very angry. He did not like the way the French and British had brought the Egyptian problem before the Security Council. Dulles had only heard of the matter in Washington on his arrival from London on the morning of 22 September, and this despite the fact that Eden had promised him not to put the issue to the UN without first getting in touch with him. He was far from pleased about being confronted with a *fait accompli*. A few weeks later I was to sense the same dismay in President Eisenhower, who was appalled by the attitude of the French and British. He thought their failure to discuss the matter with him beforehand showed a lack of confidence and was surprised by this and visibly distressed. He felt that this was not the way to treat a former Supreme Allied Commander.

Foster Dulles explained that basically he was in agreement with the French and British. Only the possibility that they might use force had caused him to part company with them. The use of force he believed dangerous, liable to set Asia and Africa on fire. It would, he said, in effect amount to a reversal of the customary roles of the West and the USSR. For the time being, the Russians had renounced the use of military force as an instrument of policy. In threatening to use force, Britain and France were putting themselves in a position not unlike that of the USSR before the death of Stalin.

My own view at the time – early October 1956 – was that it was then too late to take such an attitude. At the beginning of the crisis it might still have been acceptable, but now, a few months later and after so much negotiation, it was hard to justify.

In my view, the Suez operation was justified by Nasser's clear violation of the 1888 Treaty, the inability of the United Nations to provide an acceptable solution to the conflict, and the danger which could have arisen if Nasser, defying international law, had been allowed to demonstrate that one can best get one's own way by the use of armed force and arrogant and cynical disregard of one's obligations. Nevertheless, I prefer not to comment on the way the French and British carried out their operation, on their hesitancy in the face of reactions which ought to have been foreseen since they were inevitable, or on their shilly-shallying when confronted by opposition. The best one can say is that there were extenuating circumstances.

The military operations having started, the issue was put to the UN General Assembly. The atmosphere at the time is difficult to describe! Israel, France and Britain were in the dock. Nearly every government was against them, above all the Afro-Asians and, inevitably, the Communist bloc. But on this occasion the USA and the countries under its influence were also ranged against France and Britain. The struggle was hopeless, the more so as the accused did not defend themselves by asserting their rights and pleading the legitimacy of their actions. Suddenly they could think of nothing but how to save face in the Assembly by promising that they would comply with its recommendations and fighting a rearguard action. I felt they needed help. As I have already said, my preoccupation was to maintain the solidarity of the Atlantic Powers.

The draft resolution, submitted by twenty states, mainly African and Asian, was couched in very severe terms. Its essential object was to obtain the immediate withdrawl of the Israeli, French and British forces from Egypt. The French and British were ready to comply, and the task was to devise a formula which would allow them to do so without undue loss of face. I sought to tackle this problem by tabling several amendments which left intact the main object of the draft resolution – the withdrawal of the Anglo-French force. The French and British clutched at the lifeline which I had thus thrown them and declared that if my amendments were accepted they would vote for the resolution. A unanimous vote could have been achieved. However, this was precisely what the most influential delegates did not want. What they wanted was outright condemnation and political triumph. The Soviet delegation was particularly intransigent. Its attitude was all the more disgraceful as the Russians had just made it brutally clear that where Hungary was concerned they would take no notice of any resolutions voted by the Assembly. Soviet cynicism was total and shameless.

While procedural wrangles were going on – they now seem both incomprehensible and futile – an apparently endless debate began on my amendments. I had every reason to expect American support since before the meeting Cabot Lodge, the US delegate to the Security Council, had promised that he would vote in favour of my proposals. I would not have acted as I did had I not been sure of American backing, since my first aim was to restore unity among the member-countries of NATO.

I was first worried and then appalled when I realized that Cabot Lodge was taking no part in the debate and when he remained silent after the French and British had announced that they would support my amendments.

Taking advantage of an interminable speech by the Indian delegate, I went up to Cabot Lodge and begged him to support me as he had promised. My efforts were in vain. I have never discovered what had happened and why he denied me his support, contrary to his promise.

For an American, Cabot Lodge speaks admirable French. As a result he has acquired a reputation for being pro-European. I have often wondered if that reputation is justified. On this occasion, at any rate, he not only failed to stand by France and Britain, but behaved with a hostility which was very difficult to understand since he had merely been asked to agree to the striking out of a few words which his allies found wounding. There was no question of changing the basic nature of the motion that had been tabled.

Was he acting on his own authority or was he following instructions from Washington? I do not know. It is said that Selwyn Lloyd has never forgiven Cabot Lodge. Had I been in his place, I should undoubtedly have felt the same way. In fact, although I was not personally involved, I was angered by Cabot Lodge's inexplicable conduct.

My amendments were defeated by thirty-two votes to twenty-three, with eighteen abstentions, including that of the United States. If Cabot Lodge had made a plea for moderation, it is more than likely that the outcome would have been different.

At the time the vote was taken the matter was not, perhaps, of great importance to the French and British since they had already decided to withdraw their troops. However, the American attitude over the Suez affair gave rise to anti-American feeling among the French, which General de Gaulle was later to exploit to the full.

Having been appointed Secretary-General of NATO, I took no part in the work of the UN from 1957 to 1961. That year I returned to New York. My work was essentially concerned with the problems of the Congo, Rwanda and Burundi. As a result, I was involved in disputes which I propose to describe later.

The UN has now been in existence for more than twenty years. On the whole, it has been a disappointment for it is not playing the great part in international life which its founders envisaged. It has had three Secretaries-General who, though men of widely differing qualities, were all devoted and able.

Trygve Lie brought to his duties a calm, temperate disposition and sang-froid. He remained imperturbable, at least outwardly, in the midst of the storms of the cold war.

Dag Hammarskjoeld was more brilliant, a more complete personality; more complex, but also more ambitious. He believed in the role he was called upon to play and systematically sought to widen its scope, which was only right. There can be no doubt about his influence on the countries of Asia and Africa, and he succeeded in strengthening that influence, though at the cost of not always being entirely fair with Europe and the white race in general. He embraced the angry passions and the triumphs of anti-colonialism as if they were his own, and he did so, I am sure, not only from a sense of duty but from conviction. He was an idealist, a philosopher and, in the conduct of day-to-day affairs, an able and adroit diplomatist who pursued his aims with determination. He combined all the qualities – attractive and dangerous alike – of those who believe themselves entrusted with a mission.

Where Congolese affairs were concerned, Hammarskjoeld did not always make life easy for me, although I must admit that he succeeded in giving the UN a powerful impetus and in asserting his authority and influence, and that he was valued and admired by most people. His tragic death while on active UN service only helped to raise his reputation still further. He was without doubt one of the greatest figures ever produced by the Organization.

U Thant is much more reserved. He possesses in the highest degree that outward calm which is a striking quality of many Asians, and yet I am certain he also has firm convictions, even burning passions. While I have never known him show any flicker of emotion, anger, impatience or pleasure, I have always found him understanding, calm and fair. Since he is not of European extraction, he has no need to go out of his way to curry favour with the Asians and Africans, and this enables him to be more impartial than Hammarskjoeld. Although I have not always seen eye to eye with him about the problems of the Congo, I have found U Thant moderate and loyal, and he has always behaved with great dignity. In my opinion he makes an excellent Secretary-General.

Clearly, to function as it should the UN needs more than a good Secretary-General. I still believe the right of veto must be held responsible for the UN's partial failure, a right which symbolizes the absolute sovereignty of the Great Powers and which runs directly counter to the UN's basic concept. Moreover, many member-countries only pay lip service to the principles of the Charter. While they are ready to condemn the use of force and recourse to war where others are concerned, their cynicism when their own interests are at stake is amazing.

All in all, neither impartiality nor objectivity nor willingness to promote the rule of law are to be found in the United Nations. Whatever the issue, partisan blocs are formed, with the result that no one has time to listen to arguments counselling reason and moderation.

Nevertheless, the Organization must remain in being; undoubtedly its underlying principles if not its actions, its theories if not its practice, constitute a step in the right direction. Whenever it fails, the results of that failure are only too evident. However splendid it would be if it could act effectively in the service of peace, it will be many years before the UN lives up to the hopes cherished in 1945. Nevertheless, even though at present it cannot be relied upon to settle all the conflicts which divide mankind, it embodies a wholly valid idea with which we must keep faith.

PART FOUR

The Defence of Europe
1944–54

19

Ernest Bevin's Speech:
The Brussels Treaty

Let us now return to an earlier time in our story.

What we had feared since the end of the war had come to pass: the Great Powers had failed to maintain unity after their victory. The Russians and the Anglo-Saxons – the latter supported by the French following General de Gaulle's unsuccessful visit to Moscow – had clashed repeatedly, not only in the United Nations but also in the field – in Iran, Turkey, Greece, Poland and Germany, just about everywhere, in fact.

It seemed that the USSR was banking on a world revolution. It was ready to back subversive movements wherever they appeared, thus creating one difficulty after another for its former allies. The Russians went out of their way to rub salt into every wound. Gradually, many Westerners, concerned for the future of peace, came to regard the USSR as more dangerous than defeated Germany.

In the last twenty years a number of Western statesmen have been dubbed either 'fathers of European unity' or 'fathers of the Atlantic Alliance'. Not one of them deserves this title: it belongs to Stalin. Without Stalin and his aggressive policies, without the threat with which he confronted the free world, the Atlantic Alliance would never have been born and the movement for European unity, embracing Germany as an integral part, would never have had the astonishing success which it has in fact enjoyed. In both cases, a defensive reflex was at the root of these great achievements.

The Americans, British and French tried, during and after the war, to change the course of history. The Anglo-Soviet and Franco-Soviet Treaties, and the establishment of the United Nations, reflected these endeavours. History, however, went its own way regardless.

At Yalta Roosevelt fondly imagined he would be able to live in perfect amity with Stalin. It took the leaders of the Western Powers two to three years to realize their mistake. In fact it was only thanks to Hitler's attack in June 1941 that the Russians felt compelled to seek an alliance with the West. This step was inspired neither by their inclinations nor their doctrine, and once the danger was over they soon made this all too clear.

I have already mentioned how reserved, cautious and slow the British were with regard to the efforts to create a united Europe. For years they anxiously tried to avoid doing anything that might conceivably cause the USSR displeasure. Ultimately, however, it was the British who took the initiative.

Churchill, who was in opposition at the time, was first to sound the alarm. In his speech at Fulton, USA, on 5 March 1946, he spoke scathingly of the situation that had been created: 'From Stettin in the Baltic to Trieste in the Adriatic, an iron curtain has descended across the Continent.' He went on to call for unity among the English-speaking peoples in order to eliminate all 'temptation to ambition or adventure'.

A year later, on 5 June 1947, General Marshall, then US Secretary of State, speaking at Harvard University, made one last attempt to prevent the division of Europe. He urged its nations – all the nations of Europe including the USSR and the Communist countries – to draw up an agreed list of their needs, which would eventually be met by the United States. The Soviet reaction was so aggressively hostile, Molotov's speeches so deliberately arrogant, that Bevin and Bidault realized that any cooperation with the USSR was quite out of the question and a new course would have to be plotted by the non-Communist nations of the West.

It was Ernest Bevin who had the honour of blazing this trail. His speech in the House of Commons on 22 January 1948 was an historic event, for it marked the beginning of a new European policy and heralded a future Atlantic policy.

Ernest Bevin occupies a special place among British

Foreign Secretaries. Physically he did not at all resemble William Pitt, Lord Palmerston or Anthony Eden. It never occurred to me to admire the cut of his suits or the elegance of his ties, but I did feel tempted to envy his solid common-sense and courage. A man of rugged build, he symbolized, following as he did a succession of Foreign Secretaries who were the products of Eton and Oxford or Cambridge, the arrival of a new class in the seats of power. His outward appearance was deceptive, however, for beneath his rugged exterior there was a nimble mind, a firm will, absolute intellectual honesty, a sense of responsibility, utter devotion to the cause of democracy and a sincere love of peace. Of modest origins, having made his way up in the trade union movement, he was typical of many men who emerged during the closing years of the last century – men who, thanks to their own efforts and qualities, and without any privilege whatsoever, came to share both the responsibilities and honours of office. During the war he showed himself capable of filling the highest posts with distinction. At the Foreign Office he may well have meditated upon his un-expected destiny, his astonishing career. Despite his lack of conventional training, he succeeded absolutely, thus proving once again that for a minister technical accomplishment is far from indispensable. What matters is sound judgement, a sense of responsibility, a will to act – and to act decisively – and a fighting spirit. Bevin had all these qualities in ample measure.

In his House of Commons speech on 22 January 1948 he excelled himself. I have always thought that on that day – ministers of exceptional merit are apt to do this – he made a point of disregarding the advice of his over-cautious civil servants and decided to strike out on his own. At all events, never before had Britain been so outspoken in proclaiming her readiness to help promote the unity of Western Europe, nor has she ever shown such courage since. For one moment in her political history Britain was enthusiastic and, may I say, lucid, about Europe.

Bevin, whose speech should really be quoted in its entirety, began by outlining the situation as it then was and went on to speak of his hopes for and disappointments at the policies of the Soviet Union. He then recalled what had happened in the Balkans, in Hungary, Poland, Germany, Iran and Turkey, and how the Yalta Agreements had been violated. It seems, however, that it was Molotov's attitude at the conference that followed General Marshall's proposal which caused Bevin to abandon all hope of an understanding with the USSR. He realized that Russia was ready, as he put it, to wreck or intimidate Western Europe by fomenting political unrest and economic chaos, if need be by using the methods of revolution.

This was more than Bevin was prepared to take lying down and he resolved to speak out and act as a great European:

'But surely all these developments which I have been describing point to the conclusion that the free nations of Western Europe must now draw closely together. These nations have a great deal in common – their wartime sacrifices, their hatred of injustice and oppression, their parliamentary democracy, their efforts to promote economic justice, their understanding and love of liberty. I believe the time is ripe for a consolidation of Western Europe.'

Having proclaimed his decision, he began by saying that it was with France that agreement must be sought in the first place. He went on:

'The time has come to find ways and means of developing our relations with the Benelux countries. I mean to begin talks with those countries in close accord with our French allies. I hope treaties will be signed with our near neighbours, the Benelux countries, making, with our treaty with France, an important nucleus in Western Europe. We have then to go beyond the circle of our immediate neighbours. We shall have to consider the question of associating other historic members of European civilization including the new Italy, in this great conception. Their eventual participation is, of course, no less important than that of countries with which, if only for geographical reasons, we must deal first. We are thinking now of Western Europe as a unit.'

Bevin did not ignore Germany. He said a place would

have to be found for her in the future organization but that she would not be able to join before her former victims; also, she could be allowed in only when she had become a democracy.

Seen in the context of the situation at the beginning of 1948, this was a very great speech, a speech one must know in order to appreciate what happened in the years which followed and assess what the future may yet have in store for us. Subsequently, Britain may have shown hostility, suspicion and scepticism where Europe was concerned, but Ernest Bevin must be given credit for having been *the* Foreign Minister who gave the European movement its initial impulse. In so doing he accepted his responsibility for, and admitted his disappointment with any anxiety about, what had gone before.

The welcome in Belgium was immediate. On 23 January 1948, within a few hours of Bevin's speech, I issued a communiqué which stressed how important I considered the British Foreign Secretary's statement to be, and my intention of consulting my Netherlands and Luxembourg colleagues on action to be taken.

On 31 January, the three Benelux Foreign Ministers met. They welcomed the historic step taken by Britain and said they would be ready to begin negotiations once they had 'defined the rough outlines of a common attitude based on Western European solidarity and awareness of the role which the Benelux countries could play in the movement for unity'. This complete understanding among the Benelux countries was important. Thanks to their agreement, they were in effect able to give the treaty which was eventually signed a content rather different from that originally envisaged by the British and French.

It is my impression that Bevin, a little overcome by his own boldness, later tried to minimize the significance of his speech. However, his words allowed of no doubt. The treaty for which he had called was essentially a precaution against the Russian threat, with the German problem relegated to second place. Yet his earlier proposals had not been strictly in line with this approach.

At the beginning of February I was visited in Brussels by Hector McNeil, Bevin's chief assistant. We were very good friends, and I could speak to him quite frankly. At that time I was also on the best of terms with Sir George Rendel, the British Ambassador to Belgium. His command of French was excellent and I could thus be sure we should not be hampered by any misunderstandings due to language difficulties. He was loyal and upright, and I had every confidence in him. At the time, and indeed later, too, when we came to discuss the North Atlantic Treaty, he was much more than merely a good negotiating partner – he was a colleague in the fullest sense of the word and was just as ready to accept my point of view as to stand up for the views of his own government. Sir George was just the sort of intermediary we – the British and myself – needed to ensure the success of our efforts. He proved by his example how important a part an ambassador can still play, even in our day, provided he believes in what he is doing and has the right sort of qualities for his work. I am greatly indebted to Sir George for the important contribution he made to these important negotiations.

Events moved rapidly, though not as smoothly as one might have wished. On 19 February I received two memoranda, one from the British and another from the French. The same day the three Benelux countries sent these two Governments a joint memorandum. There were important differences between the documents exchanged. The British and French proposed a treaty which, if not identical with, was at least very similar to, the one they had themselves concluded at Dunkirk. The Benelux countries, on the other hand, felt that this document was too narrowly conceived. The Anglo-French drafts called for measures with a view to organizing mutual assistance in the event of armed aggression by Germany, as well as for joint action to put an end to any possible threat if that country were to resume a policy of aggression. These two hypotheses took no account of the facts to which the British Foreign Secretary had alluded, and the three Benelux Governments therefore considered that such an agreement was not what was required.

Although the French and British memoranda were not couched in identical terms, it was clear from the similarity of the arguments presented – even the order in which they were listed was the same – that the documents had been drafted after preliminary discussions between our two major partners.

Two arguments were advanced. The first was somewhat surprising in view of the vehemence with which Bevin had condemned Soviet policy in the Commons. It ran as follows: 'Nothing must be done to irritate or worry the USSR. Reference must therefore be made to the German threat, and it must be made clear that besides being anxious to bring about Western European unity we also wish to create conditions which will facilitate agreement with Eastern Europe.'

The second argument was even more unexpected. We were warned against a premature conclusion of a multilateral defence agreement, for, we were told, the Americans might use this as a pretext for assuming that the security of Europe was assured and, consequently, for withdrawing their troops. The French and the British therefore considered that before concluding a collective agreement, to which the Americans would adhere later, it would be wise to sign a series of bilateral treaties.

The Benelux countries took a simpler and bolder view of the situation. Scorning diplomatic caution, which can be taken too far, they were more realistic in their approach. After invoking the provision of the UN Charter which allows for arrangements to be made for legitimate collective and regional defence, they urged the conclusion of a treaty to this end. They cited as an example of what they had in mind the Inter-American Treaty of Mutual Defence signed in Rio de Janeiro on 2 September 1947. The three Benelux Governments believed that mutual aid in the event of aggression should be automatic and immediate. Consequently, they declared, a system allowing for regular consultation on all problems of mutual interest should be set up. This political agreement should go hand in hand with military and economic agreements, which, in turn, should envisage ultimate economic union.

The difference in approach was obvious. The two Great Powers were cautious, even hesitant, while the Benelux countries were prepared to draw the logical conclusions from the situation as they saw it. Ready to go beyond a conventional alliance, they sought to make the best of this chance to create a true community of the partners to the treaty.

The British and French Governments urged that discussions should begin immediately in one of the Benelux capitals. This was the most positive aspect of their attitude. Their proposal was accepted forthwith, and the talks began in Brussels on 4 March 1948. They made rapid progress and, on the 17th of that month, ended with the signing of the Treaty of Brussels. It is clear from the text of this document that several of the ideas put forward by the Benelux countries were accepted – which does nothing but honour to the Great Powers.

In my political career, which spans many years, there have been times when I believed I was on the point of realizing all my hopes. Those were heady moments! 17 March 1948 was one such occasion. That evening I gave a grand dinner reception. All in all, we were satisfied. We had responded immediately to Bevin's sensational speech of less than two months before. Diplomacy had been rapid and effective. We had gone as far, possibly even a little further, than Bevin had asked – or even wanted. It was a job well done.

The Treaty of Brussels was approved by the Belgian Parliament by a huge majority. Only the Communists opposed it, and opposed it vehemently. Just one year before they had been in the Government. There could be no doubt: a new page had been turned in the annals of history. A new chapter was about to begin in the Western World.

20

The Washington Treaty

The effects of the Brussels Treaty were immediate. The very day the five ministers were meeting to sign it, President Truman made a speech in the US Senate just as important as Bevin's in the House of Commons. Truman, in fact, took up most of the points made by Bevin and, in his turn, voiced his disappointment with, and anxiety about, the USSR.

In February 1948 it was Czechoslovakia's turn to be brought under Communist rule, in circumstances which seemed to bear out all the West's fears. President Truman spoke of the pressures being brought to bear on Finland and the Scandinavian countries, on Greece – in the throes of a civil war, with the rebels receiving direct aid from the USSR – on Bulgaria and Yugoslavia, on Italy – where the Communist minority was making a sustained effort to gain control of the country. The methods, Truman said, might vary, but the general pattern was unmistakable. He then stressed that five free Western nations had faced up to the danger threatening them by agreeing in Brussels on their future economic cooperation and the need to work together for their defence against any aggressor. He then came to the crucial point in his speech:

'The significance [of the Brussels Treaty] goes far beyond the actual terms of the agreement itself. It is a notable step in the direction of unity in Europe, for the protection and preservation of its civilization. This development deserves our full support. I am confident that the United States will, by appropriate means, extend to the free nations the support which the situation requires. I am sure that the determination of the free countries of Europe to protect themselves will be matched by an equal determination on our part to help them to do so.'

A new page in the annals of history was thus turned on 17 March 1948: the Monroe Doctrine was dropped; America's isolation was dead. The road ahead was clear and President Truman took it without hesitation. Negotiations began forthwith, and at the beginning of the following year they resulted in the conclusion of the Washington Treaty.

During the autumn and winter of 1948–9 diplomatic exchanges continued between representatives of the United States, Canada and the signatories of the Brussels Treaty. In October 1948 the partners to the Treaty, at a meeting of their Consultative Council, agreed to 'accept the idea of a defensive Atlantic pact and the measures to be taken in connection therewith'.

And how indeed could they have done otherwise? Even by adding together all their military resources and directing them jointly, they were in no position to put up any worthwhile resistance to the Soviet divisions occupying Eastern Europe, which, since the end of the war, had been able to augment and modernize their armament. Without American aid Western Europe was in no position to resist effectively. The importance of the Brussels Treaty as a symbol was undeniable, but in the absence of American and Canadian backing its practical significance was open to doubt.

In my view, the new treaty had to be an Atlantic equivalent of what the Brussels Treaty was for Europe. Our task was to choose our partners, to define the scope of the guarantees the treaty was to offer, to define the geographical limits of the area it would cover and to settle certain legal problems arising from the differences in the institutions of the countries involved.

Several months of continuous exchanges were necessary before adequate solutions were devised. The work was completed in March 1949. On the 19th of that month, the State Department in Washington published as a White Paper the text agreed by the governments. This was an unusual step of rather doubtful value, taken to prepare the American public for the new commitments which their Government had assumed by virtue of the treaty. The first result was – as one might expect – an outcry from the USSR.

On 31 March 1949 the Soviet Government handed to each

of the Governments concerned a note setting out its views. As so often with Communist documents, it was wordy, confused and intemperate. It maintained that the proposed treaty was intended to prepare the way for aggression against the USSR; that it amounted to a violation of the principles of the UN Charter, the Anglo-Soviet and Franco-Soviet Treaties and the Yalta and Potsdam Agreements.

The Belgian Government replied immediately, contesting each and every Soviet argument and stressing that the object of the new treaty was legitimate defence and that it was therefore in absolute accord with Article 51 of the Charter. The note sent to Moscow was clear, moderate in tone, but firm. Yet I am convinced that it had no effect whatever on the Soviet leaders. Thus began the dialogue of the deaf which has now been in progress for well-nigh twenty years.

The treaty was signed in Washington on 4 April 1949. In essence, the signatories pledged themselves to regard an armed attack against any party or parties to the treaty, whether in Europe or in North America, as directed against each and all. In consequence, they agreed that in the event of aggression all the signatories would come to the aid of the party or parties concerned and would take such action as the victim considered necessary, including the use of armed force, to restore and safeguard security in the North Atlantic area.

The simplicity of the wording left no room for doubt: this was a purely defensive agreement. I emphasize this because for years spokesmen of the USSR and of other Communist countries and parties have ceaselessly argued that the Treaty of Washington is an alliance for aggression. I wish to make it clear that the idea of aggression against the USSR has never been considered within the alliance. Our plans have at all times been exclusively aimed at preventing war. Our purpose has been to make ourselves sufficiently strong to deter any possible aggressor and negotiate without fear on the problems posed by the USSR. At no time have we betrayed these principles.

The Treaty of Washington does not differ very greatly in its wording from other treaties, except for Article 9 which says:

'The Parties hereby establish a Council, on which each of them shall be represented, to consider matters concerning the implementation of this Treaty. The Council shall be so organized as to be able to meet promptly at any time. The Council shall set up such subsidiary bodies as may be necessary; in particular, it shall establish immediately a defence committee.'

I do not think that at the time it was drafted the writers of this clause realized all its implications. It is from Article 9 that the entire structure of the Alliance stems, including NATO itself, its Permanent Council, its integrated commands, joint infrastructure and the post of Supreme Commander, North Atlantic.

This Article gave to the Atlantic Alliance a new character and made the treaty – which in itself is a mere collection of words – an effective instrument. It is Article 9 which has made it possible to resolve in times of peace and at leisure problems which alliances normally have to face when war is already upon them and which then have to be dealt with in haste and confusion.

The defence of Europe was at last organized and assured. Protected by the Atlantic Treaty, Europe has since experienced a long period of peace; it has in fact become the most peaceful part of the world. Such difficulties as have occurred – e.g., the Berlin problem – the countries concerned have settled peacefully and with confidence. Soviet expansion, so dangerous in the first few years after the war, has been halted. More important, the Communists have been made to realize that they stood to gain nothing from their cold war against Western Europe. As a result, they have changed their tactics and opted for peaceful coexistence, thus opening up new prospects for East-West relations.

Although I was present at the birth of the Alliance and signed the treaty on behalf of Belgium, I played no part in its affairs in its early years. In August 1949, as a result of political developments in Belgium, I had to resign my posts as Premier and Foreign Minister. In the subsequent elections my party was defeated. Contrary to my advice, it rejected the offer of cooperation made by the Christian Socialists. I thus found myself a member of the opposition, and so I remained for the next four years. I took full advantage of this opportunity to devote all my strength to the cause of European unity. I shall later describe the fascinating campaign for this cause.

21

The European Defence Community: Mendès-France in Brussels

The Atlantic Alliance developed rapidly: the first defence measures were taken; the United States gave considerable military aid to Europe; a permanent coordinating body, the Committee of Deputy Permanent Representatives, was set up.

The very existence of the Alliance was sufficient to influence the course of events. On 12 May 1949 the USSR lifted the Berlin blockade and a few months later gave up its support of the Greek rebellion. The invasion of South Korea in June 1950 showed, however, that international Communism had not really changed its policies. Having decided to abandon the struggle in Europe, where it was confronting forces of whose power it was well aware, Communism shifted its effort to Asia, where it hoped conditions would be more favourable.

In the UN, the reaction was immediate. Under the aegis of the United States, the defence of South Korea was organized. When the Atlantic Council met in September 1950, the discussion centred on a single issue: how could an act of aggression such as that to which South Korea had just fallen victim be prevented in the NATO area? It was concluded that the defence of Europe must be based on a 'forward strategy', i.e. a strategy for the defence of allied territories along as advanced a front as possible. In this, German participation was essential. Dean Acheson, the American Secretary of State, was quite firm on the subject. The United States was ready to play an active part in the defence of Europe on condition that Germany's resources, including her manpower, were used. He said it was unthinkable that the USA should contribute several hundreds of thousands of her troops to defend Europe on the Elbe while one part of Europe made no contribution to this effort. American opinion would never accept the proposition that it was up to the United States to defend Europe, Germany included, while the Germans themselves remained mere onlookers.

These views, however, troubled a great many consciences. Was it wise to rearm Germany barely five years after the end of the war? For obvious reasons, objections were particularly strong in France: memories of the war, the invasion, the defeat and the occupation were still fresh in that country.

At that time, René Pleven, who had worked with General de Gaulle in London, was the French Premier, and Robert Schuman the Foreign Minister. Both were champions of a united Europe and believed in combining their advocacy of the European cause with a policy of Atlantic solidarity. On 24 October 1950, rejecting the idea of independent German units – which would have entailed the early restoration of the German General Staff, an institution liable to become a rallying point for the forces of nationalism – they called for the creation of a European army geared to the political institutions of a united Europe. Their proposal called for a pooling of human and material resources within the framework of a single force. A European Defence Commissioner, responsible to a European Assembly, would be appointed by the governments concerned. The proposed army would be financed from a common budget and the European forces would be placed at the disposal of the NATO Command.

The French project was no doubt bold, but was it also well thought out? Did it accord with the views of most Frenchmen? This was open to question, as the events which followed were to show. The plan, far from being the fruit of long and careful preparation, was but an emotional reaction to the idea that a German army might re-emerge. However, the boldness of the project, the confidence it showed in a future united Europe, earned it the support of those who, following the establishment of the European Coal and Steel Community, came to believe in the need for a fresh advance towards European integration.

At its meeting in Brussels in December 1950, the Atlantic Council accepted the French views and the Americans renounced their own plans and gave their blessing to the project, which came to be known as the European Defence Community (EDC). Talks began in Paris immediately, with the six countries which had set up the European Coal and Steel Community (France, Germany, Italy, the Netherlands, Belgium and Luxembourg) taking part. The United States gave its approval – as did the British – but it did not enter into any positive commitment.

The discussions which ensued were protracted and difficult. The basic concept was revolutionary, but the political and technical problems involved were numerous and complex. The negotiations continued throughout 1951 and the early part of 1952. They ended in May, after Britain had offered a guarantee to the future community and the USA had pledged itself to do likewise once the EDC Treaty had come into force. The treaty itself was signed in Paris on 27 May 1952.

The document was ratified at more or less the same time by Germany, the Netherlands and Luxembourg. In Italy, the appropriate parliamentary committees also voted in favour. In France, on the other hand, progress was less promising. A section of public opinion had been alerted by a hostile General de Gaulle, who had condemned the Treaty from the depths of his exile at Colombey-les-Deux-Eglises. The Government, in which Georges Bidault had again assumed the post of Foreign Minister, was absorbed by the problems of the war in Indochina and was far from anxious to encourage a discussion in Parliament and the country at large which was liable to arouse political passions. However, the British Government, and even more so the US Administration, were calling for a solution. The question of German rearmament had been on the agenda since 1950 and since then three years had elapsed. A French plan had been adopted. There had been prolonged negotiations and finally agreement had been reached. It was time to act.

In the Belgian elections in March 1954 the Christian Socialists lost their absolute majority. In the week that followed the Socialists and the Liberals established a government with Achille Van Acker as Premier. I returned to the Foreign Ministry. In June the Laniel-Bidault Government was overthrown in Paris and on the 18th of that month Pierre Mendès-France took office as Premier and Foreign Minister.

While Pierre Mendès-France may not be the most likeable of Frenchmen, after de Gaulle he is, in my opinion, the strongest political personality to have emerged in France since the war. Immediately following the events which I shall now recount my feelings towards him were not friendly. Had he not struck an all but lethal blow at the cause of European unity? Yet, I must admit – and I do so willingly – he is a man of exceptional intelligence, strength of character and courage. In the thirties he was the infant prodigy of the Third Republic – the youngest deputy, the youngest minister in the Blum government, and an acknowledged economic and financial expert before he had a single grey hair. The war was to give him a chance to prove that his physical courage was as great as his moral courage. A member of the de Gaulle administration at the time of liberation, he left the Government in dramatic circumstances after de Gaulle had rejected his call for a policy of austerity. For most of the next ten years Mendès-France was out of office because he refused to have anything to do with the feeble and short-lived governments that followed one another in France in rapid succession, administrations in which he would in any case have been unable to gain acceptance for his views. As it was, Mendès-France showed by his conduct that, great though his self-confidence and his ambitions undoubtedly were, he refused to stoop to vulgarity.

In 1954 his hour struck at last and he became Premier. He succeeded in creating an atmosphere of confidence and hope. From the outset, Mendès-France enjoyed greater popularity than his predecessors. However, though in some quarters his qualities earned him loyal support, even absolute devotion, he also made a good many enemies.

Pierre Rouanet, his biographer and admirer, has this to

157

say about me in his book entitled *Mendès-France in Office*: 'Like so many prominent people, he is ruled by his heart rather than his head. He can understand those with whom he has to deal provided he feels he is liked.'

As M. Rouanet has never met me, let alone spoken to me, I can only assume that this is how Mendès-France, whose confidant he is, sees me. I cannot say whether this assessment of myself is right or not. However, I do think it more than a little amusing that this theory should be put forward by one who is certainly the most emotional politician I have ever met. Any discussion with Mendès-France soon takes a personal turn, with sentiment and emotion overriding reasoned conviction and argument. He wants to be – and indeed he can be – convincing, but often he seems to be more concerned with arousing the emotions of those with whom he has to deal. The fact is that his sensibility is as strong as his sense. He has a marked gift for drama and frequently succeeds in moving men's hearts.

During the Brussels Conference, he was haunted by the constant feeling that people were out to persecute him, which made his task more difficult and his contribution less effective than it would otherwise have been. He was convinced that he was not liked, that people did not trust him and that his position was that of a prisoner appearing before a biased judge.

During sessions, he never stopped doodling. Many people have this habit – some draw flowers, others animals or women. As for Mendès-France, he kept drawing vast dark prison walls. I am quite certain that he sincerely felt the others were against him, and in the end succeeded in making the French believe he had been unfairly treated. I shall have no trouble in proving that this was far from being the case.

These events are now far behind us, but even so I still blame myself for having failed to devise a formula at the Brussels conference that would have met Mendès-France's wishes and satisfied him that he had achieved the success he needed to put his policies into effect in Paris. After more than ten years I still regret the failure of that conference, a failure which resulted in the EDC Treaty being rejected by the French Parliament. I regret that failure not only because of its military implications, but above all because its ratification would have been a decisive step towards a united Europe.

Mendès-France was not sufficiently European-minded to fight the battle. If, rather than complain of his reception, he had emphasized the concessions his partners had made him and had spoken of the genuine cooperation he had been shown, events would have taken a different course. Had he been ready to fight on the battleground prepared in Brussels, I believe to this day that he might have won through and, having emerged victorious over the EDC issue, he could have fought the subsequent battles on more favourable terms.

He was victorious in August 1954, but by causing the French Parliament to throw out – without any discussion of its intrinsic merits – a treaty which France had not only signed but which she had actually herself proposed, he in fact dug his own grave. Mendès-France was overthrown at the beginning of February 1955. He proclaimed his opposition to Gaullism in 1958 and was ousted in the two parliamentary contests which followed. He was prevented from making the contribution of which he was capable. Today he must be seen as a man who has failed to fulfil his destiny. But perhaps it is not yet too late. He stands for all that is most solid and effective on the French Left. Will events, which for so long have gone against him, favour him at last? It would be a great pity if it were otherwise.

On 24 April 1954, one month after my return to office, I met Foster Dulles in Paris and together we reviewed the situation. We both reached the same conclusion: the French Government would have to submit the EDC Treaty to Parliament for ratification without further delay. Dulles made it clear to me that if the existing state of uncertainty, due to French hesitation, continued, the USA would be unable to proceed with its policy of military aid to Europe. He said the American Administration was facing not only opposition from its declared adversaries but also discouragement and scepticism on the part of its own supporters. An important section of public opinion was beginning to ask itself if Washington's European policy should not be revised fundamentally. Many thought our aims unrealistic and the vast expense involved in Washington's policy was a waste of public money. The Secretary of State assured me of his support in whatever steps I might care to suggest.

The British were equally worried and impatient. Since they anticipated a possible refusal by the French Parliament to ratify the Treaty, they were already busily working out alternative policies providing for German membership of the Atlantic Alliance on an equal footing or for the restoration of unlimited German sovereignty, which would, of course, have left Germany free to pursue her rearmament.

Such policies were bound to arouse French opposition and it was for this very reason that Pleven and Schuman had proposed the European Defence Community. If these policies were in fact applied, the divisions within the Atlantic Alliance would be aggravated and its very existence might be endangered. Certainly, such proposals were liable to cause France to leave the Alliance. It was at that time that the notion of the 'empty chair' was first mooted.

Profoundly averse to such policies and convinced that they would prevent the creation of a united Europe while at the same time endangering our security, I was determined to do all I could to thwart them. I therefore got in touch with my colleagues in the Netherlands and Luxembourg and we agreed that it would be necessary to hold a conference in Brussels at which the partners to the Treaty would review the situation. I was given the task of officially putting this proposal to the Germans, the Italians and the French, and I immediately obtained the agreement of the first two. In Paris, however, I came up against snags.

Mendès-France was then grappling with a great many complex problems, the chief of which was the war in Indochina. He had drawn up a timetable for his operations. The target dates which he had set himself gave him four weeks in which to make peace, and other problems were to be resolved thereafter in a predetermined order. As an intellectual exercise this sort of approach has its attractions, but unfortunately political life is not that easy! How pleasant it would be if only one could arrange one's problems neatly in one's diary and deal with them one by one! Events, alas, do not await our pleasure and problems tend to crop up simultaneously, in a tangle. Consequently, politicians must be able to deal with everything at one and the same time.

Important though Mendès-France's schedule might have been, the impatience of his American and British partners presented an equally pressing challenge. I was alive to the urgency of the situation but was also anxious not to give the impression of wishing to exert undue pressure on the French Premier. Through diplomatic channels I requested Mendès-France to receive me, leaving the choice of date to him. He suggested 30 June and I informed him in a brief letter that this would be acceptable.

At our meeting, Mendès-France declared that: (1) Indochina must be given priority; (2) in its existing form the EDC Treaty could not command a majority – or at least not an adequate majority – in the French Parliament, and the Treaty was of such vital importance to France that it could not be carried into effect against the wishes of a substantial minority; (3) it would be best if a compromise solution were devised as a result of discussions among Frenchmen.

In my turn, I summed up for Mendès-France's benefit the position of his partners. I reminded him that the idea of a European Defence Community had first been mooted by the French themselves and that we had accepted it to prevent uncontrolled German rearmament. I recalled further that three governments had, not without difficulty, persuaded their respective parliaments to ratify the treaty and that a fourth country – Italy – was about to follow suit. It was unthinkable, I said, that we should now begin the whole parliamentary process again from scratch.

We agreed fairly easily that it was in fact impossible for the French Parliament to amend the treaty without the agreement of the other signatories being obtained in advance. A conference would therefore have to be held to examine the French suggestions. Mendès-France did not want this meeting to take place before the negotiations on Indochina had been completed. I could see his point and we agreed that the end of July might be a possible date. Meanwhile, the French Premier would try to persuade the members of his Government to agree among themselves on the problems involved, for they were then divided on this issue. The Gaullists were hostile to the Treaty, while the other ministers, being convinced Europeans, were in favour.

We decided to remain in touch. In this way, I would keep abreast of developments in France and would be better able to prepare for the conference. It would doubtless be held in Brussels and, as Foreign Minister of the host country, I would be in the chair. Subsequently, Philippe de Seynes, whom Mendès-France had appointed his representative, and André de Staercke, Belgium's permanent NATO representative, had several meetings to draft a set of proposals which could be submitted with some chance of success.

My meeting with Mendès-France on 30 June was useful, if only because it helped to clarify our respective points of view. However, our difficulties clearly remained unresolved. Our discussions had been long and arduous, but perfectly friendly. That very evening, Mendès-France sent me the following letter, which confirms this:

'My dear Premier, I am anxious to let you know before the day is out how much I appreciated your kindness in coming to see me in Paris. Our meeting was bound to be useful, above all for me. It was, unfortunately, difficult for me to leave Paris at this time. Thanks to you, we have been able to meet, and I wish to express my gratitude for this with all my heart.

'I am happy to have been able to acquaint you with the timetable the French Government will have to observe. I hope this will convince you that a decision will be taken in the near future and that the former hesitations will be at an end. They were unfortunate in every way and must not be allowed to persist.

'Regarding the substance of the problem, it is my hope that your anxieties will prove exaggerated and that a solution will be worked out for the sake of an ideal which we both cherish equally – the creation of a united Europe.

'My attention being wholly taken up by the subject under discussion, unfortunately I forgot to thank you for wishing me success, a few days ago, in my efforts on behalf of my country and who knows, perhaps also for the good of an even greater cause. Please believe me that, coming from you, these words of encouragement are very precious to me.'

After returning to Brussels, three days later, I received a letter from Foster Dulles:

'My dear friend,
I have been watching with the closest attention your efforts on behalf of the European Defence Community. As I pointed out to you in Geneva, we are determined to give you our firm support. In our conversations here with Sir Winston Churchill and Mr Eden, we have all agreed that Europe would be cast into confusion and chaos if this creative and constructive project were abandoned. No other acceptable solution has emerged during our discussions and this has only strengthened us in our conviction that no such solution in fact exists.'

The same sentiments were conveyed to me from London by the British Ambassador in Brussels: the British were adamant that a solution must be found, that the Treaty must be ratified or, failing ratification, that the rearmament of Germany must proceed in some other way.

Besides Pierre Mendès-France, Chancellor Adenauer was to play an important role in Brussels. I had met him a few months earlier in Strasbourg, in circumstances worth describing.

The Saar, occupied by France but legally part of Germany, remained a most intractable problem. The future of Franco-German relations depended on its solution and the problem therefore had a considerable bearing on the ratification of the EDC Treaty by the French Parliament. If the Treaty were to be ratified, it was essential that relations between the two countries should be based on mutual friendship and trust – on this point all political observers were agreed. Sustained efforts were therefore made to devise a solution to the problem of the Saar. The Council of Europe had studied the question and, thanks to the efforts of the Dutch Socialist Deputy van der Goes van Naters, a compromise formula had been drafted, calling for the 'Europeanization' of the contested region.

In the spring of 1954 talks were held in Paris between Professor Hallstein and Maurice Schumann, the French under-Secretary for Foreign Affairs. The proposal put forward by van der Goes was accepted as a basis for discussion, but both sides submitted a series of amendments. The discussion was making no headway.

Towards the middle of May, the Consultative Assembly of the Council of Europe met in Strasbourg at the same time as the Ministerial Council. Chancellor Adenauer represented Germany, France was represented by Vice-Premier Pierre-Henri Teitgen, while I represented Belgium.

This was my first meeting with the Chancellor. On the other hand, Pierre-Henri Teitgen and I were old friends. I had nothing but admiration for Teitgen's devotion to the European cause and his exceptional gifts as an orator. Few men have moved me as deeply or as frequently as he has done in speaking of the last war and his desire for Franco-German reconciliation within the framework of a united Europe. Teitgen played a great part in those best years of the European Assembly in Strasbourg. Rarely has so much talent and such generous feelings been put at the service of so great an ideal and so noble a faith.

We decided to approach the Germans jointly in order to explore possible solutions to the problem of the Saar. We were convinced that this was a worthwile effort in itself, but at the same time we also bore in mind the need for ratification of the EDC Treaty.

Our first meetings were with Hallstein, who was an ardent believer in a united Europe and whose goodwill was beyond question. However, he was a lawyer and, at that time, also a civil servant. His powers to commit his Government were limited. Although we did make some progress, it was not enough. It was then that the Chancellor intervened, gaining my fervent admiration, an admiration which persisted until the moment when, led astray by General de Gaulle, he ceased to champion the European ideal with the necessary lucidity. But between 1954 and 1960 he proved that that was a quality he possessed in ample measure.

In 1954 Chancellor Adenauer was nearly eighty years old, but nobody would have thought of him as an old man. Physically and intellectually he was on top of his form and courageously pursued his grand political design, which was to enable Germany to become part and parcel both of the Western alliance and of Europe. Like Foster Dulles, he was one of those statesmen who are capable of taking the long view. Their ultimate goal may be in the far distance, but they never lose sight of it and never cease striving to achieve it. They can distinguish between essentials and in-essentials and are ready, on occasion, to make a short-term concession for the sake of their long-term objectives. Al-though there was at that time a socialist opposition in Ger-many which – wrongly – refused to support Adenauer in his foreign policy, his authority was such that he was able to take a good many risks with impunity.

In our conversations I was impressed by his lofty ideal-ism. He was above quibbling about legal niceties and ques-tions of detail. He could see his partners' point of view and was not interested in enhancing his personal prestige. Adenauer's enthusiasm and wisdom alike made it an excit-ing experience to work alongside him. We did not find over-much difficulty in making substantial progress under his direction. Teitgen and Adenauer agreed on the wording of a draft which provided for major concessions to France.

On the basis of the compromise solution put forward by van der Goes van Naters, the Saar was to become a Euro-pean territory. The Franco-Saar Economic Union would be maintained and the United States and Britain would guaran-tee the agreement.

For France this was an unexpected and unhoped-for success. It was due to the enthusiasm for European unity which then prevailed in Strasbourg and which inspired both Adenauer and Teitgen in their efforts. Unfortunately, the latter had conducted the negotiations alone on behalf of his Government. When he submitted the draft to Paris, happy with his undeniable success, the experts there started split-ting hairs and putting forward amendments which, with-out offering any real improvement, put the entire discussion back into the melting pot.

To persuade Germany to accept the sacrifices to which he had agreed, Chancellor Adenauer needed an immediate reply. A decision had to be taken in the prevailing atmos-phere of confidence and enthusiasm. Unhappily, the officials of the Quai d'Orsay were obsessed with diplomatic protocol and a ridiculous perfectionism. It may also be that they were none too pleased that Teitgen had brought these negotiations to a successful conclusion without their aid. Whatever the truth of the matter, the fact is that, instead of making the best of the exceptional opportunity within their grasp, they shilly-shallied, argued and wasted time until finally the chance of success vanished. In August of that year the French Parliament rejected the EDC Treaty and there was no longer any question of a European solution to the Saar problem. Two years later, the people of the Saar voted overwhelmingly for their region's unconditional reintegration with Germany. I believe this to have been one of the worst setbacks suffered by French diplomacy since the war.

When I met Chancellor Adenauer in Brussels, he was still the man I had come to know in Strasbourg. Throughout the conference he gave a striking display of his qualities. He was understanding, conciliatory, as well as persuasive, and did everything in his power to promote his cause, which was also the cause of Europe. Alas, our combined efforts were to prove of no avail.

The Brussels Conference did not get off to an auspicious start. A few minutes before the opening I was told of the death of Signor de Gasperi.

The first session began with a speech by Mendès-France. He spoke of his anxiety to secure the Treaty's ratification, but added that there was no chance of the document being accepted in its present form by the French Assembly. He went on to speak of the main ideas contained in the long memorandum which, a few days earlier, he had sent to each of the Treaty partners in the hope that they would accept certain major amendments. He wanted the period of the Treaty's validity and the conditions governing any annulment to be modified; further, he wanted to do away with the Treaty's supra-national character by according to all the signatories the right of veto for a period of eight years; lastly, he wished to limit the application of the clause providing for the integration of military forces to the units stationed in Germany.

It was obvious that if these proposals were accepted the governments which had already induced their respective parliaments to ratify the Treaty would have to resubmit it for ratification in much less promising circumstances. The governments concerned considered this unacceptable.

One after another, Beyen, the Netherlands Foreign Minister, Chancellor Adenauer, Signor Piccioni, the Italian Foreign Minister, and M. Bech expounded their views, each in his characteristic way. It became apparent that there was no hope of agreement on the basis of the French draft. The conference thus found itself in an impasse from the very start. In my capacity as chairman, and being the sort of man I am – always inclined to look for a compromise in such circumstances – I put forward a counter-proposal.

The objections to the French proposal were mainly of a legal nature. The way it was formulated made a modification of the Treaty inevitable, with all the various difficulties this implied. I therefore suggested that a declaration be added in a rider to the Treaty. This would make it possible to satisfy most of the French requirements while avoiding parliamentary complications. However, my proposal did not meet with Mendès-France's approval and we therefore began discussing his memorandum paragraph by paragraph. After a difficult, confused and fruitless debate lasting some hours we all realized that we could not work in this way. I considered the time had come to resubmit my proposal, and I handed to my colleagues the draft of a statement.

The attempt at mediation started badly. Mendès-France, having gone over the text, objected indignantly to the preamble, which he regarded as an indictment of France phrased in unacceptable terms. I thought he was making a great deal of fuss about virtually nothing, for the preamble was merely a review of developments from the time the French Government had proposed that the European Defence Community be set up until the opening of the Brussels Conference. It further described the efforts which France's partners had made to meet her wishes and contained not a single sharp word or aspersion. All it did was to describe, strictly objectively, the inconsistent attitude of the French.

I cannot say whether Mendès-France's indignation was

real or pretended. At any rate, he gave one of those dramatic performances in which he likes to indulge from time to time. Beyen urged the French Premier not to introduce unjustified personal undertones into the discussion and, to demonstrate our good will, we all solemnly proceeded to tear up the first page of my draft. Calm having thus been restored, the debate was resumed. After all this time it is impossible to sum it up. We clashed over hypothetical assumptions which developments have since shown were unwarranted. For instance, we spent a great deal of time trying to work out what would happen if Germany were reunified.

Mendès-France behaved with redoubtable – and, for his partners, exhausting – obstinacy, fighting for amendments the significance of which escaped us. The moment he got his way, he would minimize the importance of the concession he had just obtained. He had a difficult time, for he was facing not a hostile coalition but partners who, while trying to do their best to see his point of view, were honestly unable to share it.

Below are some notes I made in the evening of 20 August at the end of the second day of the conference. They give my impressions:

'A long harassing day, full of tension and incident. Mendès-France obstinately restates his position time and again. He believes that because he has fixed a date for the debate in the French Parliament he must be given whatever he asks for and wants everyone else to adjust their policies to suit the mood of the French Parliament. There are gross errors in his arguments. He does not know the mentality of the others, which in any case probably worries him very little.

'What exactly does he want? So far, I have no idea. He is afraid of a statement by the Five and has tried to enlist the support of the Americans. But at the moment his credit in the USA stands very low. His standing with the British is undoubtedly better.

'Adenauer is really splendid. What luck we have him here! We must definitely get the German issue out of the way while he remains in power. He knows how to stand firm, but also how to give way when necessary. There was an interminable discussion about the Treaty of Bonn.* Adenauer took a strong line. Beyen is sometimes too tough. This is a good thing where great issues are at stake but does not help with minor matters. But he gives nothing away, and Tjarda keeps egging him on to be even tougher!'

The morning and afternoon sessions on the 21st were devoted to meetings of experts, who did their best – for the most part in vain – to work out compromise solutions on the points we had left in abeyance. The ministers met again at 8 a.m. The discussion was resumed where we had left off, in very much the same way. Here and there a little progress was made, but several problems remained unresolved. Towards 11 o'clock, tired out, I called for an adjournment. Mendès-France and I stayed behind in my office. I was about to have one of the greatest surprises – and one of the most emotional experiences – of my entire career.

During the debate I had opposed the French Premier on a number of issues, but most of the time I had sought, proposed, and occasionally found, answers which met his point of view. Our relations were therefore cordial. It was this, I believe, which caused him to let me into a secret that left me dumbfounded. He said to me: 'I am certain we shall not succeed in reconciling our respective points of view.' After taking from his wallet several sheets of paper and passing them over to me, he added: 'This is what I shall say shortly, after we have duly noted the failure of our efforts.' I was thunderstruck. If this was the case, what was the point of all our efforts during the last three days, of the long hours passed in tiring and painstaking discussion of issues raised by the French; what was the purpose of our major concessions?

When I had put this to him and asked him to explain his attitude, he answered: 'I do not want to assume responsibility for a premature rupture, but I can tell you here and now that I have decided to say no.'

I was utterly stupefied. Why was he behaving in this way? Why was he telling me now, this morning, before

* This document defined the agreements with Germany (author's note).

the actual hour of decision had struck? To this day I do not know the answer, never having been able to understand such complex diplomacy.

I took my leave of Mendès-France and asked for M. Bech to be shown in. I told him what I had just learned and asked him for his advice. Just as shaken as I, he suggested I should forget all about it and that we should resume our work as if nothing had happened. This is exactly what I did, but for the rest of that night all our efforts seemed futile. I knew I was taking part in a charade.

After the document I had submitted had been examined in full, it was time to close the session. This was my task as chairman. I tried to sum up the discussion, underlining the concessions France's partners had agreed to make. In particular, I said, a period of three years would be allowed to elapse before any steps towards integration were taken. Mendès-France had been told that he might interpret Article 38 of the Treaty as providing for a slowing down of political integration within a united Europe; finally, the clauses governing any annulment of the Treaty would be drafted in accordance with French wishes. I concluded my statement by stressing that Mendès-France was now in a position to claim that his partners had made major concessions to him in Brussels and that he would now undoubtedly be able to fight his battle in the French Assembly with some chance of success.

Mendès-France then rose to reply, and in so doing made public the document he had shown me during the adjournment. There was every indication that it had been carefully prepared. This was not an improvised statement by someone forced to make a snap decision at the end of a debate. This was a declaration carefully weighed up in every detail and drawn up to serve as a brief in any subsequent discussion. In short, Mendès-France declared that none of the concessions he had obtained was of sufficient weight to win the support of undecided French deputies. He said he was returning to Paris empty-handed and that there was not the slightest chance of the French Parliament ratifying the EDC Treaty. He added, to console us, that he was still in favour of European unity, well aware as he was of the need for

German rearmament. The search for alternative solutions, he said, must begin without delay.

Chancellor Adenauer then spoke. In a moving appeal, he begged Mendès-France to realize the scope of the concessions he had obtained and to stand up and defend the Treaty. Signor Piccioni, the Italian Foreign Minister, declared that this unforeseen outcome had hurt him deeply. Bech and Beyen said nothing, but their disappointment was as great as my own.

Our entreaties were of no avail. Mendès-France had made his decision, not on account of what had just taken place in Brussels, but in response to the demands of the political situation in France.

We could only admit our failure, and this we did in the final communiqué of the conference.

In reviewing the events I have just described, I can feel once again all the disappointment and anger which gripped me then.

In comparing Mendès-France's proposals with the wording of the document agreed on by his five colleagues, no one could deny that he had in fact won tremendous concessions. We had done all we could. The interpretation of the Treaty now met the chief French objections. Mendès-France, however, wanted more. He was out for a political triumph. The position of the others – the fact that they could not be expected to return to their parliaments, which had only just pronounced on the Treaty, and demand that the deputies reverse their earlier decision – none of this made any impression on him. He was interested only in his own problems. In fact, he seemed to think the obstinacy and intransigence he had shown would serve him as a trump card in French domestic politics. For success in that sphere he was prepared to sacrifice the cause of European unity, and this is precisely what he did. However, his conduct brought him no luck. He failed in his attempts to strengthen his hold on his own country, and ultimately France consented to Germany joining NATO, something which heretofore she had always obstinately opposed.

On 22 August Mendès-France left Brussels, but instead of returning to Paris he went to London. Isolated from his

European partners and in open opposition to Foster Dulles, he needed encouragement and, if possible, new allies. Could Churchill and Eden help him?

According to Rouanet, Mendès-France's biographer, this Franco-British meeting resulted in complete agreement. He would have us believe that for Mendès-France it was a further triumph:

> 'At 17.00 hours the Premier was back at the airport. While the entire West was mourning the death of all hopes of common action for European security, Churchill, Eden and Mendès-France knew that the future London and Paris agreements were already germinating. Eventually it was to take only five weeks of sustained effort to complete the work, while it had taken the EDC project five months to die a slow death.'

Later we shall see what in fact happened at the London Conference, but I can say here and now that Rouanet's account is inaccurate. I have evidence to show that this idyllic story of the meeting between Mendès-France and Churchill is a long way off the mark. Let me add that a report of the meeting has come my way 'straight from the horse's mouth'. The following is a memorandum from Mr Churchill to André de Staercke, head of the Belgian delegation to the EDC conference in Paris:

> '1 We did our best, using what arguments we could, to emphasize what a dangerous impression – dangerous for both France and the West in general – would be created by a rejection of the EDC Treaty by the French National Assembly.
>
> 'We strongly urged him to lend his personal authority to the EDC Treaty and to M. Spaak's proposals as representing by far the best solution for France.
>
> 'He declared he would submit the Treaty to a vote by the Assembly but that he was absolutely certain the Treaty would be rejected.
>
> '2 We urged him to make it clear to the Assembly that an alternative solution would have to be found without delay in the event of the Treaty being rejected. He agreed and said he was ready to state that in his view a simple

solution would have to be found within two months. We pointed out to him that it would be difficult to find a solution and to put it into effect so soon.

'In conclusion, we stressed that he should endeavour to persuade France that the EDC was by far the best choice. We emphasized, in particular, that we were acting in concert with the United States Government and that we owed a debt of honour both to Dr Adenauer and to the European countries which had already ratified the EDC Treaty.'

There is a wide discrepancy between this account and the approbation which, according to Rouanet, Mendès-France had received in London. History is sometimes written in a singular fashion!

Back in Brussels I was at a loss what to do. I kept returning to the proceedings of the conference, asking myself where we had gone wrong and if we had allowed a chance of a reasonable agreement to slip through our fingers. I resolved to make yet another attempt.

One of Mendès-France's main objections to the Treaty had been its supra-national character. I therefore tried to devise a formula which would set the French Premier's fears at rest. Without disclosing the matter to my partners, on 24 August I instructed our Ambassador in Paris, Baron Guillaume, and André de Staercke to request an interview with the Premier, at which they were to submit the following draft to him:

'In the event of a member-state considering its vital interests endangered by the working of the Community's institutions, the state concerned may submit the matter to the Ministerial Council. The latter must take immediate steps to end this state of affairs. A member-state may at any time request the Court to rule whether or not the issue invoked is in fact of vital importance. The Court's ruling will be final.'

Although the French Premier agreed to meet my two colleagues, they were not well received. Having read the draft, Mendès-France reacted with some impatience: 'How is it,' he said, 'that I am being presented with this draft now when all is over? If it had been to hand at the beginning of the conference, things might have turned out very differently.'

I do not think much of this argument. In any case, Mendès-France lost no time in adding that the formula submitted to him did not meet his requirements fully. He wanted a rule that Ministerial Council decisions should be unanimous, and furthermore that a clause be inserted to the effect that the Ministerial Council was empowered to set aside any decision by one of the subordinate bodies of the Community. Finally, he wanted these points incorporated in a protocol which would have the same force as the Treaty itself. Mendès-France went on to insist that he could only accept the Treaty if his conditions regarding its form and substance were met and he added – no doubt frightened by the minute concessions he had made – that he would be powerless to achieve anything with these amendments alone. It would doubtless be necessary, he declared, to recall the conference with a view to examining the other points of the formula and, moreover, there was still the problem of the Saar!

Mendès-France added that he regarded the approach that had been made to him as evidence that M. Spaak was persisting in his efforts to bring about a reconciliation. He was all the more grateful for this as he had been placed in a humiliating position in Brussels, where he had had to face *organized* opposition. In response to M. de Staercke's protest at this, he corrected himself and instead referred to *spontaneous* opposition. Finally, he asked for time to think things over, adding, however, that he was not at all sure that this attempt would succeed.

The outcome of my *démarche* was thus not encouraging, but since it had not met with total failure, I decided to press on. I drafted a note in which I explained my point of view in an effort to reply to the points raised by Mendès-France. I had little difficulty in showing that my formula in fact met the main French demands.

Baron Guillaume and M. de Staercke were instructed to seek a further interview with the French Premier. This time their failure was final. They were informed of this in the following terse terms: 'There is no point in your wasting your time repeating the same old tune. I am reminded of the Brussels Conference, which was a dialogue of the deaf if ever there was one!' Mendès-France could not resist the temptation to conclude the interview with the two officials with a remark which reflected his irritation: 'I shall no doubt soon read all about M. Spaak's impression in *Le Figaro.*' This was an allusion to an interview I had given a short while before to the Paris paper. This time it was all over. All that remained was for Mendès-France to have the EDC Treaty rejected by the French Parliament. This he succeeded in doing by giving a totally misleading account of the Brussels Conference. He spoke of the humiliations he had allegedly suffered and his partners' lack of understanding.

In this atmosphere the French National Assembly began its debate on the Treaty on 29 August. What is incredible, indeed almost inconceivable, is that a French Government presided over by a man who sought to restore the authority and prestige of the executive – and who had actually succeeded in so doing – should have proclaimed itself neutral on the issue. Parliament was debating a treaty which both its friends and opponents had declared important, even crucial, to the country's future, yet the Government refused to vouchsafe an opinion. The Government eventually allowed the debate to be closed by a procedural manoeuvre and without the substance of the question being discussed at all. Nothing like it had ever been witnessed before and it is difficult to see what Mendès-France hoped to achieve by these tactics.

By 319 votes to 264, with 12 abstentions, the Assembly voted against the matter being placed on the agenda. The twenty-three members of the Government deliberately abstained from voting. There can be no doubt that if Mendès-France had taken a firm stand and fought, the result would have been different. Considerations of domestic politics made him act as he did. Yet, his prestige in France was not enhanced and abroad he lost much of his standing.

22

The London Conference
and the Paris Agreements

With the EDC dead, another way had to be found of inte-
grating Germany into the Western family of nations. On
1 September Dulles wrote to me:

'My dear friend,
The action of the French National Assembly in rejecting
the EDC Treaty without even a full-dress debate has, I
know, been as bitterly disappointing to you as it has to
me. David Bruce has passed on to me your remarks in this
connection. You have done everything possible to realize
this bold concept, which held out so much hope for the
future of Europe and our Western alliance. I want you to
know how deeply I and my fellow-Americans appreciate
your sustained and imaginative efforts throughout the
years, particularly in these last few crucial weeks. The
qualities of true statesmanship you have displayed have
won the admiration and respect of all. We must, of course,
persevere in our joint efforts to create a Europe strong
united and full of hope, despite the fact that conditions
are less favourable now.

'The United States will have to face great difficulties if
our future common efforts do not bring quick results. It
is, however, reassuring to know that men such as you are
determined to strive for our common objectives.

'I am about to leave for Manila, but will closely follow
developments in Europe in the coming days. I am aware
that you hope to be in New York for the opening of the
United Nations General Assembly and am looking forward with great pleasure to seeing you again there.'

It was a friendly letter, apparently intended to comfort me. I look upon it as further evidence that, contrary to his appearance and repuation, Foster Dulles could be understanding, human and cordial. However, it was not only his friendship which made him write to me as he did. He was worried about the political situation. The rejection of the EDC presented him with serious problems, as he made clear on 31 August in a statement containing some very stern references to France. He declared: 'France's rejection of the European Defence Community is a sad event. France is thus turning her back on the historic proposal which she herself made four years ago. This proposal, if adopted, would have meant the pooling of Europe's military resources in a single European army and would have helped put an end to the recurring European conflicts, the last two of which turned into world wars.'

He went on to declare:

'1 that the defence of Europe required a German contribution;

2 that Germany could not be expected to accept neutrality forever and that her sovereignty would have to be restored to her;

3 that, in order to prevent wars between neighbours, supra-national organizations would have to be established and accepted;

4 that United States policy had, since 1946, been based on the hope that one day Western Europe would unite.'

He followed this up with a solemn warning: France's retrograde step, unaccompanied by any alternative proposal, meant that the United States must now reassess its foreign policy, and particularly its relations with Europe.

Foster Dulles made no attempt to hide either his thoughts or his anger. He went on: 'Germany must now be given back her sovereignty undiminished. This is a promise which would have been kept had the EDC become a fact. She must not be punished for something she has not done.' He stressed in conclusion that the United States remained ready as ever to support European countries which remained faithful to the ideal of European unity and that the defection of a single country must not be allowed to prevent the rest from acting.

Rarely had the representative of a Great Power spoken out so clearly, and so incisively, in condemnation of the conduct of an ally. The American leaders made it brutally clear that they were tired of French prevarication. It looked increasingly as if Dulles was considering a European and Atlantic policy without France as a possible answer to our problems. Despite my disappointment with the French, I thought this was going too far, or, at any rate, that it was premature. I continued to believe that the search for a compromise must continue, that efforts must be made to allow the French Government to change its mind and that it should not be confronted with an impossible dilemma, causing it to lose face.

I wrote to Dulles along these lines, and this counsel of moderation may have had some influence on him, for a few days later he confirmed the receipt of my message without insisting on the need for the draconian measures he had advocated earlier. Again he declared that he would like to meet me before long.

British influence, too, was making itself felt. In London, disappointment was as marked as in Washington. However, while the British were as determined as Dulles to see a re-armed Germany, to support Chancellor Adenauer and to put an end to French hesitation, Eden did not regret as deeply as the Secretary of State the blow that had been struck at the ideal of a united Europe and a supra-national organization. In the sense in which we used the word in 1954, the American statesman was more 'European' than the British.

Eden, incidentally, was more Francophile than Dulles, more inclined to bear in mind French susceptibilities. The entente with France seemed more important to him than the creation of a united Europe – a concept in which he had never believed very strongly, at least not in the form *we* had in mind. He believed a good, solid, conventional alliance would be as good, if not better. This is one of the few issues on which we differed.

Despite this, it was to Eden I turned at the beginning of September. I sent him a long personal letter in which I set out the arguments I had earlier put to Foster Dulles. It ended with these words:

'Naturally the Belgian Government is as ready either to attend a conference in London or to discuss any of these questions within the framework of NATO. The shape of that conference would not seem to be of particular importance; what matters is that we should work out some reasonable ideas to help extricate ourselves from our present impasse.'

My letter was dated 7 September 1954. On the 11th Eden was in Brussels for a meeting with the Benelux Foreign Ministers. He had decided to take matters into his own hands and had begun a series of negotiations which must undoubtedly rank among the most successful of his entire career. From beginning to end he conducted these exchanges in a masterly fashion. He was in turn conciliatory and firm and, finally, in a bid to wrest a definitive decision, showed himself both imaginative and bold. It was mainly due to him that the crisis which began with the rejection of the European Defence Community Treaty was settled. With understanding, patience and infinite skill he moved between Mendès-France, Dulles and Adenauer, and succeeded in restoring in less than a month the position in Europe and in ending the prevailing disarray. Eden may rightly be regarded as the 'father of the London Agreements and the Treaty of Paris'.

In the morning of the 11th he explained his main ideas to Bech, Beyen and myself. He submitted them to us as projects still in the planning stage and declared himself open to any suggestion. In essence, what he had in mind was an extension of the Brussels Treaty. He wanted Italy and Germany to sign the Treaty, with the latter Power also becoming a member of NATO on a footing of equality with the other member-states.

My colleagues and I endorsed his initiative and the main features of his plan. We also agreed to take part shortly after in a conference in London with Great Britain, the United States, Canada and the six signatories of the EDC Treaty.

Having won this initial success, Eden went to Bonn. After the rejection of the EDC Treaty by the French Parliament, the German Chancellor was in a difficult position. His entire European policy had suffered a grave setback. He therefore adopted a very reserved attitude, the more so as the opposition in the German Parliament was beginning to stir. Adenauer needed help if the issue of Germany's future were to be settled satisfactorily. He did not favour the conference proposed by Eden. Like Foster Dulles, he would have preferred a NATO conference which would tender an invitation to Germany to join the Atlantic Alliance. He anticipated that certain restrictions on German rearmament would be required, and did not oppose this in principle. He had in fact agreed to this within the framework of the European Defence Community but was nevertheless afraid that measures might be adopted which would prove difficult to justify to the German public.

Eden must have displayed great powers of persuasion for before he left Bonn the Chancellor had assured him that he was not opposed to the British plan and was prepared to accept the procedure suggested by the Foreign Secretary. Eden then left for Rome, where Signor Piccioni promptly agreed to his ideas on behalf of Italy.

On 15 September Eden was in Paris, where he had a meeting with Mendès-France. Of all the politicians he had met, the French Premier proved the most reserved. Eden had the happy idea of attending a meeting of the NATO Permanent Council on 16 September at which he gave an account of his discussions in the various capitals he had visited. He explained his answer to the problem of German rearmament and his ideas were welcomed. He was thus certain of the support not only of the five countries which had ratified the EDC Treaty but of all the NATO Powers with the exception of France. This strengthened his hand in his subsequent talks with Mendès-France, who persisted in his opposition to German membership of NATO and demanded the adoption of measures which would have placed Germany in a position of inferiority *vis-à-vis* her future allies.

Back in London on the 17th, Eden could claim that, while he had not fully convinced Mendès-France, he had made sufficient progress to enable him to call the proposed conference. True, there was a risk, but it was a warrantable one.

The conference began on 28 September 1954 in a tense atmosphere. Dulles was responsible. While Eden was in Paris trying to carry Mendès-France along with him, the American Secretary of State had decided to pay a sudden and spectacular visit to Chancellor Adenauer. He also announced that from Bonn he would go on direct to London without visiting Paris. He thus made it clear that he was determined not to meet the French Premier, and in so doing gave the world a foretaste of what later came to be known as the 'policy of the empty chair'. This show of bad temper was very badly received in France. Mendès-France was hurt, the more so because in Bonn Foster Dulles had come out strongly in favour of all the German views. The communiqué issued after his meeting with Chancellor Adenauer ended with these words:

'The two sides agreed that German sovereignty must be re-established as soon as possible. They further agreed that Germany must participate in a system of collective security on a basis of full equality. Since this programme is so important for the future of both Germany and the free world, it should be discussed as soon as possible with the other governments concerned and must find expression in positive steps following a meeting of the Ministerial Council of the North Atlantic Treaty Organization.'

After this statement, making him an unconditional ally of the German Chancellor, Dulles flew off to London, by-passing Paris. His brusque attitude was due to his very real doubts as to whether he would be able to persevere with his Atlantic policy if a solution to the problem of German rearmament were not found very quickly. Both public opinion and political circles in the United States were becoming restive at the amount of time which was being wasted in fruitless discussion. Dulles had warned the French but, preoccupied with their own difficulties, they preferred to pretend that they were unconvinced by what they were pleased to call the 'American bluff'. Fortunately, the British were both more alive to the realities of the situation and more determined to work out a reasonable solution.

At the time of his arrival in London, Foster Dulles had

agreed neither to Eden's proposals nor to the tactics the latter had suggested. The meeting between the two men turned out to be decisive. In the event, the Secretary of State somewhat reluctantly agreed to a conference being called. He made it clear, however, that he would attend as an observer rather than as a participant, adding that he would be in a position to determine the attitude of the United States only when the results of the conference were known.

In London, on the morning of 28 September, the nine Foreign Ministers had three proposals before them: Eden's plan, a French proposal and a German memorandum.

Eden's plan was the one he had put forward during his tour. While its general features had been made clear, the details were still vague, in accordance with Eden's flexible diplomacy.

The French proposal called for Germany's adhesion to the Brussels Treaty but made no mention of her entry into NATO. It contained a number of complicated proposals about arms control. Several were more severe than those contained in the EDC Treaty.

Germany, in her memorandum, declared herself ready to sign the Brussels Treaty and to limit her military contribution. However, she demanded the right to join NATO and restoration of her full sovereignty.

It turned out to be a very difficult day. Fighting for his ideas, Mendès-France showed himself as dourly obstinate as in Brussels. As chairman, Eden displayed infinite patience. Whenever things looked like getting out of hand, he would adjourn the session so as to avoid an open row and would offer us all a cup of tea. A good many cups were drunk during the conference!

The lobbies were buzzing with rumours. In general, comment was critical of the French, whose attitude in the end irritated everybody. The ideas put forward by Foster Dulles, on the other hand, were gaining ground. More and more, the need to go ahead without France was coming to be seen as the only way out.

Finally, it was Eden who saved the day. We now know from his memoirs that he had foreseen and measured the difficulty we were likely to encounter. On 27 September, explaining the situation, he wrote to Churchill, and in so doing showed remarkable powers of prediction:

'In my opinion, the success of the conference depends on a new commitment by Great Britain to maintain her forces indefinitely on the Continent and not to withdraw them against the wishes of the majority of signatories of the enlarged Brussels Treaty.'

Eden added:

'I realize that this would be an unprecedented commitment for Britain to undertake. However, the hard fact is that it is impossible to organize an effective system for the defence of Western Europe – essential to Britain's security – without a major British contribution.'

These were wise words, excellent words, and they marked a bold step forward. In admitting that Britain was in no position to withdraw her troops from the Continent of Europe without the agreement of the majority of her partners, Eden was endorsing in an essential area – that of defence – the idea of a supra-national authority. What a pity his courage was confined to the military sphere and did not show itself in regard to the European Coal and Steel Community or, later, the Common Market. But for this, Europe would have become a different place.

Churchill hesitated about giving his approval. On the night of 28 September, having listened to a report from Eden which spoke of all the difficulties he had encountered during the day, the British Cabinet gave the Foreign Secretary a free hand, after what appears to have been a very lengthy discussion. Eden then went over his plans with Foster Dulles and the two agreed on the scenario to be used to give the conference a new lease of life.

During the afternoon of the 29th, after one of those long adjournments made necessary by our inability to agree, the American Secretary of State, who had until then been silent, suddenly asked for permission to speak. He began by recalling that in the spring he had made it clear that the United States was ready to maintain its troops in Europe on condition that the French Parliament ratified the EDC Treaty. He went on to remind the ministers that United

States policy had invariably been based on the hope that Europe would one day unite: that had been the object of both the Marshall Plan and the Atlantic Alliance. Dulles added that if these efforts turned out to be in vain, if Europe again furnished a spectacle of dissension threatening the outbreak of war, the tendency in the United States would be to withdraw from Europe. In that event, the commitments Washington had entered into could not be met. He then spoke of the wave of disappointment which had swept the USA, particularly Congress, after the rejection of the EDC Treaty. Many Americans, believing the situation in Europe to be hopeless, were inclined to think that the USA would be well advised not to enter into any further commitments in this part of the world.

After this display of pessimism, and having delivered his warning, Dulles changed his tone. He declared that if the conference did find a way to restore unity among the European Powers he would feel disposed to recommend to the President a renewal of the promise of American support along the lines of that given when there was still hope that the EDC might become a reality. However, the success of the conference was a *sine qua non* if the United States were to give this new undertaking.

Although these words amounted to quite a strong threat, they also held out the hope that the United States would support the British proposals provided they were accepted by the other governments. This was a possible first step out of our impasse, but it was not enough to save the day.

Eden then took up the running and made a speech which ensured the success of the conference. After thanking Foster Dulles for his words and recalling Britain's efforts to help create the EDC, he declared that something more was needed. He therefore promised that not only would the British troops be maintained in Europe at their existing strength, but also that they would not be withdrawn without the agreement of the majority of the Brussels Treaty partners. He went on:

'My colleagues will realize that what I have announced is for us a very formidable step to take. You all know that ours is above all an island story. We are still an island

184

people in thought and traditions. And it has not been without considerable reflection that the Government which I represent here has decided that this statement could be made to you this afternoon. . . . Of course, you will understand that what we have just said, and the undertaking we are prepared to give, does depend on the outcome of our work. If we succeed here then this undertaking stands; if we do not, Her Majesty's Government could not regard itself as committed to what I have said this afternoon.'

These two speeches, the first by Foster Dulles, but even more the second by Eden, created an atmosphere fraught with emotion and a sense of occasion. Everyone realized that the hour of decision had struck. If the London Conference were to fail, like the one in Brussels, not only would this mark the end of the Atlantic Alliance but the Brussels Treaty would also succumb to the blow. The entire defence policy of the West would collapse in the face of the Russian threat, which remained formidable.

The five Powers which had ratified the EDC Treaty, as well as Canada, had no hesitation in declaring their support for the British proposals. Britain's offer and that of a continuing American presence in Europe could not be rebuffed.

How did Mendès-France react? I have always been convinced that he was surprised by the British offer, surprised because it marked so radical a departure from Britain's traditional policy. Britain's desire to contribute to Europe's security was so strong that the French Premier could not continue to withhold the concessions the situation demanded. All eyes were on him. He thanked Eden, and the few sentences he spoke made everyone feel that it was virtually certain the French would change their attitude.

The meeting was quickly brought to a close. All the delegates needed time to think. On leaving, I caught sight of M. Massigli, the French Ambassador. His eyes were full of tears. He declared his country had just obtained the concession for which he had been asking Britain in vain for the last twenty-five years. All seemed to be going well. If the French were content, the conference was saved. However, this result was not achieved without further difficulty, for Mendès-France was not easy to negotiate with. There were times when Eden had to show great firmness in order to secure the long-awaited final agreement.

Eden was helped by Adenauer, who announced without prompting that Germany was ready to renounce the production of nuclear, biological and chemical weapons. Despite all these gestures of good will, it took five more days of technical discussions before the draft of the final agreement was completed. It was a lengthy document, which declared that the occupation regime in Federal Germany be wound up as soon as possible, that Germany and Italy adhere to the Brussels Treaty, that a European agency for the control of armaments would be set up within the framework of the Brussels Treaty and, lastly, that the member states of NATO attending the conference would recommend to the next meeting of the NATO Ministerial Council the immediate entry of the German Federal Republic into the Organization.

It remained for these decisions to be set out in the form of a treaty. Without further ado the task was begun on 5 October in Paris. The work, though difficult, was rapidly completed by the diplomats. The ministers met again in Paris on 21 October and it took them only one day to reach agreement on the draft texts before them. The Atlantic Council, which was informed the following day, accepted the proposals – notably the one for Germany's entry into NATO.

In most of the capitals the ratification of what had now become the Treaty of Paris was relatively easy, though this process was accomplished in an atmosphere of resignation rather than of genuine enthusiasm. The crisis which had followed the rejection of the European Defence Community Treaty by the French Parliament had been exceedingly serious. No one wanted to be held responsible for resuscitating it.

Only Mendès-France had a fight on his hands. The French supporters of the EDC were out for revenge. A number of people were still angry at the way the Premier had allowed the EDC debate to be conducted in August. Moreover, they did not have far to look for a justification

186

of their attitude; in many respects the new solution was less favourable to France than the one that had been rejected. However, this time Mendès-France fought resolutely. He did what he should have done several months earlier and emerged victorious from the parliamentary battle.

The treaties having been finally ratified by the French Parliament, Germany became a member of NATO in the spring of 1955. Thus ended a long series of negotiations, a diplomatic contest which had spanned several years, a battle that had at times been violent, full of incident, a battle in which some of the West's most important statesmen – Dulles, Adenauer, Mendès-France and Eden – had confronted one another. Their qualities and defects alike were highlighted in the struggle. Dulles, devoted to the cause of Atlantic and European unity, a dedicated anti-Communist, resolute and authoritarian in manner, aggressive and tough, sometimes to the point of brutality; Adenauer, obstinately pursuing his policy with a controlled passion, the statesman-philosopher among us, ready to take the greatest risks when it mattered but never forgetting his fundamental aim. Only a few years after the war's end he had succeeded in restoring Germany to her rightful place in the Atlantic community and had won recognition as a leader of the new Europe. Mendès-France was full of zeal and passion in his approach to politics, but he was also secretive and at times disturbing. Most of his colleagues were in two minds about him. His courage won him sympathy, but he could also be exasperating. On occasion he would move people deeply by his dramatic oratory, but he was touchy, difficult and often unnecessarily obstinate. One who knows him well has said of him: 'He hates playing second fiddle.' He had no time for ideas conceived and realized without him. His ambition was to put his personal stamp on whatever decisions were adopted. This is doubtless a legitimate aspiration but difficult to achieve when one is faced with men with strong personalities of their own.

Finally, there was Eden, in his prime as a statesman, the most experienced politician among us. He had adopted a middle-of-the-road, pragmatic position which destined him for the part of mediator, and he also acted as arbiter when necessary. I am convinced that without Eden we should have had great difficulty in reaching agreement. In 1954 and 1955 Eden saved the Atlantic Alliance.

My two Benelux colleagues, Bech and Beyen, and I formed a triumvirate, working in complete accord despite our different temperaments. Bech was notable for his moderation and ready smile, while Beyen was more determined and less conciliatory. As for myself, among the three of us mine was the hottest temperament. With our various qualities, we made up a force which allowed us to play our full part. The following year, when the time came to give fresh impetus to the struggle for Europe, we were able to prove this anew.

PART FIVE

United Europe

23

The Marshall Plan and OEEC

The first bid to organize Europe was made in 1947 by an American, General Marshall, who was then President Truman's Secretary of State.

It behoves us Europeans to be modest. Only the fear of Stalin and Marshall's bold vision enabled us to take the right road. It was on 5 June 1947, at Harvard University, which had just conferred an honorary degree on him, that General Marshall made his famous speech. He had just returned from Europe and had been struck by its deplorable economic plight. At the same time, he was disappointed in Soviet policy. He hoped he might be able to contribute to the rehabilitation of the countries devastated by the war, giving them a common goal for which to strive: reconstruction. Marshall was sincere. The offer he made to the Communists was neither a diplomatic manoeuvre nor a trap. He was hoping to extricate his wartime allies from the impasse in which they were caught by putting the accent on practical issues and promoting cooperation in the economic sphere, since cooperation was becoming increasingly difficult in the diplomatic field.

It was not true that the Americans were trying to dominate Europe by means of the Marshall Plan and to interfere in its internal affairs. Had this been their aim they would have dealt with the European countries one by one. This would have been the easiest way for them to safeguard their influence and impose their political will on Europe. The situation of the countries concerned was such that it would have been difficult for them to resist America's demands. However, far from acting thus, the Americans declared: 'The initiative must come from Europe. The role of this country [i.e. the USA] should be to provide aid in order to promote a joint programme as far as possible. This programme should be comprehensive, and drawn up by a large number of countries working together.'

These were generous and wise words. The British, through Bevin, and the French, through Bidault, responded immediately. Having consulted the other countries concerned, they suggested to the Russians that they accept the American offer. Molotov's unequivocal and brusque refusal made a deep impression on Bevin and Bidault and was the final and decisive reason why these two abandoned all thought of cooperation with the USSR. The first result of General Marshall's offers was therefore politically important. In addition, there was another effect: the offers compelled the European governments to collaborate and to consider their problems from a common point of view instead of thinking exclusively of their own narrow national interests. Marshall's offers were thus at the root of the Coal and Steel Community and, later, of the Common Market.

To put the Marshall Plan into effect, the various governments had to undertake a tremendous technical task. Following the Soviet refusal, France and Britain called a conference of fourteen European Powers, which opened in Paris on 3 July 1947. The fourteen were made up of Powers which had fought in the war on the side of the West, of neutrals, as well as of some countries which had been dragged into the war on the side of Germany, such as Austria and Italy. Only Spain was excluded from the common enterprise, for at that time there were still hopes that it might be possible to induce General Franco to retire from the political scene.

I still remember my dealings with two Ministers of Finance: Liftinck of the Netherlands and Sir Stafford Cripps of Great Britain. Like myself, they were Socialists, but unlike myself they were of a doctrinaire frame of mind and as obstinate as I, in general, tend to be conciliatory. Circumstances forced them to pursue a policy of austerity in their respective countries. Although that policy had been forced on them by events, they insisted that it had been freely chosen and wanted me to acknowledge that it was fundamentally right.

During the last few months of the war, Belgium had gathered an abundant harvest of foreign currency and had thus been able to settle her Lend-Lease accounts with the United States. She therefore had no reason to impose severe restrictions upon herself. I was ready to help the Dutch and the British to cope with their difficulties, but this was not enough for my two colleagues. They wanted me to champion a policy of economic austerity, something which would have been of no use to Belgium. We had some very lively meetings. I tried to end the debate by putting forward practical solutions. However, Liftinck and Cripps insisted that I acknowledge the fundamental correctness of the emergency measures which they had taken in their respective countries.

Sir Stafford Cripps, an ascetic endowed with a red nose as well as formidable intellect, was an able tactician and an excellent debater. An idealist who tended towards mysticism, he thought in absolute terms. At the same time he was obstinate; in short, difficult. Our relations were correct, but I believe he had little time for my enthusiasms. I was too emotional and altogether too much of a continental for him. These were qualities he did not like, as he was to show later on.

On the other hand, my relations with the two Americans who at that time played a prominent part in Europe were easy and friendly. I have known Paul Hoffman and Averell Harriman for more than twen', years, having met them repeatedly at various stages of my career, thus establishing ties of friendship which our identity of views made even closer.

In his capacity as Administrator for Economic Cooperation, Paul Hoffman was a great success, not only because his courtesy made him pleasant to deal with but because he championed the cause of European unity before it had become fully established. I have often made use of his arguments to show that if the countries of Europe could reach an understanding, their rehabilitation would be rapid and they would regain their former political importance. He was a pioneer and innovator. He gave us confidence and we owe him a great debt of gratitude.

At the beginning of 1948, Harriman was entrusted by President Truman with a special mission in connection with the Marshall Plan. He, too, is entitled to our thanks. Many

193

were the occasions when Harriman acted as our spokesman in Washington. As a former aide to President Roosevelt, he already enjoyed a great reputation at that time. During the war the President had appointed him to a post of exceptional importance – United States Ambassador to the USSR. Harriman was discreet, modest and reserved. His dignified bearing was tinged with a touch of melancholy, and he seemed a little shy. However, those who knew him well realized the strength of his convictions and the audacity of his views. Once a problem had been put to him in precise terms, he was a changed man. Suddenly he would be all attention. He would listen and make up his mind quickly. One could sense his determination and drive. He was among the few people who realized the great potential for Europe of the Marshall Plan. Like Paul Hoffman, he was able to see beyond the immediate issues and he shared Hoffman's vision of a united Europe, a Europe acting as one, and able, in the long run, to take its place beside the United States as a worthy partner. He foresaw a Europe no longer the USA's poor and weak ally, the sort of ally that constantly needs aid but only gives impatience and ingratitude in return. Harriman never gave up fighting for intelligent cooperation between the United States and Europe, a struggle he has been able to wage for many years thanks to his astonishing physical and mental resilience.

After serving as Governor of New York State, he resumed his diplomatic activity under Kennedy and Johnson. Travelling the world as special envoy of the two Presidents, or carrying out special missions for the State Department, he has been involved in all the great issues of our time. He has had dealings with all the political leaders and his experience is therefore exceptional. I met him again when I was grappling with the difficult problems of the Congo. As always, he was understanding, friendly and, when the need arose, courageous. It was thanks to him that I was able to deal successfully with a number of dangerous situations. I am both grateful and devoted to him.

It was not long before our efforts were successful. On 17 December 1947, President Truman passed a Bill authorizing an interim grant of aid to Europe. On 16 April 1948 the

European Economic Convention was signed by ministers representing sixteen European governments and the Commanders-in-Chief of the allied occupation zones in Germany. The OEEC was set up. I was elected its Chairman and Robert Marjolin, the French economist, Secretary-General.

The parties to the Convention declared that their aim was close economic cooperation. They wished, above all, to determine their respective needs and to meet them fairly, having regard to the total amount of American aid available. For the year 1948-9 the United States undertook to provide 4,875 million dollars on the basis of an agreed intra-European system of payments and trade regulations, proving that the countries of Europe were genuinely anxious to cooperate.

The effort of reconstruction thus began promisingly. It was to produce rapid and spectacular results. Thanks to the Marshall Plan the economy of the democratic part of Europe was saved. The standard of living of its population soon greatly surpassed that of the Communist countries. The aims defined by General Marshall in his Harvard speech were attained. The success was a striking demonstration of the advantages of cooperation between the United States and Europe as well as among the countries of Europe themselves.

However, the work of the OEEC was disturbed by a political controversy which began in 1948. Hoffman, Harriman and MacBride, the Irish Foreign Minister, together with a few others including myself, wanted the organization to play a more important role. We believed the OEEC should become the basis for long-term European cooperation and continue to function even after the completion of Europe's rehabilitation. We thought, too, that an attempt should be made to invest the OEEC with certain political powers. The British and Scandinavians opposed these ideas. Hoffman and Harriman wanted the organization, after it had been transformed in accordance with these concepts, to be led by a man capable of giving it the necessary drive. They decided to choose me. But at that time I was Premier and Foreign Minister. I could accept the appointment only if I gave up my political work in Belgium, and this I did not wish to do.

On 15 October 1948 Bevin sent me the following message:

'Certain rumours have come to my knowledge, according to which you might be willing to give up your ministerial appointments in order to take up a post in the OEEC. However, as Belgian Premier you are playing a major role in the renaissance of the West and I fear you may not be able to exert the same influence and authority within the OEEC. Speaking personally, I should be very sorry to lose your support and sound advice in the councils of Western Europe. However, you must, of course, judge for yourself which is the best course for you.'

I have every reason to believe that this advice was meant sincerely. At the beginning of the year Bevin had signed the Brussels Treaty and I had just made my speech in the UN criticizing Soviet policy. We were in the middle of negotiations with the Americans for the establishment of the Atlantic Alliance. Bevin realized that I shared his views and was a reliable ally in our various endeavours. It is thus understandable that he should have thought it best that I remain Belgian Premier. However, his feelings were undoubtedly influenced in part by his wish to prevent the OEEC from being led by a man whose ideas about the organization of Europe differed from those of the British Government.

At the beginning of 1949 a committee consisting of nine ministers examined, under my chairmanship, the structural reforms the OEEC would have to undergo to improve its efficiency. Three memoranda on this subject had been submitted to us – one by myself, a second by MacBride and a third by the British. The first two urged that the OEEC's area of competence should be broadened and the President vested with certain powers. The third merely called for a number of minor modifications.

The compromise reached meant that we had to make far-reaching concessions. The best we could do was to secure the establishment of a consultative committee at ministerial level, charged with examining, prior to full-scale discussions, the main problems, and laying down a programme of work. This was not much of an achievement.

In August 1949 I gave up my posts as Premier and Foreign Minister, having lost the elections in Belgium. Within the OEEC the struggle between the two factions continued. The Americans were hoping that the organization might serve as the basis for a united Europe. They still wanted it to be headed by a politician, and I remained their choice.

My own personal situation had changed. I was no longer in the Government. The question of the monarchy divided the Belgian people profoundly. The idea of presiding over an international body whose task it would be to create a united Europe appealed to me. In December I visited the United States, where I met President Truman, who informed me that his Government had definitely decided to put forward my candidature for the presidency of the OEEC. Mr Truman advised me to call on his Secretary of the Treasury, Snyder. The latter received me very kindly, declaring with some exaggeration that all the financial resources of the United States would be at my disposal in my future efforts. I returned to Europe a little heady with joy over my achievements, convinced that my career was about to take a new turn. But I had not reckoned with Britain's obstinacy and influence.

When MacBride suggested at a meeting of the OEEC Executive Committee that I should be appointed chairman with additional powers, Sir Stafford Cripps opposed the idea in the most categorical terms. Following a unanimous decision of the British Cabinet, he declared my candidature to be unacceptable. Off the record, Sir Stafford explained that I was needed to ensure a proper balance in Belgian domestic politics. I believe Bevin was sincere when he said he wanted me to remain Belgian Premier, but I find it difficult to accept that Sir Stafford really meant what he said in declaring that he thought it important that I lead the opposition in my country.

In actual fact, this incident highlighted a difference between successive British Governments, both Labour and Conservative, and myself. The Council of Europe began its activities in May 1949. It was the scene of spirited battles between the federalists on the one hand and the supporters of the *status quo* on the other. Robert Schuman put forward the idea of the European Coal and Steel Community, and that of the EDC was mooted soon afterwards. The Europe in which I believed was beginning to take shape, and the British Labour Party was hostile to it. It consequently did not want me to occupy a position where I could have exercised my influence in support of ideas to which it was hostile. This was fair enough, and I would only blame the Labour politicians for hiding their real reasons.

As it was, their opposition to my leadership of the OEEC forced me to continue my career as a politician. In pursuing that career I was able to serve Europe better than if I had accepted the presidency of an organization whose dynamism and importance were soon to decline.

24

The Hague Congress
and the Treaty of London

By 1950 the movement for a united Europe was in full swing. For centuries there had been Europeans who dreamed of a new Europe and of concord between countries which in the past had again and again made war upon one another. Many plans had been canvassed but no leading statesman was prepared to put the weight of his authority behind them. Only philosophers, economists and poets – brave men crying in the wilderness – had fought for the European ideal.

Between the two wars, Aristide Briand was the first statesman to make the attempt by taking the initiative with a speech before the League of Nations in Geneva. In somewhat vague terms he called for a European federation. Although he won a prestige success and caused something of a sensation, his initiative gained no support, for the time was not yet ripe for such experiments.

In the years that followed the end of the Second World War, when it became clear that there was no prospect of continued cooperation with the USSR and that it was essential to organize Western solidarity, the idea of a united Europe was revived and pursued with more vigour than at any time in the past. The situation had been transformed by a new element: the idea was now being championed and publicized by important statesmen. Thanks to them, the transformation of Europe ceased to be an abstract notion and became a topical political issue.

Winston Churchill, whose Fulton speech had shaken the Atlantic world, created a fresh stir in Europe with an address in Zurich on 19 September 1946. Although defeated in the previous year's general elections, he still enjoyed tremendous prestige and undeniable authority throughout the democratic world. His unexpected move caused a considerable stir. The Zurich speech was beautiful: it followed the true Churchillian tradition, being serious, dramatic and full of passion, and it combined poetical language with an acute awareness of the needs of the moment. He justified his vision of the future by his interpretation of the events of the day. When one remembers that Churchill made his speech a mere eighteen months after the end of hostilities, one can but feel boundless admiration for the man; although already old, he did not flinch from new and tough battles.

The Zurich speech galvanized all those who believed in the need for a new Europe. By making that speech, Churchill became one of the leading pioneers of European unity. And yet the speech was to become the root cause of a grave misunderstanding, for it contained an ambiguity which no one noticed at the time. After remaining hidden for some time, it was brought into the light of day when Churchill, back in power, refused to associate himself with the European Coal and Steel Community and the EDC.

Though even on a careful reading his Zurich address seems clear, Churchill, in referring to Europe in some splendid passages, failed to define what exactly he meant by Europe in geographical terms. At the time, he appeared to include Great Britain in Europe, but in fact this was not the case. The united Europe which Churchill advocated was a continental Europe, of which France and Germany were to be the joint leaders; Great Britain, the Commonwealth, the United States and, if possible, the USSR, were to befriend and support it.

Churchill wanted Britain to promote the creation of a united Europe, but he did not want Britain to be part of it. For a number of years after his Zurich speech nobody asked him exactly what was in his mind when he made it. People were only too glad of his backing for a great cause. The ambivalence of his speech suited everyone, and it was therefore unjust to Churchill when people later took him to task for his attitude. However, he was perhaps wrong not to have clarified his position when the time was right and to have allowed people to believe that there was a powerful movement in Britain ready to press for that country's integration with continental Europe. The overwhelming majority of Labour supporters were hostile to this policy. As for the Conservatives, though they were ready to follow their leader, it soon became clear that they were not prepared to go beyond expressing a measure of sympathy for the idea of a united continent of Europe of which Great Britain would not be a part.

But whatever may have been the true sense of Churchill's speech at Zurich, the impulse had been given. All the unofficial movements which championed the cause of European unity joined forces in organizing a great congress to voice their demands. It was held at The Hague from 7 to 11 May 1948, and was to become an historic landmark in the annals of Europe. A huge number of delegates attended – more than 1,200. Among those present were Churchill, representing Britain; Ramadier and Reynaud representing France; and van Zeeland for Belgium. Also present were two men who were as yet little known but who were soon to play a major role: Adenauer and de Gasperi. The unofficial movements were represented by their most dynamic leaders: Denis de Rougemont, Salvador de Madariaga and Henri Brugmans.

The congress duly ended with a vote on three resolutions dealing, respectively, with cultural, economic and political affairs.

The first called for the establishment of a European cultural centre: this was set up within a matter of years. The second proclaimed a set of principles, most of which are now embodied in the Treaty of Rome. The third urged that a European parliamentary assembly be convened immediately.

The resolutions adopted at The Hague, bold though they were, were evidently well thought out, since all of them – and this is rare where congress resolutions are concerned – were to be carried into effect within a few years.

The most urgent task – and the first that was in fact tackled because it was also the easiest and most spectacular – was the establishment of a European Assembly. Our efforts were quickly rewarded with astonishing success. Two men were responsible: Duncan Sandys and Joseph Retinger. Different though they were, the two men had one quality in common: unflagging energy. Duncan Sandys, Churchill's son-in-law and a Conservative MP, had served as a minister during the Second World War. He was one of the first Britons who – going beyond the ideas of his father-in-law – wanted to see a union established between Great Britain and continental Europe. He first devoted part of his activities to this enterprise and in 1948–9 gave up all his other work for its sake. All doors were open to him and he visited all capitals, laid siege to all the ministries and overcame all opposition.

He was accompanied by Joseph Retinger – a man of unique qualities. The politicians who had spent the war years in Britain knew him well. After a life full of incident and a variety of occupations, in 1940 he became General Sikorski's confidant and adviser in London. An intelligent, active and slightly mysterious individual, he would have luncheon every day with one British politician or another, or with a member of one of the governments in exile. He knew everybody and no door was closed to him. During those years he was one of the best informed politicians. He helped to initiate the discussions we Poles, Czechs, Dutch, Norwegians and Belgians held in order to establish new links between us. Continuing his efforts after the war, he was among the most ardent partisans of European unity and deserves to be remembered as a pioneer of that cause.

On 23 August, Robert Schuman, then French Foreign Minister, wrote to me:

'The French Government has just decided on a new initiative and would greatly welcome it if you would agree to associate yourself with it. We intend submitting to the five governments which have signed the Brussels Treaty a plan worked out by the International Committee of the Movement for European Unity. It calls for a conference which would pave the way for the establishment of a European Assembly.'

At the beginning of September I went to Paris to inform Robert Schuman of my support for the plan. Together we made it our business to try to convince our three partners. I was very pleased to be able to collaborate with Robert Schuman. I have never seen so modest and discreet a man with so much imagination and political courage. He had none of the qualities normally expected of a leader. He spoke simply, avoiding the use of flamboyant language, and made no attempt to stir the emotions of his audience. However, what he had to say was so manifestly honest, and his words so patently sincere and wise, that he succeeded more effectively in convincing people and persuading them to follow him than he would have done had he been a much more brilliant speaker.

It is strange to think that this reserved, even timid, man should have been able to put his stamp on Europe to such effect that for some years he was considered its leader. Thanks to him, French prestige was able to assert itself. Beyond doubt, France was the leader. This result was facilitated more by Robert Schuman's agreeable manner, pleasant smile and air of sincerity than by General de Gaulle's haughty and harsh diplomacy. Schuman proved that it is easier to imprint one's personality on events by one's qualities as a human being than by arbitrary claims to greatness and authority.

What we now had to do was to convince Bevin. At this time – the end of 1949 – he was already a sick man and very different from the Bevin I had come to know at the beginning of 1948. I have never understood why he changed his views as he did. I have already mentioned the importance of his speech in the House of Commons on 22 January 1948 in which he put forward the idea of organizing the Atlantic Powers and proclaimed his desire for European unity. There seemed then to be no limit to his courage. Never again was Bevin to show up in this light. On the contrary, on a number of occasions he seemed surprised and even worried when he saw the ideas he had himself pioneered being put into practice.

On 15 September he explained his views on what he called the 'Franco-Belgian initiative'. He emphasized the difficulties which stood in the way of a common European concept and expounded the arguments which have since been reiterated so often by both Labour and Conservatives: Britain has no written constitution and does not want one. As a member of the Commonwealth she can do nothing without first obtaining the agreement of her fellow members and does not wish to do anything which might loosen her ties with them. Bevin added that it would in any case be possible to set up an assembly to deal with political affairs only after the various defence and economic problems had been solved. 'It would be wrong to try to construct the roof without first having built the house.'

Happily, during our talks Bevin proved less negative in his approach than we had feared. We were supported in our work by Bech and Stikker, the Dutch Foreign Minister. The four of us proved sufficiently strong to obtain certain concessions. On 28 October 1948, at a meeting of the Consultative Council set up under the terms of the Brussels Treaty, we managed to obtain approval for the establishment of a committee to consist of representatives appointed by the various governments in the following way: five each to represent France and Great Britain; three each to represent Belgium and the Netherlands, and two to represent Luxembourg. Their task would be to examine ways and means of promoting the unity of the countries of Europe.

The committee was to examine measures proposed by the French and the Belgians with a view to preparing the ground for a European consultative assembly, as well as a British proposal for setting up a European council appointed by, and responsible to, the various governments.

The wording of these proposals highlighted the differences between the two rival concepts. Nothing was as yet decided, but discussions could now begin and that was the main thing.

The committee set about its task under the chairmanship of Edouard Herriot. On 16 December it submitted to the governments a plan for a European union which provided for the establishment of three bodies: a Council of Europe – an inter-governmental authority composed of ministers; a Consultative Assembly whose members would be appointed by the various national parliaments; and a Secretariat. After this first report had been adopted unanimously, British objections apparently vanished. However, appearances were deceptive.

When the committee met again, on 18 January 1949, Hugh Dalton, the leader of the British delegation, put forward a totally different counter-plan. Instead of the as-

sembly originally envisaged there would be a body consisting of national delegations appointed by the various
governments concerned, each headed by a minister; voting
would be *en bloc*. This was unacceptable.

This time it proved impossible to devise a compromise in
the committee and it was thus in a bleak atmosphere that
the Consultative Council began its session on 27 January.
However, a miracle happened. I must admit that I do not
recall the details of the discussion and I have forgotten
whether or not we had to struggle hard to overcome British
reservations. The fact remains that we did overcome them.

The communiqué published at the end of the meeting
announced that agreement had been reached on the establishment of a Council of Europe which would consist of a
Ministerial Council and a Consultative Assembly. The
Council would deliberate in private and its decisions would,
alas, be subject to the rule of unanimity, while the Assembly's meetings would be public. Italy was to be invited
to join. At Bevin's suggestion, Strasbourg was chosen as the
seat of the new organization. This border town, which had
so often in history been the object of Franco-German rivalry,
was selected as a symbol of cooperation and friendship.

The treaty establishing the Council of Europe was signed
in London on 5 May 1949 by representatives of the five
Powers which had taken part in the negotiations, plus the
three Scandinavian countries, Italy and the Republic of
Ireland. The Treaty of London incorporated the main points
on which the Five had agreed. Its preamble stressed the
need for international cooperation for the maintenance of
peace and reaffirmed a number of moral and political
principles fundamental to European civilization, as well as
the need for economic cooperation as a means of encouraging social progress.

Strangely enough, there was no reference in the Treaty to
any issue connected with national defence. This was due to
British influence, as well as to the hesitations of Sweden
and Ireland. These two countries were ready to play their
part in the common effort but had no intention of jeopardiz-
ing their neutrality. This omission to mention defence was
unfortunate since it was an obstacle to progress towards
European unity. How could there be any hope of such

progress in the absence of any discussion of so vital an issue?

But this was not the Treaty's only defect. The Ministerial Council was under an obligation to promulgate its decisions on all matters of importance *unanimously*. Once again, this acceptance of the absolute sovereignty of states was to prove a wretched and paralysing barrier to progress.

I have frequently attended meetings of the Ministerial Council. Of all the international bodies I have known, this is undoubtedly the most timorous and ineffectual. The fact is that the British and Scandinavians have no intention of using this new organism to help build a new Europe. They have joined the organization, and that is as far as they are prepared to go. When they joined they were determined to bide their time before taking the next step. In the years that followed, the entry into the Council of such neutral Powers as Switzerland and Austria did nothing to improve the situation.

As for the Assembly, it is a purely consultative body with no real powers whatsoever. It can only discuss matters within its sphere of competence and convey its conclusions to the Ministerial Council in the form of recommendations. The fate of these recommendations at the hands of a Council bound by the rule of unanimity soon became all too plain. Most of the recommendations were never taken up.

I did not sign the Treaty of London, not because I did not approve of it but because at the time I was detained in Belgium by an election campaign. In the event, I lost these elections and it then proved impossible for me to continue my cooperation with the Christian Socialists.

Forced into opposition, my disappointment was tempered by my satisfaction at the events which were to follow.

25

The Council of Europe:
First Session

The first session of the Council of Europe began in Strasbourg on 10 August 1949. The Consultative Assembly was good enough to postpone the election of its President by twenty-four hours in order to enable me to stand, as I first had to hand over my seals of office in Brussels.

Having thus been freed of my ministerial burdens, I was elected unanimously on 11 August, my candidature having been sponsored by Winston Churchill, André Philip, Paul Reynaud, Jacini of Italy and Kraft of Denmark. What happy days those were when I was able to serve as the rallying point around which countries and parties could unite!

I had already presided over the United Nations Assembly and the OEEC and, despite the fact that by temperament I am a fighter rather than an arbiter, I had acquired a reputation as an adept of the art of chairmanship. I practised with some measure of success what I came to call 'controlled impartiality'. This means that one must allow all opinions to be voiced without, however, surrendering the right to guide the debate in what one believes to be the right direction and to promote the necessary compromises at the right time.

For me, the election was a fortunate turning point. It enabled me to remain in touch with Europe's political leaders. Between 1949 and 1954 I devoted myself unreservedly to the cause of European unity and wrote a large number of articles in its support. I made speeches in all the member countries of the Council of Europe. This was a time of lively activity and genuine enthusiasm. My friends and I were convinced we were fighting for a cause that merited our absolute devotion. Adenauer, Schuman, de

Gasperi and Jean Monnet were our leaders. At times we followed their advice and at others it was we who drove them on. Thus, together we were able to make progress towards the Europe of our dreams. It was a fascinating experience.

I presided over a magnificent assembly. Nearly all the most eminent parliamentarians of Europe had made sure of being sent to Strasbourg. Never has a chairman had so many politicians and orators of renown sitting under him. For any connoisseur of the art of oratory these debates were a never-to-be-forgotten experience. It was also fascinating to compare the many styles of public speaking and the temperaments of the various delegates. As born orators, the French put their views clearly. They were clever at improvising and thanks to their brilliant perception adjusted themselves easily to the changing tides of fortune in our debates. The British were methodical, calm, good-humoured, lively in repartee, but, except for Churchill, rarely impassioned. The Italians were voluble, free with their gestures, ceaselessly emphasizing with their hands their fiery arguments. The Scandinavians were cool, imperturbable and avoided all showmanship or gesticulation. They were precise and always reasonable – perhaps to excess.

The most outstanding of all these parliamentarians was Paul Reynaud. His fluency as a speaker, the clarity with which he expounded his thoughts, the incisiveness of his attacks and his ready repartee made him the most effective speaker I have ever known. I had only one fault to find with him: he was pitiless towards his opponents; he simply crushed them. His victories were total, and this may indeed have detracted from their effect. People could not forgive him his superiority as a speaker, which he made no effort to hide. Less obvious triumphs would doubtless have been more helpful to his cause.

There were other outstanding speakers, too, though they may not have been Reynaud's equals; André Philip, for example, who could be wise and mistaken in turn but who always defended all his beliefs ardently, right or wrong. There was Teitgen, who had no equal when it came to infusing an element of drama into a debate and who combined strong feeling with compelling logic. There was Guy

Mollet, less flamboyant, more detached, who always presented his solid arguments methodically. Then there was Michel Debré, a brave, lone figure, fighting for his ideas as if it were a matter of life and death.

As for the British, there was Churchill with his special brand of oratory. He delivered his carefully prepared speeches as if they had been improvised. He used his sonorous voice, imparting a special weight and a strangely moving inflection to certain words, and interspersed his speeches with brilliant passages, gleaming like freshly minted coins. Churchill knew, too, how to make skilful use of his prestige.

Macmillan, calm, lucid, a good debater, refuted the arguments of his opponents, or sustained his own, with efficiency and skill, illustrating his thoughts at times with humorous asides and at others with biting irony. There was Boothby, full of fire and conviction, and Julian Amery, who added a continental flavour to his special brand of British eloquence. There was Lord Layton, charming, loyal, a good European, whose support was most valuable to me, and finally McKay, that astonishing Labour MP from Australia, who, alone among his group, advocated Britain's entry into a federal Europe.

Lastly, there were the Dutch, the Germans and the Scandinavians, with their serious approach, punctuated occasionally by a burst of feeling from Strauss or Gerstenmaier.

It was, in truth, a splendid spectacle, a festival of eloquence, skill and parliamentary expertise. The first session saw a discussion on the alterations to be made to Europe's political structure. From the outset, differences emerged. The Assembly was in fact divided into three camps. A federalist minority, which demanded the immediate adoption of a European federal statute. At the other end of the spectrum there was the prudent faction, which insisted that Europe should be built up step by step, stage by stage, without undue haste. Most of the delegates, including myself, took up a position in between these two extremes. We agreed in principle with the federalists but were anxious not to lose touch with the British.

All in all, the results of this first session were satisfactory.

Many of the speakers had expressed views reflecting a genuine European awareness. However, the final goal remained in question and no agreement was reached on the methods to be employed to attain it. Though the enthusiasm we felt at the beginning of August had not diminished, we were now more alive to the difficulties which would have to be overcome if we were to realize our ideal.

26

The Council of Europe:
Second Session

The second session of the Assembly turned out to be important. Three principal subjects were dealt with: Europe's organizational structure, the defence of the free world and the Schuman Plan.

During the ensuing debate, a clear distinction emerged between the attitudes of the bold and the prudent factions. The future division of Europe was taking shape.

The federalists launched a major offensive. In their camp were some of the best speakers in the Assembly: André Philip, Pierre-Henri Teitgen and Gérard Jacquet. One after another, they mounted the rostrum to state their views. They did so with verve, advancing in turn arguments based on reason and on sentiment. Their impassioned pleas contrasted with the pragmatic attitude of the British and the Scandinavians, but their ardour failed to melt the hearts of the Nordic delegates, nor did their Cartesian logic have any effect on the prudent patriotism of their opponents. While they took endless pains to paint vast political frescoes, to advance bold ideas and draw up plans for the future, Miss Bacon, an authoritative figure in the British Labour Party, with both her feet firmly on the ground, declared that 'no one should try to run before they can walk. There must be no undue haste in building a united Europe.'

Macmillan said roughly the same thing, though he clothed his arguments in somewhat more elaborate language. To explain what divided his compatriots and himself from the continentals, he declared:

'Our differences are, above all else, a matter of temperament and intellect. They are based on an age-old contrast

211

between two ways of thought and methods of argument. The continental tradition seeks to reason *a priori* and descends, as it were, from the summit to the plain; it proceeds from general principles, which it then applies to practical issues. This is the tradition of St Thomas Aquinas, the tradition of scholasticism, the tradition of the great continental thinkers and scholars. The British, on the other hand, prefer to discuss problems *a posterior*, ascending from practical experience towards the summit. This is the tradition of Bacon and Newton.'

There is a great deal of truth in this – as can be seen from the history of the efforts to create a united Europe. European unity had to be seen to be succeeding before the British gave any thought to becoming part of it.

In 1950 those who were anxious to go ahead without further ado urged that supra-national authorities be established forthwith in the key sectors: defence, human rights, coal, steel and power. European ministers were to be placed at the head of each department. These proposals were rejected by a united front of the British and Scandinavians. If the other delegates had insisted on these proposals, this would merely have served to harden the division of Europe. Since most delegates wished to avoid this, the proposals were rejected by very large majorities.

In their speeches, the British insisted again and again on what they called the 'functional approach', contrasting it with the 'legislative approach'. Their idea was that a united Europe should be created by solving one by one the practical problems of the moment. They also repeatedly advanced a new – and dangerous – notion. They said: 'Let those who wish to take the federal path do so by all means. We, for our part, have no intention of following their example, though we do see their point of view.' Thus the idea of a 'Little Europe' took shape, comprising France, Germany, Italy and the Benelux countries.

When, at a later date, the British refused to join the Schuman Plan – which was the first attempt to apply their 'functional approach' in practice – the moderate faction in Europe was left with no option but to go ahead and build the new Europe without Great Britain.

Personally, I had not yet arrived at that stage in 1950. I had hoped too fervently for Britain's participation to give up easily so long as there seemed the slightest chance of its realization. But when the Conservatives returned to power the following year and merely continued where Labour had left off, I finally realized that to try to make Britain the cornerstone of our efforts would be to renounce the very idea of a united Europe.

On 9 May 1950, at the Quai d'Orsay, Robert Schuman gave a press conference at which he outlined the plan that was to constitute the basis of the European Coal and Steel Community. That plan had been drawn up by Jean Monnet. In saying this I do not in the least wish to detract from the part played by Robert Schuman. His contribution – and it was essential – was to have accepted political responsibility for Monnet's ideas.

I met Jean Monnet for the first time in Washington in 1941 and remember the occasion very clearly for two reasons: first, because of what he said to me and, second – dare I admit it? – because of the excellent dinner he offered me: chocolate profiteroles – creamy and light, rounded off a splendid meal prepared by his French chef. The dinner made an agreeable contrast with the austerity of British cooking to which I was subjected at that time.

Having tasted these material delights, we went for a walk which took us along a route from which we were able to admire the panorama of Washington. We spoke of the post-war period, of what would have to be done to safeguard peace and Europe's future. Monnet gave me an account of the underlying philosophy, and explained the rough outlines of what later became known as the Schuman Plan.

It is this continuity of thought, this perseverance in pursuing his ideas, that I feel is Jean Monnet's most characteristic trait. Like Robert Schuman, he is a man of modest bearing, in fact he even seems shy. But though Monnet may not be an impressive public speaker, in his day-to-day work he is incomparable and the strength of his convictions is unequalled. I have seen him deal with individuals as different from one another as one could wish to find: captains of industry, government leaders, trade union militants, Members of Parliament of every political hue. By the time Jean Monnet had finished with them, they were all convinced of the rightness of his views. Thus he made converts one by one.

In the immediate post-war years, he played a crucial part in the efforts to create a United Europe. We all looked up to him as our master and relied on him for advice. Nothing was done without him in this connection at that time. His untiring and selfless efforts earned him our devotion, respect and admiration.

In the spring of 1950, Robert Schuman and Jean Monnet, realizing that the endless discussions in Strasbourg were a sheer waste of time and that there was no chance of a federal solution ever being adopted, decided to approach the problems of European unity from another angle. They became advocates of the functional approach. Robert Schuman declared: 'Europe will not be created all at once, nor will it be a unitary structure. Europe will be the result of specific measures. To begin with, our solidarity will take the shape of practical ties.'

There was, however, a great deal of courage behind this apparent moderation. The French Government was in fact proposing that the whole of French and German coal and steel production should be placed under a joint authority which would enjoy supra-national powers and would 'create the first practical basis for a European federation, essential if peace is to be preserved'.

The final goal had thus not been forgotten. Though the idea was to approach it stage by stage, the supra-national principle was to be applied from the outset. For my own part, I accepted this proposal enthusiastically. To support it, I wrote an article in which I gave it my full blessing.

Our problem was to discover what the British reaction was likely to be. We did not have long to wait. The negotiations began and some rather subtly-worded memoranda were exchanged. Two points of view emerged: the French were asking for a conference of countries 'ready in principle to pool their coal and steel resources and to establish an authority whose decisions would be binding on the governments concerned'. The British, on the other hand, were unwilling to accept such obligations. They proposed a general discussion which would 'throw light' on the nature of the plan and all its political and economic implications.

It proved impossible to devise a compromise since Robert Schuman remained adamant. He called a conference. It was held in Paris, with France, Germany, Italy and the three Benelux countries taking part. Britain held aloof. Little Europe was taking shape. Schuman and Monnet wanted this to happen, convinced as they were that the only thing that would persuade the British to change their minds was the success of the enterprise.

On 13 August 1950, Robert Schuman defended his plan before the Consultative Assembly in Strasbourg on behalf of the Ministerial Council as well as in his own name. He gave numerous technical details to justify the plan and, on the most crucial matter of all – that of the supra-national character of its institutions – he declared:

'I accept a renunciation of sovereign rights not for its own sake, not as an end in itself, but as a necessity, as the only means at our disposal to overcome national selfishness, the enmities and narrow-minded prejudices which are ruining us.'

He concluded by saying:

'We do not think we are being presumptuous in claiming that if our proposal, which you have accepted, becomes a reality in the form in which it has been submitted to and accepted by you, forces will have been set free whose potential cannot as yet be measured. One thing, however, is certain: they will promote rapid and complete economic and political unification of Europe.'

The speech led to prolonged discussion which showed that the functional approach was bound to give rise to difficulties just as hard to overcome as those of the legislative approach.

The British were not only outspoken, they were united: there was no difference in this respect between Conservative and Labour. Macmillan made an important speech justifying their attitude. His refusal to accept the Schuman Plan and the very notion of supra-nationality was reflected in the following passage:

215

'At all events, one fact is certain, and we had better face it frankly. Our people will not hand over to a supra-national authority the right to close down our pits and steelworks. We shall not permit a supra-national authority to reduce a large section of our fellow citizens in Durham, the Midlands, South Wales and Scotland to unemployment. These fears may be imaginary, but their existence is a fact, and a fact, moreover, which no British Government can afford to ignore.'

Thus the gulf was created which divided most of the continentals from virtually all the British. Yet it would be wrong to say that all the continentals took the same view. General de Gaulle, emerging from his retreat at Colombey, addressed the members of the Council and the mayors of the Moselle Department in the following terms, in the style which is so very much his own:

'When de Gaulle says there is need for a new national economy, he is answered by a proposal calling for a sort of a mishmash of coal and steel. Those who have made this proposal have no idea where they want to go, and all they can do to justify their scheme is to talk of some kind of an industrial complex.'

De Gaulle was only speaking for a minority, though one which even at that time embraced both the Communists and the extreme Right.

The discussion on the Schuman Plan had important repercussions in Strasbourg. It brought out fundamental differences, the existence of which had until then only been suspected and which it was hoped to overcome by means of skilful compromise solutions. Many people were coming to realize that it would be impossible to create a united Europe with the British.

The same session saw the beginning of a debate on defence. Despite the fact that the Treaty of London had expressly excluded defence from the Assembly's area of competence, the Ministerial Council had instructed the Assembly to define its position with regard to the 'problems of the defence of peace-loving peoples against aggression'.

Those delegates who were eager to expand their field of activity could not pass up such a splendid opportunity. What had happened to justify 'this imprudence', as some called it? The fact is that war had broken out in Korea and the United Nations had intervened. The United States had proclaimed its readiness to send troops to Europe, but was also calling for the rearmament of Germany. It appeared advisable to sound out European opinion on these issues, and the Assembly seemed as good a place as any for this.

Once again, it was Churchill who took the initiative in calling for the immediate establishment of a united European armed force. The most audacious among the deputies went even further and expanded Churchill's draft as follows: 'The force shall be under the authority of a European Minister of Defence. It shall be subject to European democratic control and shall act in cooperation with the United States and Canada.'

This revolutionary provision was adopted by eighty-nine votes to five, with twenty-nine abstentions. It was the most important decision yet taken by the Consultative Assembly. It reflected the state of disquiet which prevailed in Europe, as well as a desire for progress towards unity. Among those who abstained were the Scandinavians, the British Labour delegates and the German Social Democrats. The opposition of the latter to Adenauer caused them to make mistakes in matters of foreign policy. It was only after these had been put right that the way was open for them to return to power. It took several years before they managed to emerge from the blind alley into which they had strayed.

The debate on European defence was resumed at the autumn session. In the meantime, the French Government, with Pleven as Premier and Schuman as Foreign Minister, had put forward the idea of a European Defence Community.

At the Assembly's meeting on 24 November 1950, Schuman gave an account of French policy. He ended his speech with an impassioned peroration which contrasted strongly with his usual sober tone. But then, the subject was indeed important.

After Schuman's speech there followed a debate on a report submitted by Duncan Sandys. A great many speakers representing all countries and political parties took part. The discussion was dominated by Paul Reynaud, Macmillan and Guy Mollet. On behalf of the German Christian Democrats, von Brentano announced his support for the French plan. A resolution, the chief clauses of which were based on the draft adopted in response to Churchill's initiative in August, was passed by eighty-three votes to seven, with nineteen abstentions.

The second session of the Assembly thus came to a satisfactory close. The discussions had been interesting. There had been many speeches – too many perhaps – but some of them remarkable. The Assembly had proved to be a real forum of international opinion. The confrontation between the views of some of the most important political leaders of the various countries had been fascinating. However, it was becoming clear that there were difficulties in store for us. The Europe of the Eighteen was soon to clash with the Europe of the Six, and the dynamism of the latter was to contribute to the former's decline.

27

The Council of Europe: Third Session

The third session of the Assembly, in autumn 1951, began auspiciously for me, but ended on a less happy note. I was re-elected President – without discussion, which was a creditable personal achievement. However, on 11 December I tendered my resignation, discouraged by the faint-heartedness of most of the delegates and their refusal to take the decisions I considered essential. As far as I was concerned, the session proved one long series of disappointments.

The interminable debate on the aims and prospects of European policy began anew. Its most striking feature was the attitude of the British. The Tories had succeeded Labour, Churchill had replaced Attlee. Much was expected in Strasbourg of this change, for Churchill's Zurich speech was still fresh in everyone's memory. In the two earlier sessions, the Conservatives had seemed more European-minded than their Labour opponents. People were hoping that now that they were back in power, the Tories would cooperate with the continentals. It was not long before the latter realized their mistake. The disillusionment was cruel. As regards the organizational structure of Europe, the Schuman Plan and the European army, the Tory Government and its delegates in the Assembly continued the previous Government's policy without the slightest change.

On 28 November, Sir David Maxwell-Fyfe (later to become Lord Kilmuir), who in earlier years had been a most ardent advocate in Britain of the need for European integration and had acquired a considerable reputation in this context, made a disappointing speech. In effect, he said that while the Churchill Government was ready to give friendly support to the movement for European integration, there was no question of the British taking an active part in it.

Let us be fair: this was precisely the thesis Churchill had put forward in Zurich. True, his attendance at The Hague congress, his speeches in the Consultative Assembly, his call for the creation of a European army, all these had given rise to illusions. But once he was back in office he made sure that his attitude was understood: Britain had no intention of joining a united Europe, nor even of taking part in the efforts then being made to promote a partial integration of our continent.

Sir David's words allowed of no doubt in this respect. Speaking of the federal solution, which he described as 'an illusory concept', he said: 'We do not believe that it is open to a country such as ours, in our situation and with the responsibilities I have indicated, to adopt such a solution.' Referring to partial agreements, he added: 'Our policy will always be to support the conclusion of partial accords under the auspices of the Council of Europe and to strengthen our links with other countries. While it may be impossible for us to accede to such agreements, we should never dream of opposing them or of wishing them anything but every success.'

By way of an example of what was in his mind, he mentioned that if the Schuman Plan was ratified, HM Government would appoint a 'permanent delegation accredited to the High Authority in order to keep in contact and discuss trade matters with it'. Regarding the European Defence Community, he promised to study how Britain could best associate herself with it in practice. 'We have,' he said, 'as a first step, strengthened our team of observers in Paris so as to assist the work of the conference and to place our knowledge and experience at its disposal.'

Summing up his position, he declared: 'I hope I have succeeded in convincing many of my friends that we are trying, honestly and sincerely, to help Western Europe's advance along the road to unity. Our intention of establishing close and lasting links with the Coal and Steel Community is an earnest of our good faith.' That was the extent of Britain's part in the bid to establish a united Europe. It was derisory.

The effects of Maxwell-Fyfe's speech were immediate. A large section of the moderate delegates, who had up to then insisted on the need not to lose touch with the British, realized the futility of their hopes. They came to see that if progress were to be made towards European integration, all hope of British participation would have to be abandoned.

In 1948 it seemed obvious that Bevin must be the leader of a future united Europe. By 1951, with Churchill in power, it had become evident that any attempt to unite Europe could only succeed if Britain took no part in it. The views put forward by Sir David Maxwell-Fyfe were repeated in more or less the same terms by all the British delegates, Conservative and Labour alike.

As for the continentals, they were divided into two groups: those who thought it their duty to make one last appeal to the British to take an active part, and those who, taking note of Britain's refusal, urged that it was necessary to go ahead without further ado.

In this confused situation, there was no question of decisions of any importance being taken. People were even afraid to call for the establishment of a European organization with real, if limited, powers. An anodyne resolution was therefore adopted. It noted that it had not been found possible to agree on a common course of action and left everyone free to act as they saw fit. Despite the extreme moderation of these views, the resolution was only passed by sixty votes to ten, with twenty-nine abstentions. The disarray of the Assembly, and its inability to act, were glaringly obvious. It was no use looking to this organization for help.

Simultaneously with this debate in Strasbourg, another had begun in Paris, on the plan for a European Defence Community.

At the Assembly's session on 10 December, an unusual event occurred: four Foreign Ministers – de Gasperi, van Zeeland, Schuman and Adenauer – had spoken in support of the concept of a European army in the hope of obtaining the Assembly's backing for this project. The delegates' response was, however, disappointing. Not only did the British declare that they were determined to stay aloof, not only did the German Socialists raise a whole series of objections, but some of the other delegates, too, made it clear that they had reservations about a course of action in which Britain refused to join. Sitting at the chairman's table, I had to watch this fiasco in silence, angry and discouraged.

On the night of 10/11 December, I made up my mind to resign the chairmanship of the Assembly. I was anxious to regain my freedom of speech and action. I had had enough of being referee and wanted to play an active part once more. I thought I had some useful ideas to contribute and that the time had come to do so. The Consultative Assembly had lost some of its former importance. No longer was it in the forefront of the struggle. Its debates had a habit of closing with ineffectual compromises, and I was covering up this state of helplessness with my authority as President. I was determined to strike out in a fresh direction. I hesitated for several hours before finally making up my mind. Despite the fact that in Belgium I was a member of the opposition, my duties as President of the Strasbourg Assembly had enabled me to keep in touch with the leading figures in international politics. If I gave up this position, I would have to fall back on my own resources, stripped of any official authority. I might be in for a difficult struggle. However, my desire for freedom of action overcame all my scruples, and on the morning of 11 December I wrote to Lord Layton to inform him of my decision.

Within a matter of hours, I was back in my seat in the Belgian Parliament, and making a speech in which I did not mince my words. It was violent both in tone and content. On hearing a recording of my own words, I was surprised at the passion and fierceness of my attack. I accused the Strasbourg Assembly of being hesitant:

'Sitting at the desk which I occupied until yesterday, I could not help noticing something which has often filled me with sadness: I was astounded by the sheer ingenuity displayed in that Assembly to explain why nothing need be done. Nowadays, everyone seems to have a good reason for wanting to mark time. Certain Germans say they will not help build a united Europe until they have built a united Germany. Certain Belgians will help only if Britain joins in the effort. Certain Frenchmen will have nothing to do with a united Europe if this means that they will have to sit down at the same table with the Germans. As for the British, they will not help until they have found a solution acceptable to the Commonwealth. Our Scandinavian friends are watching all this with an air of disillusion. I am convinced that if a quarter of the energy that is now being wasted in this Assembly on saying "no" were devoted to saying "yes", we should not be in our present plight.'

I went on to protest against the lack of urgency shown in certain quarters and stressed the need for action.

'The Europe of which we are speaking is a Europe which we have allowed to be grossly mutilated. Poland, Czechoslovakia, Hungary, the Balkan countries, Eastern Germany – all these have gone. It is a Europe against which Asia and Africa have risen in revolt. The largest and strongest among us is at this moment being defied in Iran and Egypt. It is a Europe which for the last five years has been living in fear of the Russians and on the charity of the Americans. Faced with such a situation, we prefer to do nothing, as if history would wait for us, as if we had time in plenty to remould our thinking at leisure, taking dozens and dozens of years, as if we had plenty of time to do away with our tariff barriers, to discard our national egoisms, as if we had all eternity before us.'

I then tried to draw up a balance sheet of the Assembly's third session. My language was plain:

'During this last fortnight, we have missed all our chances. To begin with, we have failed to take stock, courageously, of the frank and clear statements made by all the British delegates. But this much ought to be said to them – and I hope you will forgive me if I do so now: when we met in Strasbourg we did so cherishing certain hopes. We believed that the political changes in Britain would give us a fresh opportunity for closer cooperation. We were looking forward with bated breath to what the spokesmen of the Conservative Government would have to say to us, and were also awaiting with impatience the statements of the Labour Party, now that it has gone into opposition. You have never been more outspoken and clear – and I feel I ought to compliment you on this – than when you said to us, realizing as you did what this must mean for Europe: "We shall never go along with you on this road."

'I say this not without some disappointment, not without some bitterness, but I say it without any wish to be offensive: the statements for which we had been waiting, on which we were relying, for which we were hoping, those statements never came. It is therefore up to us to display the courage and strength of character necessary to face up to reality. . . . Since the beginning of this session, my mind has been made up, my attitude clear. I do not say to you: "Let us build Europe, taking our lead from Britain," for to rely on Britain, whether Conservative or Labour, means, in the present situation, to give up the very idea of building Europe. I say to you: "Let us face the facts and take our courage in both hands."

'Gentlemen, I have not the effrontery to say to you: "No one is better aware than I of the dangers inherent in any attempt to create a purely continental Europe." Why, indeed, should I make such a claim, for in fact all those who have now resigned themselves to building a continental Europe realize the risks attendant upon such a policy. But has there ever been a policy with the slightest pretensions to greatness which has been free from risk? Life itself is a constant succession of choices between various risks, and those who are never prepared to take a chance, whether it be in their private or their political life, will never achieve much.

'Instead of facing up to the British situation with courage, we have been trying to devise a formula on which we could all agree. But these are formulae for helpless inaction. In the last few days, new ambiguities have appeared in regard to certain grave issues, and this has once again caused some people to believe that the "no" of the British was not final and that if only we persist in our policy of inaction and passivity we may still persuade Britain to join us.'

I went on to complain of the lack of response to the speeches made by the foreign ministers the previous day, of their timid reception and the lack of encouragement given to the ministers. I concluded by saying that since the Assembly had lost all ability to act, it was necessary to resume the struggle outside its precincts by appealing to public opinion.

This speech proved an important landmark in the part I was to play in European affairs. From 1942 to 1951 I had persistently advocated Britain's participation in the building of Europe and had even urged that she should be Europe's leader. However, after Churchill's return to power I came to realize that we must do without Britain's support if we were to make any headway. This was a severe disappointment. I decided to support Jean Monnet's view: 'Create a united Europe and Britain will join. It is by succeeding that you will convince her.'

My resignation created something of a stir in European political circles. A section of opinion in the Assembly urged me to reconsider my decision, but I refused to listen to these kind promptings. The British Labour delegates did not associate themselves with this demand. To make it quite clear where they stood, they thought it necessary to send me an open letter in which Gordon Walker declared on their behalf that though they regretted my departure and were convinced that no better President could be found, it was up to me to decide how I could best serve the cause of European unity.

This was fair enough; in my speech I had not minced words in referring to Gordon Walker. But we have met frequently since and, as true professionals, have recalled with pleasure our tussles in the Assembly.

This was the end of my tenure of office as President, a tenure which had twice been renewed. By giving up this position I regained my freedom of action, which I used to fight for the idea of a united Europe and, more particularly, for the aims which the Six had set themselves. However, I did not give up my activities in Strasbourg altogether. I have addressed the Consultative Assembly since then in my capacity as spokesman for the Political Commission and, later, as Minister. However, henceforth my principal sphere of activity was to be in the Joint Assembly of the European Coal and Steel Community.

The various political moves towards a united Europe which took place in 1952 are difficult to disentangle since a number of efforts were made simultaneously.

In March, Eden addressed the Ministerial Council of the Council of Europe in support of a number of new ideas. He had no doubt been impressed by the criticisms levelled at Britain and was also worried by developments on the continent of Europe: the treaty instituting the European Coal and Steel Community had been concluded and, in Paris, the talks on setting up the European Defence Community were making progress. In Eden's view, while it would be wrong for Britain to become part of Europe, she must not become isolated as a result of the establishment of a coalition of Western Powers. Eden thus remained faithful to the concept of a European balance of power guaranteed by Britain. His aim was to ensure – while maintaining Britain's sovereignty intact – that his country was not cut off from the Europe which was beginning to take shape, and to help it retain a measure of influence on this process. Eden's aim was to establish organic links between the Council of Europe on the one hand and, on the other, the institutions foreshadowed in the treaties setting up the European Coal and Steel and the Defence Communities.

His proposals were well received. The Consultative Assembly established a commission with the task of studying and defining them more closely. However, the work of this body proved fruitless. The Council of Europe was in a state of crisis. Despite all the kind words, despite all the declarations of desire for close collaboration, the bridges had been burned. The Six, full of dynamism and hope, were determined to make their own way and to ensure that their progress was not hampered by waverers.

28

The Messina Conference

The conference which laid the foundations of the Common Market and Euratom was held at Messina on 1 and 2 June 1955.

Why did we choose this Sicilian town for our meeting place? It was a favour for our colleague Martino. An election campaign was in progress on the island, which was his birthplace and which he represented in Parliament. He was by no means displeased at the added publicity he gained from being seen in the company of his European colleagues. For our part, we were happy to be of service to him and we had the additional pleasure of working in a wonderful setting. We stayed in the magnificent San Domenico Hotel in Taormina. Each morning we prepared the day's agenda in the hotel gardens, surrounded by flowers, and each evening we ended our work there. Throughout the conference, I remained in constant touch with Bech and Beyen. We maintained full agreement and joined forces to make sure of attaining our aims. The result surpassed our expectations.

I do not remember the details of our discussions, which were long and serious. On the last day of the conference we had to work through the night, drafting the final communiqué. The sun was rising over Mount Etna as we returning to our rooms, tired but happy. Far-reaching decisions had been taken.

The resolutions adopted by the Foreign Ministers of the member-states of the ECSC at their meeting in Messina on 1 and 2 June 1955 runs to several pages. It begins with a statement which is perhaps its most crucial part:

'The Governments of Belgium, France, the German Federal Republic, Italy, Luxembourg and the Netherlands believe the time has come for a new stage in the building of Europe. They hold that the first step must be taken in the economic sphere.

'They are of the opinion, furthermore, that the work of establishing a united Europe must be accomplished by developing common institutions, by a gradual amalgamation of the various national economies, the creation of a common market and the progressive coordination of their social policies.

'They believe such a policy to be essential if Europe is to retain its present position in the world, if its influence and radiance are to be restored and if a continuous rise in the standard of living of its people is to be ensured.'

The document goes on to enumerate the aims on which the ministers had agreed. It reflects the various views which had been put forward as well as – let it be admitted frankly – a certain degree of confusion. So many ideas had been advanced and so many problems examined that the ministers were unable to make an altogether rational choice.

Mention is made in the document of Europe's main traffic arteries, of a joint study of plans for a European network of inland waterways, motorways and electrified railways, and of the provision of more ample and cheaper sources of energy.

The document then goes on to deal with the problems of atomic energy. It calls for the study of plans for a joint body to be responsible for the development of the peaceful uses of atomic energy. The fundamental aims of what was eventually to become the Euratom organization were thus outlined. This section of the resolution was based on ideas put forward in my original draft.

The resolution then declares without further ado – as if the ministers were unaware of the significance and extraordinary audacity of their views: 'The six governments agree that the establishment of a European common market free from tariff barriers and all quantitative restrictions on trade must be the aim in the economic sphere. They consider that this objective should be attained in stages.' This passage was a triumph for Beyen. His colleagues had agreed that this should be our goal, but it was he who had put the idea forward.

On matters of procedure, the ministers decided that treaties or any other arrangements to deal with the problems under discussion would have to be elaborated at one or more conferences. Not that there was anything sensational in that. But what was far from commonplace was the ministers' agreement that this task should be carried out by a group of governmental delegates assisted by experts under the chairmanship of a politician, whose task it would be to coordinate the various operations. The decision meant that yet another proposal put forward by the Benelux foreign ministers had been accepted. Bech, Beyen and myself had discussed the matter at length and concluded that the difficult undertaking we were suggesting could be brought to a successful conclusion only if our final goal was always kept in sight. We knew that there would be numerous and difficult technical problems to overcome. Though we had every confidence in our experts, we wanted to be sure that they would bear our political aims in mind. We thought it essential to select a man who shared our convictions and hopes to take charge of the negotiations.

I speak frankly about this for we had no idea at the time that I myself would be chosen to undertake this task. We had other names in mind. It was only after our approaches had failed that my colleagues asked me – as a last resort – to take on the job.

At first sight, I was the last man to choose. I had never been considered an economic expert and was a stranger to the mysteries of the tariff system. Nevertheless, I accepted the offer, well aware that I could obtain expert assistance and eager to put our ideas into effect. I thought I would be able, despite my lack of expertise, to inspire those around me with my enthusiasm and determination to succeed.

Now that this undertaking has indeed succeeded, I am bold enough to claim that my ignorance was in fact a blessing in disguise. I approached none of the problems with preconceived notions. I had no pet theories regarding the issues involved, but examined each with an open mind as it arose, my only aim being to secure a common-sense agreement and to see fair play between the many diverse and mutually opposed interests. Those working under me soon came to realize my impartiality. It was this quality which finally allowed me to acquire an authority I should probably never have enjoyed had I been more familiar with the problems concerned. The presence of a politician in the midst of experts was an advantage. No expert, however knowledgeable, would have shouldered the responsibilities which I assumed, and he certainly would not have enjoyed my authority *vis-à-vis* the other ministers.

There is a clause in the resolution adopted at Messina which deserves a special mention. It provided that as a member of the Western European Union and an associate member of the European Coal and Steel Community Britain should be invited to take part in the negotiations. This was another earnest of our hope that we might yet see Britain marching side by side with us along our chosen path. We wanted to prevent the Europe which was taking shape from being confined to the Six.

The resolution adopted in Messina was so bold that many people thought it unrealistic. There were many sceptics about at the time. But most people were not hostile, merely indifferent. The work accomplished was the achievement of a minority which knew where it was going.

The negotiations lasted from June 1955 to May 1957. They were fascinating, arduous and full of incident. At times we were on the brink of failure, but in the end we succeeded.

It can never be said often enough that our success was due to a common unflinching determination. This alone enabled us to overcome technical difficulties which at first seemed insurmountable. It was the foreign ministers of the Six who shared this determination: Pinay, and later Pineau and Maurice Faure; von Brentano, Martino, Bech, Beyen and myself – we were all resolved to make a success of our efforts, for we realized the political importance of our goal and knew that what we were out to achieve was nothing short of a revolution. The fate of Europe depended on our success. We never allowed ourselves to be discouraged. Each time we met an obstacle, we found the necessary degree of imagination to overcome it.

I had strengthened my personal staff by appointing von der Groeben and Pierre Uri to it. The former brought to his task all the single-minded devotion and skill of a first-rate German expert. He believed in the importance of the work. Pierre Uri deserves a special mention. He had been recommended to me by Jean Monnet, for whom he had worked. In advising me to call in Uri, Monnet made no secret of his belief that our relations would at times be difficult. Uri, he said, was not easy to get on with, and in this there may be some truth. Aware of his own intelligence and ability, Uri is certainly not a model diplomatist in dealing with other people. Nevertheless, one can only pay tribute to his knowledge and original mind. He has given me invaluable service. Without his help and ingenuity many of our problems would never have been solved.

The 'Spaak Report', an important document, is largely the fruit of his efforts. Uri was one of the principal architects of the Treaty of Rome. If I may put it somewhat cynically, I believe that my achievement was to get the best out of him; not everybody could have brought this off. Our cooperation was a success. He had many more ideas than I, though I may have been better at gaining acceptance for them.

The civil service heads of delegations, as well as their aides, were men of exceptional quality both in terms of skill and, in general, their devotion to the European cause. It was a great privilege to coordinate their efforts.

29

The British Refusal

Before describing in detail the salient features of the negotiations which led up to the signing of the Treaty of Rome, I propose to deal with Britain's attitude at that time.

When the talks began in Brussels after the Messina Conference, those who had attended the Messina meeting called on Britain to join in. Britain's response was one of qualified agreement. An official observer – a Mr Bretherton – was sent to attend the Brussels talks. Throughout our early discussions his attitude was one of discreet scepticism. While the representatives of the other Powers went about their work with a will, he remained silent for the most part. When he did join in our discussions it was only to express doubt as to whether his country could accept whatever idea looked like becoming the basis of agreement at any given time. This wait-and-see attitude of his persisted until the decisive conference, held in Venice in April 1956. When we resumed our work in Brussels, the British observer was nowhere to be seen. His government did not try too hard to explain, let alone justify, his absence. The fact of the matter was that the British were not yet ready to take part in our European venture. The overwhelming majority of them believed that it was more important for them to strengthen their Commonwealth ties than to bring Britain closer to the Continent. They considered the supra-national tendencies which were emerging among the Six unacceptable and thought European unity a good subject for wistful speeches rather than a realistic proposition.

Little by little, the British attitude changed from one of mildly disdainful scepticism to growing fear. As I have said, they had no wish to become part of Europe, but neither did they want to become too isolated from the Continent. They were alive to the dangers inherent in such a situation. Before the end of 1955, I became aware of the first signs of this evolution. The British were becoming increasingly hostile to the Brussels talks. Having first refused to take part in them, they now made them out to be a danger to European unity.

Their chosen instrument for their offensive was the OEEC. They contrasted the efforts of that organization to reduce tariff barriers with those being made in Brussels to establish a customs and economic union – intended, in due course, to lead to political unity. There was, in fact, a tremendous difference between the two projects, which the British either failed to see or pretended not to see. They brought diplomatic pressure to bear on each of the Six one by one, varying their approach according to the particular policy of the government concerned. In a memorandum dated 19 December 1955 and addressed to the German Government, London declared that, 'having given the matter full consideration, it is our view that Britain cannot join in such a project' (the one under discussion in Brussels). It stated that the common market envisaged in the Brussels talks was incompatible with Britain's economic and political relations with the rest of the Commonwealth, nor could it be reconciled with her free trade policy. Finally, the British Government warned that nothing should be done to provoke a clash between the interest of the Six and the OEEC countries.

This line of argument ran counter to the promises made by them a few years earlier in the European Assembly. The British had then declared that while they were unable to join a united Europe, they would do nothing to hamper the integration of those who wished to take part in the venture. I was worried by Britain's attitude, considering it both a danger to our efforts and a warning that relations between the Six and the British might well become worse.

As it has always been my view that candour is the best means of avoiding friction and resolving difficulties, I decided to write another letter to Eden, who was Prime Minister at the time, to warn him of my misgivings.

The letter was written on 7 February, and some days later, on the 13th, I received his reply. It was cordial but vague. He thanked me for writing to him, said that it gave him great pleasure to discuss these important issues with me and promised to consider my views carefully. He evidently did not wish to take up a firm position without first consulting his colleagues, and this I could well understand. Before the month was out Eden wrote to me again. This time his letter was somewhat more explicit, at least on how we should go about setting out our respective attitudes. He declared:

'My colleagues and I have reviewed the issues under discussion [those which I had raised in my letter of 7 February], and we have given close attention to your views. Harold Macmillan intends meeting you in Paris and will inform you of the results of our discussions. I believe you will find this a better means of exchanging views than if I were to write to you at length. Even though we cannot agree with everything you say, you may be certain that we are none the less determined to try in every possible way to promote what we consider to be Europe's true interests.'

As far as I was concerned, Eden's letter left no room for illusion. Behind this show of good will, there were fundamental differences of view.

From then on, it was with Macmillan that I conducted my negotiations, first in Paris and later in London. On 14 March I wrote to the Belgian Ambassador in London to inform him that I had had a good meeting with Macmillan and that since the British had not raised the issue of the Common Market in the OEEC I had thought it best to follow their example. I went on to say:

'My position remains unchanged. If the British have misgivings about the integrationist policy of the Six, fearing that some of their interests may be imperilled by our future Common Market, I am ready to discuss the matter with them and this, I believe, could be done within the framework of the Western European Union. You may convey this to Sir Ivone Kirkpatrick, [then

Permanent Under-Secretary of State at the Foreign Office].

For reasons best known to themselves, the British did not follow this up. Once again they hesitated at the decisive moment. This same indecision was to be seen later, notably after General de Gaulle's press conference in 1963, when they made no attempt to make the best of the other five Powers' desire to help Britain.

I had a very important meeting with Macmillan on 4 September 1956. Baron Snoy, who was my principal aide in the Brussels negotiations and presided over the OEEC working party, accompanied me. Snoy, incidentally, was a strong advocate of economic cooperation with Great Britain. Also present was M. Sergent, at that time OEEC Secretary-General. The meeting was our last attempt to prevent a clash between the efforts being made within the OEEC and those about to culminate in the creation of the Common Market. It was my impression that the British were playing for time. I believe I put my views in a manner that was both conciliatory and firm. I felt success was far too near in Brussels to brook any prevarication. This is what I said should be done:

1 An attempt should be made to discover whether the Brussels programme for reducing Europe's internal tariffs would be acceptable to the partners of a future free trade area, should one be created.

2 We must discover whether – given the exemptions and guarantees envisaged – there were any problems in connection with the institutions we were planning, and if so what those problems were. In Brussels we had found that the more flexible a system the more necessary it is to arm its institutions with extensive powers.

3 A method must be devised whereby a check can be kept on the member countries' customs revenue.

4 Measures must be taken – and this is crucial – to ensure that the efforts being made on Britain's initiative within the framework of the OEEC do not affect the success of the Brussels conference, which, in my view, cannot go on for more than two or three months. It must be brought to a close before the German elections

in 1957 in order to help Adenauer in his courageous policy.

The talks ended pleasantly, but no real decisions were taken.

I was to have one last meeting with the British, in January 1957, when Mr Thorneycroft was Chancellor of the Exchequer. The British Government had not modified its position on the main problems and had reaffirmed its views in a memorandum which it submitted to the OEEC Council on 13 February 1957. While that document welcomed 'the approaching conclusion of the negotiations begun in June 1955 with a view to creating a customs and economic union comprising France, Germany, Italy, Belgium, the Netherlands and Luxembourg', it reaffirmed that 'serious factors prevent Britain from becoming a member of such a union.' The reasons were still the same – in the main, Britain's relations with the Commonwealth. In view of this, the memorandum proposed a scheme which, had it been adopted, would have submerged the Common Market in a free trade area.

As time went on, it became increasingly difficult for me to go along with the British. Success in the Common Market negotiations was virtually certain, and I was not prepared to sacrifice such an achievement to a much more modest enterprise which offered no prospect of a European political union. All I could promise – and this I did gladly because to do so accorded both with my own convictions and a decision adopted in Messina – was that clauses would be inserted in the future treaty which would enable new member of such a union'. The reasons were still the same Common Market. This promise was kept.

The treaty of Rome was signed on 25 March 1957. A few weeks later I became Secretary-General of NATO. The negotiations within OEEC continued without my taking part in them in any shape or form. They dragged on for more than a year, only to fail in the end.

A comparison between these two series of negotiations is instructive. The talks in Brussels succeeded because the negotiators were inspired by a common political goal. Those involved used their skill and knowledge to solve their problems. The negotiations in Paris, on the other hand, were caught up in a tangle of largely academic complications. The difficulties proved insoluble because not all the negotiators were inspired by the same ideal.

I drew an important lesson from these events and have often stressed it since: 'Where there is a political will, there are no insurmountable technical obstacles. Where such a political will is lacking, every technical obstacle becomes a pretext for those out to wreck whatever negotiations are in progress.'

30

The Treaties of Rome

I must now revert to the talks which culminated in the drafting of the Treaties of Rome. These negotiations went on for nearly two years, and we repeatedly came close to failure. It was a tremendous task we were facing.

After we had defined our goal at the Messina Conference and issued a number of general directives, we held our first meeting in Brussels in July 1955. The delegation leaders were Ambassador Ophüls for Germany, Baron Snoy for Belgium, Félix Gaillard for France, Ludovico Benvenuti for Italy, Lambert Schaus for Luxembourg and Professor Verryn Stuart for the Netherlands.

I believed in the task we were about to undertake and was most eager to carry it through, and this gave me courage. We did not get off to an easy start. How were we to approach so vast an enterprise? We began in the classical manner by setting up a number of committees functioning independently. In this way a great deal of material was assembled but little progress made. I was compelled to admit as much to my colleagues when we met at the Dutch resort of Noordwijk in September 1955. They were patient and sympathetic and encouraged me to carry on with the work. I soon made up my mind that a change of method was called for. I realized that if I became ensnared in endless technical discussions without first laying down specific guidelines and taking out certain political options, I should get nowhere. I therefore decided to wind up the committees, while reserving the right to call in the experts again at a later date, and to deal directly with the various heads of delegation.

The delegation leaders all helped me greatly in the task of preparing the ground. Our discussions were often heated, but they enabled us to define our fundamental principles. These, in turn, were to become the basis of the Common Market. The chief problems were listed. When I felt that sufficient progress had been made I sent Pierre Uri, von der Groeben and Hupperts to the south of France, where they could work in peace. Their job was to draft a report in order to formulate the conclusions at which we had arrived during our discussions. This proved an excellent method. The draft they prepared – a task so difficult that it would probably have proved unmanageable had it been left to the six heads of delegation – was accepted as largely correct. It was discussed point by point, and the text finally adopted did not depart from the original draft either in general content or style. This is how the document eventually to be known as the 'Spaak Report' came into being.

I must in all honesty admit that I am not the author of this vital document. I can only claim to have directed the negotiations which made it possible for the draft to be prepared. I may also have rendered some service in assuming political responsibility for the document and in submitting and recommending it to my colleagues. It is a remarkable document, well written, clear and readable – a rare feat in this type of literature. It carried all the more weight for being unanimously approved by the heads of delegation. Although the governments were not bound by it, there was every hope that they would give it their official approval since the various administrations had been consulted in advance.

The essential feature of this work is the fundamental choice it reflects. There were two alternatives before us: we could establish a simple customs union or a common market. We decided to go for the bolder of these two courses. The report defined what was meant by the common market we had in mind, and it did so, not in vague, general terms but by setting out the various problems that would have to be tackled, the difficulties that would have to be overcome, and by defining in advance the answers to these questions.

Compared with the communiqué issued after the Messina Conference, the progress accomplished on this occasion was considerable. The ideas which had only been outlined vaguely at Messina were this time listed, defined and explained. The governments were now in a position to assess accurately the implications of a policy which they had up to now endorsed in principle only.

The report also contained a chapter dealing with the creation of an 'atomic community'. We had been helped tremendously in this work by Louis Armand, who may rightly claim to be the father of Euratom. Incidentally, it was Armand himself who invented this name and who was the organization's first President. I shall always treasure the memory of the few meetings I have had with him.

The 'Spaak Report' was discussed by the foreign ministers in Venice on 29 and 30 May 1956. Baron Snoy was right in calling this the 'miraculous conference'. Never before had agreement on questions of such importance been reached so swiftly. The document on which we based our negotiations had been distributed, read and carefully analysed in advance. There was no need for me to explain or to defend it. Agreement was general. In less than two hours, the six partners decided that the document should be adopted as the basis for our future negotiations. Having thus proved all the pessimists wrong, we entered upon a new stage in our work.

A fresh conference was due to open in Brussels on 26 June and, at Pineau's suggestion, I was asked to carry on with my task of giving encouragement to the others involved in this work and coordinating their activities. Our job on this occasion was to draft two treaties – the one which established the Common Market, and the Euratom agreement. To complete our task, we were bound to have much to discuss, for, as our ideas crystallized, new difficulties and clashes of interest emerged. Several months were necessary to see this work through to its conclusion. It was a harassing task, but I found the work fascinating and shall never forget it. It is not often one can say to oneself that one is expending one's energies to ensure the triumph of a great ideal. It would take a whole book to give a detailed account of these negotiations.

One day that book ought to be written, for a great many lessons can be learned from this great confrontation. However, all I wish to do now is to describe those events which struck me most forcibly at the time and which I therefore remember best of all – first and foremost, my contacts with the many experts involved.

For some reason I have acquired a reputation for not liking technicians. This is quite wrong. I do believe, however, that one must take care not to encourage them to stray from the subjects they know best, and above all, one must not ask them to deal with political matters. Politicians who lack the courage to shoulder the responsibilities which are properly theirs all too often resort to this device to provide themselves with an excuse for their failures. Experts, especially civil servants, only work well when given a clearly defined brief. Left to themselves, they are apt to complicate matters. Frequently they are dangerously intolerant in defending their own pet theories. Sometimes they fear their superiors may let them down and fail to cover them with their authority; in such circumstances they tend to stick to their guns. On the other hand, when the objective to be attained has been clearly defined for them, they make every effort to find a solution and use their skill and ingenuity to hammer out an agreed plan in the end.

During those long weeks of negotiation I learned to appreciate the work done by technicians at its just worth. As experts, their knowledge of their specialized fields is admirable. They move with ease even in highly complex situations, and stand up for their views with praiseworthy assurance but not always with complete good faith since they are often more intent on imposing their views than on devising compromise solutions acceptable to all.

It was at such moments that I had to intervene to cool their ardour and make them accept a compromise for the sake of our ultimate success. One interminable debate stands out in my memory. Our task was to decide at what stage an agricultural product becomes industrial, i.e. in which category we should place such commodities as bread, beer, spaghetti, sardines and bacon. This was an important issue since major interests were at stake and the decisions taken were bound to have repercussions on the entire tariff system. The experts from the various countries pleaded their case with knowledge and conviction, though it could scarcely be said that they did so without bias. I listened to them for hours on end as they made their mutually conflicting pleas. We spent whole days in fruitless debate. Wearied by these futile proceedings, at the end of an exhausting day I requested full powers for myself to deal with these problems. I promised that the following day I would submit a complete list of agricultural products which could be considered to have been processed into industrial commodities. My request was accepted. I retired to my office for the night, locked the door and, together with two or three aides, quite dispassionately, regardless of which countries stood to gain and which to lose, we completed the promised list. The following morning it was adopted without demur in a matter of a few minutes. This is the sort of service an honest layman can render.

Such incidents happened quite frequently. Another dispute I remember concerned the tariff for bananas. There was an interminable wrangle about a few per cent this way or that. Having run out of both arguments and patience alike, I announced that I was prepared to allow the various protagonists two hours to settle their differences. If they failed, I would call a press conference and announce that the cause of European unity would have to be abandoned since we could not agree on the banana problem. I also made it clear that the responsibility for this situation rested with all the parties involved. I then made a stately exit from the conference chamber. On my return, two hours later, the whole thing had been settled. Europe was saved!

These were some of the minor ups and downs in what were essentially very serious discussions. Moments of crisis occurred in the negotiations when we had to deal with such matters as the military uses of uranium, when France announced the conditions she considered indispensable in this context, and when we had to settle the fate of the former colonies. This list should in itself suffice to show that our problems were essentially political.

There was disagreement on the military uses of nuclear energy from the very outset of the negotiations. As far back as the autumn of 1955, at the Noordwijk conference, M. Pinay took me to one side to impress on me that the treaty which was being prepared would never be passed by the French Parliament if it looked like threatening France's military progress. Félix Gaillard reinforced this warning. Both were very insistent that I should do my utmost to avoid this snag. I took their warning seriously and, against my personal convictions, did my best to devise a compromise formula. This was not an easy task since Germany did not want France to enjoy a privileged position. The other parties to the negotiations, anxious to promote the cause of general disarmament, thought that the use of nuclear energy for military purposes should be banned altogether.

On the eve of the Venice Conference, on 24 April 1956, I took it upon myself to write to each of the foreign ministers concerned and put to them the following compromise suggestion:

'In order to further the cause of world disarmament, the member countries should declare themselves ready to give up, for an agreed period, the manufacture of strategic nuclear weapons of mass destruction. In the event of a change in circumstances, necessitating a different approach, they are prepared to leave the matter in the hands of the Community's Ministerial Council. Any decisions by that body would have to be unanimous.

'Such a renunciation of the right to manufacture armaments must not, of course, be confused with an abandonment of the right to receive supplies of nuclear arms from other Powers.

'After the expiry of the said period, member-states would agree not to manufacture such weapons except with the agreement of at least two other member-states. Euratom would be responsible for supplying the requisite nuclear fuel for any weapons produced in accordance with these provisions. The manufacture of these weapons would be subject to the same controls as those in force for other uses of nuclear energy. In the event of a shortage of nuclear fuel, a unanimous decision of the Council would be required for a state to receive an allocation from the common pool for the manufacture of nuclear weapons. In the absence of such a unanimous decision the allocation of nuclear fuel would be geared to current civilian requirements, so that States operating a military programme would have to draw on their allocation of nuclear fuel for civilian purposes.'

My proposal was not adopted. The problem of the military uses of nuclear energy was to remain an insurmountable obstacle for a long time to come. It took an intervention by the Heads of Government at the end of 1956 for agreement to be reached. This agreement was incorporated in the treaty which was eventually concluded: under its terms the various countries enjoy a measure of freedom in regard to the military uses of nuclear energy, though subject to certain controls. In actual practice the treaty is nowadays being respected in the breach rather than the observance. France has taken advantage of the concessions that have been granted her, but refuses to accept any controls. As usual, her partners have bowed to her demands.

The crucial stage of the conference was reached when Maurice Faure, who was at that time French Under-Secretary of State for Foreign Affairs (Pineau was Foreign Minister and Guy Mollet Premier), explained the French demands.

I had first met Maurice Faure at the Strasbourg Assembly. Not only did I like him as a person but I trusted his devotion to the European idea. I admired his gifts as a negotiator and found him helpful, ready to understand the other man's point of view, generous and modest. I also admired his easy eloquence, seasoned – though not to excess – with his native Toulouse accent.

I well remember the meeting at which he put his cards on the table. The negotiations were making headway only slowly. Though we had made a little progress, we were all aware that some people were beginning to have second thoughts, especially the French, who found the changes entailed in the establishment of the Common Market most difficult to accept. France's traditional protectionism, as well as her economic and financial troubles, made it least easy for her of all the Common Market partners to accept the rules we were in the process of drafting.

Guy Mollet, Pineau and Maurice Faure were 'convinced Europeans', but they had to cope with very real practical difficulties in addition to a political opposition to which General de Gaulle was no stranger. The fundamental changes to which the French delegates were expected to consent were far-reaching, and it took a great deal of courage and good will on their part to agree to them, but agree they did.

In a speech which was listened to with rapt attention, Maurice Faure enumerated all the questions which the French Government would wish to see solved first, as well as all the guarantees he felt to be essential. It was a long and impressive list. Its principal items were: harmonization of social legislation; France's continued right to subsidize certain types of exports; her right to maintain a surcharge on imports and, finally, the inclusion of overseas territories in the Common Market. Another French proposal was that there should be no fixed time-table for the establishment of the Common Market by stages; instead, the introduction of each successive stage should be subject to the attainment, one by one, of specific objectives defined in advance.

As Maurice Faure went on with his speech I could see the faces of the other delegates growing longer and longer. Although I recognized that there was a good deal of justice in the French requests, I realized how difficult their acceptance was bound to be. Because of their very extent, there was a danger that these requests would be rejected out of hand.

After Maurice Faure had wound up his speech with some words of hope – words I knew to have been spoken in good faith because of Faure's well-known sincerity and because of the candour with which he had addressed us

– there was total silence in the hall. No one wanted to be the first to comment. We all realized the implications of the French demands and the danger they posed to our cherished project.

Remembering Eden's successful tactics, I adjourned the meeting. We needed time to think things over and to prepare the ground for a decisive debate. The miracle happened the following day. Fortunately, the heads of delegation did not regard themselves as adversaries but as colleagues working for the same cause. The troubles of one were the troubles of all.

I will not pretend that we were altogether happy about Maurice Faure's statement, but while it would have been easy to reply with a brusque rejection of his demands – some of which would have given France a privileged position had they been accepted – everybody reacted with moderation and understanding. So far from the delegates taking an uncompromising stand, the negotiations were resumed on a more hopeful note. Maurice Faure's complete frankness had made a good impression. Once it was clear that all was not lost, it seemed easier to make progress on the firmer ground that had now been gained. As we went over the problems one by one, we came to realize that some were of minor importance while others could be dealt with by means of provisional solutions and measures of control. Acceptable compromise formulae were devised. This was not an easy task, but it was tackled with determination.

However, the heads of delegation, no matter how high their personal standing, were not armed with the necessary powers to commit their governments on certain crucial issues. It was therefore decided to hold a meeting of foreign ministers in Paris. These talks proved difficult and finished badly. The negotiations had reached the point where people are tempted to look back at the concessions they have had to make. At such times, negotiators tend to give more thought to what they have given than to what they have received and to feel that the time has come to call a halt. Points of detail then loom larger than life and men who heretofore have been reasonable and conciliatory begin to prove intractable and refuse to give that final inch needed to achieve agreement.

The talks became even more difficult when the French delegation suddenly came up with the demand that member countries of the Common Market should be entitled to opt out. This request ran diametrically counter to the entire spirit of our project. From the outset of our talks we had all agreed that the effort exacted from each of the participating countries would be so great that they could only be expected to make it if the organization to be set up were of a permanent character. It seemed unthinkable that the member countries should be asked to submit to such profound changes – changes amounting to an economic revolution – unless the permanence of these arrangements were assured.

Despite all our efforts, we failed to reach agreement. The communiqué published at the close of our talks inevitably noted this fact. At once, pessimistic commentaries began to appear in the press. However, our cause was not yet lost since the ministers had asked their experts to carry on and had decided to hold a further meeting as soon as possible. In effect, they wanted time to consider. Fortunately, too, the experts – who were in fact the members of the old Brussels team – felt their courage surging back as success, at first so dubious, began increasingly to seem within their grasp.

Finally, the last few obstacles were overcome and soon the only problem remaining was that of the association of the overseas territories with the Common Market. At this point it became necessary to call a meeting of the Heads of Government. It was held in Paris on 18 and 19 February 1957. Though the financial implications were important, the political and psychological aspects were even more vital. The Italians and Germans, who after the two world wars had been stripped of their colonies, some of which now belonged to their new partners, were to be asked to contribute to development schemes drawn up by the new owners of these territories. This was not an easy concession for the Germans and Italians to make. The resistance of the Germans, supported by the Dutch, had proved impossible to overcome at the heads of delegation level. The difference, therefore, became a matter for the governments to settle and hence the prime ministers were bound to intervene. They all gathered in Paris – Adenauer, Guy Mollet, Segni, van Acker, Bech and Drees – assisted by their Foreign Ministers – von Brentano, Pineau and Maurice Faure, Martino, Luns and myself. A debate of epic proportions ensued. It went on day and night. I had to go from delegate to delegate, pleading and looking for compromise solutions. Finally, in the small hours of 20 February, a solution was found. Once again it was Adenauer who showed himself to be a true statesman. Germany's contribution, it was decided, was to be equal to that of France, and yet it was the territories associated with the latter which stood to gain most from the new arrangements.

The final communiqué noted that agreement had been reached. The last sentence still rings in my ears, not unlike an announcement of victory: 'Reviewing the meeting, the Ministers agreed that their efforts, thanks to the active encouragement of M. Spaak, have now reached a stage sufficiently advanced to allow the results to be shortly submitted to the various governments. It is hoped that the two treaties will be signed in Rome before long.'

For me, however this was not the end of the story. I still had two obstacles to surmount. During the negotiations over the association of overseas territories with the Common Market, I tried to impress on all concerned the need to make reasonable concessions. Carried away by my enthusiasm and in order to set an example, I had accepted a financial formula which provided for a Belgian contribution larger than that expected of the Netherlands. When I put the facts to the Belgian Government, trouble ensued. In fact, the issue was trivial – a matter of a few million Belgian francs. But Brussels and The Hague have a habit of comparing closely the contributions exacted from each country. I considered the concession I had made negligible when seen in the context of the agreement I had been able to obtain. However, my colleagues insisted that I should make an approach to the Dutch – a task I found rather distasteful. I was forced to ask the Dutch if they would be prepared to agree to a revision of the agreement and to make the same contribution as Belgium. I no longer recall whether I pleaded my brief with much conviction. Anyhow, my *démarche* failed and my colleagues finally resigned themselves to this outcome.

The second obstacle to be overcome was perhaps rather more serious. During the course of the protracted negotiations which had taken place since the Messina conference I had enjoyed considerable freedom of action. Only my colleague M. Rey, who was then Belgian Minister of Economic Affairs, kept a close watch on these developments. Excellent European that he is, he supported my efforts. Van Acker, the Premier, however, took a rather more detached and sceptical view. While he allowed me to go ahead without interfering, he had, on the other hand, never shown much enthusiasm for my efforts.

The treaty was due to be signed in Rome on 25 March. A few days before that date I found myself in hospital, having been laid low by an attack of gout. While on my sick-bed, I was informed that van Acker wished to see me urgently. Although I was in pain, I answered his call. With his usual mixture of good humour and firmness he announced that, having examined the treaty carefully, he had come to the conclusion that it was unacceptable. It was out of the question for Belgium to shoulder such obligations. I must admit I was dumbfounded and, for a few minutes, I feared the worst had happened. However, with a fresh access of courage, I defended what was to some extent, at any rate, my own handiwork and sought to convince the Premier that his opposition to the treaty was ill-founded and, moreover, that our international position would be impossible if he maintained his veto.

We had a conversation during which feelings ran high on both sides, but in the end all was well. The Premier conceded I was right. I believe he did so out of friendship for me rather than from genuine conviction.

The Premier's fears were unfounded. Admittedly, the treaty was not perfect, for it bore obvious traces of the conflicts of interests which we had had to settle. Each of the partners could well have insisted on the magnitude of the sacrifices to which he had submitted, but this was not

the way to read and assess the treaty. If one were prepared to appreciate the effort accomplished as a whole
and to disregard the minor blemishes, one was bound to
admit that new trails had been blazed for economic and
social progress. If one were prepared to look at the treaty
in this spirit one could not but give it one's approval.

It is not my intention at this time to discuss the treaty
in detail. All I wish to do now is to recall some of its
outstanding features. I am thinking, above all, of its supra-
national character. There has been a great deal of talk
about this particular aspect of it – an essential feature inasmuch as it implies the abandonment of the absurd rule
of unanimity. This rule, which requires that all decisions
be taken unanimously, is the plague of international
organizations and the cause of their partial paralysis.
Since its application would be inconceivable in the internal life of the nations, one wonders why it should be
applied in international affairs. No organization can
function without power, nor can it work if the will – and
sometimes the ill-will – of a single member can nullify the
will of the rest.

The rule of unanimity was responsible for the bank-
ruptcy of the League of Nations. The right of veto – a
watered-down version of the same principle – has rendered
the UN Security Council powerless. It has also enabled
General de Gaulle to provoke crises of the utmost gravity
in the European Community itself.

The authors of the Treaty of Rome were aware of these
dangers. They held that the will of the majority should
as a rule prevail and that unanimous decisions should
only be mandatory in exceptional circumstances. This
was a major advance, the importance of which was further
enhanced by the application of the 'weighted vote'.

The equality of states is a purely academic concept.
To say, as is being said in the UN, that the vote of the
smallest Powers must carry the same weight as that of
the greatest is to fly in the face of reality. The only way
to make the Great Powers surrender the right of veto
is to apply a system which would give their vote an
importance in line with their real status.

After laborious discussions, we succeeded in having

these principles incorporated in the Common Market treaty. The association of overseas territories with the member countries of the Common Market within the framework of the treaty was another notable success. The Yaounde Convention, which was subsequently signed by eighteen African countries, must be considered one of the Community's greatest achievements. It placed the wealthy countries of Europe and the economically underdeveloped countries of Africa on a footing of equality in their relations. By taking this course, the authors of the treaty tried to indicate that they did not see the Common Market as a selfish enterprise and that it was not aimed at promoting Europe's economic autarchy. They wanted to show they realized that the prosperity of their own countries was inseparable from that of the rest of the world. In so doing, they were proclaiming both an economic truth and a moral principle.

On 25 March 1957 we signed two treaties in Rome which established, respectively, the Common Market and Euratom. It was an unforgettable ceremony, which the Italians had organized in the grand manner. We met in the Capitol, and all the chief architects of the great enterprise whose completion we were formally to record were there: the ministers who had supplied the initial impulse; the heads of delegation, who had done a tremendous job, as well as the experts who had aided us all. The bells of Rome rang out to salute the birth of the new Europe. My own heart was full of joy, emotion and hope, and I made a speech which reflected my feelings.

The Treaty of Rome symbolizes the triumph of the spirit of cooperation over national selfishness. Those who had brought the exercise to a successful conclusion were inspired by the same convictions and the same ideals. They were aware of the economic changes they had brought about. But however great these changes might be, so far as the architects of the Common Market were concerned, they were of secondary importance or, at any rate, only the first stage of an even more important revolution which was still to come – a political revolution.

Ten years later this ideal remains as valid as it was

then. It is the only ideal which does justice to our age, the only ideal capable of restoring Europe to her rightful place, a place to which she is entitled by virtue of her illustrious past.

PART SIX

The Atlantic Alliance

31

The Three Wise Men

The year 1956 was important for NATO. While we were discussing the European Defence Community and trying to overcome the crisis which its collapse had provoked, other grave events were taking place in the world. The Korean war had occurred, along with its various repercussions, its defeats and its victories. The armistice had been signed. In Europe, the Big Four had held their summit meeting in Switzerland, and later their Foreign Ministers' Conference – both without success. In Asia, there had been a war between France and Indochina. Mendès-France had put an end to it by signing the Geneva Agreements, but France also had to deal with the revolt in Algeria.

The demand of the Cypriots for independence gave rise to a conflict between Britain, Greece and Turkey. Communist China was threatening the Chinese Nationalist Government installed in Formosa and shelling the Quemoy and the Matsu Islands.

Stalin had died in 1953. Three years later, Khrushchev had made his momentous speech at the Twentieth Party Congress. The USSR's policy was changing.

I had met Molotov at San Francisco at the celebrations of the tenth anniversary of the UN Charter. For the first time ever he was affable and even friendly. He invited me to dinner and we spent a few pleasant hours together. For once, I had a chance of meeting him informally. I was struck by the mild and gentle look in his myopic eyes. So far, I had never heard him say anything other than 'niet', and in a disagreeable tone of voice at that. This time he was doing his best to show me a side of his character that I had never seen before. With the utmost charm and courtesy, he went out of his way to please me,

255

and he succeeded. He was attentive, understanding, receptive to new ideas and conciliatory. All of a sudden the barriers which had divided us for so long seemed to have collapsed.

The events I have just described did not bring the countries of the Atlantic Alliance closer together. They confronted one another at too many points of the globe, and the conflicts to which these differences had led left their mark – one might even go so far as to say scars.

Meanwhile, public opinion was overjoyed at the new Soviet policy. There is nothing the democracies would like better than to live in peace and reduce their military burdens as soon as possible. Some people now began to question the need for the Atlantic Alliance.

We met in Paris in May 1956 to review the situation. Some of us were determined to strengthen the cohesion of the Alliance. The Organization was sufficiently flexible to adapt itself to the new conditions.

We used as the basis of our discussions a report by the chairman of the Information Committee, Mr Wilgress, who at that time was Canada's permanent NATO representative. He was likeable, always good-humoured and smiling, and his advice was invariably sound.

There are few countries, I believe, which, having regard to the size of their population, have produced so many outstanding statesmen and diplomats as Canada. Many Canadians have a turn of mind which I personally find attractive, made up in equal parts of idealism and realism. Though capable of enthusiasm for and dedication to a great cause, they keep their feet firmly planted on the ground. They never indulge in daydreams; they are too efficient for that.

Mr Wilgress's report posed a number of questions which we had to answer: did the international situation call for a continued military effort on our part? Was it not necessary to extend and enhance the importance of our political consultations in order to avoid – both inside and outside the area covered by the Atlantic Alliance – confrontations liable to weaken our solidarity? Should we not place more emphasis on the economic and cultural aspects of the Alliance? Lastly, was it not necessary to modify its administrative structure?

A long, in fact a very protracted, discussion ensued in which the foreign ministers took part. It lasted no less than two whole days. Finally, an important communiqué reviewing the international situation was published. It declared that the Alliance remained essential and that while the military effort could not be reduced, account must at the same time be taken of the recent changes in Soviet policy. The fact that the Communists were now saying that war was no longer inevitable must be welcomed and the necessary conclusions drawn from this new development without, however, losing sight of the need for prudence. An improvement in East-West relations was now possible, and the Western world was ready to play its part in helping to bring it about.

The strength of the Alliance did not depend solely on its military resources but also on the political unity of its partners. In order to define the conditions necessary to safeguard this cohesion more accurately, the Council appointed a committee of three ministers. They were instructed to recommend measures designed to improve and develop our cooperation in various non-military fields and to strengthen unity within the Atlantic Council. These are the circumstances which led to the appointment of the officials whom we later came to call the 'Three Wise Men'. They were Pearson, Lange and Martino, the Canadian, Norwegian and Italian Foreign Ministers, respectively.

Their report was submitted to the Atlantic Council during its session in December 1956. It was a remarkable document which, for a number of years – in fact until the time of General de Gaulle's return to the political arena in 1958 – was regarded as a sort of bible to which we referred when in difficulty or in doubt.

The three men did a tremendous job in elaborating their report. They circulated a questionnaire on the issues under discussion to each of the member governments of the Alliance. When they had received written replies to their questions, they held repeated meetings with each of the other foreign ministers in turn. They then drafted their joint recommendations, which summed up the views expressed so well that their text was adopted as it stood. No doubt, not one of those concerned was wholly satisfied with it, but, all in all, the document was so objective and constructive that it was accepted as being as good a compromise as could possibly be devised.

Three propositions put forward in this lengthy study are worthy of particular note: (1) that, for the good of the Alliance, extensive and searching political consultations were necessary; (2) that an appropriate procedure must be devised to facilitate the settlement of any conflicts among member countries; and (3) that the powers of the Secretary-General should be strengthened.

In making their point about the need for consultations the Three Wise Men put forward a new and bold idea. First, they said, the area to be covered must be extended. No longer were these consultations to be confined within the geographical limits set out in the Washington Treaty, but they were to range freely throughout the world. They were, moreover, envisaged as serious discussions, instead of merely as an opportunity for informing one's allies of *faits accomplis*. What the Three Wise Men had in mind were consultations on plans and projects still in the course of preparation. It was made clear to the member countries that in pursuing their national policies they must not lose sight of their common membership of NATO and must consequently take account of their partners' legitimate interests.

As regards relations between member countries, the point was made that any differences between them should be settled peacefully. If such a settlement could not be achieved by direct contact, mediation should be sought within the framework of NATO, and this should be done before recourse to any other international organization.

Finally, it was recommended that the Secretary-General should in future preside over the meetings of the Council of Ministers. He should be empowered to offer his good offices to any member-states involved in a dispute. With their agreement, he would be authorized to order an inquiry, to mediate or arbitrate. The Secretary-General was thus to be vested with the right – and in fact the duty

– to draw attention to any issue which in his view was liable to endanger the cohesion or effectiveness of the Alliance.

All these recommendations were adopted. There was some discussion but in the end agreement was unanimous. There was a good reason for this, for by then the Suez crisis had occurred. I have already described its effect on the Atlantic Alliance. All the ministers realized that a repetition of such events would be disastrous. One fact which had not been sufficiently appreciated in 1949 became crystal clear in 1956: it is very difficult for Powers to act as allies in one part of the world while they are locked in violent conflict in another. International affairs are not a random succession of isolated incidents – they are an indivisible whole. This unity must be appreciated.

The crisis we had undergone taught us a lesson. In December 1956 none of the ministers sought to insist on total independence. They all hoped that a formula would be found which would make it possible for member-states to act in concert and to act effectively.

At this point it should be remembered that while the events in Egypt were still in progress, a revolution broke out in Hungary. The world has not forgotten the brutality of the Soviet Union's intervention. Our hopes for peaceful coexistence were shattered. Once more, relations with the East were tense. At one time it looked as if we might be able to bridge the gulf, but now it was as wide as ever.

In December 1956, the foreign ministers of the member countries were therefore more NATO-minded than ever before. The recommendations of the Three Wise Men – though they entailed some bold innovations – far from giving the ministers cause for concern, were in fact exactly what they were waiting for.

So far as I personally was concerned, the adoption of the report of the Three Wise Men was to have momentous results. The role of the Secretary-General had been expanded. He was now empowered to initiate action and was to be the effective head of the Alliance. Lord Ismay filled this part successfully. His experience, his good nature, the affection and the respect in which he was held – all these assets enabled him to overcome a great many obstacles. But in 1956, feeling that it was time to give way to a younger man, he announced his intention to resign. He put it rather charmingly: 'I have been the "nanny" of the Alliance; what it now needs is a tutor.'

André de Staercke thought that I might succeed Lord Ismay, and I must say I was tempted by the idea. I like changing jobs and facing fresh challenges. These changes make one's life so much richer! Moreover, I was a little tired of Belgian politics. At the time I was Foreign Minister in a government presided over by Achille van Acker. It is not easy for one who has been Premier – and I had held that post twice – to serve under another man. I had gathered my own experience and had my own ideas. In the position I was in I had to comply with the methods of another man, to support loyally a policy with which I did not always see completely eye to eye. Although Achille van Acker is a man with a strong will of his own, he was kind enough to allow me virtually total freedom of action in the conduct of Belgium's foreign relations. On the whole, we got on extremely well. Nevertheless, what I wanted was independence. At that time my party's prospects looked good and I was therefore able to leave the Government with a clear conscience. I had just been in charge of – and brought to a successful conclusion – the negotiations which ended in the signing of the Treaty of Rome. I was increasingly attracted by international problems and less and less interested in our internal squabbles. I therefore asked André de Staercke to conduct on my behalf the delicate negotiations which culminated in my becoming Secretary-General of NATO. He accomplished this task with his customary tact and finesse. Soon he was able to inform me that his efforts had been successful. This outcome was partly due to the fact that Lester Pearson, who would no doubt have been greatly preferred to me had his services been available, did not figure as a candidate. During a cordial meeting we had in New York at the time of a UN session, he informed me of his decision not to stand and wished me the best of luck.

On 14 December 1956 I was unanimously chosen to

The Three Wise Men

succeed Lord Ismay. For me, it was a pleasant occasion. In accordance with custom, fulsome tributes were paid to the new incumbent, and I do not propose to recount these eulogies. They are part and parcel of a type of oratory which follows its own rules – rules which it is considered bad manners to disregard. Recipients of such praise would do well to bear this in mind.

I should like to recall just one sentence of the speech I made in reply, for it expresses one of my strongest convictions:

'In accepting – with my Government's agreement – the post you have been good enough to offer me today, I do not feel I am abandoning Europe. My view, rather, is that I am completing – albeit in another sphere and on another plane – the task I have been pursuing all along. I am convinced that the united Europe we want must have a shield if it is to live and survive. I have long been deeply convinced, too, that only the Atlantic Alliance can be that shield.'

I still hold this conviction, as I did then, in 1956. I took up my new duties on 16 May 1957.

32

My First Atlantic Council:
Eisenhower in Paris

I remained Secretary-General of NATO for the best part of four years, until the beginning of 1961. For me, it was a fascinating time.

Thanks to my duties, I was in close touch with the leading statesmen of the West. The Atlantic Council consisted almost entirely of outstanding men. We were at the very centre of international affairs. The problems we dealt with were of genuine importance and our work of undeniable benefit. I was free of all the petty drudgery which inevitably forms part of every country's domestic politics, and was able to concentrate on a handful of major issues. I could devote myself to these matters without being harassed by obligations of either parliament or party. And finally, I was living in Paris, in itself a piece of good fortune not to be disdained. I had two exceptional aides who were soon to become my friends – André Saint-Mleux, my principal private secretary, and Aubrey Casardi, the Italian Ambassador, who acted as my deputy. When I think of these two men, I feel bound to contradict those who say that one makes one's real friends in one's youth. It is indeed a wonderful experience to find new friends in one's maturer years.

Within NATO I devoted myself, above all, to non-military matters, and when I did deal with defence issues it was only insofar as they were connected with political affairs. The relationship between civilian officials and the military has always seemed to me to present a difficult problem. I found this to be the case during the war and, in different circumstances, in NATO. By the time I had arrived in Paris, Lauris Norstad had succeeded Generals

262

Eisenhower, Ridgway and Gruenther – the first and last of whom carried out their tasks with great distinction – as NATO's Supreme Commander. Norstad, as it turned out, was one of the best. A tall man, fair-haired, slim and looking much younger than his age, his appearance reflected his Scandinavian origins. Eisenhower said to me one day that he considered Norstad to be the best organizer he had ever met. I know of no reason to question this judgement.

I was determined to follow Norstad's advice in all defence matters. I could not but bow to his technical expertise and very soon became convinced of his utter loyalty to the Atlantic Alliance. Norstad loved his job and was well aware of its importance. He never hesitated to plead NATO's cause in Washington and, since he was popular with the Republican Administration then in office, his influence was very real.

Norstad was fascinated by politics – perhaps more so than I am by the art of war. However, I gladly turned a blind eye to his interference in matters I considered to be within my own sphere of competence rather than his. I readily acknowledged the integrity of his intentions and it was with pleasure that I noted the success he had with some of his efforts. André de Staercke was extremely effective as liaison officer between the two of us and showed great skill in preventing potential trouble. This was one of the stages in its history – I am referring to the period from 1957 to 1961 – when NATO played an important part. I am vain enough to think that both the Secretary-General and the Supreme Commander were not altogether unconnected with this happy state of affairs.

The regular session of the Atlantic Council in December 1957 aroused particular interest, for it was held at Heads of Government level.

By a lucky coincidence, during my official visit to Washington on taking up my duties as Secretary-General I was there at the same time as Macmillan, who was then British Prime Minister and whose purpose was to discuss the international situation with President Eisenhower.

I had met both men before. My first meeting with General Eisenhower occurred towards the end of the war, when he was in Belgium. M. Pierlot, the Premier, welcomed him as he entered Parliament with these magnificent words: 'Fortunate indeed is the military leader who, having been carried to the highest rank by meritorious service, has found, in a just war, a field of battle equal to his ability, who has led his armies to victory and has earned the title, not of conqueror, but of liberator.'

Eisenhower was a simple, cordial and pleasant man, and he received this tribute modestly. Later, when he became the military chief of the Atlantic Alliance, I was to meet him again in Brussels. Although I was not in the Government at the time, we had a long meeting. His commitment to the Atlantic Alliance was total, but at the same time he was a convinced partisan of European unity. We understood one another perfectly in regard to these two issues. It was thanks to Eisenhower's support that President Truman succeeded in convincing the American people of the need to station large numbers of US troops permanently in Europe. This was not an easy victory to win. It took the prestige of a victorious commander and the firm resolve of a president to secure this decision.

Eisenhower's experience as a member of various international military staffs stood him in good stead as leader of NATO. I had no occasion to work directly with him at that time, but heard nothing but praise of his methods. His presence at the head of the Atlantic forces at a time when Europe was to all intents unarmed gave us all confidence and contributed decisively to our success.

During my service with NATO, I was to meet Eisenhower several times although my American counterpart in those years was really Foster Dulles, and after Dulles's death Christian Herter.

In my meetings with the President, the agreements I had previously hammered out with the Secretary of State were invariably endorsed. Never did I have the impression that there was the slightest difference of views between these two men, at least in regard to the Atlantic and European policies of the USA. Only once did I have a setback in my dealings with the American Administration: it arose out of my attempt to find a solution to the problem of French policy after General de Gaulle's return to power. I propose to deal with this topic later on.

Macmillan I knew better than Eisenhower. We had worked together twice: the first time was at Strasbourg, when I was President and he a member of the European Consultative Assembly; the second was during the negotiations which culminated in the signing of the Treaty of Rome, when I was trying to persuade the British to join us. Macmillan is one of the finest parliamentarians I have ever met. He was certainly one of the best of those who sat in the Consultative Assembly in 1949 – and yet that body boasted many such men. His brand of eloquence was typically British – at least as we continentals understand the term. He was calm, phlegmatic, but at the same time witty and incisive. Long years in Parliament had given him an imperturbable assurance. In this European Assembly, the simplicity of his manner, the distinction of his gestures and the complete absence of any exaggeration in his speeches stood out against the flamboyance of the Italians and the French.

He was one of the most ardent advocates of close British cooperation with the Continent and repeatedly spoke in this sense at Strasbourg. True, he allowed a number of good opportunities to slip through his fingers, but it must be remembered that he was not Prime Minister in those days. In 1963, when he did occupy that position, he made a genuine effort, despite the difficulties involved, to bring Britain into the Common Market.

My contacts with Macmillan were easy and agreeable. He was blessed with that courtesy and ease of manner which are an asset of so many Britons. Discussion with him, however searching and spirited, always remained on a gentlemanly plane. Later on, when he was Prime Minister, he was at first strikingly successful. Subsequently, however, luck forsook him. He then chose to retire with dignity rather than carry on a difficult and hopeless struggle. In so doing he set an example of wisdom which others might do well to ponder.

While I was in Washington, he asked me to come to

see him, and I did so gladly. He put an idea to me –
at that stage still in rather vague terms – which was
that we should invite President Eisenhower to attend the
next Atlantic Council. This, we thought, would not only
lend added weight to the occasion but would automati-
cally result in all the heads of NATO governments coming
to Paris. I liked the idea as it promised to add lustre to
the beginning of my tenure of office as Secretary-General.

The two of us, therefore, called on Eisenhower to put
the suggestion to him. We had no trouble in convincing
the President, and he accepted our invitation. Thus it was
that from 16 to 19 December 1957, presiding over a
meeting of the Atlantic Council for the first time, I was
surrounded by the heads of fifteen NATO governments.
The international situation at the time may not have
warranted such an effort. After the serious crisis sparked
off by the Hungarian rising, we were once again caught up
in the toils of the cold war. Happily, peace did not seem
to be in any danger at that time from any specific
development, although there were plenty of contentious
issues about. Each time a problem arose, a sterile dialogue
would start across the Iron Curtain, with the two sides
endlessly repeating the same arguments.

We used this summit meeting to issue a declaration,
some of the passages of which were not without distinction. It stressed the determination of all concerned to
make the alliance more effective and to expand its
activities in some areas. The meeting undoubtedly
strengthened Atlantic solidarity. But over and above these
general statements, the document reaffirmed the need to
strengthen the machinery for political consultation in
accordance with the report of the Three Wise Men. A
considerable part of the final communiqué was devoted
to scientific, technical and economic cooperation. This reflected one of the chief aspirations cherished by the most
fervent advocates of the Atlantic Alliance: i.e., that
NATO's excessive emphasis on the military aspect of the
Alliance should be reduced and the Alliance fashioned
into an instrument serving a common foreign policy, thus
giving real content to Article 2 of the Washington Treaty,
which calls for economic cooperation among the signa-

tories. The term 'interdependence of interests' occurs several times in this document. This was an implied condemnation of national selfishness and an expression of the philosophy which led us to establish the Common Market. The document was particularly explicit in its references to the need for scientific cooperation.

A truly important decision had thus been taken. The declaration was undoubtedly a step in the right direction. Had this course been pursued with real determination, our Alliance might well have been transformed into a genuine community. The early stages of this scientific cooperation looked promising. We had a number of meetings in Paris, attended by delegates of high standing. Alas, the initial impulse was gradually dissipated and the results achieved never lived up to our hopes. Nevertheless, the year 1957 ended well for the Atlantic Alliance. Our desire to adapt it to its new tasks had been forcefully affirmed and our solidarity seemed beyond doubt. I felt I was on solid ground and, after this first success, buckled down to my task.

33

The German Question

I have retrieved my files relating to this period and have re-read my notes, my many speeches and a large volume of correspondence. Since so much work was done in those years it is clearly out of the question to give a detailed account of it here. To do this would in fact require a separate book. I must therefore make a selection from among the many events of that period and the many memories crowding in on me.

My work in NATO may be divided into two periods: the first lasted from 1957 to 1959 – i.e. from the time I joined the Organization until the time when General de Gaulle's policies began to give rise to the difficulties which eventually resulted in the crisis the Organization was to experience from 1967 onwards. The first of these stages was a happy one – a period of progress during which the Atlantic Alliance grew stronger, political consultation improved, the problems of defence were resolved and the solidarity of the West became closer. The second stage, which lasted from the middle of 1959 until my departure in 1961, was much less satisfactory. It was dominated by two events: the destructive activities of the French President and the inability of the Alliance's members to react to them effectively. They did not succeed in implementing the 'ten-year plan' project put forward by Mr Herter.

For months on end I did all I could to reconcile the French and American viewpoints. Though I did my utmost to support the French, I failed both in my attempts to convince the Americans that something must be done to meet the French half way and in my efforts to make them see that if they did nothing General de Gaulle would not hesitate to strike hard at the Alliance. I could foresee what was coming and tried to arrest this march of events, but my efforts proved in vain. The situation was made worse by my failure to get the Organization off to the fresh start it needed.

Irritated by the hesitations with which I was grappling, and aware that my credit and authority suffered – possibly through my own fault because I may have advocated certain ideas with excessive fervour – I tendered my resignation in a fit of anger and discouragement. I did this following the final meeting of a Ministerial Council session in December 1960. I might have gone back on this decision had not the political situation in Belgium, which had deteriorated as a result of the events in the Congo and of grave social unrest, turned my thoughts at that time to events in my own country. My political friends were urging me to rejoin them. Such promptings are only too tempting – praise always sounds pleasant to the ear.

During my first – happy – period in NATO I had a large measure of success with my efforts to promote, in accordance with the advice of the Three Wise Men, the cause of political consultation, especially in relation to events in Europe. I was able to make a useful contribution to the settlement of two quarrels in which member countries of the Alliance opposed one another: the Icelandic fishing dispute and the Cyprus issue.

In 1958, 1959 and 1960, our attention in NATO remained focused on the German problem, the Berlin question and the various conferences held by the USSR, the United States, Britain and France. The three main members of the Alliance had special responsibilities in Germany and Berlin. They had reaffirmed their acceptance of these responsibilities in 1954 when the German Federal Republic joined NATO. All the member countries gave their approval and proclaimed their solidarity with the three Powers. The situation made it necessary to establish an equilibrium between the three and the other NATO Powers, which were in danger of becoming involved in the repercussions of a policy determined by others.

The first duty of the Secretary-General was to maintain unity with regard to the chief problems facing Europe:

Germany, Berlin and relations with the USSR. I believe I succeeded in this. Our system of political consultation operated smoothly during this time. I acted as spokesman for the other Powers *vis-à-vis* the three great partners in the Alliance and made sure nothing was done which had not been agreed in advance by all.

Speaking in Boston in September 1958, I was able to declare, in reviewing the state of the Alliance:

'Happily, we have been able to achieve much more in the political than in the economic sphere. The "Three Wise Men" have said to us: "In matters of foreign policy, you must consult one another." I can assure you that we have done precisely this, and have done it very sincerely and exhaustively. The mass of the public have no idea how much has been achieved in this context within NATO in this past year. Take, for example, the preparations for the summit conference. I am now able to reveal, without betraying any confidences, that during the entire past year not a single Note was sent by the United States to the Soviet Government about the summit conference which had not first been submitted to the NATO Permanent Council. I have specifically mentioned the United States Government because I want to emphasize that of all the countries of the Alliance it is the United States which has applied this policy of advance consultation most conscientiously and consistently. The US Government has not been content with merely announcing its intentions in more or less general terms but has been ready to submit to its allies for their comment and criticism the actual wording of its Notes.

'You realize, I am sure, that this new situation amounts to nothing short of a revolution in international diplomacy. The fact that the world's greatest Power is prepared to accept such a wide measure of consultation and applies this approach in a most liberal spirit, enabling even the smallest and weakest of its allies to take part in mutual discussions on a footing of full equality, and that, moreover, in the vast majority of cases, that Power is ready to take into account the comments made – this is indeed a development of the utmost importance for the continued existence and further development of the Alliance. Clearly, if this method proves successful, this must be the beginning of something new and significant.'

These few words of mine were not the expression of what one might term dutiful 'official' optimism. They were inspired by a trend which was then still in full swing.

On 10 November 1958, Khrushchev, in a statement which had every appearance of being an ultimatum, announced that the USSR intended to cancel the Four Power agreement on the status of Berlin. At the same time he made it clear that it was his intention to cede the USSR's rights of control in Berlin to Eastern Germany by 27 May 1959 at the latest. This action created a situation full of danger since its result was bound to be – if these things really came to pass – a face-to-face confrontation between the three Western allies and the East Germans, whose regime they did not recognize.

A few weeks later, the USSR, the United States, Great Britain and France decided to hold a conference in Geneva to review the situation. In the circumstances it was vitally necessary to maintain agreement among the allies in view of the threat with which they had been confronted. It was essential, too, to maintain the same harmony with regard to any proposals that might be submitted to Russia. All this required an unremitting diplomatic effort. The United States, Great Britain, France and Germany consulted one another many times. I was kept informed as a matter of regular routine. My task was to prepare – on the basis of the documents submitted to me – and, up to a point, to guide, the discussions in the Atlantic Council, which met at least once a week. The permanent representatives, speaking for their respective governments, emphasized their anxiety not to be presented with *faits accomplis*. In general, the discussions were based on papers drafted by my aides and myself. We drew up many such documents at that time. They summed up the views of the Great Powers, but I also used them as a vehicle for my own opinions. The following text may serve as an example:

I If the Russians, on 27 May 1959, put their scheme for Berlin into effect, the Western Governments will be placed in a difficult, and potentially dangerous, situation.

'It is in fact probable that in that event we should have to face a somewhat confused situation. The danger is that it is not the freedom of Berlin which would become the central issue, but who is to have control over access to the city. In my view – having regard to the state of public opinion in the West – this would be the worst of all possible contingencies. I believe the overwhelming majority of the Western public realize that the people of Berlin must not be left at the mercy of the Communists and are convinced that our people are prepared to take a firm line over this issue. I doubt, however, if they would be equally ready to be firm over a matter which might seem to them of minor importance, in fact a mere matter of procedure.'

II This being the case, it must clearly be *the prime object of Western diplomacy not to allow the West to be manoeuvred, on 27 May, into taking up dangerous positions.*

'We must therefore do everything within reason to avoid this happening. We should first have talks with the Russians, aimed at widening the issue, i.e., while discussing Berlin we must seek to deal with the German problem as a whole, and also with European security.'

III This is bound to prove difficult.

'It would seem that the Russians want priority to be given to precisely the two subjects we wish to avoid: Berlin and the peace treaty. They maintain that they will only discuss reunification and security after these issues have been dealt with. This Russian attitude is logically absurd and politically inadmissible.

'*It would seem, however, that in the circumstances it would be better not to be too exacting or too specific in our demands. We shall have to accept a deliberately vague agenda, which in actual fact will have to entail discussion of all these problems.'*

IV What should we say to the Russians?

'A simple repetition of all our customary arguments will not suffice since there is no chance of their being accepted. If we do this the result may well be a complete fiasco and we may find ourselves, on 27 May or soon thereafter, face to face with the problem of an isolated Berlin, i.e., precisely the situation we must seek to avoid.

'It may be a matter for regret that the Western Powers have left it so late before undertaking a thorough examination of these issues and that they have taken a course bound to lead to a conference with the Russians without having first reached agreement among themselves.

'However, it is now necessary, despite all this, to try to make up for lost time.

'*In essence, what must be done is to reverse the order in which our demands are presented.* Up to now, what we have been saying is this: (1) Reunification of Germany; (2) European security. What we must now say is: (1) Security; (2) Reunification.

'In my view, our proposals should be put to the Russians in the following terms: our attitude with regard to European security would undoubtedly be entirely different if we had been able to agree on the reuinification of Germany. Many concessions which appear to be of interest to the Russians and which we have hitherto always refused would have been possible in that event. However, provided agreement can be reached on security, we might go so far as to modify our views on reunification and give up the idea of free elections.

'Germany could be reunified by a joint decision. She could even be reunified by stages, confederation being the first. (Personally I do not believe this to be the right approach, but it must not be rejected *a priori* since the Germans themselves do not seem to be wholly opposed to it.)'

V What could we offer the Russians in terms of

security, in the event of a reunified Germany coming into being?

'1 Genuine disengagement. Not only would Eastern Germany be demilitarized, but given compensatory moves in Poland and Czechoslovakia, the demilitarized zone might be extended.

'2 The stationing of nuclear weapons in certain areas, which would have to be defined, might be prohibited.

'3 The Germans might renounce certain types of nuclear, especially long-range weapons.

'4 The NATO Powers might reaffirm both their determination never to support an aggressor and sign a non-aggression pact with the Warsaw Treaty Powers.

'5 Germany could recognize Czechoslovakia.

'6 Germany could recognize Poland, which would imply the conclusion of an agreement on the Oder-Neisse line.

'It thus seems possible to go a fairly long way to meet Russian wishes on all these matters. Two points, however, remain, on which we must insist absolutely:

'a Nothing must be done liable to lead, directly or indirectly, to the departure of the American troops from Europe;

'b We must not agree to Germany being neutralized.'

VI The most important element in the Western reply to the Soviet Note of 10 January – apart from the offer to hold a conference – was the suggestion that experts from the two Germanies should be called in to attend the proposed conference. This seemingly innocuous proposal was in fact a decision of fundamental importance which, in my view, was bound to have far-reaching consequences.

'I know that it was the Germans themselves who were the first to suggest this, but this only adds to the importance of the proposal. It would in fact seem that the authorities of the German Democratic Republic are to be allowed to put their views on the German problem to an international conference on an equal footing with the representatives of Western Germany.

'I fail to see how, if that were to happen, we could go on speaking of "the so-called East Berlin authorities" or how we could continue to ignore the state they represent when we finally come to settle the German problem.

'I do not know if the Germans have considered all the implications of the concessions they have made, but it seems to me that now that they have taken up this position there is no reason – and probably it would in any case be impossible – to oppose the holding of direct talks between the two Germanies on reunification.'

VII We must consider the consequences of the foregoing, in the event of our being compelled to discuss the Berlin problem in isolation.

'If the Russians cede their rights to the GDR, the latter, clearly, cannot be granted prerogatives greater than those previously enjoyed by the Russians themselves. The Russians have undertaken to respect West Berlin's lines of communication, and the GDR would consequently be in duty bound to do likewise. The GDR is thus subject to an obligation it cannot evade by unilateral action.

'In the event of our taking the course of a *de facto* recognition – and we have set out on that course – the situation could be discussed directly between the GDR and the Western authorities.

'Evidently, this is all very different from what we have been saying up to now, but it seems to me to flow logically – and perhaps fortunately – from the Western Powers' proposal that East German experts should be officially admitted to an international conference.'

VIII We must be clear in our minds what we mean by 'taking a firm stand over Berlin'. To me this means that we must accept no solution that would deliver the people of West Berlin into the hands of the Communists. We must not forget that West Berlin is but a small island in a vast Communist sea and that if it is left to its own devices nothing would be easier for the Communists than to submerge it.

'Whatever solution is proposed must, therefore, include real safeguards, and the only real safeguard is the presence of Western troops and freedom of access. At present, the legal basis of that Western armed presence derives from the military victory of the allies and the occupation. However, I do not think this is what matters. In my view, the occupation could in future be founded on a new agreement the details of which could be discussed either directly with the USSR or, alternatively, with the GDR.'

IX In sum, the foregoing shows that on many issues formerly regarded by us as non-negotiable, we are now ready to make fresh proposals. The following points are crucial:

'1 The Western Powers most directly concerned must reach in advance a large measure of agreement among themselves.

'2 All these matters must be kept absolutely secret. It would greatly weaken our position if the Russians got to know of our new proposals prior to the opening of the conference. If that were to happen our room for manoeuvre in the negotiations would be greatly restricted.'

I believe this somewhat lengthy document reflected accurately my state of mind at the time. My object was to ensure that we modify our tactics to suit our new ideas while at the same time standing firm. For a long time, our discussions with the Russians had been confined to a stubborn repetition of stale arguments. The Russians may in fact have shown more imagination than we did, though even they did not make any concessions of real substance. Since there was agreement on the need for talks, it was necessary to think of something new to say. Action was also needed to avoid being caught in a blind alley, which was certain to be our fate if Khrushchev carried out his declared intentions.

I must admit that I was both too pessimistic and too impatient. The disasters I foresaw never happened, and the ideas I put forward called for an effort which Western diplomacy was not ready to make. Either from caution or inertia, it preferred to put up with a vague state of affairs, with all problems left unsolved. This, however, seemed preferable to the risks inseparable from any change. My proposals were not adopted. We continued to go from conference to conference, indefatigably but in vain.

On 11 May 1959, the Four Powers held a summit meeting in Geneva to discuss the German question. They adjourned on 19 June and resumed the conference on 13 July. On 5 August they went their several ways without having taken any decisions. However, the perseverance with which they had conducted their discussions proved how much importance they attached to the need to remain in touch.

Eisenhower therefore invited Khrushchev to visit the USA. The two statesmen met at Camp David. The atmosphere improved and there was a mood of optimism in the air. It was decided that a new summit conference should be held in Paris in 1960. Yet hardly any preparations were made for that meeting. Was it to be a courageous attempt to deal with the real problems by means of fresh proposals or was there to be only a vague agenda on the need to improve East-West relations in general? It was the second of these alternatives which was chosen. It was decided to draft a declaration of principles which could be submitted to Khrushchev.

All these plans, all these preliminary discussions, as It turned out, proved a sheer waste of time. The shooting down of an American U-2 plane over Soviet territory on 1 May 1960 upset all our schemes.

Khrushchev did his best to get Eisenhower off the hook, hoping the President would pretend he knew nothing of the whole affair. However, Eisenhower, contrary to normal practice, thought it necessary to defend his intelligence service. Thus the summit conference never got off the ground; Khrushchev refused to take part.

I cannot say whether the conference, had it taken place, would have produced any positive results. The fact that it was never held gave rise to a good deal of resentment at the time, but I feel bound to say that in my view this failure did not aggravate the situation.

The sterile exchanges on the German question were resumed and are continuing to this day. It is difficult to see just how this situation can ever change. The respective attitudes of the West and the Communist camp are so wide apart that it seems out of the question that these differences will ever be reconciled. No compromise can be found, no bridge built across the gulf separating the two parties. One side says that we should allow the German people as a whole to decide their fate by means of a single referendum; the other says that there are two sovereign German states, each master of its own destiny.

The Communists cannot allow such a referendum to be held since it would show that even after twenty years the majority of the people of Eastern Germany do not support the regime. The entire system that has been established in Eastern Europe would be shaken and a fatal blow dealt to the policy the USSR has been pursuing since the end of the Second World War. For the West Germans, on the other hand, it is just as difficult to accept the *fait accompli* that has been created and to recognize the existence of the GDR *de jure*. If they do take this course, it is hard to see how the reunification they are seeking can ever be achieved.

The way things are, patience would indeed seem to be the highest virtue.

34

The Icelandic Fishing Rights
Dispute and the Cyprus Question

The year 1958 was a particularly busy one for me. Apart from my work on the German question, I had to deal with two conflicts between member countries of the Alliance. The first was between Great Britain and Iceland, about fishing rights; the second between Great Britain, Greece and Turkey, over Cyprus.

I am bound to admit that in neither case did my efforts produce a solution accepted by all the parties involved. Invariably my proposals were rejected by one or the other. Despite this, the negotiations held under the auspices of NATO proved useful and helped to allay some very deep resentments and to prepare the ground for the solutions which were eventually adopted.

During the course of a Council of Ministers in Copenhagen on 7 May 1958, the Icelandic Government announced its intention to extend, by a unilateral decision, to twelve miles the limits of the zone within which the right to fish was to be reserved exclusively for its own nationals. In terms of the real situation, the Icelanders had some justification for their action since the fishing industry is vital to their economy. Their intention to protect it was entirely understandable. In law, on the other hand, their position was weak. Nothing entitled them arbitrarily to violate their obligations. In acting as they did, they were clearly prejudicing the interests of a number of countries, above all Britain. British fishermen had been working the grounds off the Icelandic coast quite legally since time immemorial.

For a number of months I strove to devise a compromise formula. On four or five occasions I submitted to the countries concerned draft documents which took account of the reasonable interests of both sides. I went to considerable trouble to urge the need for moderation on the representatives of the two countries involved – Sir Frank Roberts for Britain and Mr Anderssón for Iceland.

Sir Frank I found an outstanding diplomatist, intelligent, a good debater and a man of inexhaustible energy. He invariably carried out his instructions without delay and passed on any replies received forthwith. He was prepared to wake me up in the middle of the night if need be – and this is precisely what he did on one or two occasions – to pass on messages addressed to me. He added to his thoughtful and lucidly presented arguments a personal touch and would sometimes invoke reasons of sentiment. This not altogether typically British approach only made his arguments the more convincing. During his time on the Atlantic Council he enjoyed very considerable prestige.

His Icelandic counterpart was a man of a very different stamp. He was distinguished by his outstanding knowledge of jurisprudence and, above all, his stubbornness. I thought at least ten times that I had persuaded him to accept a compromise formula, only to discover, the day after a heated discussion, that he remained as firmly attached to his convictions as ever, refusing to yield an inch.

I succeeded for four months in preventing the Icelandic Government from taking unilateral action, but in the middle of September 1958 I had to concede defeat. The Icelandic Government presented the world with a *fait accompli* when it claimed the right to call upon vessels fishing inside a limit which it had determined unilaterally to heave to for inspection. The British Government's reaction was to have its fishing vessels protected by naval units. Fortunately, no serious incident occurred.

In 1960, the Icelandic Government accepted in principle the need for bilateral talks, and the conflict was settled along lines which did not differ substantially from the solution I had proposed two years before. Thus we saw another example of the healing effects of time, which enable people to accept proposals they have fiercely opposed in the past.

The problem of Cyprus was both more serious and more difficult to solve and posed a real danger to the Alliance.

It faced each of the three countries involved with major issues of principle. In two of these countries it unleashed passions of the kind which are always roused by hurt national pride. The negotiations were thus held in a tense atmosphere. The repercussions any decision was bound to have on Greek and Turkish domestic affairs alike complicated matters in both Athens and Ankara. The relative moderation of the leaders was swept aside by an overwrought public opinion.

As this is not the place to go into the history of the entire problem, all I should like to say here is that the difficulties we were facing date back to 1949, when, in a referendum organized by the Archbishop of Cyprus, of the 225,000 Cypriots who took part, 215,000 declared themselves in favour of the island's union with Greece. At that time the British Government exercised sovereignty over Cyprus, which was then a Crown colony.

The situation was not improved by the Greek Government's decision to place the issue before the UN General Assembly. This body was clearly incapable of finding a solution to the problem. In the Assembly, there was no chance of the issue being treated on its merits; in fact, it was certain to be dealt with in accordance with preconceived notions. The resolutions voted in the General Assembly were, moreover, merely recommendations which those who disagreed were determined to ignore. The final upshot invariably was that these resolutions would be invoked by one or other party as and when it suited its purpose and that was as far as it went.

In March 1956, Lord Ismay, rightly anxious about the effects of the dispute on NATO, called a private meeting of the Atlantic Council. He suggested in vain that a committee be formed to mediate in the conflict. Britain and Turkey did not favour an intervention by NATO. As for Greece, she preferred to stick to the terms of a resolution, recently voted in the United Nations, which accorded to the Cypriots the right of self-determination.

My attention was drawn to this problem as soon as I took up my duties as Secretary-General. I had no intention whatever of trying to achieve a spectacular coup since I realized the delicacy of the situation, as well as the fact that anyone seeking to promote specific solutions might easily find himself caught in a trap. On the other hand, I was also aware how dangerous a worsening of relations between Great Britain, Greece and Turkey might prove to the Alliance. I therefore decided to act with all due discretion. I was encouraged in this by a letter from M. Mercouris, a Greek deputy whom I had met in the Council of Europe at Strasbourg and who had been to see me in Paris. He wrote to me on 31 May 1957:

'Immediately after my return I had several long meetings with Archbishop Makarios, who has asked me to convey his sincere thanks to you for the interest you have taken in this matter, as well as for your efforts towards a solution of the Cyprus problem. He is most anxious to discuss the issue with you and believes that only good can come from this. Unfortunately, he is unable to leave Athens for the present, and cannot see, moreover, how such a meeting could be held in conditions of absolute secrecy. Nevertheless, he reserves the right to request such a meeting at the first possible opportunity.

'Archbishop Makarios has no wish to turn down the good offices of any organization, and even less your own personal offer of help, provided such efforts can be made in confidence and provided they are based on recognition of the principle of self-determination and on the UN resolution.

'The Archbishop's views are set out in his letter of 28 May 1957 to the British Government calling on the latter to resume the negotiations with him which had been interrupted by his exile.

'Our recent meeting in Paris was most pleasant and I hope that another can be arranged in the near future.'

A few months later I had a secret meeting with Archbishop Makarios in New York. It was a most agreeable occasion. I immediately felt drawn to him for what I must admit was a purely personal reason: Makarios looks remarkably like my father. He has the same open face, the same somewhat large nose, the same black beard, the same look in his eyes – sombre and kindly at one and the same time – the same air of severe dignity. Moreover – and more importantly – he seemed to me to be a man of moderate views despite his very set convictions. The arguments he put to me encouraged me to continue my efforts. The letter I sent to the Turkish Prime Minister, M. Menderes, on 16 July 1957, explains the lines along which I thought we could work:

'My dear Prime Minister,

'I understand your reactions to the paper on the Cyprus problem – a wholly unofficial document – which I drafted a few weeks ago have not been favourable. I should therefore like to explain to you the reasons which led me to act as I did and to put some further arguments to you.

'I believe the Cyprus issue may in the long run do grave harm to NATO since it is rendering relations between three member countries of the Alliance difficult. I therefore hold that it is the duty of the Secretary-General – in accordance with the directives given me in September 1956 – to deal with this situation. But I believe equally strongly that the Atlantic Alliance must not be involved, nor its authority put at risk, unless there appears, from the outset, to be a good chance of success. By this I mean – and this will no doubt go some way towards reassuring you – that I have no intention of taking any step unless I receive in advance the formal consent of all concerned. None of the parties involved must be made to feel that it may be placed in a difficult position as a result of my intervention.

'In view of this, you will understand that in the first place I am trying to establish a basis for discussion. So long as one of the parties involved insists on integration and the other on partition, it seems to me a complete waste of time to attempt any solution whatever. What is the point of starting a dialogue between two parties neither of which is prepared to listen?

'Could not the concept of an independent Cyprus be

the agreed basis for discussion? By this I do not mean independence pure and simple, but an independence limited by an international statute free from the disadvantages which one of the parties involved sees in integration. Such a statute would cater both for the rights of the minorities and for the military requirements of the Atlantic Alliance.

'Before explaining why I believe it to be possible to devise such an independent status and why I think it would be effective, I should like, if I may, to give you the reasons why I oppose partition – a solution which, though theoretically possible, would in fact be difficult to put into practice.

'What I have learned about the situation on the island leads me to believe that any demarcation line would have to be wholly artificial. It would correspond neither to the demographic realities of the situation nor to economic facts. Having regard to the relative size of the two communities on the island, any decision on the respective areas to be allocated to them would inevitably give rise to endless haggling and futile squabbles, for it would be quite impossible to apply any rational criteria in determining such a boundary.

'If I may mention another argument in a purely personal capacity, may I say that I believe partition would inevitably involve large transfers of population – a procedure which does not appear to me to be in tune with present-day thinking.

'Finally, if I may be allowed for a moment to look at the issue from the Turkish angle, I should like to point out that I find it difficult to see why a solution has been chosen which would result in establishing, for the first time, Greek sovereignty over a large part of the island. On the other hand, I can quite see why some say that the proclamation of the island's independence would in practice prove to be but the first step towards its integration with Greece.

'The problem could therefore be defined quite simply as follows: is there any means of preventing such a two-stage integration? I believe very sincerely that there is. The independence I have in mind is an independence granted as a concession and circumscribed by a statute the implementation of which would be internationally guaranteed. Under the treaty in which the independence of the island would be anchored, the Powers concerned would renounce all sovereignty over Cyprus. In other words, they would undertake not only never to lay claim to such sovereignty, but also to reject any offer of sovereign rights were it to be made.

'The fact that a number of Powers would be associated with the treaty as guarantors – and the United States would, of course, be one of these Powers – should enable us, I firmly believe, to make entirely satisfactory arrangements.

'On this general foundation, a number of clauses regarding the detailed execution of the treaty could be superimposed, and these would provide additional safeguards. I believe these matters could be discussed at a later date.

'I also think it pointless, for the time being, to discuss minority rights and military bases. These two problems are admittedly vital, but solutions for them can be found by drawing on the many existing precedents. In fact, even better arrangements could be devised, using these precedents as a model.

'Here, then, my dear Prime Minister, is what I have to say with regard to these matters. May I assure you once again that my aim is to seek, first and foremost – and in the most complete confidence – a common basis for discussion, for without such a basis all our efforts at mediation are bound to fail. If such a common basis is not found, NATO should not, in my view, intervene. True, the lack of any participation by NATO would entail certain risks, but this would be less dangerous than a premature intervention, which could only result in widening the profound differences which exist between certain member countries of the Alliance.

'If you think these ideas mistaken or unacceptable, you need not fear, I repeat, any public intervention on my part. In that event, I should renounce my efforts at mediation at least until such time as, in my view, it

had become possible to resume the discussion on another
basis.

'Lastly, I do not need to tell you, I am sure, that
should you feel some useful purpose could be served
by my discussing these ideas with you in person, I
am entirely ready to call on you in Ankara. I should, in
that event, look forward to being able to renew the
personal contacts we have established in Paris.'

I received no written reply, but this lack of reaction
did not seem to me to be sufficient reason for abandoning
our efforts. Though I was not exactly encouraged, I had,
nevertheless, not met with a formal rebuff. There was still
a chance we might succeed, a chance we could not allow
to slip through our fingers.

I therefore called a semi-official meeting in my office,
attended by the permanent delegates to NATO of Britain,
Greece and Turkey – Sir Frank Roberts, M. Melas and
M. Sarper. All three were able diplomats. I have already
spoken of my high regard for Sir Frank. As for M. Melas
– a big man, broad-shouldered, of rugged yet fine features,
he looked every inch a true son of his native mountains.
He was full of ardour yet loyal, passionate in his beliefs
yet wise. He was deeply convinced of the rightness of the
views held by the majority of Cypriots and by his own
Government. At the time, he was sufficiently aware of the
international implications of the problem to realize that
it was our duty to try to find a compromise solution and
he greatly helped me in this.

I had met Ambassador Sarper in New York, where he
served for many years as his country's representative. He
had rightly acquired a great reputation and undeniable
influence in the UN. This was due to his experience and
moderation, his ingenuity and skill. Sarper was a colleague
– and at times an adversary – with whom it was a pleasure
to deal. Any discussion with him was bound to be on a
high level. We had our occasional difficulties, but this
has never detracted from my feelings of friendship for
him.

The four of us met in my study, the large salon of the
Villa Said, round a centre table, away from prying eyes,

where we attempted to sort out our problem. We tried to define our difficulties, eschewing passion and prejudice. We even tried to devise certain solutions then and there. While we were a long way from achieving any final results, the atmosphere was pleasant, our efforts constructive, and there was no denying that we were making headway. But, unfortunately, while we went about our task with patience and prudence, passions were being stirred in Greece and Turkey. In Cyprus, Britain was facing what was nothing short of a revolution.

The British Government could afford to wait no longer. It took a step which, from its own point of view, was undoubtedly justified but which gave rise to a crisis in the Alliance. On 9 June 1958, the British deputy representative to the NATO Council handed me in confidence a summary of a plan Mr Macmillan was due to announce in the Commons on the 19th. The plan was an honest attempt to settle the dispute. The idea was to establish a 'partnership' between the two communities on the island and the three governments concerned – Britain, Greece and Turkey. The solution put forward was to be provisional: after seven years it was to be reviewed. It was based on a representative system of government, communal autonomy and the existence of two elected chambers – one chosen by the Greek and the other by the Turkish population.

All in all, these proposals were both ingenious and liberal, but in my view they suffered from one grave defect. I knew enough of the state of mind of the various parties involved to realize that the notion of asking the Turkish and Greek Governments to appoint one representative each to assist the Governor-General would prove unacceptable to Greece. The reason was that acceptance of such an arrangement would in effect have amounted to recognition of partial Turkish sovereignty over the island. I made it my business to put this point to Mr Macmillan, who replied that this arrangement was crucial if Turkish cooperation was to be secured. It thus became clear just how delicately poised the whole situation was. It seemed difficult to devise a system acceptable to Greeks and Turks alike.

Though Mr Macmillan's statement was received coolly in Ankara, it was clear that this Turkish reserve was merely tactical. In Athens, his speech unleashed a wave of indignant protest. Courageously, Macmillan visited both Menderes and Karamanlis to defend his proposals in person. Back in London on 14 August, he sent me a note in which he informed me that he had decided to modify his original scheme in several particulars. The main change related to the status of the Greek and Turkish representatives to be attached to the Governor. Macmillan said he had reflected on the proposal I had put to him, i.e. that it should in fact be the chairmen of the two elected assemblies who should assist the Governor. While admitting the force of my argument, Macmillan objected that insistence on such an arrangement would mean the end of Turkish cooperation. The idea would, therefore, have to be dropped. The only solution open to him was to limit the powers of the two representatives. He added that the plan was due to come into effect on 1 October.

Macmillan ended his message with these words:

'We were greatly encouraged, in June, with the Atlantic Council's reply to our declaration. We propose to circulate our additional statement to the members of the Council and are ready to give any further explanation that may be required. At the same time, I hope that we may count on you to bring your great influence to bear by encouraging cooperation among the interested parties. Without this we cannot hope to overcome the problems and dangers inherent in the current situation.'

I sent my reply to London that very day:

'1 I find it difficult to give my views on the new procedure now being proposed as I am not in a position to assess accurately the results of Mr Macmillan's latest talks.

'2 I cannot help but think, however, that suddenly a very precipitate procedure is being adopted, and I do not know if the Greek Government will feel any more inclined to agree to the new formula regarding the status of the Governor than it was ready to agree to the old one. What will happen if the Greek Government does not appoint its representative?

'3 It seems essential to me that the legal problems which arise be solved without delay. Above all, we must have a clear definition of what is meant by "communal" and what by "internal" affairs. In the present situation there is a danger the parties concerned may not understand the system and the reforms which are being proposed.

'4 There would seem to be no point in calling a meeting of the Council at this time.'

It is obvious from the foregoing that I was sceptical. Since, however, I could see no way of reconciling the various points of view of the parties involved, I thought it preferable that the discussions should not be carried on within the framework of the Atlantic Council, at least not for the time being.

The publication of the new British proposals immediately raised the temperature in Athens. On 8 September, M. Melas sent me a memorandum on the latest developments. The document ended with these words:

'The Greek Government believes itself in duty bound to draw the attention of the member countries of the Alliance to the dangers which the application of the British plan would entail both for the cohesion of the Alliance and for peace in the Eastern Mediterranean.'

On 22 September this grave warning was reaffirmed in a personal message from M. Karamanlis:

'I should like to thank you for your unremitting efforts to promote a fair solution of the Cyprus problem.

'Greece has given proof of her devotion to the Atlantic Alliance by her patience and moderation in the face of the injustices to which she has been subjected by certain members of the Alliance. However, the insistence of the British Government on applying its plan unilaterally – a scheme we consider unacceptable – is bound to come as such a shock to Greek public opinion as to render Greece's continued membership in the Alliance problematical.'

Should such statements be taken at their face value? Were they, in fact, not partly intended to bring pressure to bear on us? Were they part of a tactical plan? It was difficult to decide just how matters stood, but the Secretary-General of the Alliance could certainly not afford to ignore the Greek declaration. I therefore resumed my efforts and called a meeting of permanent delegates representing the member countries not directly involved. I called on them to urge their governments to join me in appealing to the British to postpone the implementation of their plan. Having failed to win unanimous support, I made up my mind to burn my boats. Acting, perhaps, a little spectacularly, I decided to go to Athens myself to review the situation on the spot. In the Greek capital I had long talks with Premier Karamanlis and Foreign Minister Averoff. Karamanlis was a forceful man, direct in his ways, but on this occasion he gave the impression of having been driven to take certain decisions by an overwrought public opinion which he was no longer able to control.

I knew Averoff very well, having met him frequently in the Atlantic Council. He was a shrewd, subtle, re-sourceful politician. He had one weakness, however: he was occasionally imprudent in that he was apt to make promises which were difficult to keep. Both men were categorical: the least that must be done, they declared, was to try to gain time. Both said they were afraid they might either be forced to resign – in which event they would be replaced by extremists – or to give effect to the will of the Greek people by opting out of the Alliance.

Back in Paris, acting under the impact of what I had just learned, I decided that it was my duty to call a meeting of the Council. It was held on 24 September, and I submitted to it the draft of a scheme I had prepared:

'A conference will be held as soon as possible, the British, Greek and Turkish Governments being repre-sented, as well as the Greek and Turkish Cypriot communities. The Secretary-General will make his good offices available. The document below could serve as a basis for discussion:

I

'The problem of Cyprus must be settled. This must be done for the good of the people of the island and in order that mutual understanding and friendship may be restored between Great Britain, Greece and Turkey.

'It would, of course, be highly desirable if the solution adopted were to settle the problem once and for all. Unfortunately, this appears impossible owing to the passions aroused by recent events and the political attitudes that have been adopted. An attempt will therefore have to be made at devising a provisional solution. In order that the latter may be acceptable and effective, it must in no way prejudge the final solution which will eventually have to come. The detailed application of the provisional solution should, therefore, in no way either help or hinder, directly or indirectly, the adoption of any of the solutions that have been put forward.

'Any provisional solution adopted must facilitate a marked advance towards enabling the Cypriot community to govern itself, and must also provide all the guarantees required to protect the rights of the minority. At the same time, such a provisional solution must safeguard the bases and installations needed by Britain to meet her international obligations.'

II

'The new institutions should be based on the following principles:
'1 A Chamber of Representatives shall be established for each of the two communities. This assembly shall be competent to deal with all communal affairs (education, religious affairs, justice – in short, all matters appertaining to the rights of the individual in society).
'2 In addition, a representative institution shall be set up to deal with matters of common concern to both communities (internal affairs).
'3 A Governing Council, presided over by the Governor, shall be established. It shall have a Greek Cypriot majority and shall be empowered to deal with internal affairs.

'4 The Governor shall be responsible for the conduct of foreign defence and security affairs.

'5 The Governor shall be British. He shall be assisted in his executive duties by the Presidents of the two Chambers of Representatives.

'6 Either Chamber of Representatives shall be entitled to submit to an impartial tribunal any measure which it considers discriminates against or is detrimental to its respective community.

'7 The provisional solution shall remain in force for seven years.'

My desire, clearly, was to gain a few months in order to make it possible for a solution to be devised that would be acceptable to all parties concerned before 1 October, the date the British plan was due to come into effect. My scheme was, in fact, inspired by the British plan, but in one crucial aspect – the status of the assistants to the governor – it was based on the plan I had originally put to Macmillan.

The meeting of the Atlantic Council on 25 September was the liveliest I have ever attended. I was most violently taken to task by M. Sarper, the Turkish delegate, who accused me of being biased in favour of Greece, of having exceeded my rights, and of putting forward proposals unacceptable to Turkey. Finally, he declared that I no longer enjoyed his Government's confidence, adding that the latter rejected any thought of a conference on the Cyprus problem.

The discussion thus got off to a very bad start. The Greek representative replied that his Government had allowed itself to be swayed by my arguments and was ready to negotiate with the Turks and the British on the basis of my proposals. He also remarked – and this was an important new element in the situation – that Archbishop Makarios was ready to join in this course of action. As for the British delegate, he announced that he was without instructions as Mr Selwyn Lloyd, then in New York, had been unable to formulate any views on the issues before us.

I had no trouble at all in refuting M. Sarper's

accusations and in justifying both the need for action on my part and the form that action had taken. I mentioned the success I had achieved in persuading the Greek Government to enter into discussions with the Turks – a course which up to then it had resolutely refused to contemplate. I also stressed the importance of Archbishop Makarios's new attitude. Finally, I warned the Turkish Government of the responsibility it was taking upon itself by refusing to attend the proposed conference and urged M. Sarper to consider whether he was prepared to face up to the situation which was liable to arise on 1 October and to all the unpredictable consequences this was bound to entail.

The permanent delegates of the countries not directly involved supported me and expressed their Governments' gratitude for my efforts. Although my position had at first been weakened by the Turkish delegate's violent speech, it was now much stronger. Somewhat out of his depth, M. Sarper declared that his Government would determine its definitive position once Britain's attitude was known.

Thus, after a poor start, the atmosphere at the conference improved and we could now breathe a little more easily. That same evening I flew to the United States to address a meeting in Boston, together with Foster Dulles. Dulles wholeheartedly endorsed my attitude and advised me to return to Paris immediately to take the chair at a further meeting of the Atlantic Council, due to be held shortly.

On 1 October I wrote a long letter to M. Karamanlis to let him know what had happened. After giving him an account of the events of 24 and 25 September, I continued:

'On Saturday last I met Foster Dulles in Boston and discussed the situation in Cyprus with him at length. I gave him an account of my visit to Athens and made it clear to him how serious I thought the position to be. The Secretary of State did not contradict me. He agreed with me that the British reply to my proposals would probably be neither a "yes" nor a "no" and that we should presumably be confronted with a set of counter-proposals. He advised me to return to Paris so that I might be able to take the chair at the Council meeting due to be held in the afternoon of the following Monday. I decided to follow his advice.

'At the meeting on Monday afternoon, the British delegate did indeed make a declaration along the lines we had foreseen. He stated that the British Government, after having given full consideration to the matter, had decided that it could not give up its plan. His chief argument was that such a renunciation might create an extremely confused and dangerous situation. In fact, he said, such an action might fail to win the support of the Greek Cypriots while at the same time dangerously provoking the Turkish Cypriots, with the result that the Governor General would be placed in a critical situation. The British delegate added, however, that his Government was ready to attend a conference to be held on the basis, and within the framework, of the British plan.

'The Turkish delegate, who on this occasion took a much more moderate line, declared that his Government had decided to appoint its Consul General in Nicosia to carry out the duties outlined in the British plan. The ensuing discussion centred, above all, on two issues:

'1 What, exactly, was to be the role of the representatives to be appointed by the Turkish, and possibly also by the Greek, Government under the terms of the British plan?

'2 On what basis would the discussion be conducted and what would be the terms of reference of the proposed conference?

'There then followed a long discussion, during the course of which the majority of delegates representing countries not directly involved took a line that was both conciliatory and constructive. This discussion produced a number of new elements which I believe to be of great importance, especially in regard to the precise role to be played by the representatives of the two governments. At the Council meeting, we examined the formula used by Mr Macmillan in his speech of 19

June and compared it with the one he employed on
15 August. After examining these two speeches carefully,
we came to the conclusion that while Mr Macmillan
had modified his position considerably, there was an
element of confusion in his attitude. On being asked
by M. Melas to clarify matters to the best of his ability,
the British Ambassador thought he could give what one
might call a negative definition of the British position,
and it is to this negative definition that I should like to
draw your attention. Referring to the British Government's statement, he declared that the two representatives mentioned in the British plan would not be vested
with either sovereign or administrative powers. He felt
he could go no further, but this statement seemed to
me both very important and probably adequate. If I
understand the viewpoint of the Greek Government
correctly, its opposition to the British plan is due,
chiefly, to its unwillingness to see any sovereign or
administrative powers in the island accorded to the
Turkish Government. There thus seems to be no fundamental clash between the attitude of the Greek and
the British Governments on this matter. On the other
hand, there does appear to be a misunderstanding, due
to the fact that the British declaration is couched in
very general terms. However, it would seem that this
misunderstanding can be dissipated.

'In any case, if I may be allowed to say so, I do not
believe that it would be wise for the Greek Government to take up a definitive position without first having
obtained a clarification on this point. Thanks to our
discussion, we were able to define – I believe successfully – the terms of reference of the proposed conference.
Although it is true that the British Government felt
unable to abandon its plan altogether, that plan is now
only one of several elements in the situation. My own
proposals could be debated on the same footing as the
British scheme itself. I should like to add that the
discussion could range quite freely and that any proposals or amendments could, with the agreement of all
concerned, be placed on the agenda.

'I fully realize, Mr Prime Minister, that, from the

Greek point of view, the situation which has thus emerged remains fraught with difficulties. I am certain, however, that an extremely important advance has in fact been made. I am also becoming increasingly convinced that if a conference were held along the lines suggested by me, a solution would be found which would be both favourable to the people of Cyprus and beneficial to the Atlantic Alliance.

'During the session held yesterday (Tuesday) afternoon, we drafted a report on our talks and decided that the Ambassadors would submit this document to their respective Governments. If its conclusions are accepted by all the various Governments the proposed conference could be held at an early date.

'It is my hope that, in view of the points I have put to you, the Greek Government will see its way to agreeing to this proposal. I believe the explanations that have been given with regard to the real role of the Turkish representative (provided this solution is upheld by the conference) could be accepted by the Greek Government without the latter laying itself open to accusations of having given way on any issue of the slightest consequence. I think that, in fact, this representative could be regarded as a diplomatic envoy, as it were, of the Turkish Government, accredited to the island authorities, and this seems to me to be contrary neither to the Treaty of Lausanne nor to the Greek point of view.

'I shall be at your disposal at any time to give you such further explanations as you may require, and remain ready to travel either to London or Ankara if this can serve any useful purpose.'

At the same time M. Melas sent M. Karamanlis the report agreed by the permanent representatives. On 4 October M. Karamanlis sent me the following reply:

'Thank you for your letter of 1 October. May I express my gratitude, above all, for your tireless efforts to promote a solution of the Cyprus problem. I believe these efforts to be justified both morally and politically: morally, because justice is of vital importance in international relations, and politically, because it would be both unthinkable and reprehensible if we were to base our alliance on injustice and contempt for the rights of the weakest.

'Four out of every five members of the people of Cyprus are Greek, and we are all well aware of the rights, in this twentieth century, of a people in such circumstances.

'You remember, no doubt, that the Greek Government and the representative of the Greek Cypriots decided to accept your compromise proposals of 24 September only after grave hesitations. What you are now asking us to do, by virtue of the draft resolution which you have been good enough to pass on to me through M. Melas, is, in effect, to accept, at our own expense, a further compromise on your earlier compromise.

'Nevertheless, after having given full consideration to your letter, the Greek Government, ever mindful of the sufferings of the people of Cyprus, has decided not to refuse to attend the conference proposed by you, with the proviso that the Council accept two amendments to your draft of 30 September, amendments which M. Melas has been instructed to define during the course of the next meeting.

'The recent exhausting bargaining, the fact that blood continues to be spilt in Cyprus, the tension which is continuing both in Greece and in Turkey, are all matters which have given us much food for thought. It seems quite inevitable to us that even at the very best, within two or three years from now at most, unrest will break out anew in Cyprus, Turkey and Greece, with all concerned jockeying for position prior to the negotiations which will inevitably follow the next stage of this tragic affair. Even if by some extraordinary stroke of good luck public feeling does not cause new troubles to erupt, we can always rely on Soviet propaganda to incite ill will. I believe, therefore, that any statesman in my position would be bound to ask – as I ask – that the current conference should be used, in addition to discussing the British plan and your scheme, which are both concerned with a transitional period, to lay the foundations of a final solution. This is the first amendment M. Melas has been instructed to put to the Council.

'You are aware of the proposals Archbishop Makarios

has made to this end, proposals which the Greek Government has decided to endorse. Our aim is to guarantee the independence of the island as well as – and on a very generous scale – the rights of the Turkish minority, by excluding both Enosis and partition.

'I need hardly stress the magnitude of this concession, made at the expense of a prerogative that should by rights be treated as inalienable. I am bound to admit that I cannot see how a denial of this right can in all honesty be justified.

'Our second amendment concerns the composition of the conference. The Greek Government believes it to be essential that, in addition to the British, Greek and Turkish Governments and the representatives of the two island communities, the conference should also include a number of impartial delegates who could be relied upon to exert a conciliatory influence and to promote a solution of this problem.

'Naturally, I consider your participation in your capacity as Secretary-General of NATO essential as the Alliance may be gravely affected by this dispute.

'The United States Government has just informed us – without any prompting on our part – that it would be happy to participate in the conference. We naturally feel that this can only be helpful. Finally, it seems to us that the two other Mediterranean Powers which belong to the Alliance – France and Italy – should be invited to take part.

'I feel that, for reasons which I am sure you appreciate, it would be best if the conference were held at the Heads of Government level. As for the date, the conference should begin as soon as possible, for while the Greek Government is prepared to delay any appeal to the UN until the end of the present Assembly, it cannot altogether renounce the right to do so in the event of a failure to find a solution outside the UN.

'Finally, as regards the venue, the Greek Government considers that a town on the French or Italian Riviera or on one of the Italian Lakes would be most suitable.

'Mr President, may I thank you once again for your impartiality, which we believe to be particularly valuable at a time when those who are prepared to treat us without bias are few indeed.'

This reply was full of promise. Provided all the parties concerned were ready to agree to the area of discussion being expanded and to seek a definitive solution of the Cyprus problem, I was prepared to go along with such a plan. With regard to the proposed increase in the number of participants, I could see no objection and felt that no difficulty would arise in this context. However, I was proved wrong on this latter point. It was this issue, which seemed to me of very minor importance, which proved the stumbling block that wrecked my efforts.

Great Britain and Turkey would not agree to the participation of other governments in the conference. The Greek Government, on the other hand, insisted on this point and finally decided to break off the talks. By acting in this way, it gave much pleasure, I am sure, to London and Ankara, whom I had persuaded to accept my proposals with such great difficulty. I thus saw my efforts brought to nought by the very people for whose benefit I had made them.

On 29 October, M. Melas wrote to me to explain the reasons for his government's attitude:

'Dear Mr President,

'I am instructed by the Hellenic Government to thank you most cordially for your truly indefatigable efforts to bring about a conference on Cyprus. I am also to express our gratitude to the Council both for its efforts to promote a reconciliation and for the patience it has shown.

'Unfortunately, as you will have been aware since Saturday, I am also instructed to inform you that my Government no longer wishes, in view of the circumstances now obtaining, to pursue the idea of the proposed conference. As you know, the immediate reason for our disagreement relates to our proposal that the conference be augmented. I do not think any useful purpose would be served by covering once again the ground over which we went during our discussion. May I simply reiterate that the Greek Government sees in the refusal of the other parties involved to accept a proposal it deems reasonable and to which it attaches particular importance an indication that the desire for a reconciliation – essential if the conference is to succeed – is lacking.

'When this entire series of events comes to be examined impartially, the conclusion will undoubtedly be drawn that the turning point was the statement made by the British Secretary of State for the Colonies at Blackpool on 10 October in addressing the members of his party. That day, the British press announced under banner headlines that Mr Lennox Boyd had just torpedoed the conference on Cyprus. Not surprisingly, many people in Greece, and above all the Cypriots themselves, who realize that their fate depends on this minister, share the view of the British press.

'There have, moreover, been other signs that the conference was doomed to fail. As regards the seven-year transitional status for the island, on which we were prepared to negotiate despite the fact that we knew that it would at best give the island a breathing space of a mere three to four years of relative calm, the Turkish Government left us in no doubt as to the prospects of these negotiations.

'Our Turkish colleague made it clear, in this very Council, that his Government intended to demand that the island's executive council should comprise an equal number of Turkish and Greek representatives, despite the fact that the Turkish minority accounts for a mere eighteen per cent of the island's population and the Greek majority for eighty per cent. Even the British plan – while it did not provide for proportional representation – allowed the majority community a larger number of representatives. In these circumstances there seemed little hope of agreement being reached on the transitional period.

'You are aware, moreover, of the importance which the Greek Government attached to the need to find a definitive solution to the Cyprus problem at the proposed conference. We now learn that not only has the Turkish Foreign Minister declared, quite recently, that his country is not prepared to accept any solution other than partition – and this solution is unacceptable to the Greeks of Cyprus – but all the British and Turkish politicians and diplomats of whose views my Government is aware have made it clear of late that, in their opinion, there has never been any chance of agreement on a definitive solution acceptable to all parties concerned being reached at the conference.

'In this context, I must once again emphasize that the Greeks of Cyprus – as well as those on the mainland – believed that in renouncing a right as natural as that which people have come to call "Enosis", they were making a great sacrifice and hence an important conciliatory gesture. When it became clear that, after having for years violently inveighed against Enosis, the British and Turks were now disposed to take this sacrifice lightly, this, too, did much to persuade those of us in responsible positions that the other parties involved in the dispute were not really interested in reconciliation.

'The Hellenic Government was thus faced with the following dilemma: either it must break off the preliminary talks and thus lose the chance – in fact negligible – that this conference, like any other, might produce an agreement despite the fact that it was destined to be held in unfavourable circumstances; or it had to give way once again, this time over its demand that the conference be enlarged. In this latter event, the Hellenic Government would have had to sit down at the conference table with partners clearly determined to be intransigent. After considering this grave matter at great length, the Government decided to opt for the first alternative, i.e. in favour of breaking off the talks. Its view was that the chance of success were too small to justify the very serious risks inherent in a failure.

'In the view of my Government, the inevitable outcome of that failure would have been to make relations – already tense – between the three governments involved even more difficult. However, for Greece such a failure would have had a further, and very serious, consequence. As you are aware, Communist and neutralist propaganda has been at great pains to take advantage of the Cyprus issue in order to drive a wedge between Greece and NATO. As you no doubt realize, the success of this propaganda has been very disturbing to my Government.

'However, since your visit to Greece, your press conference in Athens and the action of a number of allied governments in giving proof of their impartiality with regard to the Cyprus issue, there has been some movement in favour of NATO among the Greek public. My Government is concerned lest a conference held under the auspices of NATO – quite apart from any other dangers – cause this advantage to be lost.

'I am well aware, Mr President, that this decision of the Hellenic Government will come as a disappointment to you, who have worked so hard to promote an agreement, and that it will also cause disappointment to some of our allies. However, on reflection you may agree that this decision is in fact the best course open to us in the present circumstances.

'I should like, if I may, to comment on our meeting of 23 October. My colleagues have drawn my attention to the fact that at this meeting our British colleague reproached Greece with having rejected the British plan for Cyprus without even having studied it, and he mentioned the Radcliffe plan in this context. I am sorry I did not hear this remark and that I can therefore reply to it only now.

'Sir Frank Roberts will find among the papers of his own delegation proof that he was mistaken. His predecessor, in fact, circulated to all of us a document which explained the advantages of the Radcliffe plan. I replied to this document in a letter dated 7 January 1957. I tried to explain in detail the reasons which caused us to reject that plan, and also made it clear why we thought that there were errors in the arguments set out in Sir Christopher Steel's letter.'

This long document was a strange mixture of serious and relatively trivial arguments. In the eyes of the Greeks some of the details seemed to loom very large indeed, and there were also sentimental reactions reflected in the letter which appeared to carry more weight with the Greeks than well-founded arguments. But did the letter tell the whole story? I do not think it did. The Cyprus issue was still on the agenda of the UN, and Athens was hoping that ultimately Britain and Turkey would be impressed by the Assembly's resolutions. In believing this, the Greeks were persisting in error.

I was cruelly disappointed by the failure of these protracted negotiations during the course of which I had had to plot a careful course between touchy and suspicious adversaries. All in all, Mr Macmillan's British Government, albeit hard pressed by events, had shown good sense, although it was, in my view, too inclined to favour the Turks, some of whose arguments seemed to me weak. I found it difficult, in fact, to accept the military argument invoked by Ankara. True, Cyprus is close to the Turkish coast, a fact which may have carried some weight at the beginning of the century but which had become quite unimportant in the present context, now that Greeks and Turks alike were both members of the Atlantic Alliance, and effective guarantees could easily be provided against any such danger. It was also wrong to disregard the views expressed by the overwhelming majority of Cypriots.

It was once again Foster Dulles who consoled me in my troubles. He wrote to me as follows on 6 November:

'I should like you to know how much I appreciate and admire your efforts to bring about a compromise between the two parties involved in the dispute over Cyprus. Although I share your disappointment at the decision of the Greek Government not to take part in a conference for the present, I am encouraged by the undeniable progress that has been made during the five weeks the matter has been discussed in NATO. These conversations in the Council have not only greatly helped to reduce the differences of view with regard to a conference on Cyprus; they have also, in my opinion, had a salutary effect on the Greek attitude to NATO. As a result of your efforts, the Greek Government seems to have overcome its suspicions of NATO in regard to the Cyprus issue. This improvement in the Greek attitude will make the forthcoming discussions in the Alliance easier. It is our firm hope that the Council will be able, under your guidance, to resume the discussions on Cyprus, although it seems unavoidable that we shall have to await the end of the debate in the UN. I am certain you will continue to exert your resourceful leadership to this end and we, for our part, will continue to be ready to aid you in this extremely difficult but vital endeavour.'

I believe Foster Dulles was right. As it turned out, my efforts were not, in fact, useless. While I had not succeeded in resolving the Cyprus problem, I had prevented it from resulting in serious trouble for the Alliance. After what had happened, after the proposals I had put forward and the support they had received from a large majority of the members of the Council, the Greeks could no longer argue that there was any lack of sympathy and understanding for them. There could no longer be any question of their indulging in talk about leaving the Atlantic Alliance. From my point of view this was a valuable result.

After this we had no further occasion to deal with the Cyprus problem in NATO. At the beginning of 1959, the British, the Greeks and the Turks drew up a new statute for the island and signed the Zurich and London Agreements. I have no wish to comment on these documents. At all events, they do have the merit of existing. However, the arrangements for which they provide are complicated and the system has proved difficult to operate.

The calm which had been restored proved short-lived, and to this day the island's peace remains precarious and has been maintained thanks only to the presence of UN troops. A definitive solution is yet to be found.

The day after the London Agreement was signed I received three telegrams – from Selwyn Lloyd, from Karamanlis and from Christian Herter, the latter having just succeeded Dulles. They were good enough to say that I had contributed to the success achieved. At the beginning of 1959 my position as Secretary-General of NATO was thus excellent.

Let us now turn our attention to other developments. General de Gaulle had in the meantime resumed power in France after a long spell in retirement. A new phase in the history of the Atlantic Alliance was about to begin, and it was not to be a happy one.

35

General de Gaulle

I find it difficult to give an impartial judgement on General de Gaulle. True, I was a Gaullist in London during the war and again in 1958, but for the last ten years I have seen in him the most dangerous adversary of the two ideals for which I have fought for nearly a quarter of a century: the Atlantic Alliance and European unity.

It may well be that General de Gaulle has wrecked both these ideals. If this turns out to be the case he will have helped to destroy the international achievements which have been my hope and pride. Yet, in defining my views of him and his conduct, I feel that it is only right that I should try to do him justice.

I concede unreservedly that de Gaulle has rendered tremendous service to his country. It was he who, in 1940, was mainly responsible for ensuring that France retained her place in the camp of the victors. No doubt, other members of the Resistance ran greater risks and made greater sacrifices, but by his proclamation of 18 June de Gaulle took upon himself a historic responsibility which must be neither denied nor belittled. On that day he became the living symbol of a great cause. He played his part with determination and dedication. That aspect of his life and achievement seems to me to be beyond criticism.

In 1958 he very probably saved France from civil war. No one else would have been able to govern the country successfully in those critical hours. It was his authority, and his shrewd patriotism, which were needed at that time to win acceptance for the liberal solutions that alone could end the war in Algeria.

At the beginning of May I was due to leave Paris for Ottawa to meet the Canadian Government. Like so many others, I was deeply worried about the internal situation in one of the principal member countries of the Atlantic Alliance.

Before leaving, I decided to seek a meeting with Vice-Premier Guy Mollet, the Socialist leader. I found him discouraged and pessimistic. He told me that in the event of riots there would be no one to defend the Republic and its institutions. Neither the army, nor the police, nor the Republican Security Squads (CRS) could be relied on. The mass of the people were disappointed and their reactions uncertain. It was no use counting on them.

His assessment agreed with mine. I took it upon myself to advise him to support General de Gaulle if the latter came to power. I do not know whether my advice influenced him in any way, nor can I now be sure that it was sound advice.

True, civil war was avoided and the Algerian problem solved – in circumstances and by ways and means on which I prefer not to comment. This apart, General de Gaulle's leadership does not seem to me to have had a particularly salutary effect on France's domestic affairs; as regards the international situation, I would call it downright disastrous. We are thus faced with a record which is difficult to assess, and I prefer to leave this task to future historians.

Having done justice to what I consider to be the positive elements in his work, I now propose to examine his achievement as a whole. The first impression that comes to mind is one of a man who inspires strong yet ambivalent feelings. They range from the total – and in some ways touching – loyalty of a Michel Debré; from the absurd flattery of a François Mauriac, to the merciless accusations of the journalist Jacques Laurent and the writer Fabre-Luce.

Is there not room for a more considered judgement? I have often asked myself: is he truly a great man who will bequeath to posterity an impressive achievement? When the history of our times comes to be written, much will be said of him. Yet when the final reckoning is made, people will realize that nothing of lasting value has been achieved.

When Churchill was at the height of his fame, he said

with unfeigned modesty: 'During the war I was merely the interpreter of the will of my people.' Churchill's work and his personality became part of the fabric of British history. He was but one link in a long and solid chain, as was indeed his ambition – the ambition of a true statesman serving a great country.

But when de Gaulle steps down into the political arena, he says: 'After me there will be chaos.' I consider this to be a confession of his own failure. In the history of France he figures neither as one who has carried on an existing tradition nor as the first of a new line of statesmen. He is a freak, astonishing admittedly, but a mere fleeting phenomenon for all that. This is why he is not a truly great man but merely an exceptional figure – and that is the measure of his achievement. Hence what he is is more important that what he does.

To understand de Gaulle, it is useless to rely either on the statements of his admirers or those of his enemies. The best book about him is his own *The Edge of the Sword*, which he wrote in 1932. It contains an amazing chapter, entitled 'About the Human Character' – amazing because it has proved prophetic. This virtually unknown colonel described in it what he was to become later, when events made him the leader of Free France and subsequently the Head of the French State.

Let us look at these pages, which bear the stamp of a writer of outstanding merit. We find in them, above all, the reflection of his lust for power, defined as 'a passionate will and an eager, even jealous desire to make decisions'. This gives us some idea of what the events of 1940 and 1958 must have meant to this man. He probably found the second of these occasions even more intoxicating than the first. It offered him something like a revenge for a long, unexpected, and rashly sought retirement and enabled him to regain the power he loved so dearly. It was restored to him in dramatic circumstances which enhanced his triumph and flattered his pride. How can one believe that such passion could possibly diminish with the passing of time or that age could ever dull the edge of such desire, a desire quite impervious to the vagaries of universal suffrage? The fact that half the people of France refuse to follow him has made no difference either to his resolve to rule or to his will to act.

Moreover, success or failure in what he does matter little to him; he is, as he says, 'willing to shoulder the burden of any setback, and to do so with a certain bitter satisfaction'.

The fact that he takes pleasure in misfortune is one of the stranger aspects of General de Gaulle's personality: he is aware that he is at his best in adversity. In the midst of danger he shows a singular firmness of purpose, a strength of character that is quite out of the ordinary. He likes to stand up to the mighty and derives tremendous satisfaction from doing so. To be surrounded by opponents, and even enemies, does not worry him in the slightest; on the contrary, it gives him profound pleasure. In general such courage is bound to be a tremendous asset, but does this apply with equal force to a political leader? I do not think so. People want happiness, as is indeed their right. It is the duty of their leaders to try to give them this happiness without seeking the bitter pleasure of misfortune. In any case, de Gaulle regards misfortune as a result of the failings of his political opponents rather than of his own errors of judgement.

Such a man must of necessity be a lonely figure, though de Gaulle realizes that no one can act alone and achieve great things. Hence he allows that 'others do have a share in one's activities – persons who are not devoid of the merit of self-abnegation and obedience and take endless trouble to do as they are told'. I can only suppose that General de Gaulle's ministers have read and pondered this sentence before taking office. They have been warned; they have no right to complain. They will always be mere executants – never counsellors. Obedience is the only virtue expected of them.

The type of man de Gaulle describes, and whom he quite clearly would dearly love to resemble, must keep his distance, 'because authority calls for prestige, and to enjoy prestige one must be remote'. Hence the General's haughty courtesy, which those who have had dealings with him know only too well. But at the same time de Gaulle's hero can be kindly. 'He is a born protector of the weak, and their trust uplifts him for he feels he owes a duty to those who place their humble faith in him.' This is not a brutal dictator speaking but a stern father whose benevolence grows in direct proportion with the obedience he is shown. This is why he is prepared to mingle with the crowd and to shake the hands that are held out to him.

Such is de Gaulle's view of his inferiors, but his attitude towards his superiors is just as characteristic: 'The ordinary run of events does not suit him [de Gaulle's hero]. Sure as he is of his judgement and aware of his strength, he does not put himself out to please others. He knows his own mind, and his incisiveness and firmness frequently cause him to eschew passive obedience.'

Marshal Pétain no doubt glanced only cursorily through Colonel de Gaulle's book. Had he read it more carefully, he would have foreseen that in the event of a serious crisis he had better not rely on the cooperation and loyalty of a man – even though that man was his favourite – who was convinced of his unerring judgement and his superiority over those around him.

The strangest – and certainly the most revealing – passage in this chapter of *The Edge of the Sword* – a book by a serving officer – is that in which he eulogizes military indiscipline. 'Those who are involved in great enterprises must often disregard the empty fiction of a false obedience.' He expresses his approval of the conduct of Pelissier at Sebastopol, of Lanrezac at Charleroi and of Lyautey in Morocco – all of whom had disobeyed orders given them by their superiors. To justify his view, he quotes the words of Lord Fisher, who, on receiving a signal from Admiral Jellicoe regarding the Battle of Jutland, declared: 'He has all of Nelson's qualities bar one – he does not know how to disobey.'

In 1932, Colonel de Gaulle thus gave warning of what General de Gaulle would later have the temerity to do in 1940. What he failed to make clear, however, was that in his eyes an act of disobedience is not necessarily justified by the soundness or otherwise of the reasons which have prompted it but rather by its success or failure. This he was to show later when he ordered the rebellious French generals who had staged a rising after being misled by de Gaulle's own speeches and promises to be court-martialled.

Haughty, aloof, severe with his inferiors, sure of himself, certain of his superiority to others, bold in action, passionately attached to power, refusing to acknowledge any limits to his command or exercise of authority, kindly in a slightly patronizing way – this is how de Gaulle has struck those who have had dealings with him, observers free from either excessive adulation for or unfair aversion to him.

His loyal followers are apt to describe de Gaulle as a great political thinker able to foretell the shape of things to come. I believe this judgement to be wrong.

When he surrendered power in 1945, he told the United States Ambassador in confidence that he would be back in the saddle before six months were out. His retirement at Colombey lasted twelve years. During one of my visits to Paris in 1957 he assured me with an air of disillusion that it would be at least ten years before anything could be done to restore France's greatness. The following year he was back at the head of the French Government.

He restored peace in Algeria, but achieved this by doing the opposite of what he had promised and, I believe, of what he had hoped, to accomplish. Having wanted to partition Germany in 1945, he subsequently concluded a friendship treaty with the Federal Republic and, publicly at least, called repeatedly for German reunification.

Having tried, in 1958, to bring about a rapprochement with the United States and Great Britain, and having gone so far as to propose the establishment of a triumvirate which would settle world problems on behalf of the whole of the West, he later adopted a policy akin to neutrality. As regards the USSR, he showed himself in turn unyielding and exaggeratedly optimistic. Having first opposed the idea of an East-West rapprochement, he subsequently became its champion. He claimed to be an advocate of European unity but wanted to see it achieved only if this could be done under French leadership. By his intransigence and brusque diplomacy, he provoked crises which went close to wrecking this great project.

To be honest, I have not been able to discover either

in his actions or his doctrines anything like a consistent grand design. In fact, he seems obstinately wedded to out-dated concepts. In the execution of his day-to-day policies, on the other hand, he is a tactician of outstanding and undeniable skill. He is a great diplomat in the conventional sense, but has earned that title by his skilful conduct of affairs rather than by the nobility of his aims. He is apt to conceal his intentions only to reveal them unexpectedly, mostly amidst a burst of publicity. He is a disconcerting partner to negotiate with because of his attitude: he is in turn contemptuous, kindly yet sceptical, and at times utterly ruthless. He is a master of the art of equivocation and takes pleasure in provoking misunderstandings. I have seen many a man – and some important figures too – fall for his guile.

Finally, he is without equal in investing everything he does with an aura of importance and concealing his changing thoughts behind a mask of self-assurance. Such was the exceptional and redoubtable man with whom the Atlantic Alliance and Europe had to deal from 1958 onwards. Neither the one nor the other had any reason to rejoice at his coming to power.

It was on 23 June 1958 that I resumed contact with General de Gaulle. In the memorandum I drew up after our meeting, I included the following passage: 'Physically and in terms of his morale, he is altogether different from the man he was a year ago. He struck me as being relaxed and to the point, putting his arguments firmly, clearly, and without emotion. When I thanked him, he replied: "For the present we are safe." He then immediately turned to NATO problems.'

We had a long talk. I realized that there were a great many problems of which he knew nothing. He was poorly informed of the background of the issues under discussion. He did not know the men in power, notably Adenauer and Dulles. Up to a point, having been out of politics for twelve years, he was a beginner in international affairs.

I asked him to allow me to reflect on what he had said and suggested that I should draft a memorandum of our meeting. He agreed, and I sent the document to him on 3 July.

36

The French Memorandum
of 17 September 1958

Two months later, on 17 September 1958, General de Gaulle wrote to President Eisenhower and Mr Macmillan, then Britain's Prime Minister, enclosing a memorandum in which he outlined his attitude to the Atlantic Alliance.

His letter to the President of the United States was most cordially worded. He remarked on the situation in the Far East and the concern with which developments there were bound to be viewed by the American public. He went on to assure the Americans of his sincere friendship and trust and expressed his desire for closer co-operation to make the Alliance more cohesive and effective.

De Gaulle's memorandum of 17 September – a document of exceptional importance – has, so far, unfortunately never been published. I say unfortunately, because it has given rise to comment inevitably based on incomplete knowledge and to a good many misconceptions. It would, of course, also be of the utmost interest to know what proposals General de Gaulle was at that time putting to his American and British partners, what motives inspired his action, and to see how wide was the gulf which separated the policy he would have liked to pursue from that which in fact he followed.

I once had in my possesion a copy of this memorandum which had been passed on to me in my capacity as Secretary-General of NATO. I was most grateful for this token of confidence. But my copy has disappeared from my files. I have never been able to clear up this mystery, but I should like to emphasize that all I am about to say is in strict accord with the document sent by the General to the Americans and British.

The analysis of the situation which General de Gaulle made in his memorandum was admirably to the point. He began by saying that the area covered by the Atlantic Alliance as originally conceived no longer corresponded to political and strategic realities. It was impossible, he said, to regard an organization which confined itself to the security of the North Atlantic – as if events in the Middle East and in Africa were not of close and direct concern to Europe – as being suited to its purpose. The range of modern warships, aircraft and missiles had rendered that concept out of date from the military point of view. The original system had been adopted, he went on to say, because nuclear weapons – clearly of crucial importance – were then the monopoly of the United States, and all decisions on defence, concerning every part of the world, were therefore in effect left to the Government in Washington. However, it had to be recognized that such an assumption, acceptable though it might have been at the time, was no longer in accord with the realities of the situation. As a result, the General continued, France could not agree that in its existing form, NATO was capable of meeting the security requirements of the free world and especially those of France herself.

So far, so good. The memorandum accurately described the situation as it had evolved since 1949 and set out admirably the need for Western solidarity. It stressed the arbitrary nature of an alliance confined to dealing with events in a particular area of the world while the foreign policy of the various governments was in fact clearly being conducted on a global scale.

Proceeding from this premise and constructive criticism, General de Gaulle, instead of drawing conclusions which had they been jointly put forward by himself and the Anglo-Saxons would have strengthened the Alliance, proposed the adoption of a system liable to destroy it. To eliminate the defects he had described, General de Gaulle asked that a system be adopted for the conduct of world policy and strategy based solely on the United States, Great Britain and France. These three Powers would set up an organization responsible for taking joint decisions on policy matters arising in connection with international security, as well as for drawing up and, should the need arise, for putting into operation, plans for military action, notably in regard to the use of nuclear weapons. Under this system, theatres of operation could be defined and organized, subject to the overall policies of the Alliance, for such areas as the Arctic, the Atlantic, the Pacific and the Indian Ocean. As and when necessary, these areas could be further divided into sub-theatres.

General de Gaulle went on to declare outright that the French Government considered such security arrangements essential and made it clear that France's participation in NATO depended on the adoption of this system. He went on to say that, should it prove necessary, he was ready to invoke the procedures for a revision of the NATO arrangements outlined under Article 12 of the Washington Treaty. He then proposed that negotiations should begin immediately between the United States, Great Britain and France.

While the arguments set out in de Gaulle's memorandum of 17 September 1958 resembled those he had put to me a few weeks earlier as regards the nature of the problems discussed, his conclusions and the procedure which he was proposing for dealing with these issues were new and, in my opinion, open to serious objections.

I could not accept these arguments either in my capacity as a former Foreign Minister or as Secretary-General of NATO. If de Gaulle's proposals for a triumvirate were adopted, if international policy were left to three members of the Alliance, I was convinced we should see a revolt of all the other NATO countries.

There were other reasons, too, why, in my opinion, the triumvirate scheme was not viable. It seemed unlikely that de Gaulle would always be prepared to bow, in the conduct of international affairs, to the decisions of his two Anglo-Saxon partners. If, on the other hand, the decision-making process were made subject to the rule of unanimity, the resulting system would quite clearly be inefficient.

The day after I had received the memorandum, I left Paris for Boston, where I was to meet Foster Dulles. This gave me a chance to sound out the views of the

Secretary of State regarding these proposals, which were unexpected and in fact sensational. Inevitably, Foster Dulles's views did not differ very greatly from my own. We both attached great importance to the need to strengthen the Alliance and thus realized only too clearly the dangers inherent in the course of action suggested by the General.

While Foster Dulles was certainly not opposed to the idea of France playing a more important role, he had made himself a champion of the system of consultation devised by the 'Three Wise Men' – a system which had begun to prove its worth. In his view, this experiment should not only be continued but extended. In his memorandum, General de Gaulle was asking that the existing alliance of fifteen be replaced by a three-power alliance of doubtful efficiency. For a variety of good reasons, the United States was opposed to this. The British reaction to de Gaulle's ideas was similar.

On my return to Paris, I drafted a reply to de Gaulle's memorandum. Since the latter was confidential, I did not feel free to place it before the Atlantic Council. Had I done so, it would have had a poor reception. There had, in fact, already been certain leakages of information. Macmillan had been to Bonn, where he had met Chancellor Adenauer. The latter was utterly opposed, not to say violently hostile, to de Gaulle's ideas. The feeling in Rome was much the same.

Although my memorandum of 15 October expressed my own views, I am convinced that in fact it reflected those of virtually all the members of the Alliance.

I began by stressing my agreement with the French diagnosis and recalled that in my own public utterances during the previous six months I had put forward the same views. In 1950, the Communist threat was chiefly military, and confined to Europe. It had since shifted, above all, to Asia and Africa and had become economic and social rather than military. It was therefore up to the West to begin considering an expansion of its area of action to other parts of the world. I also spoke of the need to revise NATO's organizational structure. The development of strategic nuclear weapons and, above all, the installation of intermediate range ballistic missiles in Europe had changed the nature of our problem. Europe's inevitable direct involvement in any nuclear war was a fact which had to be taken into account. The authority enjoyed within the Alliance by the European partners had to be strengthened in line with their new responsibilities.

I then went on to outline my many objections to de Gaulle's arguments. I emphasized the efforts that had been made, as well as the fact that a measure of success had already been achieved. I went on to say that the shackles imposed by the geographical limits of the Alliance had already been broken. The area of political consultation and, as a result, the area to which Atlantic solidarity applied, had been enlarged so as to cover every part of the globe. It was out of the question that a system be set up based on the assumption that only France, the United States and Great Britain had any interest in problems arising outside Europe. Portugal, the Netherlands and Belgium had colonies in Africa and Asia, while other member countries of the Alliance had economic interests of such importance in these areas that they could not possibly remain indifferent to political developments there.

I therefore deplored the idea of 'creating a political and strategic organization on a world scale with the United States, Great Britain and France as its only members.' This was neither a practicable nor a helpful idea, I declared. If that scheme were adopted, it would be the end of the Alliance. 'I am convinced,' I said, 'that Italy and Germany will never agree to this and, rather than submit to such a tutelage on a global scale, they would resume their absolute freedom of political action, with all the dangers this would entail for Europe and Western solidarity.'

I went on to say: 'I am equally certain that were the minor member countries of the Alliance to be deprived of the vehicle of discussion and consultation which NATO – their only means of standing up for their views and interests – represent for them, they would, rather than accept the orders of this triumvirate, look to neutrality for their salvation.' Finally, I predicted that the reply of the United States and Great Britain to de Gaulle's memorandum would be negative. Without opposing the idea of conversations between the Ambassadors in Washington, I strongly advised against these consultations being held behind the backs of the other member countries of NATO. I declared that such talks could never be kept secret and that the indiscretions which would inevitably ensue could only exacerbate feelings and increase distrust. I noted in conclusion that I thought it out of the question to involve the permanent military group in these discussions – a body which was subordinate to NATO and on which all the fifteen member countries were represented. To give such an organism an assignment on behalf of three governments only, with the other twelve being kept in ignorance of what was going on, could, in my view, lead to serious trouble.

It was quite obvious from certain of the General's ideas that he was completely ignorant of the machinery of the Alliance. I am convinced his memorandum was drafted without the Quai d'Orsay's help, for it would otherwise never have been allowed to go out containing the glaring mistakes it did.

We were thus face to face with the first outward signs of a policy determined by one man alone, acting without the advice of parliament or even of a minister. This kind of situation was henceforth to arise time and again.

However, I did not wish to end on so negative and critical a note. I made it clear that I thought it advisable for some of the ideas outlined in General de Gaulle's memorandum to be put up to the Alliance for discussion: ways of expanding the geographical area covered by the treaty would have to be examined, as well as methods to improve the machinery for political consultation. We would have to see what could be done in the military sphere to lend the European Powers a weight of authority commensurate to the dangers facing them and, above all, I said, we must establish a strategy embracing the entire world.

I declared that not all these questions need be discussed in the Atlantic Council from the outset by all countries represented on it. More flexible solutions could be devised, such as the establishment of committees with restricted representation, which could be entrusted with specific tasks. The main thing was not to face the member countries of the Alliance with *faits accomplis* but to enable them to make their voices heard at all times in the defence of their interests.

I thus tried, in my reply, to single out those arguments from de Gaulle's memorandum of 17 September which I thought acceptable, leaving the remainder to be dealt with by means of compromise solutions.

I now realize that at that time I was still labouring under too many illusions. I thought I could talk to General de Gaulle as I was used to talking to the American, British, German and Italian leaders. The fact is, however, that one does not discuss with General de Gaulle: one either does as he says or one stands up to him – there is no halfway house.

There was no reply to my memorandum. However, it is only fair to say that my relations with the French Government were not affected by the candour with which I had opposed General de Gaulle's ideas.

The British and Americans rejected the proposals put to them by de Gaulle and that seemed to be that. At that time we did not yet realize how redoubtable a diplomat we were dealing with. Hiding his disappointment, de Gaulle never mentioned his proposals again. But he is not a man to forget or forgive easily. Thereafter, he calmly turned down all offers of special cooperation, put to him repeatedly by the Americans, disdaining to react in any way at all to the approaches made to him. His mind was made up. Since his views on how the world should be run had been rejected, he was determined to destroy the organization which was the chief obstacle to his schemes. From that time on, NATO was under sentence of death so far as de Gaulle was concerned. He was resolved that it should never be said that he had accepted without alteration a scheme as important as the Atlantic Alliance in the shape and form it had been created under the terms of the Treaty of Washington, nor that he was prepared to follow a policy conceived without him.

However, by October 1958 matters had not yet quite reached that pass. De Gaulle had resumed power too recently to be able to indulge in the spectacular political coups which were maturing in his mind.

His allies' mistake was not to have realized the dangers implicit in his views, the state of mind these views reflected, the perils inherent in the revival of these old concepts and, above all, their failure to see that in opposing de Gaulle they were making an enemy for ever of a man whose pride exceeds his wisdom, who never forgets a setback and who never forgives those responsible.

37

The French Nuclear Demands

Although the deplorable plan of 17 September 1958 had been rejected, I was under no illusion that this was the end of our troubles. I felt convinced that it was my duty to seek solutions which would meet the justified demands of the French. I did my utmost to this end throughout 1959 and 1960. The crux of the problem was to convince the Americans that General de Gaulle had made up his mind regarding the nuclear issue and that no argument – political, military or financial – would induce him to change it. His reasoning was simple, and might best be summed up in the form of a syllogism: a Great Power must possess a nuclear capability – France is a Great Power, hence France must possess a nuclear capability.

This, then, would have to be the starting point in our search for a solution. In July 1959 I drafted a memorandum defining France's relations with NATO. I stated, to begin with – and this was the underlying reason for my concern – that during the preceding few months the French Government had repeatedly expressed its opposition to proposals made by the NATO military authorities. I was referring to France's refusal to agree to the integration of the NATO air forces, her refusal to apply the agreed arrangements for financing the IRBMs, her decision to withdraw the French Mediterranean Fleet from NATO, and her refusal to permit the US Air Force to stockpile nuclear arms on French soil. France had thus created a difficult situation which was disturbing to most of her allies. Under the heading 'Aid to be accorded to France in her nuclear test programme', I declared:

'As I understand it – contrary to what is sometimes said – the United States would be ready to apply *vis-*

à-vis France a system identical to the one the US has introduced in relation to Great Britain. However, before this can be done, France must make the "substantial progress" in nuclear research required under American law. What, exactly, is meant by "substantial progress"?

'Would it not be useful if the United States were to give at this point some indication of this, and even some guarantees? Personally, I believe it would be advisable to go even a little further. The American legislation to which I refer probably made sense while the United States still had a monopoly of nuclear knowledge. Its validity is, however, much more open to doubt now that the Russians have made the advances in this field with which we are all familiar. To solve this problem, we must, I believe, base our reasoning on the following propositions:

'a France has decided to acquire possession of her own nuclear bomb and, I am convinced, nothing will persuade her to relinquish this plan.

'b There is no doubt that she will succeed sooner or later, after spending more or less money.

'c Would it not be better to enable her to save herself some of the considerable effort involved and to persuade her that, in return, she should devote to other aspects of our joint defence all or part of the savings thus achieved? If this were done, we should all benefit.

'French participation in global strategy

'1 France is right in speaking of the need for a global strategy.

'It is obvious that the flank of NATO's defence has been turned in the Middle East and Africa. We cannot afford to indulge in a "Maginot Line" complex.

'2 France is also right – particularly in view of the outstanding importance of her location on the Europe-Africa axis – in saying that she must play a part, in the event of a world war, in helping to determine strategy even outside the territorial limits of NATO. It is at this point that our problem becomes difficult. What, precisely, is meant, in the situation we are facing, by the words: "France must be allowed to play her part in world strategy"?

'a There has been talk of a directory. A genuine directory is out of the question and cannot be made to function either by applying the majority rule or the rule of unanimity. Such a concept would be opposed not only by all the NATO Powers but also by a number of other states such as Australia and New Zealand. Moreover, the establishment of an effective directory would set off a powerful neutralist current in Europe.

'b Can we reallocate the military commands on a world scale? Within the limits of NATO, this is a problem which can, no doubt, be re-examined, and I can see no reason why this should not be done. On a world scale, however, an agreed allocation of command responsibilities would imply the existence of a genuinely common foreign policy – and this is not a realistic notion at this stage.

'Would it, therefore, not be possible to establish within the framework of NATO, with a view to examining the political and military problems which arise outside the geographical limits of the Alliance, special committees with a restricted membership, whose task it would be to study these problems in detail and to work out agreed directives? The latter could be submitted, either in whole or in part, to all the NATO countries for their information. It might, for example, be thought useful to set up such committees for Africa, the Middle East, the Far East and South-East Asia. This would have the advantage that the main partners of the Alliance – who would be represented on all the committees – would have a complete picture of the world situation, in keeping with their interests and responsibilities. The other partners, on the other hand, would be in a position to make their voices heard on problems of direct concern to them (Belgium and Portugal on Africa; Turkey on the Middle East; the Netherlands on South-East Asia). Perhaps it might also be possible to establish a special committee for nuclear problems.'

Nearly ten years have elapsed since this document was

drafted. The ideas outlined in it have proved correct. There was no denying that account had to be taken of the fact that, rightly or wrongly, General de Gaulle had taken an irrevocable decision. He had made up his mind to give France a nuclear strike force and there was no point in trying to prevent him from carrying out his intention. We should have helped him in his efforts and taken advantage of our assistance to him to strengthen the defensive power of the Alliance.

Far be it from me to think that my papers provided an adequate answer to all these questions. All I can justly claim is that I had the courage to ask them. I was trying to counteract the tendency, all too often found among diplomats, to stick to the status quo and to delude oneself that problems are solved by sweeping them under the carpet.

I was received by General de Gaulle on 16 July 1959 and presented my memorandum to him. I asked him to let me know whether, in his view, I had defined any of the questions dealt with wrongly and if any of the solutions proposed by me seemed inadequate to him. This attempt at direct diplomacy evoked no echo whatever. I was clearly attaching greater importance to the office I held as Secretary-General of NATO than the General was prepared to accord to it.

However, I did have the impression that I had succeeded in clearing up certain issues during our meeting. De Gaulle said to me: 'I am not against NATO. In fact, I am convinced that in the event of war NATO would prove indispensable. There are, however, three issues I find disconcerting [I was rather struck by his choice of words!]: 1 Africa; 2 responsibility for the use of atomic weapons; 3 military integration.'

As regards Africa, the General held that since the Treaty of Washington did not cover the African continent, it was essential to conclude a supplementary agreement. In regard to the use of nuclear weapons, he said resort to the use of the nuclear bomb should be subject to consultation. Referring to military integration, he said it was necessary to define precisely the difference between what he termed 'intensive cooperation' – an alliance of the conventional type, he declared, was no longer sufficient – and outright integration, which he considered contrary to French interests, for he declared, 'integration does away with one's sense of responsibility'.

All these ideas should have been examined by the Alliance. There was nothing here to give rise to irreconcilable differences. At that time, all could still have been saved. What was needed, however, was the will and the courage to discuss these matters, to give up the habit of artificial optimism and of believing that everything would come right in the end of its own accord.

I have no wish whatever to criticize Christian Herter, who succeeded Foster Dulles. He was a charming man, courteous, well-intentioned, moderate, devoted to the Atlantic Alliance, but he lacked his predecessor's clear vision and, above all, his sense of purpose. He had no wish to face up to the problems posed by French policy. Suddenly, American diplomacy, which under Dulles had occasionally been brutally forthright, became timid.

I remember a visit to Washington at that time. At the State Department I met a great many officials and advisers who were busily working out all sorts of schemes. However, I had the impression that these tasks had been allocated in a somewhat artificial way and that specialization had been taken to excessive lengths. I remember saying at the time: 'I have seen a number of teams at work. They all seem to be busy fitting together the pieces of a jigsaw puzzle but no one seems to know whether the picture they are meant to compose is supposed to represent the early Christian martyrs or a twentieth-century naval battle.'

My efforts at least to define the problems before us met with indifference on de Gaulle's part – for the General was pursuing his own policy – and with hesitancy on the part of the Americans, who were unable to determine their own aims. In this way, another year was lost amidst confusion. We all knew that there was a problem to be tackled. The General made no secret of his dissatisfaction and the situation was slowly deteriorating.

In the spring of 1960, Mr Gates, US Defence Secretary,

put forward on behalf of his Government a plan for the stationing of IRBMs in Europe. It took no account of French views on the matter. In fact, they were not even mentioned. To ignore France in this way was a grave psychological error. From then on, de Gaulle inevitably opposed this policy with contempt. It was essential that something be done. In a note to the Americans, I once again drew their attention to the gravity of the differences between themselves and the French, and put a proposal to them. If it were impossible, I declared, in view of the MacMahon Act and congressional policies, to assist France in the production of an atomic bomb, would it not be possible to promise her that assistance would be forthcoming once she had succeeded in this operation by her own efforts? Could France not be helped with the production of missiles? In this way, American legislation would be respected while, at the same time, valuable assistance would be given to France. In that event France could no doubt be persuaded to take part in a joint organization for Europe's nuclear defence within the framework of NATO. This seemed to me an ingenious solution, calculated to bring the two points of view together.

My illusions were soon to be shattered. On 4 June 1960, Mr Nolting, the American assistant permanent representative to NATO, called on me to tell me that he had studied my note and felt that my suggestions would not be acceptable to his government. Two arguments, he said, would doubtless be put forward by the latter: first, if the USA were to help France establish a nuclear strike force, it would one day undoubtedly be confronted with a similar request from Germany. Second, if it adopted the policy suggested by me, this would be liable to influence the Soviet Union's attitude to the East European Communist countries and to China.

I thought these arguments weak. Hypothetical German demands could not be put on the same footing as those of the French. On no account must the impression be given that the arrangements adopted under the London Agreements – by the terms of which Germany had undertaken not to produce nuclear arms – could conceivably be called into question. No such demands had in fact ever been made by the Germans and it would be unwise even to suggest any such thing. As for the USSR and its allies, I was convinced that the European Communist countries had neither the desire nor the financial resources to manufacture such weapons. The Chinese, on the other hand, were perfectly capable of such an effort.

Nolting listened to me attentively and with evident sympathy. He was well-informed, perfectly familiar with the situation in Paris and the dangers General de Gaulle's unsatisfied ambitions represented for the Alliance, but he gave me little hope. Nolting called on me again on 4 July, and this time he brought me the official American reply. As he had predicted, my proposals had been rejected. At the same time, he asked me to arrange for a postponement of the discussion on Mr Gates's proposals due to be held in the NATO Council, as they were to be modified.

I drafted a memorandum on this meeting, which concluded with the following passage: 'The news conveyed by Nolting is obviously bad. It shows that the Americans remain obstinate on the basic issues and that the military problems have not been examined adequately.' Despite my great disappointment, I thought it wrong to abandon my efforts. On 6 July I wrote to Mr Herter as follows:

'Mr Nolting came to see me to convey the reply of the United States Government to my suggestions regarding Mr Gates's proposals. Need I point out that this reply has come as a great disappointment to me and has made me deeply anxious about the future of NATO? I think it would be no exaggeration to say that we have reached a crucial point.

'I am firmly convinced that if we do not succeed in finding a solution to the problem of Europe's nuclear armaments along multilateral NATO lines and with the effective participation of all countries, we shall move towards a state of confusion and helplessness in the military field while also endangering our solidarity in the political sphere.

'In particular, would there be any point in drawing

up a ten-year plan unless we reach agreement on our immediate problems? True, it is an excellent thing to think of the future, but care must be taken that this does not become a pretext for neglecting the very real difficulties of the present. May I emphasize once again – and I hope you will forgive me for pressing this point with such insistence – that to deny France the right to create her own nuclear strike force would be to set one's face in vain against one of the main objectives of General de Gaulle's policy. Also, to refuse him the aid to which he considers himself entitled would be to create an atmosphere in which it would be impossible to ensure the ability of the Atlantic Alliance to develop in the way it should.

'The point is not whether France is wise or unwise in wishing to create such a force. The fact is that she wants to create it, that she will create it and that, moreover, if I may say so, as far as I can see this entails no danger for the Alliance. I regret that the opportunity which now arises to assist France – provided she modifies her military policy *vis-à-vis* NATO – is not being seized.

'In view of the direction in which the current discussions are moving, I greatly fear that Europe will not be able to create her own nuclear force, that France will continue pursuing her own costly policy and that the cohesion of the Atlantic Alliance will suffer grave damage as a result.

'Mr Nolting, realizing my disappointment and – I say so advisedly – my anxiety, did his best to reassure me by suggesting that the new American proposals for the deployment of Polaris missiles may meet with France's approval. I should very much like to be able to say that I agree with him; however, I cannot honestly say I do.

'If the French persist in their refusal, as I fear they will, all the results I can foresee ensuing will inevitably materialize and our Alliance will little by little lose its cohesion and effectiveness. You may well think my insistence exaggerated and inopportune. If this is the case, all I can do is to ask your forgiveness, in the hope that you will bear with me since what is at stake is the future – happy or otherwise – of NATO. I shall do what the United States Government has asked me to do; that is, I shall postpone the debate on Mr Gates's proposals in the hope that the time thus gained will be usefully employed.

'In conclusion, I should like to make it clear to you that my initial contacts with the French were on the whole encouraging. The French officials with whom I have been in contact seemed interested in my proposals. I have met M. Couve de Murville and am due to see M. Debré at the end of the week. I have also requested an interview with General de Gaulle, on whom, when all is said and done, everything clearly depends.

'On reflection, and despite the negative response I have had to my proposals, I feel it would be advisable for me to continue my attempts at sounding out opinion. At least this will enable us to know precisely the position of the various parties involved. I shall, of course, not fail to keep the United States delegation informed of developments.'

My pessimism proved well founded. I had assessed the General's policies correctly and realized the danger threatening us. Unfortunately, I failed to convince the Americans.

Yet, as I had pointed out in my letter, my contacts with the French had not left me without hope. While Couve de Murville had reacted with some reserve, Michel Debré, on the other hand, had shown real interest, and General de Gaulle's attitude, as it turned out, was not completely negative either. I called on the General on 21 July 1960. That same day, I drafted the following memorandum:

'I was received by General de Gaulle on 21 July. The aim of the meeting, which took place at my request, was to inform the General of my attitude to Mr Gates's proposals.

'I explained to the General the ideas set out in my note to the United States Government, which I had submitted to them during the course of my last visit. The General listened to me attentively. His attitude was one of polite scepticism. He declared, in effect, that he did not believe there was any chance of my efforts succeeding. According to him, the United States Government is not prepared to shift from its position with regard to the French nuclear strike force. He went on to say that the United States Government was determined to remain the sole possessor of a major strike force and had no intention of doing anything that might allow its allies either to acquire such a force or to share its possession with the United States. He made it quite clear to me that, in his view, there was absolutely no chance of my efforts succeeding and that I should fare no better with my efforts over missiles than he had done in his approaches regarding the atomic bomb. He added that he had repeatedly thought he had succeeded in enlisting President Eisenhower's interest in his endeavours but that, for one reason or another – exactly why he could not say – the final decision of the United States Government had invariably dashed his hopes.

'He added that in view of all this he had made up his mind: he considered he had no alternative but to establish unaided a French nuclear strike force, which he believed to be essential to his country.

'When I remarked that his views were rather pessimistic and that such an attitude would make it difficult to strengthen the Alliance, even on the political plane, he made an unmistakable gesture of resignation, to indicate that, in his view, there was no use denying these regrettable, but unfortunately, true facts.

'During the course of our conversation, I asked him if he had any objection to my continuing my efforts. His reply was that he would, of course, not dream of preventing me from doing something which was in accord both with French views and interests. He reaffirmed, however, that in his opinion these efforts would prove vain. When I asked him if France were interested in having missiles supplied to her, his answer was a clear "yes", and he added that if this could be done it would present a considerable gain, especially from the financial point of view.

'I thus came away from my meeting with the

General convinced that his mind was made up and that the United States' refusal to help France build her own nuclear strike force must be seen as final. The General obviously regretted that this was the case but had drawn his own conclusions, both military and political.

'Personally, I am convinced he could be induced to change his mind if it were found possible to grant him a substantial concession. He is, however, determined not to make any such request himself.'

I must in all fairness admit that General de Gaulle had predicted American reactions accurately. He was in a better position to do so since, in conversation with me on a number of occasions, he made no attempt to disguise the fact that if he had been in the Americans' place he would have done precisely the same. When one enjoys so marked a superiority, he declared repeatedly, one does not share it with anyone, not even one's best friends.

I have recounted these incidents at some length since I believe them to be significant and at the root of General de Gaulle's decision to leave NATO. There can be no doubt that the General was disappointed and angry when, in 1958, the British and Americans refused to join him in setting up the triumvirate he had suggested. Despite this, all could still have been saved if the Americans had realized that General de Gaulle was utterly determined to set up his own nuclear strike force. I do not believe this decision to have been wise and am convinced that France would have been much better advised to have tried to prevail upon the United States to arrange for effective French participation in the formulation of nuclear strategy. However, my advice carried little weight. Once it was clear that General de Gaulle would not give way, it would have been better to attempt a compromise between his obstinate demand and the interests of the Alliance by offering him a solution which made adequate allowance for such of his requests as were legitimate.

The American Administration did not make the necessary effort. I do not know what they were hoping for – probably that the magnitude of the financial sacrifice required would deter the General. However, the Americans did not know their de Gaulle, as events were to show only too clearly. When it was too late, they tried to retrieve the position by means of their multilateral force (MLF) project. However, by then France was no longer able to modify her attitude and, in any case, the project did not meet her main requirements.

The remarkable feature of this whole episode is that the two partners never really tackled their dispute frankly. Instead, we witnessed a typical demonstration of over-complex diplomacy, with everybody flattering himself that he was cleverer than the next man and acting on hidden motives rather than openly declared intentions.

What was the outcome of it all? France now has a nuclear strike force, but its usefulness is becoming increasingly dubious, and its power in relation to the resources of the USSR and the United States is steadily diminishing. The *force de frappe* requires enormous expenditure and thus hampers France's economic and social progress. As for the United States, it proved unable to prevent a development which is rightly feared: the partial disintegration of NATO. A more forthright approach, greater candour and imagination, would have enabled us to avoid this situation.

During 1959 and 1960 my relations with the French Government were on the whole good despite my declared opposition to some of its activities. I never left Paris in any doubt as to my intentions, and the French could not but acknowledge my efforts to persuade the United States to make certain changes in its policies to meet French wishes.

The following episode – which might have developed into a serious clash – illustrates the degree of understanding I had reached with the French.

On 14 July 1959 M. Debré, who was then Premier, requested me to call on him. My relationship with M. Debré is a strange one. We have not, I believe, a single idea in common. At Strasbourg, during the meetings of the European Consultative Assembly, I have had some extremely lively exchanges with him. And yet, I have always felt a certain sympathy for Debré. His loyalty to General de Gaulle is unquestioning and has led him into some strange contradictions. However, I am convinced he has never been guided by personal ambition or actuated by underhand motives. Such utter devotion is so rare a phenomenon in politics nowadays that one cannot help but admire it.

On that 14 July 1959, Michel Debré was visibly worried. As soon as I entered his study, he said to me:

'I have something very serious to tell you, but first let me explain what is happening in Algeria. Things are going much better. General Challe has been completely successful in the Oran region and has also had some success in the Algiers area. The guerrillas are running short of ammunition. We have found stock-piles of unusable weapons. There can be no doubt about the accuracy of these reports.

'Now, on my return from Madagascar, I am told that two ships carrying cargoes of arms are about to land in Morocco. One of them has slipped our blockade but we have managed to stop the other one. However, the fact remains – and that is the tragedy of it all – the Americans and the Norwegians are on the point of supplying millions of rounds of ammunition and thousands of grenades to the rebels *via* Tunisia. The Tunisian army has no need of these supplies. There can thus be no doubt that they are intended for the rebels. This France cannot permit. If these arms reach their destination, I shall have to take fresh military measures and will be forced to make my reasons public. The result will be a grave crisis in Franco-American relations. For me personally this is a tragedy. The United States Ambassador in Paris has not been kept informed, while Alphand, our Ambassador in Washington, is being treated in an off-hand manner. The Americans are violating an agreement with France. If I do not get a satisfactory reply very soon, I shall have to inform NATO.'

All this was said to me in a tone of considerable anger, and I could only agree with the French Premier. It was intolerable that two of France's NATO partners should help the Algerians in this way. Although it was doubtless regrettable that the French Government had never put the Algerian situation on the agenda of the Atlantic Council, on the grounds that this was a French internal affair – an attitude which was clearly excessively legalistic and in stark contradiction with the facts – this failure on the part of the French Government could in no way justify two of France's allies in giving aid to the rebels.

I promised Debré I would use my influence to put an end to this situation. The next day I met the permanent representatives of Norway and the United States. The Norwegian delegate immediately saw my point of view and promised to report our conversation to his Foreign Minister forthwith. The American was less forthcoming and merely gave me an assurance that the United States was operating a special service in Tunis which was keeping an eye on these matters. He added that he did not believe the arms were intended for the rebels.

The following day the Norwegians assured me that the delivery would not be made. The Americans refused to give me such an undertaking, and I therefore made it clear to them that if they persisted in this attitude I would have to put the matter to the Council. They evidently did not relish this prospect. A few days later Michel Debré wrote to me:

'Allow me to send you a personal word of thanks for your intervention. This was most useful, particularly where our American friends are concerned, with whom, after having clarified the situation, we have resumed bilateral talks which look promising . . . for the moment!'

I have recalled this incident to show that the Secretary-General could intervene usefully in certain circumstances, and also in order to emphasize the extent to which good Franco-American relations were endangered by the constant refusal of both sides to discuss frankly the whole range of their mutual problems.

Why did the French not take advantage of the facilities offered by the Atlantic Council to explain their policies and enlist the support of their allies? I have never been able to understand their attitude and am certain that, had they acted differently, they would have received the aid – the moral aid at least – they required and that a good many difficulties could thus have been avoided.

38

Chancellor Adenauer

It was in 1959 and 1960 that my contacts with Chancellor Adenauer were at their closest and most frequent. The struggle we had waged jointly at the Brussels Conference on behalf of the EDC, the similarity of our views at that time on the need to create a united Europe, our efforts to secure the adoption of the measures which eventually saw the light of day as the Treaty of Rome – all these had helped to establish close ties between us.

In August 1959 and September 1960 I met him in the villa which Stikker – at that time the permanent delegate of the Netherlands to the Atlantic Council – owned at Menaggio on Lake Como. It was a magnificent place in a splendid setting, and combined the beauties of the Italian landscape with traditional Dutch comfort. There was a splendid view of the mountains and the lake, a well shaded terrace and a lovely garden. Cool drinks, the wise views of trusty friends – the master of the house, as well as André de Staercke, General Norstad and Ambassador Blankenhorn – all these were there for the asking.

I was struck during these meetings by an outstanding feature of Adenauer's mentality: there was an impressionable side to his character, and he was ready to adopt extreme views based on sentiment rather than fact. I have seen him violently anti-British, anti-American and anti-French in turn. Most often on these occasions his judgement was emotional and based on a false interpretation of events.

I recall that during a meeting with Foster Dulles we decided that false information and deliberately slanted comment must be at the root of Adenauer's opinions because they were so glaringly at variance with the facts.

In August 1959, it was Britain that he distrusted and

Macmillan who was the object of his suspicions. He maintained that Britain was not a reliable ally. The arguments he used were childish and we did our best to counter them. Finally, we succeeded, I believe, in making him see how wrong he had been.

The freedom with which the Chancellor expressed his views on events and people alike made any conversation with him fascinating. He told us, for instance, that Khrushchev, apparently very disturbed at events in China, had said to him: 'What are we to do about this vast mass of people growing at the rate of twelve million a year? You ought to help us with this problem instead of fighting us.'

Adenauer repeatedly assured us of his faith in Europe. Smilingly, he said to us: 'I do not think General de Gaulle's Europe is the same as my own, but I think he is learning fast.'

The Chancellor's views on the entire complex of Atlantic and European problems were unexceptionable, and our meeting ended amidst an atmosphere of confidence and friendship.

At that time General Eisenhower, who had been elected President of the United States, was about to tour Europe and to visit France. The prospect of a meeting between the two soldier Heads of State had its worrying aspects as far as I was concerned. I thought the preparations for the meeting inadequate: there had been no frank diplomatic exchanges to discuss the real issues. Fresh misunderstandings were therefore to be feared. After the cordial meeting I had had with Chancellor Adenauer in Italy, I felt free to write to him as follows:

'My dear Chancellor,
    'I have, of course, given a great deal of thought to our recent conversation, during the course of which I neither could nor would hide from you my concern at the unrest which now bedevils the diplomatic scene. It seems to me that the Atlantic Alliance is passing through a crisis which, though not as serious as the one we experienced at the time of Suez, may well become so unless vigorous action is taken. I therefore

feel I should neither be committing an indiscretion nor trespassing on your kindness if I were to ask you to devote some attention to the three or four problems which seem to me particularly important.

'During these last few weeks the Americans have, I feel, made two mistakes. The first was when they invited Mr Khrushchev to visit the United States without any genuine attempt at consulting the views of their allies as to whether they thought the invitation opportune. Their second mistake was when, in order to soften the impact of the first, they organized President Eisenhower's trip to Europe. They thus succeeded in first arousing misgivings and fears in some quarters and then, by what they intended as a counter-measure, only underlining still further the potential importance of Khrushchev's visit. In so doing they gave rise to some lively reactions – scarcely favourable to the Atlantic Alliance – especially in France.

'If the Americans are not prepared to discuss the fundamental issues with Khrushchev, Eisenhower's consultations in Europe will be pointless since both sides will merely reiterate the views outlined in Geneva. If, on the other hand, this is to be the start of a major diplomatic initiative, I fear the President's lightning visit is bound to prove inadequate. Personally, I believe the first of these contingencies applies and that it is only in the unlikely event of Khrushchev putting forward some new proposals during his visit that talks among the Western Powers should be resumed.

'If my view of the situation is correct, by far the most important part of the President's tour will be his meeting with General de Gaulle, for, while there are at present no new problems affecting the West as a whole, there are problems – difficult ones at that – affecting relations between the United States and France.

'The latter is utterly dominated by the personality of the General. There is, in fact, no longer any such thing as French policy – neither in the press, nor in Parliament, nor even in the Government. There is solely the policy of the General. This being the case, the General's character is the key to the whole situation.

Those who fail to see this are liable to commit the gravest of errors. In discussing this problem with General Norstad I once heard him say: "In his meetings with General de Gaulle, the President will be calm, friendly and generous." I must admit that the last of these epithets fills me with apprehension. The Americans must not be allowed to delude themselves that they can succeed with General de Gaulle by means of a few minor concessions. It is essential that they meet his chief demands. The General is not the sort of man to be satisfied with a diplomatic *pourboire*.

'There are, I believe, three principal issues to be faced:

'1 France's participation in formulating strategy throughout the world.

'2 Political responsibility for any use of nuclear weapons outside the framework of NATO.

'3 Support for French policy in Algeria.

'First of all it must be acknowledged that these three problems are real. A strategy strictly confined to the areas covered by the Washington Treaty clearly fails to take full account of the magnitude of the Communist threat, which is just as much present in Africa and Asia as it is in Europe. In view of this, France is rightly concerned – since her interests in Africa are considerable – at the fact that this essential effort to co-ordinate the defence of Europe and that of Africa is at present lacking, and she intends to play a role here commensurate both with geographical position and her interests.

'In his various recent messages, General de Gaulle has spoken of this problem and has posed it correctly. However, his solution – the establishment of a three-power directory – seems to me wholly mistaken. There are many reasons why I think as I do, but one may suffice for the present: the creation of a genuine three-power directory would quickly result in the demise of the Atlantic Alliance. It would inevitably cause the small Powers of Western Europe to look to neutrality for their salvation, and this would seriously weaken the West. The directory is both an unworkable and a wrong-headed scheme. Something else must therefore be found. Personally, I am not yet quite sure what exactly should be done, but I do feel that a solution could be devised by means of more systematic, flexible and restricted consultations. At all events, what is needed is that the Americans, and more especially the President, should show some understanding of, and interest in, this problem and make it clear that they are prepared to help in the search for a solution. I am sure that this would be enough to see us through our difficulties.

'This problem of world strategy is linked with that of the possible use of nuclear weapons outside the NATO area. If I understand General de Gaulle rightly, it is not his wish that France should enjoy a right of veto over American policy. What he is asking for is advance consultation with regard to any such action, and he says that if the Americans were to disregard any advice by him against such action, they would by this very act create a new situation which might have a bearing on the application of the Washington Treaty. This faces us with a very important and delicate problem. I do not believe this is the right time to raise it, since we are probably dealing with hypothetical situations which will in any case never arise in practice but the discussion of which might nevertheless create doubt in certain quarters regarding the strength of the Alliance. However this may be, I feel President Eisenhower should be warned that some such question may be raised during the course of his talks with General de Gaulle. We must make sure that no such surprise is sprung upon the President, and he must, therefore, be given time to consider his reply.

'Lastly, as regards Algeria, I do not believe the General will be in a position to determine his policy between now and the end of the month. If I am right, it would be best if the Americans promised not to vote for any resolution in the United Nations which France is not prepared to accept, and they should use their influence to persuade their friends to follow suit. In this context we must bear in mind the all-important fact that only General de Gaulle, and he alone, can devise and impose a liberal solution to the Algerian problem. It is therefore our duty to help him. If, contrary to my prediction, the French Government does succeed in defining its policy, it would be highly desirable for the Americans to support it publicly and unequivocally.

'If, in their conversations, the President and the General do not deal with this problem, these talks will not only be pointless but positively harmful, for they will allow ambiguities to persist which might have serious consequences for NATO.

'You will be the first, Mr Chancellor, to meet the President of the United States on his European tour. I therefore believe that what you say to him will be of exceptional importance, and this is why I have taken the liberty of writing to you at such length and so frankly.'

The day after his meeting with President Eisenhower, the Chancellor sent me a brief note which read as follows:

'I have discussed at length and in considerable detail the subject of France and Algeria with President Eisenhower. I stressed Algeria's importance to Europe. I believe my efforts will prove successful provided de Gaulle makes his intentions as regards Algeria clear, at least in rough outline. Eisenhower stressed the importance he attaches to NATO and to European integration. He also declared that the era of two-Power control, as it existed during the war, has gone for good.'

I had done my duty. I had tried, within the limits of my means, to point out the dangers ahead and to be helpful. I had drawn the attention of the 'top brass' to the real issues. I had warned them of the difficulties that lay ahead and had managed to do so while remaining loyal and impartial towards all concerned. My only regret is that my efforts were not more successful.

I was to meet the Chancellor again at Stikker's villa in Menaggio in September 1960. All those who had been present at our meeting the previous year were again there. On this occasion it was not Britain's attitude which disturbed the German Chancellor, but France's. He had just met General de Gaulle at Rambouillet. After a long talk with the General, he was by no means reassured about the future of Europe and NATO.

As regards the European community, the General had made clear his objections to the type of organization provided for in the Treaty of Rome and, more particularly, to the role the EEC Commission was intended to play. He believed that all this must be changed, if necessary by revising the treaty. Referring to the Atlantic Alliance, he had put to the Chancellor all the grievances – relating to nuclear armaments and military integration – with which I was so familiar. 'One only fights well under one's own flag' – those had been his words. He had then touched upon a rather more personal matter – the independence with which NATO was conducting its affairs on French soil – and had mentioned as an example the fact that Herr Strauss, who was then German Defence Minister, had paid a visit to General Norstad without requesting an interview with de Gaulle himself. In the Chancellor's eyes, de Gaulle was altogether too touchy – an aspect of his personality for which, he thought, we must all accept some part of the blame. He advised us to bear this point in mind and not to forget to show the General the proper degree of deference.

The Chancellor thought it best not to oppose the General's views too strongly. He told us he had asked de Gaulle to indicate what changes he thought should be made in NATO, and the General had handed him a memorandum dealing with the subject, which, however, seemed rather vague. The Chancellor had written a long letter in reply to which he had not yet received an answer.

After this account of his meeting with the French Head of State, the Chancellor turned to General Norstad and vigorously criticized American policy. He said the Americans were not firm enough. The State Department was leaving its delegate to the Atlantic Council without instructions far too long. This was the reason why it was impossible to counteract de Gaulle's dangerous centrifugal tendencies.

General Norstad replied by developing certain new ideas regarding the military organization of the Alliance. He suggested that a NATO nuclear strike force should be established which would be under the control of the Atlantic Council and at the disposal of the Allied Supreme Commander. Having listened carefully to this recital, the Chancellor said how pleased he was and readily endorsed this formula. I then remarked that I doubted very much if General de Gaulle would be prepared to accept it, but the Chancellor said I was wrong and that a force which would enable NATO to act independently would undoubtedly be acceptable to the General.

The future was to show that the Chancellor was wrong and I was right. I have often been amazed at the inability of General de Gaulle's partners to understand him. They showed an incredible degree of optimism and continually deluded themselves that it was possible to convince the General or work out an agreement with him. De Gaulle made the best of these illusions. Stage by stage he pursued his policy, aimed at the destruction of the Atlantic Alliance, and he managed to bring about the situation which eventually arose in 1967 without those who did not share his way of thinking ever having forced him to show his hand. During these prolonged exchanges, the General's superior diplomatic skill was always in evidence. I detest his ideas, but I am bound to acknowledge the skill with which he ensured their triumph.

The agreement between Chancellor Adenauer and General Norstad created an atmosphere of optimism. The two men were only too glad to think they had found a solution to the most urgent problems then facing the Atlantic Alliance. Only de Staercke and I were sceptical.

Subsequently, Chancellor Adenauer was to remain blind to the facts of the situation even when events had shown that he had been wrong to believe that the General had changed his mind. In fact, it was Adenauer who, little by little, adopted his partner's ideas about European and NATO issues. He failed to resist de Gaulle's deliberate bid to seduce him. Joint prayers in Rheims Cathedral; joint reviews of French and German troops marching side by side; embraces from yesterday's enemy in front of the television cameras – this was enough to confuse a man whose advanced age had weakened his powers of judgement.

39

My Resignation

The latent Franco-American dispute was my major pre-occupation in 1959 and 1960. My disquiet was increased by a growing premonition that I would never solve this problem. At times I allowed my impatience, and worse, my displeasure, to show through. I became more deeply disillusioned still when it fell to my lot to deal with Mr Herter's 'Ten-Year Plan' in the Atlantic Council.

At the meeting of the Ministerial Council in December 1959, Mr Herter – with the best of intentions, I am sure – proposed that we should draw up a plan for the Alliance's activities during the ensuing ten years up to 1969 – when the partners to the Alliance would be free to give one year's notice of their intention to quit. Mr Herter merely mooted the idea and left the detailed elaboration to the Atlantic Council. For the Secretary-General this was a difficult task and a heavy responsibility. Not only did I fail, but in failing I came up against so many difficulties that I lost heart. As my hopes grew dimmer, my interest in the work I was doing gradually diminished. I came to realize that the Alliance would never live up to my earlier expectations and was forced to conclude that it was now past its peak. In the circumstances, I thought it best to make room for another. I was coming to feel more and more that all I was achieving by my repeated efforts was to exasperate the ministers concerned and that they, for their part, thought my insistence on the need to discuss controversial issues exaggerated and, at times, out of place.

Before the Council meeting due to be held in December 1960, I had many more talks with my colleagues. In September, October and November, I presided over meetings of the permanent representatives at weekly intervals. The idea was that we should draft NATO's ten-year plan on the basis of a document I had put before them. I made virtually no headway.

On the political plane, several of the permanent representatives rejected all proposals aimed at strengthening the system of consultation. Their governments were afraid they might be forced to shoulder new responsibilities and possibly even to take upon themselves fresh commitments.

As for the economic problems, most of the governments were opposed to any real NATO involvement in this field. In response to my repeated pleas, they objected that nothing must be done liable to hamper the work of the OECD. There was thus a fundamental difference of approach between them and myself. Without wishing to detract from the importance of the OECD and the value of its work, I was convinced that, in view of its composition, it would never be able to evolve a genuinely united policy. I was certain at that time – as indeed I am to this day – that economic issues, whatever they may be, but more especially those connected with the relations between the Western Powers and the underdeveloped countries and the Communist world, must be seen as merely one aspect of a global policy. On no account must they be treated as a purely technical matter. To me it seemed that NATO was the right place to settle these issues. It was therefore my constant endeavour to divest the Alliance of its excessive emphasis on military problems and to ensure that all aspects of peaceful coexistence were discussed within its framework.

In the event, the rule of unanimity foiled my efforts and all I could do was to take note of our differences and, whenever possible, to suggest compromise solutions. I was only too aware of their inadequacy.

I stressed repeatedly how discouraged and disillusioned I was. I found the meeting of the Council of Ministers in December 1960 particularly disappointing. After all the trouble we had been through, the document which it finally fell to my lot to present to the Council was bad. It reflected our inability to make any progress. The ensuing discussion, too, was mediocre. Mr Herter made a speech which was in the main devoted to the military effort of the Alliance. In a few very terse sentences he rejected all the French views. The United States opposed the creation of new nuclear forces – a development which, according to Washington, would result in new diversions among the members of the Alliance, duplication of effort and hence waste of resources. It would, he went on, give rise to rivalry in the nuclear sphere within the Alliance. Mr Herter proclaimed himself categorically in favour of a 'multilateral' effort and gave a rough outline of what was in his mind in this context.

So far as I remember, the French representative did not even trouble to speak up for his government's point of view – so wide was the gulf which separated it from the ideas Mr Herter had outlined on behalf of the United States.

General de Gaulle's decision was irrevocable. He was determined to pursue his policy without taking any further note of his partners' wishes. We were going through a crisis without, apparently, most of the ministers realizing its gravity at the time.

In his statement, which consisted of forty-eight paragraphs, Mr Herter only devoted one to the subject of political consultation. He promised that there would be consultations within NATO without limit as to the geographical areas involved. In another part of his statement he dealt with economic affairs. In this context, he said the United States would seek to cooperate with the other Powers within the framework of the OECD rather than NATO.

It was now clear to me that the ten-year plan must be considered a failure, that the dispute with France had been accepted as a *fait accompli* and that there was no question of our pursuing any sort of activity in the economic sphere in the Atlantic Alliance. Mr Herter's speech only served to increase my concern and seemed to bear out my most pessimistic forebodings.

At this meeting of the Ministerial Council an incident occurred which made my cup of bitterness run over. The Portuguese Foreign Minister made a vigorous and emotional plea on behalf of his country's colonial policy. Although personally I was rather doubtful whether this was a wise thing for him to do, I thought it only right that the Council should not allow such a plea to go unanswered. What sort of a system of political consultation was it if one of the members of the Alliance could make a speech on a question of vital importance to his country without any of the other allies so much as opening their mouths to approve or reject his views. This silence was much more disturbing than any reply, however negative and critical, would have been. It reflected a lack of interest which could not but endanger the cohesion of the Alliance.

During this Council of Ministers I experienced one disappointment after another. I believe that when I made this clear I did so with rather too much emphasis and, for the first time, I sensed that the members of the Council disapproved both of the tone and the content of my arguments.

As so often in my life, my reaction was immediate. As soon as the session was over, I requested the permanent representatives to join me in my office, and I informed them that I wished to resign. They were kind enough to protest and assured me that I enjoyed the entire confidence both of the representatives and of their ministers. They asked me to think the matter over and as I was anxious not to harm the Alliance in any way and did not wish to give my gesture undue publicity, I agreed. But I had made up my mind to go.

A month went by, however. It was taken up by various negotiations. I felt some hesitation in confirming my decision to resign. When one has held a position of some importance one always tends to think oneself indispensable. I continued to believe in the need for the Atlantic Alliance and now I also nurtured a secret hope that the announcement of my impending departure would act as a spur to the governments which were holding back. My hope was in vain.

On 31 January, with the agreement of the permanent delegates, I issued a statement announcing my decision, which I justified by a reference to my desire to return to Belgian politics. This, while not exactly untrue, was not the whole truth.

On 13 February 1961, I sent a long letter to President

Kennedy in which I explained my views. I quote the text below, omitting only some paragraphs dealing with the military situation of the Alliance:

'Dear Mr President,

'I greatly regret that circumstances have prevented me from cooperating with your Administration and that my work in NATO is to be cut short by my return to Belgium. However, before relinquishing my post, I thought I should put to you, with complete candour, my thoughts on the Atlantic Alliance and the problems which confront it. Perhaps – and certainly this is what I would wish – my few remarks will prove useful to you.

'In 1949, the Western Powers, by signing the Treaty of Washington, gave a fitting reply to the Communist threat as it then was. The treaty was a reaction essentially confined to Europe and to the military sphere. Since 1949 the Atlantic Alliance has attained its main objective: it has put a stop to Communist expansion in Europe. This is a great success. Were the Alliance to be destroyed or even merely weakened, the conditions which for ten years allowed Soviet imperialism to expand victoriously in Europe would undoubtedly recur. It would be a grave mistake to allow this to happen.

'However, in 1961 we no longer face the same problems. Having been halted in Europe, the Communist offensive has continued in Asia, Africa and South America. The nuclear monopoly which the United States once enjoyed is a thing of the past. The Communist offensive has shifted to the economic field and has found fertile ground in the underdeveloped countries. I believe Mr Khrushchev is telling the truth when he says that Communism, at least for the present, does not wish to expand by force of arms. At the same time, however, I am convinced he has not abandoned the hope of seeing Communism dominate the world. His aim is to isolate free Europe and North America. If we are encircled in twenty-five years' time and reduced to the position of a small minority surrounded by vast

347

masses of humanity indifferent towards or even hostile towards us, the fate of our civilization will rapidly be sealed at our adversary's time of choosing.

'The Atlantic Alliance – admirably though it answered its purpose in 1949 – must therefore adjust itself to the new conditions without delay. This problem of adaptation is the basic issue to be faced. It would appear that some of the members of the Alliance are averse to taking part in the effort required.

'Countries such as Canada, Norway and Denmark feel that they cannot go beyond their splendid effort in 1949. At all events, they refuse to undertake any fresh military commitments and are even reluctant to associate themselves closely with the policies of their allies in areas beyond the geographical limits set by the Treaty of Washington. While they are prepared to take part in a search for a common stance on European problems such as those of Berlin and Germany, they are disinclined to do so in regard to issues arising in other parts of the world. And yet, it is these issues which nowadays are the most numerous, the most pressing, and perhaps the most important, of all those facing us.

'Since nothing can be done in NATO except by a unanimous vote, the reluctant attitude of some of the partners hampers the necessary process of adaptation or, at the very least, prevents that process from being accomplished with the requisite speed.

'It would be unfair to put all the blame for our shortcomings on these three Powers alone. The France of General de Gaulle – for reasons that are well-known – is angry with the organization and treats it as an instrument of minor importance, making no effort to hide that she would greatly prefer a three-Power policy to the fifteen-Power version the Alliance has forced on her.

'Only vigorous US leadership can enable us to solve this problem. If the United States fearlessly wagers everything on the Alliance, it may succeed in persuading all the others to follow suit. Is the United States ready to play this part? That is the crux of the problem.

This is the background against which we have to examine our various activities.

'*Political situation:* The effectiveness of the Alliance depends on our success in the area of political consultation. During these last few years, some real progress has been made, but much remains to be done. As the field covered by the processes of consultation expands, so our difficulties increase.

'As regards the problems which arise within the geographical limits of the Alliance, results have been good. We have been able to agree on a joint policy on such issues as Germany and Berlin, and this policy has been maintained and applied by our joint efforts. This is doubtless a very important achievement.

'In relation to the problems arising outside the geographical limits of the Alliance, the need for consultation has, in general, been accepted, but the results have so far not been very satisfactory. Member countries on occasion act without consulting their partners. Above all, consultation, where attempted, has failed to produce a common policy.

'The latest instance, occurred quite recently in connection with the Congo. America's ideas on this subject as we know them have been such as to make it impossible for the French, the Belgians and the Portuguese and, I believe, the British also – in other words the Powers most immediately concerned with African problems – to endorse them.

'What has been termed the "American plan" has not been discussed at all within the framework of NATO. In fact, the allies of the United States were informed of it at the same time as its adversaries. This gave rise to a somewhat difficult discussion in the Permanent Council, both as regards the tactics to be adopted and the substance of the problem. Such episodes are dangerous for the future of the Alliance. Commonsense tells us that one cannot be united in one part of the world and at odds in another.

'I am well aware that all this creates problems and difficulties for a great country such as the United States which has interests to defend in every part of the world, but I am none the less convinced that a crucial choice must be made between two alternatives. At this time, this choice could be defined as follows: does the United States attach more importance to the UN than to NATO? In other words, is it ready, in order to win the support or the friendship of the non-aligned countries, to go so far as to sacrifice the interests or to hurt the feelings of its NATO allies? This did in fact occur in connection with the Suez affair and Algeria. More recently, the same thing happened in connection with the Congo and the Portuguese territories in Africa. The repeated occurrence of such situations greatly weakens the cohesion of the Atlantic Alliance.

'A balance could probably be struck. Personally, I am certain that this can only be done by means of increasingly close, trusting and, above all, prompt, consultations so that a situation is reached where no government is ever made to feel that it has been faced with a *fait accompli*.

'In theory, this may seem very complicated, but in fact it is not. It is best to talk things over before taking a decision since a discussion must in any case take place sooner or later; delay often only makes things more difficult. If I may, I should like to repeat that the future of the Alliance and its efficiency depend on the way we conduct our political consultations. In this matter also, the example set by the United States will be decisive.

'*Economic problems*: For years, those who have had occasion to discuss the future of NATO have insisted on the importance to be attached to Article 2 of the Washington Treaty, i.e. to economic problems. There is no denying that our success in this area has been very uneven. During these last few months economic problems have been causing us growing concern. Though the work of the Economic Committee of the Alliance has made progress and certain important problems have been submitted to it and are now under examination – for example the oil policy of the USSR – we are not yet able to say if this work will produce any positive results. There are, however, other problems to be faced

– crucial in my view – posed by the Communist offensive in the underdeveloped countries. What we must decide is whether these matters should be dealt with within the framework of NATO or submitted to other international organizations. For myself, I have always believed NATO to be the right place. I must admit, however, that this view is far from being shared by all the NATO governments. Several of them – probably a majority – are of the opinion that NATO is not the place to discuss these problems and they would rather see this agenda entrusted to the OECD [Organization for Economic Cooperation and Development].

'I fear, however, that this body, which numbers several neutral countries among its members, would prove a difficult, if not an impossible, venue for such a discussion. The fact is that the problems we are facing are as much political as they are economic. I fail to see how Austria, Sweden or Switzerland could take part in measures to counteract the policies of the Communist bloc. Their refusal to undertake any such commitment would seem to rule out any such notion.

'Even if it is decided that NATO is not to have executive powers in the economic sphere, it ought nevertheless to remain the place where Western policy *vis-à-vis* the underdeveloped countries is laid down, though it may be left to another organization to carry it out. For my part, firmly convinced as I am that the battle against Communism will in the immediate future be fought in the economic rather than in the military sphere and that it will take place in Africa rather then in Europe, I believe that NATO is doomed to fail in its efforts if it is denied the right to deal with these issues in a comprehensive way.

'The more NATO is treated as a purely military organization, the weaker it will be – at least in Europe. The Organization would, on the other hand, be vastly strengthened if it were allowed to play its part in the solution of the most vital issue of our time – that of the underdeveloped countries. We shall have to define our position in regard to this problem in the long-term plan for political action due to be submitted to the conference in Oslo next May.

'If I were asked to sum up my remarks in a single sentence, I should say that the question that must be answered is whether the members of the Alliance are prepared to show greater willingness than hitherto to act in concert. The reply the United States gives to this question will be absolutely decisive. It will determine our entire future. It is my fervent hope that its answer will be "yes".'

This letter, dated 13 February 1961, was the political testament I bequeathed to NATO. My position as Secretary-General had enabled me to examine the problems facing the Alliance more consistently and impartially than most ministers. I was at the hub of a great organization and was aware of the scope which existed for extending its activities. I was also in a better position than others to predict future developments.

The years I spent in Paris taught me many lessons – interesting and, on the whole, agreeable ones – even though it remains true that I did not succeed in every facet of my task.

Speaking at the farewell dinner which the permanent delegates gave in my honour, André de Staercke, their doyen, declared:

'Your constant aim has been to reduce the gap between what NATO is and what it could be. Called upon as you were to choose between two alternatives – a vast Ministry of Defence serving an international alliance or an instrument of the Atlantic Community to be used on a steadily expanding scale – you followed the call of your convictions and your temperament. You have worked unsparingly to promote the progress of our community, and your presence amongst us has been both a challenge and an achievement.

'Responding to what our Norwegian colleague the other day called the "duty to be impatient", you urged upon us the need for solidarity. You made us confront the pressing problems facing us while, at the same time, giving us hope that we would indeed solve them if only we were prepared to translate our sense of unity into action.'

These few sentences were dictated by de Staercke's loyal friendship for me and his excessive kindness. However inaccurate, they describe well the goal I had set myself. Perhaps it was an ideal which was too far removed from reality, but I do not regret having believed in it.

I left my post on 31 March to return to Belgian politics. One month later I was reappointed Foreign Minister.

PART SEVEN

Minister for the Last Time

40

Africa

In 1960, during my absence from Belgium, I was in no way involved in the Congo crisis. Personally, I did not feel that the matter had been handled well. I was opposed to the calling of a round table conference, since it seemed obvious to me that a discussion conducted along these lines was bound to end in victory for the extremists. In the circumstances, the moderates dared not show themselves less eager for immediate independence than the most violent extremists. The Belgian Government, for its part, submitted to the pressures, which it knew to be irresistible. The results of these negotiations exceeded our worst fears. Independence was promised for 30 June 1960. This was a decision taken on the spur of the moment, and it was made all the more dangerous by officially inspired optimism in Belgium and the joyful amazement of the Congolese.

Once these decisions had been taken, the King called a Crown Council – a constitutional procedure only rarely employed in Belgium. The ministers are hardly ever consulted by the monarch as a body. I have somewhat painful memories of the occasion. Van Zeeland and I were the only ones to express our fears and doubts. De Schrijver and Rolin, speaking in reply, sought to justify the action that had just been taken. Rolin delivered a lyrical speech about the historic event in which he had just taken part. With the lack of realism so characteristic of him, he eulogized his Congolese negotiating partners, attributing to them every conceivable political, civic and human virtue, and proudly claimed responsibility for the adventure into which Belgium had been plunged. It was one of his most typical and, I feel bound to say, objectionable speeches. All we could do was to bow to the new realities and to wish those responsible good luck. Their motives were complex. Some of them were perfectly honourable, others less so. To understand why they acted as they did, one has to bear in mind the following facts of the situation: the trend towards decolonization; the war in Algeria, which seemed a warning example to be avoided at all costs; and the fact that the vast majority of Belgians were not prepared to spend one single sou, let alone lose one single man, in defence of the colony.

Those who thought they were responding to the spirit of the times – or even imagined they had stolen a march on it – were actuated by generous political motives in granting its independence to the Congo on terms more favourable than those accorded by France and Britain to some of their former colonies. On the other hand, there were some Belgians, too clever by half, who thought they would be able to hang on to all their possessions while at the same time pretending they were giving them up. Between them, the idealists, the weaklings and a few calculating individuals managed to put an end to a venture – amidst an officially-inspired atmosphere of euphoria – which, for a small country like Belgium, had not been without its moments of greatness.

The awakening which was to follow was as harsh as the earlier illusions had been pleasant. The independence celebrations were rendered embarrasing by an insolent speech made by Patrice Lumumba in the presence of the King. The mutiny of the police force – the *force publique* – the following week was the first of a series of events which saddled Belgium in the eyes of the world with a deplorable reputation for incompetence and hypocrisy.

The treatment we received in the United Nations was disgraceful. Our best intentions were distorted and our mistakes – unfortunately we did commit some – were exploited beyond measure.

I watched this tragedy from Paris and did my best to help the Government, trying to secure for it the assistance of the member countries of NATO. One of the mistakes of the Belgian Government was that it had failed to make sure of the support of its allies in determining its policy for the Congo.

André de Staercke shared my feelings on the subject. He went to Brussels before the final decisions were taken to try to convince the Belgian ministers of the need to seek the help of the members of the Alliance. He failed in his mission; his advice was rejected. The men responsible for Belgium's policy were convinced that they were about to give the world a new great lesson in wisdom.

When the UN was informed of the situation in the Congo after Belgian troops had been sent there to protect the lives of their compatriots and the most violent and unjust accusations were levelled against Belgium, not one of her allies spoke up in her defence. The friendliest among them kept quiet. Their silence bore witness to their embarrassment. The United States opposed us. In the United Nations, the USA all too often took the side of the Afro-Asians regardless of the legitimate interests of its NATO partners. At that time, the dream of swift decolonization, which dated back to the Roosevelt era, still inspired the policies of the State Department!

Let us recall the facts: during the first days of July 1960 the police mutinied at Thysville, Leopoldville, Luluabourg and Elisabethville. The Congolese authorities were unable to cope with the situation and the life of some tens of thousands of Belgians seemed to be in danger. As a result, the Government in Brussels felt compelled to send out troops to the Congo. President Kasavubu's response to this legitimate move was to request the aid of the United Nations. The situation was made still more complex by the fact that Katanga, under the leadership of Moise Tshombe, had proclaimed its secession. This event greatly added to our difficulties. Many people accused the Belgian Government of having secretly aided and abetted Tshombe's move. Some denounced the alleged duplicity of the Belgians who, at the very moment they were granting its independence to the Congo, were evidently making sure they would be able to stay on in Katanga, the colony's richest province.

The full facts of this event are not yet known. For myself, I am convinced that in July 1960 the Brussels Government had no intention whatever of trying to retain its rights in Katanga. The policies adopted subsequently, however, were not always as clear as they might have been and the benevolent sympathy with which Tshombe was treated seemed to justify the accusations of duplicity levelled at Brussels. There can, moreover, be little doubt that when the troubles broke out in July, big business looked on the secession with favour. What mattered to the companies was the maintenance of order and their ability to carry on their lucrative activities. To what extent did they intervene? How far were they involved in inspiring these events? I would not wish to pronounce too categorically on these matters, but I do believe the companies cannot be absolved of all guilt. For a number of years they pursued a policy which differed from that of the Government, as I was to find out to my cost.

In the Security Council, which had been called to discuss the Congolese complaint, the Belgian delegate supported Kasavubu's request for intervention by UN troops. Was this intelligent, and was it good diplomacy?

On 13 July 1960, the Security Council adopted a resolution calling on the Belgian Government to withdraw its troops from the Congolese Republic and authorized the Secretary-General to 'take, in consultation with the Government of the Republic, the appropriate steps with a view to furnishing to that Government the requisite military assistance until such time as the local security forces are in a position fully to meet their responsibilities'.

The Congolese adventure was about to begin for the United Nations, and it was to assume even larger proportions at the instigation of the Secretary-General, Dag Hammarskjoeld, whose role in the affair was to prove decisive. He was anxious that the United Nations should play as important a part in the Congo as possible. For this he cannot be blamed, but one may well ask if Hammarskjoeld did not indulge in risky policies and take too much upon himself. He invariably put as wide an interpretation as possible on the resolutions of the Security Council. His idea was to chance his hand in an experiment which, if it succeeded, would perpetuate the glory of the UN. In actual fact, the operation was beyond the Organization's means. It soon became obvious that Hammarskjoeld was bent not only on helping to re-establish order, but that he wanted to play a decisive part in the administration of the new state. His ambitious ideas were reflected in his report of 6 August 1960 to the Security Council. He put forward a vast scheme. The UN civil affairs chief was to be backed by a large group of experts who were to have powers to deal with virtually the entire field of administration.

Events were to show that the UN did not have enough men at its disposal competent to meet all these tasks. Some of the UN personnel were poorly equipped for their duties, while others went about their business without showing the necessary measure of impartiality.

The basic philosophy of the Secretary-General led him to adopt an anti-Belgian attitude. By acting as he did he thought he was doing his duty as an opponent of colonialism. For instance, he advanced the untenable proposition that the whole of the considerable technical assistance which Belgium was continuing to render the Congo must pass through the hands of the UN. He also covered with his authority those of his colleagues who were doing their best to drive out the Belgian experts who had stayed behind in the Congo to cooperate with the local government and who enjoyed its confidence.

This policy was soon to land the UN in a series of grave disputes, not only with the Government in Brussels but also with Leopoldville.

When I became Foreign Minister again on 25 April 1961, the situation was bad. The Congo had broken off diplomatic relations with Belgium. The Katanga secession was giving rise to grave concern and the UN intervention was causing serious problems.

A Government statement issued in April 1961 defined Belgium's position with regard to the Congo. It underlined that we were determined to draw all the legal and political consequences which flowed from our recognition of the government in Leopoldville as the only government of the Congo. I felt that, given skilful diplomacy, the desired objective should be within our reach.

I intended to cooperate loyally with the United Nations, to meet all its reasonable demands, but knew that the attitude of the Secretary-General and, even more so, that

361

of some of his officials, was bound to cause a good deal of friction.

I was determined to complete the repatriation – which the UN was insistently demanding – of the Belgian political and military advisers in Leopoldville and Elisabethville; on the other hand, it was also my duty to protect my compatriots and to safeguard our right to deal directly with the Congolese Government.

My first aim was to explain my policy to the members of NATO, since I felt it essential to put an end to Belgium's isolation, which had persisted since July 1960. At a meeting of the Atlantic Council in Oslo in May 1961 I therefore made a comprehensive statement on the situation and defined our immediate aims.

I began with a general observation, noting that it was beyond Belgium's resources to settle the problems of the Congo unaided. I said Belgium could only act effectively if her motives were understood and if she were supported by her allies. I expected to be advised and informed by them and was ready to listen to criticisms of our policies. In brief, I made it plain that I intended to apply, in my capacity as Foreign Minister, the principle of thorough consultation which I had advocated while I was Secretary-General of NATO and explained that I was also anxious to cooperate with the UN in implementing the resolutions of the Security Council.

My statement was well received and there was general agreement that the principles I had put forward were correct: what I wanted was a neutral Congo which would respect Western interests; a stable and independent federation established by the Congolese themselves, with the UN playing an important part on condition that it cooperated with the Kasavubu Government and refrained from imposing its solutions by force.

Dean Rusk, speaking for the United States, and Lord Home, for Britain, supported my views. I knew that I would be able henceforth to count on their cooperation and left Oslo well satisfied.

The second stage of my diplomatic action led to a meeting with Hammarskjoeld in Geneva on 12 July. It went off rather better than I had feared, although I had some difficulty in persuading the Secretary-General to see my point of view. He was hostile towards Belgium, very critical of her policy for the Congo and, I believe, he did not much like me personally. Up to then our relations had always been cool but correct. There were thus a good many obstacles to overcome. Nevertheless, we succeeded in agreeing on the terms of a protocol setting out the conditions for the repatriation of the Belgian military and political advisers from the Congo and Katanga. With regard to the Congo, the list of those concerned was to be drawn up by the Central Government. As for Katanga, the list was to be compiled by the UN. It was to be comprehensive, and its publication was intended to reassure those not included and thus to help calm the atmosphere. As it turned out, no problems arose in Leopoldville, since the Government there did not ask for a single Belgian to be withdrawn. In Katanga the protocol was not applied because the UN never presented the list it was to have drawn up.

Far from wishing to exploit this failure of the UN, I took vigorous action. By the beginning of September, of the 200 regular officers and NCOs serving with the Katanga gendarmerie, 145 had been repatriated; twenty-seven were on their way home; seventeen remained in Elisabethville to assist in running the Katanga gendarmerie in a temporary capacity, while twelve were directly subordinate to the Belgian Consulate, ready to help with the evacuation of Belgian civilians – a contingency that had to be borne in mind.

With regard to the mercenaries, despite the fact that it had never had any control over them, the preceding Belgian Government had issued a communiqué making it clear that the recruitment of Belgian citizens for service in foreign armed forces was a punishable offence. If those responsible were identified, they would be tried and sentenced. We went on to declare that we were determined to confiscate the passport of any Belgian who continued serving with the Katanga gendarmerie. No one could expect us to do more.

Between the beginning of July 1961, when I met Hammarskjoeld, and the beginning of November, when the UN undertook its first military operation in Katanga, the situation became increasingly complex. Interminable negotiations began between Hammarskjoeld, Premier Adoula of the Congo and Tshombe. It would take up too much space to go into the details of these exchanges.

One of the reasons why the attempts to bring about a reconciliation failed – attempts in which I took part by ceaselessly advising Tshombe to meet Adoula and to do so in a conciliatory spirit – was the presence in the Congo of Mr Conor Cruise O'Brien, the senior representative of the Secretary-General. Mr O'Brien was an Irish diplomat who had joined the UN staff. In my opinion he lacked both tact and judgement. His dream was to defeat Tshombe. It may well be that he thought he would thus prove himself a loyal servant of the Security Council, and he may even have sincerely believed that he was helping the Congo. For my part, I find it difficult to determine just what his motives were, never having met Mr O'Brien. At all events, he appeared maladroit and interfering. O'Brien was a principal supporter of the UN troops' armed intervention and to justify himself, he never hesitated to make inaccurate reports on his activities. He was not I think a man who inspired confidence and showed few of the qualities one is entitled to expect of a senior international civil servant. However, Hammarskjoeld, and later U Thant, covered him with their authority despite the fact that he seemed to be interpreting their instructions as he pleased. His chiefs were left to face the consequences of his actions, which often gave the appearance of having been decided on his own responsibility and without adequate reflection.

At dawn on 13 September, the UN troops – about nine thousand strong – launched an offensive aimed at occupying Elisabethville. They were engaged by the Katanga gendarmerie, a force of about eleven thousand men commanded by mercenaries. The offensive was not a success and was halted after a few days.

On 17 September, Hammarskjoeld left New York to meet Tshombe in order to conclude a cease-fire. The accident in which he met his death was announced on the 18th. On 20 September, the talks between Tshombe and the representative of the UN were resumed and an agreement was signed.

Why did the UN act as it did? The reasons given have always been confused. Belgium was put in the dock by O'Brien's public statements and his reports. He claimed that the first shots had been fired from the windows of the Belgian Consulate and that Belgian officers were behind certain local attacks on UN troops. He never submitted any proof to support his allegations, which I easily refuted in the Security Council. The fact is that O'Brien was ready to grasp at any pretext to justify his own pet schemes and personal policies.

The cease-fire was not well received by all the members of the United Nations. The Government in Leopoldville, too, had certain reservations. It did not welcome the direct contacts which were taking place between the UN Secretary-General and Tshombe.

At the beginning of November, a number of African countries demanded that a meeting of the Security Council be called. They included Ethiopia, the Sudan and Nigeria. In a telegram addressed to the President of the Assembly, the Emperor of Ethiopia expressed concern at the situation that had arisen and disappointment at the fact that the UN had failed to put an end to the Katangan secession. He went on to call on the Security Council to give the UN troops 'clear and precise directives defining their duties and responsibilities'. It was becoming obvious that certain governments were prepared to see the problems of Katanga resolved by force of arms.

The Security Council met on 13 November and I asked to be allowed to attend it. It was essential that Belgium be represented. My country was liable to be subjected to violent criticism. On 15 November I made a speech to explain the Belgian Government's policy in reply to the attacks to which Belgium was being subjected from all sides.

The events of the preceding year – the hostility and malice with which so many countries had treated Belgium; the accusations levelled against us by O'Brien; the bias shown by several members of the 'tribunal' before which

I was to be arraigned – all this was bound to make my task difficult. However, my brief was well prepared and my intentions upright. I was not afraid of the battle that was to come.

Moreover, I still held several trump cards. I had been present in San Francisco when the Charter was drawn up and signed. I had been President of the Assembly and, during its early years, had played an important part in it. True, there were now new faces in the Security Council, but there were also some I had known for a long time, men with whom I had worked and who trusted and liked me. Among the UN officials were some of my former colleagues and friends. I was therefore not isolated, as my predecessor had been.

It was on this occasion that I first met Justin Bomboko, the Congolese Foreign Minister. During the riots of July 1960, he had taken a courageous stand to protect my compatriots. Although we had our disagreements, I realized immediately that here was a man I would be able to work with and one who was anxious to come to an understanding with me. Our relations were therefore good, and they were to get better still and to turn into friendship during the years which followed. It was this which enabled me to save the situation the following year.

My speech was long, impassioned, very frank, even brutally so in places. After I had finished, a good many people came up to me to say that they had not heard a European speak out so clearly and vigorously for a long time against the accusations – which had become a sort of ritual exercise – levelled against the former colonial Powers. They also praised me for having spoken my mind with regard to certain UN officials and made no secret of their pleasure at the stand I had taken.

I began my speech by taking the offensive. I referred to 'the obvious bias of certain UN officials in dealing with various Congolese issues arising out of Belgium's responsibilities and difficulties'. I went on to say that I had not come to New York with a persecution, and even less with a guilt, complex. I then proceeded to plead my country's cause. I recalled that my policy was based on two essential principles – recognition of the Leopoldville

Government as the sole legitimate authority in the Congo, and Belgium's readiness to cooperate with the United Nations – and went on to deal with the accusations made against Belgium. I believe that I succeeded in convincing those of my listeners who were impartial. Widening the scope of my speech, I severely criticized the draft resolution before the session, pointing to the dangers entailed in the possible resort to force which the resolution contemplated with a view to solving the Katanga problem, dangers to the white community in the Congo and the UN alike.

I concluded this part of my speech with these words:

'What you will do today – if you adopt the resolution as it now stands, if you accept the definition of a mercenary and "hostile element" proposed by M. Bomboko, if you go ahead with the operation you are organizing in Elisabethville – what all this amounts to in fact is a bid to hunt down the white man. The white man is to be left defenceless, he is to be deprived of a chance to plead his cause, he is to be left helpless. We would never accept such a situation in a civilized country, and what we cannot tolerate from a civilized country we can tolerate even less from the world's most important organization.'

Finally, I tried to show that, rather than use violence, the United Nations should attempt a diplomatic initiative to bring about a reconciliation. I then listed the factors which seemed to me to make such a policy possible.

My intervention ended in partial success. A resolution was adopted on 24 November and, for the first time for several months, it contained no accusations or condemnations of Belgium. This was an undeniable advance. On the other hand, I had not succeeded in persuading the Council to delete, or even to water down, the clause regarding the possibility of a resort to force. The Security Council decided to 'authorize the Secretary-General to act vigorously and, if need be, to use such force as may be necessary in order to apprehend forthwith, detain with a view to their eventual prosecution, or to expel, any foreign military or para-military personnel or political advisers not subordinate to the UN Command, as well as all mercenaries as defined under Paragraph 2 of the Security Council resolution of 21 February 1961'.

The Security Council thus prepared the ground for the action that was being plotted in New York by those who were out to avenge themselves for the defeat they had suffered in September. They were not slow to take advantage of the situation.

The results – predictable in view of the atmosphere that had been created – followed in due course. On 5 December 1961 the United Nations launched its second military operation against Katanga, and this time it ended in victory.

No doubt Tshombe had been unwise. His hesitations, his bellicose statements, his vacillating policy, the few acts of violence which he was unable to prevent or to put down, all this furnished those who were bent on using violence with the pretext they were looking for, if not with a genuine reason. On 5 December the UN officials announced that a plan for a military attack on the 'Blue Helmets' had been discovered. They said it provided for a general offensive. The same day the UN forces opened fire on the Katangan road block in order to restore communications between Elisabethville airport and the town. Thus began the hostilities, which in a matter of hours became widespread, U Thant having authorized his subordinates to take such military action, by land and air, as they deemed necessary. It was the chance O'Brien had been waiting for.

I have no desire to defend Tshombe's policies. I believe them to have been ill-advised because they were ambiguous. His ambivalent and inconsistent attitude was bound to irritate and worry all those who had dealings with him, even his most ardent well-wishers. However, I have always been convinced that the UN offensive was started deliberately by certain officials of the Organization and that the reasons invoked by them did not hold water.

When the famous plan for the general offensive was published at my express and repeated demand, it emerged that the document was dated September 1961. It had thus been drawn up three months before the start of the

UN operation. One glance at the plan was enough to show that it merely listed the defensive measures to be taken by the Katangan gendarmerie in the event of an offensive by the Congolese army or the UN forces. There was nothing in this document to indicate that the Katangan gendarmerie intended to start hostilities.

The plea that the UN forces had merely exercised their right of self-defence was equally feeble. The incidents which had occurred at the beginning of December, deplorable as they were, were in fact trivial and might have justified a police operation but certainly not the UN military offensive which eventually engulfed a large part of Katanga. The means employed by the United Nations both on land and in the air were considerable. The fighting continued until 20 December and ended in complete victory for the UN forces. The war was waged with great violence, without any effort being made to spare the lives of non-combatants or to avoid damage to private property. In Belgium, it gave rise to deep resentment and violent protest. Many Belgian civilians fell victim to these operations, which were executed with utter ruthlessness. Addressing the two Houses of Parliament when they met in joint session on 12 December, with the fighting still in progress, I had this to say:

'In actual fact, there can be no question of the UN forces exercising their right of self-defence. The resources employed are out of all proportion to the incidents which have occurred. What we are facing today is a warlike action in pursuit of which the UN has had no hesitation in bombing the centre of Elisabethville, art treasures, bridges and tunnels. The UN is waging its action a long way from Elisabethville, deep in the province of Katanga. It has ordered industrial installations to be bombed, and if the present operation continues for even a few days more, the UN may well restore to the Central Government a completely devastated and impoverished Katanga which will no longer be able to play its former important role in the Congo's economy. I believe this to be an intolerable situation, to say the least. It seems to me that when a Foreign Minister says to the United Nations that its methods are intolerable, that is as far as he can go.'

My speech was unanimously approved by Parliament, except for the Communists. My relations with the United Nations became very strained. I exchanged many telegrams with the Secretary-General, and their tone became increasingly ill-tempered. I felt displeased for a good many reasons. The UN was waging its military operations without observing the most rudimentary rules of warfare. Civilians were being killed and wounded, hospitals bombed, and industrial installations endangered. U Thant's reply was to invoke the resolution of the Security Council and the UN troops' right of self-defence.

While I was continuing my exchanges with the Secretary-General, I tried at the same time to persuade Tshombe to adopt a more constructive attitude. The fact that he finally agreed to meet Adoula at Kitona on 20 December was largely due to my sustained pressure. At Kitona, an agreement was hammered out between Tshombe and the Central Government. Tshombe agreed that the Congolese Constitution should apply to Katanga, he recognized the unity of the Congo in perpetuity and accepted Kasavubu as Head of State. He conceded that the authority of the Central Government should apply throughout the Republic. Finally, Tshombe undertook to see to it that the resolutions of the UN General Assembly and the Security Council were observed.

This agreement seemed to indicate that Katanga's secession was over. In fact, this assumption turned out to be false and the tragicomedy was to continue for another year. After the events at the end of 1961, relations between Belgium and the United States took a turn for the better and the two governments began to cooperate effectively. In July 1960 the United States had strongly supported the UN intervention. Without US support, the policy pursued first by Hammarskjoeld and then by U Thant would have been impossible. While it would not be true to say that the United States was hostile to Belgium during this difficult time for my country, we did not receive the support from our great ally which we had a right to expect.

After the UN troops had won their victory and Tshombe, by his attitude at Kitona, had given us all hope that a solution had been found to the problem of Katanga's secession, a rapprochement occurred between Washington and Brussels. This was made possible by the efforts of US Ambassador Douglas MacArthur, who helped me tremendously during that period. Our relations, which had at first been purely professional, soon turned into solid, trusting and lasting friendship. I felt free to reveal my thoughts to him, and MacArthur not only accurately conveyed my ideas to the State Department but, I am sure, pleaded my cause on many occasions. We would meet several times a week and, at times of crisis, several times a day. Thanks to his lucidity, I knew exactly what his Government wanted. I knew, too, that he had a clear idea of my aims and that my views would be conveyed to Washington undistorted. MacArthur became one of my team, which also numbered among its members Robert Rothschild, my Principal Private Secretary, and Etienne Davignon, my assistant secretary, as well as Albert Hupperts, the Head of the Congo Department, and Jean Van den Bosch, the Permanent Secretary of the Foreign Ministry.

Thanks to MacArthur, our relations with the American Administration continued to improve. Dean Rusk, Ambassador McGhee, Under-Secretary of State Mennen Williams, Harriman, and finally President Kennedy himself, all helped me greatly.

It was at that time that my relations with Kennedy were at their closest. I had met the President for the first time in 1959 at Harvard, the day I received my honorary doctorate of the famous university. What struck me above all was how incredibly young he looked. One had the impression that here was a shy young man. Later, after he had been elected President, I was astounded again and again at each of our meetings by the remarkable change in his personality. Never before had I seen the proposition that wisdom comes with responsibility confirmed so strikingly. I summed up my view of the President as follows: 'The first time I saw him he listened to me, the second time he questioned me, the third he gave me his views and the fourth he let me know his decisions.'

Much has been said about the charm he radiated. It was very real and was soon to be coupled with an air of quiet authority which was all the more impressive because it emanated from a young man. One felt he was bringing a new quality to politics, that thanks to him a new generation was making its mark. For those who in terms of years could have been his father or elder brothers, there was something refreshing in his personality, like a promise of a new dawn.

The culminating moment of our acquaintance came at the end of November 1962. I was in Washington at the time to try once more to find a solution to the Congolese problem. I had had a long discussion with Dean Rusk and his aides about a particularly involved diplomatic situation. We had agreed on the objective to be aimed at but differed as to the tactics to be adopted. We therefore decided to ask the President to arbitrate. He received us in the afternoon of 27 November. Instead of asking us into his study, he received us in the adjoining great drawing-room, where the Cabinet normally meets, and grouped around him were top officials of the State Department. Sitting opposite the President, I was a little intimidated by the impressive setting and the number of people ranged on the other side of the table. Dean Rusk first reviewed the situation in general terms with his usual courtesy and clarity and then proceeded to expound his own views. Having listened attentively to the Secretary of State, the President asked me to put my point of view, and I did so as best I could. The President reflected a while and then announced that he agreed with me. I must admit this gave me profound satisfaction.

I was to meet Kennedy for the last time a few weeks before his death. Our conversation was informal and friendly. It was a beautiful day and we stepped out into the garden which adjoins the presidential study. As we walked up and down, he spoke to me of his worries: the pending increase in the price of steel, which he had decided to veto, and China's progress in the nuclear field. Somebody took a photograph of us. To this day I have a print of it, sent me by the President with a cordial dedication.

Our meetings had been more informal, more intimate than at any time in the past and my sympathy and admiration for Kennedy greater than ever. I sensed that I was in the presence of a strong, responsible statesman, bent on achieving something great, and capable of so doing. I left him believing I would soon see him again and that I could always count on his support in the pursuit of our Atlantic and European policies.

Then came the sad day at Dallas. With countless thousands, I heard of the tragedy, and my tears mingled with theirs, tears shed over the loss of this young life, over this destiny unfulfilled. However brilliant his career may have been up to this point, Kennedy had not yet reached the limit of his potential. Instinctively, people throughout the world, stunned by the news of his death, felt that a great hope had died with him. History would have been different had Kennedy lived longer.

From the beginning of 1962 onwards I had many discussions with Washington. The hopes to which the Kitona agreement had given rise were soon to wane. Once the danger was over, Tshombe reverted to his equivocal policies, showered assurances of good will on all and sundry but never made any clear-cut promises. Adoula was not strong enough to impose his own views, and the UN representatives on the spot were caught up in a welter of chaotic activities.

Several meetings were held between Belgian and US representatives and at the beginning of the summer the US State Department, with my agreement, issued a long document which was sent to U Thant. The latter accepted it as it stood. Its provisions covered: a federal constitution for the Congo; the allocation of the tax revenue and foreign currency receipts among the central and provincial governments; the introduction of a single currency; the integration of the military forces in the Congo; the proclamation of a general amnesty and the re-establishment of a central government in which all political and regional groupings would be represented.

To achieve these ends, a four-stage procedure was envisaged. The first two stages provided for a gradual reconciliation: the third for economic sanctions to be imposed in the event of Katanga refusing to carry out the plan within the stated time; and the fourth for further measures, which were not clearly defined but which allowed for recourse to force in the event of the steps taken during phase three failing to achieve the desired result.

It was agreed that the document should be presented first to Adoula and then, if he accepted the plan, to Tshombe, and this was in fact done. On 23 August, Adoula accepted the plan with certain reservations regarding the action to be taken if unexpected difficulties were encountered in the execution of the plan. On 24 August the plan was presented to Tshombe in Elisabethville. In a note dated 2 September, Tshombe announced his agreement but, as was his wont, added a whole series of riders. Once again we felt – as we had felt after Kitona – that there was reason for hope, but once again these hopes proved vain. It was Tshombe who was mainly to blame, and even more so his European advisers, some of whom unfortunately were Belgians. Their policies bristled with reservations, ambiguities and contradictions. They thought they were proving their mettle as 'subtle diplomatists', but since they lacked any genuine political experience all they actually achieved was to irritate everyone concerned. Even those who were most anxious for a reconciliation finally lost patience. An interminable exchange of diplomatic notes began between Adoula, Tshombe, the UN and the US and Belgian Governments.

The worst snag was the allocation of resources and currency receipts between Katanga on the one hand and the Central Government on the other. This was also the problem which involved the Belgian Government most directly. The latter had to use its influence with the Union Minière Company to persuade it to take part in the search for solutions to our problems. This did not prove an easy task. The company's management was in a difficult position. It had to protect major economic and financial interests and depended for its continued ability to function on Tshombe, who was the only politician in sight capable of maintaining order. On the other hand, the Union Minière was beginning to realize that, politically, Tshombe was bound to lose out in the end and that before long the Government in Leopoldville, backed as it was by the United Nations, would re-establish its authority in Elisabethville and that the company would therefore be well advised to come to an understanding with the Central Government. They were thus on the horns of a dilemma, having to decide whether to pay more attention to the immediate facts of the situation – and in this context Tshombe was still the main figure to be reckoned with – or to the prospects in the long term, when he would no longer play any role at all.

I tried hard to persuade the company to cooperate in applying the U Thant plan. It agreed to do this, but in fact did so neither sufficiently quickly nor resolutely enough. Relations between Tshombe and the United Nations soon deteriorated. It became more and more difficult for U Thant to feel that the President of Katanga was being honest with him. By the beginning of December 1962 the situation was once again extremely tense. The UN official in charge of relations with the Congo informed Tshombe that the Secretary-General was disappointed with his attitude and felt obliged to consider applying the sanctions for which his plan provided. Tshombe continued to shilly-shally and to indulge in childish tricks. He went so far as to claim that he knew nothing of the various phases outlined in the plan. Then, quite suddenly, he left Elisabethville and thus made it impossible for the negotitations on the distribution of revenues to continue.

Showing himself singularly ill-informed as to the balance of the various forces in the field, despite the fact that he had been duly warned by the Secretary-General, Tshombe allowed incidents to occur which resulted in clashes between his gendarmerie and the UN forces. Clearly, the events of the previous year had taught him nothing.

Exasperated by Tshombe's tricks and his failure to keep his word, the UN started a new offensive on 28 December at Elisabethville 'to restore the security of its troops and their freedom of movement'. Results were not slow in coming, and they were spectacular. This time Katangan resistance was virtually non-existent. It only took a few days to break it completely. The UN troops pressed on with the campaign and on 4 January – contrary to orders received from New York – occupied Jadotville. It was a military joyride rather than a genuine operation. Happily, only nine people were killed and ninety-two wounded.

Tshombe made himself look ridiculous with his inflammatory appeals to his troops to resist and to the people to rise. There was no response from either the one or the other. Tshombe himself had left Elisabethville on 28 December for Northern Rhodesia, and from there he went on to Kolwezi. On 8 January, in the company of the Belgian Consul, he returned to Elisabethville, declaring that his aim was to bring back peace and to apply the U Thant plan without bloodshed and unnecessary destruction of property. Tshombe's return was largely due to the constant pressure I had brought to bear on him, and even more to the direct intervention of Colonel Van de Walle, the Belgian Consul at Elisabethville. It is only right to stress the part played by the Consul. He was firm in defending Belgian interests but at the same time proved an effective intermediary between myself and Tshombe, whose confidence he had gained. The Consul, who was a real man of action, showed courage and initiative although he knew he would be disowned should he fail. His part during the crisis, and later during the Stanleyville campaign, was both important and useful. This modest man has not received the recognition which is his due.

On 14 January, Tshombe executed a new volte-face. He left Elisabethville once more after having taken – or at least so he claimed – all the steps necessary to carry out a scorched earth policy. But once he had arrived at Kolwezi he declared, in agreement with his ministers and to the amazement of all, that he was 'ready to announce to the world the end of Katanga's secession and to allow the UN troops complete freedom of movement'. He added that he was prepared 'to return to Elisabethville once more so as to settle there the details of the implementation in full of the U Thant plan'. At the same time he demanded the immediate proclamation of an amnesty. This time it was indeed the end of the Katangan secession. It had taken two years to achieve this result.

I fear that this account does not give a complete picture of what happened during this time of abortive manoeuvres, moves and counter-moves, childish tricks, bad faith and temper tantrums, which, in their sum total, added up to a series of incidents comic and tragic in turn. On looking back on these events after the passage of some years, one is bound to say that Tshombe was the chief culprit. His advisers, unfortunately, were unwise. They encouraged him to engage in useless resistance and ill-considered policies. Nor did the conduct of some of the UN officials on the spot help matters. In New York, Hammarskjoeld had accepted – and up to a point solicited – responsibilities which it was beyond the power of the UN to discharge.

U Thant, who had inherited this policy, was less ambitious and more restrained. He was unable to go back on the policies put in train by his predecessor but once he was in a position to pursue his own ideas he showed himself both more impartial in assessing the situation and more prudent in his policies. I have often had to oppose U Thant but have never had any reason to doubt his good will, his good faith, or his desire to devise peaceful solutions to our problems. It was not his wish to use force. Later, when I had to settle with him the many problems which arose in connection with the loss of life and property in Katanga, I found him both accommodating and fair-minded. I have great respect for U Thant.

Adoula and Kasavubu proceeded cautiously. They had few resources at their command and depended on the United Nations. Although they never rejected counsels of moderation, they had no choice but to fight Katanga's secession. Deprived of its richest province, the Congo saw its future imperilled, and this was a situation they could not allow to go unchallenged. However, they were neither intransigent nor vindictive during our search for a solution to the crisis, and for this they deserve praise.

For me personally, the Katangan situation was most difficult. I was fundamentally and profoundly opposed to the secession, but my aim was to put an end to it without violence or bloodshed. I could not support Tshombe from the legal, political or moral point of view. Despite this, I went on believing for a long time that he had to be treated with consideration because he stood for a force which the Congo needed. I went out of my way to be patient with him and to give him 'sound advice'. There were times when I thought I had succeeded in persuading him to adopt a course that could have saved him. However, my hopes invariably came to nought. Instinctively, left to himself, he was able to see the situation as it really was, but unfortunately he was too ready to listen to flattery and dishonest advice from people who did not wish to see Katanga back under the authority of the Central Government.

I had to plot a difficult course between Tshombe, Adoula and U Thant, and also had to take into account the state of public opinion in Belgium, which was divided over this issue. Moreover, I had to defend certain legitimate interests and, more importantly, the lives of some thousands of my compatriots. I had to be careful of international opinion, which had shown itself very hostile to Belgium and had to be pacified by slow degrees. All in all, the policies we followed proved successful. The secession came to an end and, apart from the events of December 1961, force was never used on a large scale.

I was successful in convincing the Congolese Central Government of my good faith, and in December 1961 Belgium and the Congo resumed diplomatic relations. I was able to work well with Adoula and Bomboko and to restore Belgium's standing in the United Nations. This was to prove a valuable asset later on when I had to deal with the problems of Rwanda and Burundi, and even more so when I had to defend our action at Stanleyville.

It would have been impossible to restore Belgium's prestige without the good relations which I maintained with the United States. That country has been treated unfairly in Belgium. The tendency there has been to impute to the USA intentions which in fact it has never had. It is just not true that the Americans wanted to supplant the Belgians in the Congo. This would, of course, in any case have been a very foolish thing for them to attempt. All the United States wanted was to prevent the Congo becoming yet another area of East-West confrontation. To this end, it was essential that there should be a strong government in command in Leopoldville, able to control the situation.

From 1962 onwards, the Americans proved faithful allies, and their senior officials, including the American Ambassador in Brussels, as well as Dean Rusk and his aides and the President himself, showed a great deal of understanding for Belgium's problems and stood by her in her difficulties.

The fact that we finally succeeded was largely due to this collaboration. The leaders of that great country have always allowed me to put my views to them candidly and never tried to use their power to impose their own policies. In our discussions, I was always treated as an equal. When we disagreed on a particular point, we invariably tried to settle our differences honestly. While I cannot say that the United States has always behaved in this way in its international dealings, its conduct *vis-à-vis* Belgium has been irreproachable. It is with gratitude that I recall the help we have had from America.

The events at the end of 1962 struck a fatal blow at Tshombe's standing. He stayed on in Elisabethville for a few months despite his diminished standing and then decided, tired and sick as he was, to go to Europe for medical treatment. His career seemed at an end, but the history of politics has seen strange twists of fate. Eighteen months later he became Prime Minister, this time in Leopoldville. In 1963, even though the Katangan affair had been settled, our troubles were not yet at an end. The Adoula Government was in no state to exercise authority over the whole of the Congo and, despite the efforts of its leader, the country's economy was in a sad plight. At the beginning of March, Adoula visited Belgium, where he was warmly received. He was pleased, Belgo-

Congolese relations were restored and cooperation between the two governments was resumed.

There were three problems on which we had to concentrate: the settlement of the legal dispute pending between the two countries over financial claims arising as a consequence of decolonization, Belgian financial aid to the Congo and cooperation in reorganizing the Congolese army. This help was necessary due to the rising in Kivu Province and the departure of the UN forces.

The claims raised many issues. Most of them were settled during my visit to Leopoldville in 1964; the remaining problems were cleared up at the time of Tshombe's visit to Brussels in his capacity as Premier. On this latter occasion, I had to take a firm line with the big companies with interests in the Congo, which were not always identical with those of the state. The financial problem kept us busy during the whole of that year. A devaluation of the Congolese currency was considered necessary by all the experts. In a country whose government and administration are weak and disorganized, such an operation is particularly difficult to carry out. Belgium was directly involved, since the devaluation could not be accomplished without her help.

Together with the Americans and the International Monetary Fund, we were ready to play our part in this operation, but there were delays in drafting the necessary measures since the experts were at odds about what needed to be done. The devaluation was finally carried out, but by then the best chance of success had gone. As a result, the measure did not fundamentally improve the situation.

The reorganization of the army posed political problems which were even more difficult to overcome. On 26 February 1963, Adoula wrote to U Thant:

'Within the framework of the technical aid which the Congo will require after the departure of the UN troops, the Government of the Republic has decided to make use of assistance in modernizing the Congolese National Army from the following countries: Canada, Italy, Norway, Israel and Belgium. The latter will modernize the Army's technical services, staffs and operational formations. Belgium will also deal with our bases, the gendarmerie and military training establishments.'

The Secretary-General accepted this Congolese plan, on condition that the UN would remain responsible for organizing the modernization programme as agreed in December 1962, and that the programme submitted be put into operation without delay.

Of the countries mentioned by Adoula, only Israel and Belgium agreed to the Congo's request. Israel trained a parachute regiment, while Belgium assumed the important task of reorganizing the army.

This question of military aid to the Congo kept me busy throughout 1963 and 1964. The situation showed no sign of improving. After a revolt in Kwilu Province, there was the rising instigated by Soumialot in the Ruzizi Plain and Gbenye's revolt at Stanleyville. The Governments in Leopoldville – at first the one presided over by Adoula and then that under Tshombe – insisted that Belgium increase her military aid. We were thus in danger of becoming involved in operations for which we would be held responsible, with our international reputation once again at risk.

My instructions to the Belgian officers on the spot were not easy for them to carry out. Their job was to cooperate in reorganizing the Congolese Army but they were not allowed to take part in the fighting against the rebels. Our airmen were allowed to carry troops but not to take part in military operations.

At the end of 1963, Tshombe, who was then living in Madrid, asked me for permission to spend a few days in Belgium to see his children. While I could not refuse such a demand, I had to take care not to arouse the displeasure of Adoula, on whom I continued to look as the most effective Congolese politician. I therefore informed him of my intention to permit Tshombe's visit. Adoula was not particularly pleased, but left me free to go ahead with my decision. In December 1963 I thus met Tshombe for the first time. Until then, my contacts with him had been frequent but indirect. He did not make a bad impression on me. While Adoula was serious, severe and reversed, Tshombe was extrovert, ready to laugh, and undoubtedly radiated great charm. However, he was fickle and unreliable. I had made sure he was left in no doubt that he would not be allowed to indulge in political activities while in Belgium, to have contacts with journalists or to take any public statements whatsoever. As a result, he was discreet in his conduct. When he left the country he sent me a letter of thanks for the hospitality he had received:

'As you know, my visit to Belgium has been of great benefit to me. Not only have I been able to meet you, but I have come to understand how different the past might have been had we been able to establish personal contact at the crucial stage of the events in the Congo.'

I should like to believe that his regret was sincere and that he realized what opportunities he had lost by refusing to follow my advice. When Tshombe became Prime Minister I had the impression that he did in fact occasionally listen to me.

At the beginning of 1964, Adoula wrote to me in reply to a good will message that I had sent him:

'The fact that friendship between Belgium and the Congo has now been restored after the storms of 1960 is, beyond any doubt, due to your efforts. It is to you we are indebted, and I shall do everything in my power to make your task easier.'

I was touched by these words. My task had indeed been hard since the spring of 1961. I had to go about it with patience and prudence, and to cope with difficult, and at times tragic, situations. What saved me – I think I may be allowed to claim this – was my moderation and realism, as well as my absolute good faith in dealing with Congolese affairs. I had shown that Belgium could not be fairly accused of neo-colonialism, that her intentions were honest, that what we were seeking to do was to establish a balance between our continuing aid, which remained essential to the Congo, and our refusal to become involved in the internal affairs of that country.

Adoula was seeking our help, U Thant believed that help to be necessary and Tshombe, in his exile, was not hostile to us. Could anyone have done more?

Among the chief events in 1964 were my visit to Leopoldville, the overthrow of Adoula and the airborne operation at Stanleyville.

My visit to the Congo made a deep impression on me. I discussed with Adoula the legal issues pending between our two countries and was struck by the progress the Congolese Premier had achieved. In our talks, in which he played the leading part, he behaved as a real states-man. He knew his brief inside out – highly technical and complex though it was – put his views clearly, and effectively combined firmness with a readiness to look for compromise solutions. In a mere three days we made considerable progress, which was in large measure due to his good sense and competence. While I was happy at the results achieved, I was even more pleased by the enthusiastic welcome – certainly not stage-managed – I had received from the native population of Leopoldville during a triumphal tour of the city. I was the first Belgian minister to come into personal contact with the Congolese people since 1960. I made four or five stops in the city. Wherever I halted, large crowds gathered to give me a moving welcome. The slightest mention of Belgium and of cooperation between our two countries was cheered. Not only could I see no trace of resentment at the coloni-alist past, but, on the contrary, I had the feeling that our former rule was receiving rather more than its due share of praise. My whole visit passed in an atmosphere of euphoria.

President Kasavubu received me magnificently. He lived in a villa on the outskirts of the city – a large house in a splendid setting, with an admirable view of the river. The Head of State impressed me as a simple man who was nevertheless jealous of his prerogatives, well disposed to-wards Belgium, and who trusted Adoula as his Prime Minister. Behind this good-natured exterior, however, there lurked, as events were to show, a personality more complex, ambitious and calculating than surface appearances would have led one to believe. Kasavubu succeeded in getting rid, in turn, of Lumumba, Adoula and Tshombe. The three men never knew what had hit them. I myself saw the sheer amazement on the faces of Adoula and Tshombe. President Kasavubu had first given them assurances of his good intentions and then deceived them with remarkable skill. He was determined to be, and to remain, top man in the Congo. Whenever anyone looked like assuming any real authority or acquiring genuine prestige, Kasavubu would get rid of them. His quarrels with Lumumba are well known since the incidents to which they gave rise took place in public. In his dealings with Adoula, and later Tshombe, he was more secretive but just as ruthless.

To attain his ends, Kasavubu acted single-handed. Neither the Americans nor the Belgians helped him. The latter did not welcome Adoula's departure in 1964 nor that of Tshombe in 1966. On the contrary, what Belgium wanted was some continuity in Congolese affairs, and Kasavubu's action came as an unpleasant surprise to the Belgian authorities. In the end, however, his excessively individualistic policy came to grief. Kasavubu was in his turn eliminated by General Mobutu with singular ease. The former President was not fond of day-to-day work and it was only on big occasions that he was prepared to exert himself. The political alliances he contrived after Tshombe's downfall were fragile and dangerous. His career came to a sudden end amidst complete indifference in the country. And yet he was one of the principal architects of Congolese independence and, for a number of years, the embodiment of the new Congo.

Despite my efforts and Adoula's good will, despite the determination with which he went about his business, the general situation deteriorated rapidly. To be able to carry out the necessary economic and financial policy – which involved devaluation – the Prime Minister needed an efficient administration. This, however, he lacked. Moreover, owing to rebellions by the followers of Mulele and Soumialot, the intrigues of the exiles in Brazzaville and the hostile intervention of certain neighbouring countries, he was unable to impose his authority through-

Africa

out the Congo. His position, was, in fact, becoming increasingly untenable: prices were rising, there was widespread unemployment and rebellion was spreading.

Tshombe's popularity, on the other hand, was growing. He had maintained his connections not only in Katanga but throughout the whole of the Congo. More and more people were beginning to speak of him as the coming man. He was in fact benefiting from his years of absence: people had forgotten his faults. The mass respected Adoula but it was Tshombe's name that it cheered.

Kasavubu and Adoula agreed that Tshombe would have to be recalled from Spain and, in due course, to the amazement of all, Kasavubu appointed Tshombe Prime Minister. This no one had foreseen.

In Brussels and Washington, the governments were surprised and worried. While Tshombe's assumption of power might be useful in the Congo itself, because of its shock effect, it was bound to make the situation worse from the international point of view. Tshombe was highly unpopular with many African Heads of State and had acquired a reputation for being pro-white, pro-Belgian, pro-Western. People were not prepared to forgive him the Katangan secession and he was also being accused of having had a hand in the assassination of Lumumba.

The military situation deteriorated very rapidly and the rebellion which had begun in June 1964 while Adoula was still Prime Minister was spreading dangerously. By the end of July, the insurgent forces were in control of the whole of Maniema Province; Bukavu was encircled; Kabongo, 175 km. from the Kamina army base, had been occupied. On 7 August, Stanleyville was taken by the rebels. The National Liberation Committee in Brazzaville was doing its utmost to step up its subversive activity. It was only because of the internecine quarrels and rivalries which divided Gbenye, Soumialot, Gizenga and Bochley-Davidson that the rebellion failed to achieve decisive results. Several foreign Powers officially sided with the rebels, and Algeria, Egypt, the Sudan and the Congo (Brazzaville) supported them openly.

Tshombe then turned to the moderate African Powers such as Senegal and the Ivory Coast for help. I strongly encouraged him in this, stressing that he must not allow himself to appear to be a creature of the Belgians and Americans in Africa and must secure African support and repay it loyally. This policy produced good results. Soon Tshombe seemed less isolated. The military situation, however, was still worrying, and it was to Belgium that Tshombe turned for more aid. In so doing he put the Brussels Government on the spot.

If the National Liberation Committee, thanks to the foreign aid it was receiving, managed to extend its activities, it would no longer be a rebellion that we should have to deal with, but a war. In a letter to Tshombe dated 17 September, I set out the conditions which would have to govern our cooperation:

'1 The Belgian Government will, at the request of the Congolese Government, provide it with air support in order to give logistical assistance to the Congolese military forces, to provide them with transport facilities and to contribute in this way to the security of the population and especially to that of the Belgian personnel engaged in furnishing military and technical aid.

'2 This aid by the Belgian Government will take the form of the dispatch to the Congo of a unit of the Belgian Air Force.

'3 As stated under point (1) above, this unit will be solely authorized to carry out transport missions, including the evacuation of personnel, as well as reconnaissance, to the exclusion of any direct participation in support missions involving the use of offensive weapons (bombing, strafing, etc.).

'4 The officer commanding the unit or his deputy will carry out such missions as are proposed to him by the Congolese military authorities, subject to the condition that such missions shall be consistent with the arrangements defined under points (1) and (3). He alone will be authorized to issue instructions to the air crews and to order sorties. He will be empowered to take the initiative in ordering missions designed to ensure the security of Belgian citizens.'

I had no illusions about these provisions. The operations that had been authorized could easily go beyond the limits foreseen. Belgian officers were reorganizing the Congolese army, the Belgian Air Force was ferrying Congolese troops, Belgian responsibilities were increasing dangerously. It is for this reason that I pressed on with my policy of reconciliation, in which I had never ceased to believe. I wanted Tshombe, whose Government was weak, to seek the cooperation of such men as Adoula and Bomboko. I also hoped that he would try to make peace with the moderate wing of the Liberation Committee, headed by Gbenye. The latter had got in touch with me. He had sent me a letter in which he spoke of his friendly feelings for Belgium, urged that I should intervene and support him, and complained of the aid I was giving the Tshombe Government. I replied on 3 August and, a few days later, Gbenye requested that I receive him. I agreed, and we had two meetings in complete privacy. We met in the Ardennes, where I was spending a holiday.

Gbenye put his ideas to me at length. I tried to refute those I thought unreasonable. He left me several detailed memoranda to which I replied point by point. The views I expressed might perhaps best be summed up as follows:

I A military settlement of the conflict which is rending the Congo asunder seems impossible.

II In the event of the civil war continuing or of a divided Congo coming under the control of several authorities, there is every likelihood of large-scale foreign intervention. Neither the Congo nor Africa as a whole stand to gain anything from the creation of a new Korea or Vietnam.

III Since a military solution is out of the question, and would in any case be too costly, we must seek another way out. There is only one: a political solution resting on as broadly based a reconciliation as possible.

IV A political solution can only be found if the parties involved in the dispute do not insist on preconditions. Instead, they should agree on a positive programme of action.

V No solution will be wholly consistent with the law. Neither the Fundamental Law nor the new Constitution can be applied *in toto*. The legality of the new Government which will emerge will be based on the simple fact that it exists and will receive foreign recognition. The goal to be aimed at is the establishment of a government based on as wide a measure of unity as possible. The Congo, in any case, needs the help of all who are able to help, both in Leopoldville and in the provinces.

VI This formula should be treated as a transitional solution which would remain in force until such time as calm has been fully restored in the country and elections held. After the elections it should be possible to adopt a more settled form of government.

During our talks Gbenye did not impress me as either intelligent or far-seeing. He was certainly not an acceptable choice as Prime Minister of the Congo. On the other hand, he did seem to be ready to listen to advice and to adopt a sane view of the situation. However, once he was back in Stanleyville he again came under the influence of bad advisers and eventually brought disgrace upon himself.

The autumn of 1964 turned out to be a time of heavy responsibilities for me. I had to take decisions which must rank among the most difficult I have had to face in the whole of my political career.

The occupation of Stanleyville by the Congolese rebels at the beginning of August triggered off a succession of events which ended with the dispatch of Belgian paratroops to that city during the period from 24 to 27 November.

The young Patrick Nothomb, the Belgian Consul at Stanleyville, whose courage throughout was beyond praise, has given an account of the fate suffered by the 1,500 European civilians who had been taken prisoners by Gbenye and were later treated as hostages, beaten and tortured, and whose lives were threatened.

Once he was back home Gbenye quickly forgot his promise to me that he would behave with moderation. His conduct became more and more dangerous and his views seemed to indicate a complete lack of any sense of responsibility. The way he incited the passions of his fellow Congolese entailed the gravest dangers for the Europeans he was holding prisoner.

My attention was drawn to the situation at the end of August. From then on I did all I could to save the Stanleyville hostages from the fate that threatened them. I made a sustained diplomatic effort on several fronts and knocked on every door to alert whoever seemed likely to be able to help. In this way I hoped to avoid the worst. Soon, however, I realized that such methods would not be enough in the circumstances. It was no use reminding Gbenye of international law or appealing to his feelings as a human being. As events took their course and Gbenye's position in Stanleyville grew more and more precarious, he revealed himself increasingly as a primitive creature liable to act with violence and brutality.

At the end of the summer, during a visit to Washington, I discussed the situation with Harriman. It was during one of our meetings that the idea was conceived of an airborne operation to save the hostages of Stanleyville. We did not take this decision lightly since we were aware of the technical difficulties involved and the international repercussions to which the operation was bound to give rise. We therefore agreed not to intervene in this way except as a last resort in the event of all other attempts to save the hostages failing. From that moment, my diplomatic action and the military preparations went hand in hand.

On 6 November I wrote to the Secretary of the Organization of African Unity. I asked him to urge the Stanleyville rebels to allow humanitarian measures to be taken on behalf of my unlawfully detained fellow citizens. On 20 November I sent another letter to Gbenye in an attempt to persuade him to show reason. In the meantime, I asked the Red Cross to help and issued instructions to the Belgian Ambassadors in Ghana, Algeria, Guinea and Mali to make it clear at the highest level that no Belgian personnel were involved in the military operations proper, to denounce the disgraceful acts of oppression to which foreign residents in Stanleyville were being subjected and to stress that the city had at no time been bombed. I also asked the Ambassadors of the African countries in

Brussels to see me. I gave them my view of the situation and expressed my astonishment at their governments' lack of action, which I urged them to make good, informed the United Nations of the gravity of the situation and requested the Organization to assist us. All this diplomatic activity proved fruitless. Some of those I had approached were unwilling to do anything to help, while the remainder were powerless.

The situation in Stanleyville was getting worse, with Gbenye's verbal excesses becoming more extravagant. The treatment inflicted on foreign nationals, especially Belgians and Americans, was growing steadily more brutal. Outrages, including beatings of foreign residents and other humiliations, were becoming more and more frequent until the violence reached a crescendo. On 29 October Radio Stanleyville declared:

'We shall henceforth be unable to guarantee the security of Belgian and American citizens. So far, the People's Liberation Army has always protected foreigners, but this will be impossible from now on in regard to citizens of certain countries whose governments are aiding Mose Tshombe, the lackey of imperialism.'

On 5 November Gbenye said: 'In view of the bombing, all Americans and Belgians in the liberated areas will be considered prisoners of war.' An article signed by Gbenye, published in the paper *Le Martyr* on 14 November, said:

'We have more than three hundred Americans and over eight hundred Belgians in our hands. They are in safe custody. In the event of the slightest attempt at bombing our areas or the capital of the revolution, these people will be dispatched to the hereafter – in other words, they will be massacred. We shall make the hearts of the Americans and Belgians into fetishes and clothe our bodies in their skins.'

A broadcast by Stanleyville radio on 20 November declared: 'The Youth Wing of the Congolese national movement demands the lives of the nationals of all countries whose governments are giving aid, in kind or in personnel, to Tshombe.'

On 23 November a message from Gbenye to Kenyatta was intercepted. In it, President (sic) Gbenye threatened that 'all foreign prisoners will be eaten or petrol drums will be set alight outside their doors to burn them alive.'

The situation had thus become critical. The troops of the lawful government were advancing on Stanleyville and the hour of decision had struck.

During the first days of November 1964, we were giving serious consideration to having Belgian paratroops air-lifted to the scene in American aircraft. We did not want to make a premature decision, but nor did we want to risk being too late. We therefore decided to proceed in several stages. The British had been informed of our plans. They approved them and gave permission for the aircraft to land on Ascencion Island in the first place. We had also approached the Congo. We were thus free to press on with our operation if we so decided, but on the other hand we could also cancel the operation in the event of our diplomatic efforts proving successful.

On 23 November, after final consultation with the USA, we decided that there was no point in losing any more time in the hope that our various moves might yet produce some result. We realized that the arrival of government troops on the outskirts of Stanleyville might lead to the hostages being executed in accordance with Gbenye's warnings and made up our minds to act. During the night of 23–24 November 1964 I hardly slept a wink. When the telephone rang in the small hours of the morning, I grabbed the receiver after two rings. It was my principal private secretary announcing that the first parachutists had been dropped on Stanleyville. The die had been cast. I was convinced that our decision had to be carried through, but fully realized the dangers involved in our venture.

The vast majority of the Belgian public reacted to the news splendidly. On 24 November I went out to dinner with a friend. As we entered the restaurant most of the people present rose and applauded. The news of our military operation was good. The paratroops had landed as planned. There were virtually no untoward incidents and the troops pressed home their attack towards the centre of the city without losing any time.

Patrick Nothomb has given an account of the events in Stanleyville. The hostages were assembled and marched off from the hotel where they had been kept prisoner. They were escorted by Congolese troops, who were obviously in a high pitch of excitement, to the foot of the Lumumba monument that had been put up in the city. On the way they heard some of the 'simbas' ask the commander of the detachment if he would not let them kill at least a few of the prisoners. At this moment the paratroops were already close at hand, only two streets away. Suddenly a few shots rang out. It seems that a Congolese, a major in the rebel army, had lost his head and emptied his tommy-gun into the column of prisoners. His example was immediately followed by his men. Some twenty Europeans were killed by these bursts of firing. The arrival of the paratroops, which followed almost immediately, fortunately prevented any further massacre. Their presence was enough to cause the rebels to scatter. The hostages were set free. The Belgian troops had no casualties and those of the enemy were negligible.

On 26 November the paratroops, after a brief stop-over at Paulis, took off again, taking with them the few dozen Europeans resident there. On the 27th, in accordance with orders, they were back at Kamina, and by the 29th they were all out of the Congo, their mission completed.

Even at this distance in time I still believe the operation to have been essential, for it enabled us to save the lives of nearly 1,500 people. There is no knowing what might have happened had we not acted; in fact, there is every reason to believe that the Congolese rebels would have carried out their threats. Gbenye's inflammatory speeches had had the expected result. His troops, incited to a high pitch of fanaticism, were capable of anything. This they had shown on a number of occasions by their savage butchery of innocent Europeans. What we did was entirely consistent with international law and, more important still, with moral justice. I have no regrets other than that I failed to prevent the death of the victims murdered in those tragic hours.

The military operations had been carefully planned, and equally detailed preparations had gone into our diplomatic effort.

On 21 November I instructed our permanent delegate to the UN, Ambassador Loridan, to send a letter to the Chairman of the Security Council to acquaint him with the situation in Stanleyville. The Ambassador noted the critical plight of the Europeans and gave an account of my many attempts to save their lives. The final passage read as follows: 'My Government must reserve the right to request an emergency meeting of the Security Council in the event of an examination of the problem becoming necessary in order to save the lives of the innocent civilians in the Stanleyville area.' We thus made sure that no member state of the UN could later complain that it had been taken by surprise by the events at Stanleyville. The letter made it quite clear that the Belgian Government was ready to act if need be.

The US and Congolese Governments, whose attitude was similar to our own, also wrote to the UN. Before taking action, I secured the agreement of the Government in Leopoldville to our plans as was my duty, and received the necessary assurances in a letter sent by Premier Tshombe on 21 November to the Belgian Ambassador in the Congo, Comte de Kerchove. We were thus covered from that angle also.

On the morning of the 24th, at the request of Ambassador de Staercke, the Atlantic Council held an emergency meeting. My principal reason for requesting it was to keep our allies informed, since I realized that we should need their help during the weeks to come. The meeting was entirely satisfactory. One after another the permanent representatives assured the Belgian Government of their sympathy and gratitude for its efforts to prevent the loss of human life. All that could be done to prepare for the meeting of the Security Council – now certain to be called – had thus been done.

On 25 November, the Soviet representative, Fedorenko, sent a letter to the President of the Security Council denouncing 'the action of Belgium and her NATO allies, which constitutes a threat to the freedom and independence not only of the Congolese people but of other African countries as well'. Without expressly requesting a meeting of the Council, he drew its attention to the dangers inherent in the measures taken by the 'colonialists' and demanded that an end be put immediately to Belgian, US and British intervention. However, it was only on 1 December – and all the Belgian troops had been withdrawn from the Congo on 29 November – that twenty-two countries requested that a meeting of the Council be called. Twenty of them were African; there was also one Asian country (Indonesia), and one European (Yugoslavia). The meeting took place on 10 December.

I remember the few days I spent in New York on that occasion as being some of the worst of my entire life. The representatives of several African countries made carefully prepared, hate-filled speeches, bristling with false accusations. Their accounts ran counter to well-authenticated facts. They imputed the most absurd intentions to Belgium and vied with one another to see who could display the most prejudice and use the most violent language. For two days on end they took turns in speaking and subjected me to a tough ordeal. I was not free to interrupt them. All I could do was to allow the torrents of abuse to flow over me. I was familiar with the facts of the situation in Stanleyville and eager to reply immediately to establish the truth and give vent to my indignation. However, I had to await my turn to speak. I really suffered during those forty-eight hours. I knew then what it must feel like to be an innocent man on trial, to have one's every action and intention twisted and distorted.

For instance the representative of the Congo (Brazzaville) accused us of having deliberately evacuated the Europeans from the rebel-controlled parts of the Congo in order to be able the better to machine-gun these areas and to massacre the Africans. At the end of the second day, sickened by these speeches, the lies, the malice, the incomprehension and hate, I left the hall.

I was due to speak first at the following day's session. I spent part of the night walking the streets of New York to gather my thoughts and prepare my counter-attack. Finally, the hour struck when I was to speak in reply. I think the speech I made was one of the best of my whole career. I was tense with excitement, hurt, convinced of the justice of my cause, full of indignation at the accusations that had been levelled against my country. My cause was just, my brief excellent. I was to put my adversaries to rout as much by the solidity of my arguments as the sincerity of my feelings. As I went on with my speech, I felt my strength welling up within me. There was no mistaking that my words were striking home. The embarrassment of those who had shown themselves so unjust, and the approval of those who had remained impartial, were growing visibly. I was aware of this, as all speakers must be when they feel that they have succeeded in establishing a link with their audience.

Finally the battle was won. As I sat down I was aware of a flutter of excitement in the midst of the silence which had suddenly come over the auditorium. I could feel that it was all that some of the delegates could do to restrain themselves from applauding, while the rest were confused and at a loss what to say.

In Belgium the speech made an enormous impact. It had been broadcast in full and, at the request of many listeners, had to be repeated by the radio – an unusual occurrence. I was to have my reward a few hours after I had finished the speech. It was a telegram from King Baudouin, who said: 'Thank you for having defended the honour and just cause of our country so well.' Nothing could have given me greater pleasure or moved me more deeply.

In the Security Council the debate went on. Those who had suffered a moral defeat refused to acknowledge the fact and, for some days thereafter, continued to argue their case – still in the same aggressive and abusive vein. However, it is only right that I should recall the speeches of Mr Wachuku of Nigeria and M. Usher of the Ivory Coast. Showing true impartiality and nobility of spirit, they dissociated themselves from the exaggerations of their African colleagues.

In the resolution adopted by the Security Council on 30 December 1964, neither Stanleyville on the one hand nor Belgium, the United States and Britain on the other were mentioned and no one was condemned. The United States representative, Adlai Stevenson, and Lord Caradon, for Britain, both of whom had helped me with their advice and comforted me with their friendship throughout those days, were able to vote for the resolution without any qualms since its recommendations were in accord with our own ideas. The diplomatic battle thus ended well and the success gained in New York complemented that won by the paratroops in Stanleyville. Our good faith and bold determination to save life had carried the day.

While the outcome of the Stanleyville affair had lifted a great burden from my shoulders, the situation in the Congo was still showing no sign of improvement.

At the beginning of January 1965 I went to Paris to attend a meeting of the Atlantic Council which I had requested. I was anxious to keep Belgium's allies informed of the situation, which seemed to me full of danger. In my speech I noted that the rebellion, which until a few weeks before had been an internal affair of the Congo, was turning into an international incident, since it was clear that the USSR, acting through the intermediary of Egypt, Algeria and Ghana, as well as Communist China, using Burundi and the Congo (Brazzaville), were stepping up their assistance to the rebels.

In the circumstances, I said, Belgium thought it right to help the Leopoldville Government maintain order. Since there was a risk of full-scale war, Leopoldville could no longer be expected to act unaided. All the countries involved must face up to their responsibilities. In view of this, I thought it necessary both to support the Kasavubu-Tshombe Government and to try to work for a reconciliation among the principal Congolese leaders so as to enable them to govern the country jointly. I had therefore advised Tshombe to work towards this end, to seek the support of the French-speaking African countries, to fill the vacant posts in his government, prepare the ground for elections and announce his readiness to allow the elections to be supervised by representatives of friendly African nations. I had also urged him, I went on to say, to appeal for foreign technical and military assistance while, at the same time, keeping the Organization of African Unity informed. I had further advised him to see that a generous amnesty was proclaimed and, finally, to make it clear what his plans were in the economic and social fields. All this was quite good so far as it went, but was probably too logical.

I reaffirmed yet again my anxiety to work with the United Nations and the Organization of African Unity, in accordance with the resolution recently voted by the Security Council.

My speech seemed to meet with the approval of the majority of the delegates present. Lord Walston for Britain and Mr Harriman for the United States put forward similar arguments. M. Habib Deloncle, the French Under-Secretary of State for Foreign Affairs, on the other hand, was less positive. While he expressed approval of Belgium's action at Stanleyville, he drew a clear distinction between military aid and all other forms of technical assistance, condemning the former and approving the latter. In so doing he was clearly forgetting that France herself had not hesitated in intervening repeatedly in her former colonies to maintain or restore order and that one cannot possibly send teachers, doctors and technical experts to a country in the throes of a civil war without seeking to ensure their security. All in all, however, the meeting was a success and I left it in a better position to deal with Tshombe, who was shortly due to visit Brussels.

His visit, too, went off well. Although our talks, which were designed to clear up once and for all the legal claims pending between Belgium and the Congo, proved difficult, I am bound to admit that the Congolese were frequently right in their demands on the big companies. I repeatedly had to take the side of the Congolese and to use my influence to pave the way for a reasonable settlement. However, at the end of the day we reached agreement, and the outcome was undoubtedly a success for the Congolese. They had now become the majority shareholders in most of the important companies operating in their country. They ought to have used this as a starting point for their country's economic resurgence. However, Tshombe was incapable of taking such action.

On the political side, things were still worrying. Kasavubu's mandate as President of the Republic was due to be renewed that year. I had a feeling that Tshombe was toying with the idea of standing against Kasavubu. This was dangerous, since the cooperation of the two men was clearly essential. I therefore tried hard to persuade Tshombe to desist, but it was difficult to assess to what extent he was in agreement with my views, and even more difficult to believe that, regardless of what he said, he would not change his mind anyhow.

I was only too right. Tshombe, vacillating and secretive, finally announced that he would be a candidate for the presidency. This was enough to revive the fears of Kasavubu, in whose eyes Tshombe, from that moment on, was an adversary to be eliminated. Once again, Leopoldville was alive with intrigue. I do not know exactly who was plotting against whom, but the final upshot was Tshombe's eviction after he had emerged victorious from the elections. Once again Kasavubu proved himself a master tactician. However, this time he was to be hoist by his own petard. His choice for the office of Premier, Kimba, enjoyed neither authority nor prestige. He made statements which were unfortunate in every way and gave rise to misgivings and disappointment on all sides. In the small hours of 24 November 1965, the Congolese radio announced that the army chiefs, headed by their Supreme Commander, had deposed both the President of the Republic and Premier Kimba. Lieutenant-General Joseph-Désiré Mobutu became the new Head of State.

The coup took place without bloodshed, with startling ease. Kasavubu made no attempt to resist. All of a sudden, he was completely isolated and ultimately retired to his native province of the Lower Congo.

We in Brussels were both surprised and pleased by what had happened. During the final months of his presidency Kasavubu had seemed ready to do anything, however preposterous, to cling to power. Mobutu, on the other hand, had always shown himself moderate, reasonable and well-disposed towards Belgium. There was every reason to believe that, under his leadership, our two countries would be able to cooperate to our mutual advantage. A new chapter in the history of the Congo was about to begin. Personally, I was to play no part in it, for a few months later I resigned from the Government.

In general, I have enjoyed good relations with the Africans. Most of those who know me are, I believe, prepared to concede that I have tried to understand and assist them.

It is not always easy to understand them. I am entirely free of the slightest trace of racial prejudice. The very notion that I might look down on a person because the colour of his skin differs from my own is utterly foreign to me. In saying that there are differences between the Africans and ourselves, I make no value judgement; I merely state a fact.

What I have always found the greatest stumbling block in my relations with Africans has been my inability to get them to show any concern for the future. To govern is to foresee. While this tenet of political wisdom is universally accepted in the West, the Africans I have met seem to attach no importance to it. I have found many of them able debaters when it was a matter of discussing precise issues of immediate interest. I do not think that in this respect they are in any way inferior to the best European speakers. On the other hand, whenever it was a question of the more or less remote consequences of their actions, I invariably found them inattentive and uninterested. This crucial distinction in our respective attitudes and mental habits is undoubtedly partly to blame for the difficulty which we often experience in understanding one another.

After five years of experience in this field, I am convinced that we must not intervene in the Africans' internal affairs. We must allow them to make the running and confine ourselves to giving advice when asked. Above all, we must beware of thinking that what is good for us is necessarily good for them. When Belgium left the Congo in 1960 we bequeathed to that country a splendid Constitution. We included in it such provisions as our own experience made us deem necessary. For Belgium, this would have been a perfect Constitution, but it had no place in the Congo.

Our parliamentary democracy is a difficult form of government. It works well in our own country because it has come into being as a result of a slow process of evolution and protracted conflict. Democracy is a prize to be fought for – it is quite wrong to try to force it on anyone.

Our cardinal mistake in Africa – regardless of the fact that our good will was beyond doubt and our motives free from the taint of self-interest – was to try to induce the Congo to follow a policy fashioned after our own image. In this respect we – as so many before us – pursued what one might call 'democratic imperialism'. It would have been wiser to have allowed the Congolese to work out their own solutions or, alternatively, to have drawn on their ancient institutions and traditions. There was never any chance that the excellent system we devised for them would succeed in practice.

We must not take offence at the fact that forms of government have sprung up in Africa which do not accord with our own ideas of what is best for that continent. Africa will go on looking for the right path for a long time to come. She will find the right balance, I believe, neither in democracy nor in Communism. Africa seems to me to be hardly suited either to democracy's untrammelled liberty or to the authoritarian discipline of Communism.

Do not let us be too hard on her because of her errors and let us admit by all means that Africa's faltering experiments have neither been more extravagant nor more numerous or bloody than those which have marked our own history.

The consequences of colonialism will burden our relations with the Africans for a long time to come. It may well be that future generations of Africans will judge us Europeans more severely than those who lived under our rule. The *memory* of past injustices sometimes gives rise to greater resentment than the actual injustices themselves. The time will come, however, when events will be seen in their true light, even colonialism. When that time has come, the injustices to which it gave rise will be felt to have been balanced by the material and human progress which it has undoubtedly engendered and promoted. The time will come, when, with all our various superiority and inferiority complexes having been dissipated, we shall be able to live side by side in an atmosphere of equality, dignity and mutual respect.

41

East-West Relations

For my generation the Russian Revolution was one of the landmarks of our lives, whether we were for or against. As the First World War drew to its close and I began to take part in politics, I followed the ups and down of the Revolution with passionate interest. I was opposed to Tsarism and to its system of political oppression, but I was not a Communist. Even as a militant on the extreme Left of the Socialist Party, it never occurred to me to join the Communist Party. The fact that at one stage I advocated, in all good faith, very advanced ideas was more a response to certain events than an expression of my beliefs or my real nature. Intellectually I am a liberal and as regards my social beliefs I am a moderate. I could not be happy in a society in which the state or, worse still, one party, had the right to impose a moral yoke on me. I am not enough of a fanatic to believe that it is right to inflict privations and horrors on generations of men in order to create a society which might conceivably be better than the one in which we live now. I am a Social Democrat rather than a socialist. I say *social* democrat because I should like to see certain privileges brought to an end, with everybody enjoying as equal an opportunity in life as possible, for this would enable us to create a genuine elite. I say *democrat* because to me freedom is the only social climate in which a man can live in honour.

During the forty-five years of my political career, I have had many opportunities to speak and write about the Russian Revolution and Communism. There have been times when I spoke out violently against Moscow's foreign policies. From 1948 to 1958, I helped to halt the advance of Soviet imperialism into Europe. After the twentieth congress of the Soviet Communist Party, when the USSR decided to practise a policy of peaceful coexistence, I changed my attitude. I was among the first to seek a new relationship with the countries of Eastern Europe, without, however, ever losing sight of reality. While the Soviet danger in Europe has lessened, Communism as a way of life and system of government remains, despite the evolution it has undergone, a doctrine we must fight.

The most accurate definition of my attitude to Communism can be found in a speech I made in Oslo in June 1960 addressing the Atlantic Council. I began by dismissing the wrong reasons, invoked by so many people, to justify their opposition to Communism: some are emotionally hostile to the Slavs or to the Chinese; others condemn Communism because it has come to power as a result of a bloody revolution – forgetting that we in the West are the first to have had such revolutions. Others again advance questionable views on the organization of the economy in the Communist countries. Hostility to Communism is justified least of all when it is based on opposition to the great efforts which have been made in the Communist world to remove, or at least to lessen, social inequality and injustice.

Justifying my opposition to Communism, I said:

'It is not a matter of choosing between two different social systems; the alternatives are much more important, and our choice is a more serious and fundamental one: we have to choose between two types of civilization. The economic and social system conceived and brought into being by the Communists has led them to adopt a definite form of government. This, in turn, has caused them to adopt a certain way of life and, by the same token, a way of thinking. It is thus in the way of thinking, of government and of life, in the general concept of the place of the individual in society where the real difference lies, it is this which distinguishes the Communist system from Western society. As for myself, the essential point about Western civilization is its respect for the dignity of the individual. To safeguard that dignity, the liberties of the individual must be secure, and this the Communist regime has

403

proved incapable of achieving ever since its inception. On the contrary, it is this respect for the individual which Communism is trying to destroy in the world.'

I went on to say:

'It is up to us to realize the magnitude of the danger which confronts us. As I see it, Communism has three ambitions: it wants to rule the world; it claims that its coming is inevitable; and it aspires to absolute rule.'

Ideological experts and students of Communism will no doubt consider this a somewhat naïve summary. Be that as it may, it represents the simple reaction of many to an historic event the consequences of which for mankind have been even more important than those of the French Revolution.

My first contact with Soviet reality occurred in 1932. That year I was able to visit the USSR thanks to the generous help of the paper *Le Soir,* which advanced the funds for my trip and promised to publish a series of articles giving my impressions. This was kind, as I was quite unknown at the time except to a very few, in whose eyes I enjoyed the somewhat unfortunate reputation of being a drawing-room Socialist of the extreme Left.

Le Soir published these articles without insisting that I make the slightest change. In so doing, the paper showed considerable independence, for in the middle-class and industrial circles where it mainly circulated, my views – some of them highly complimentary to the Communist revolutionaries – naturally did not go down at all well. The editor has since admitted to me that he was relieved when the series came to an end for the number of cancelled advertising contracts was beginning to worry him.

During my first few years as Foreign Minister I had little contact with Soviet representatives. In 1935, the Belgian Government presided over by M. van Zeeland resumed diplomatic relations with Russia, which had been broken off at the end of the war. This was one of the conditions on which the Socialist Party insisted before entering the government. I thought this demand reasonable: it was time to take note of an established fact.

Rubinin, the first Soviet Ambassador in Brussels, was a pleasant young man with whom I had no political talks of any consequence. However, I did intercede with him to save a Polish Jewish Socialist friend of mine, Alter, who had been abducted to Moscow as a prisoner. The Russians had got hold of him when they invaded Poland in 1939. It was only natural that I should approach the Russians on his behalf, but Victor Serge reports in his memoirs that my request was very badly received and was the root cause of the Soviet leaders' hostility towards me, notably when the UN General Assembly elected me its chairman.

When war broke out between the USSR and Finland towards the end of 1939, the sympathies of virtually all Belgians were on the side of the Finns. Their courage and unexpected resistance aroused our admiration. I had no hesitation in voting for the USSR's expulsion from the League of Nations. Later I made a speech in the Belgian Parliament to justify the stand I had taken in Geneva, which was approved by all, with the inevitable exception of the Communists.

After the *débâcle* in the spring of 1940, Moscow, at that time a faithful ally of Hitler's, broke off diplomatic relations with Belgium and asked our Ambassador to leave the USSR. It was only after June 1941 that the Soviet Government changed its attitude and Bogomolov was accredited as Ambassador to the Belgian Government in London. My contacts with him were fairly frequent. He asked me several times to dine with him *tête-à-tête*. On these occasions he was cordial, well-informed and ready to speak reasonably freely. In the course of one of our conversations he repeatedly stressed that Hitler's great mistake had been to think, after his initial victories, that the Soviet system was bound to collapse. The fact that this prediction had proved wrong was evidence, Bogomolov maintained, both of the patriotism of his fellow countrymen and of their loyalty to the Communist regime.

I have already spoken of my attitude to the USSR at the end of the war. Earlier, without being prepared to make any concessions to Communism as a doctrine, I hoped it would prove possible to maintain the alliance we had concluded in 1941. I did my best to prove this by taking Molotov's side in San Francisco over the issue of the Argentine's entry into the UN, as well as by offering to Vyshinsky, in 1945, the conclusion of a treaty of friendship between Belgium and the USSR. Little by little I was forced to abandon these intentions. My attitude changed, as did that of Bevin and Bidault. We gradually came to realize that the USSR was bent on pursuing its objectives without paying any heed to even the most legitimate interests of the Western democracies. Moscow was not interested in the offers of cooperation which were being held out to it; on the contrary, it was determined to hamper our political and economic rehabilitation.

As Chairman of the UN General Assembly in 1945 and 1946, I played a more important part than would have been the case had I merely been Belgian Foreign Minister. I had to stand up to Molotov, Vyshinsky and Gromyko, whose behaviour in New York was most objectionable and intransigent. Their policy inevitably led to their country's isolation while, at the same time, causing the West to unite – first in Europe through the Brussels Treaty, and subsequently in the Atlantic Alliance. It took us three to four years to wake up to the fact that our illusions had been vain and to realize the dangers inherent in Stalin's policies.

I took an active part in promoting the revival of Western strength and encouraged Belgium's integration in the processes of European and Atlantic cooperation. A convinced champion of this policy, I advocated it in my speeches and writings. The speech I made in Paris in 1948 and the role I played in helping to fashion the London agreements, as a result of which the German Federal Republic became a member of the Western European Union and the Atlantic Alliance, were not calculated to endear me to the Soviet leaders.

Nevertheless, I carefully followed the evolution of Moscow's policies. As far back as the 1955 meeting in San Francisco to mark the tenth anniversary of the UN, I was struck by the changed attitude of the Russians towards me. I was therefore not surprised when, in the autumn of 1956, Avilov, the Soviet Ambassador in Brussels, conveyed to me an official invitation from his Government. A visit to Moscow by the Premier and myself would be welcomed, we were told. We agreed immediately since such a visit fitted in well with the policy of relaxation and peaceful coexistence in which we wished to play our part.

Avilov was one of the best Ambassadors ever to represent the USSR in Belgium. Unlike so many Soviet diplomats, he was prepared to take part in – and even to encourage – conversation and discussion instead of being content with a mere repetition of slogans, a practice apt to change every meeting into a propaganda exercise, with the most infantile and threadbare arguments being trotted out again and again. There seemed to be some point in talking to Avilov because one felt one was helping to bring about a *rapprochement* between our two countries, to remove old misunderstandings and prejudices and thus to pave the way for a new policy. The invitation conveyed to us by Avilov was undoubtedly the result of our earlier conversations.

Premier van Acker, myself and our aides left for the USSR on 22 October 1956. Van Acker was to remain only three to four days and took part in our talks in the Kremlin at the outset of our visit. I, on the other hand, stayed on until the middle of November, visiting Tashkent, Samarkand and Stalingrad. It was during this trip that I met Bulganin and had my first encounter with Khrushchev, who was then Secretary of the Communist Party of the Soviet Union. When the two were together at the negotiating table it was immediately obvious that Khrushchev was the real leader.

Bulganin looked pleasant, with his white hair, open countenance and soft, blue eyes. His general demeanour gave an impression of great kindness and gentility. He seemed a mild, quiet *petit bourgeois*. However, as our discussions grew more spirited, his eyes became hard and one soon realized that behind Bulganin's apparent bonhomie there was a very different, and more formidable, person.

No need to tell how Khrushchev struck people. All-powerful though he had been in his own country for some years, there was nothing in his outward demeanour reminiscent of a Hitler or a Mussolini. He was small, stocky, heavy, negligently dressed and, at first sight, there was nothing in him to capture one's attention. You had to look twice before you caught sight of the crafty glint in his eyes, and you had to do business with him to appreciate his shrewdness, his gift of repartee and his sense of humour. He seemed to be sincere and cunning in turn. Not for him the supposedly mystifying and pregnant silences of the conventional diplomat! He liked the sound of his own voice and when he felt people were listening and appreciating his arguments or anecdotes, when he felt you liked his jokes, he took pleasure in his success. As a result, talking to Khrushchev was not only a useful exercise; it was fascinating. I could not help feeling a real liking for the man.

It is not my intention to pass judgement on Khrushchev's conduct as a whole. No doubt his life contains many a disgraceful episode, but it remains a fact that when the burden of responsibility rested on his shoulders he changed Soviet policy for the better. He was convinced Communism would finally emerge victorious throughout the world but was prepared to abandon the pursuit of this goal by methods liable to lead to war. He realized that war would be as great a disaster for Russia as for her adversaries and that the result was bound to be the doom of the economic and social experiment to which he had devoted his life. He also knew that in the event of war the USSR would lose to the Chinese its leadership of the Communist camp, which it had bought so dearly. These were risks he did not wish to run. It was Khrushchev who put an end to the absurd notion, frequently advanced by Communist propaganda, that the atomic bomb was only dangerous to the capitalist countries.

Peaceful coexistence as defined by himself seemed to Khrushchev the best of all available alternatives. By proclaiming this doctrine forcefully and presenting it as a fundamental principle, he rendered the world a great service for which he is entitled to our gratitude. Because of certain prejudices, excessive caution and lack of imagination, the West failed to make the best of the opportunities offered by Khrushchev's policy.

I am not so simple as to believe that he was completely sincere during his talks with me. I am in fact convinced that he confided in me not so much because he thought I was the sort of man who understood and approved his views, but, above all, because he wanted me to repeat to others what he had said to me. There was a time when I was prepared to act as intermediary between Khrushchev and the member countries of NATO, convinced as I was that there were certain advantages to be gained from following up his proposals. I am thinking, above all, of my meetings with Khrushchev in 1961 and 1963. Our talks in 1956 were, in fact, comparatively unimportant.

Throughout the whole of two long sessions nothing new or important was said. We had to put up with a long speech by Khrushchev, who once more went through the whole catalogue of accusations the Communists habitually level against the West. What he said was neither original nor convincing. We had to listen to all the usual rigmarole about Munich and the treaty with Hitler, the lack of a second front during the war, and to a long tirade about NATO's aggressive policy. A particularly violent passage was directed against Federal Germany and her 'revanchist' leaders.

None of this held the promise of any progress, despite the fact that Khrushchev again and again proclaimed his desire for peace. In the only positive idea in his speech he referred to a non-aggression pact between the NATO and the Warsaw Treaty Powers. Speaking in reply, I merely noted that such a pact must be seen as the culmination of a policy of *détente* and could certainly not be its starting point.

All in all, the impression I took away with me was not a good one. The Soviet leaders appeared to be clinging fast to their positions. They were violently opposed to the very idea of Atlantic or European unity, extremely hostile to the United States and even more so to Western Germany. There seemed to be no hope of any *rapprochement*. Yet, strangely enough, these disagreements had not poisoned the atmosphere. Khrushchev and Bulganin remained cordial, and only Shepilov seemed at times aggressive.

We signed a treaty of cultural cooperation and published a communiqué. It contained one sentence which, even though it repeated a form of words customary at the time, was of some slight importance. It referred to mutual non-interference in internal affairs.

I broadcast a brief and banal statement over Radio Moscow in which I spoke of my hopes of seeing peaceful coexistence take the place forever of the cold war and declared that the vast majority of democratic countries shared this wish.

My tour of the Asian part of the USSR was to prove more interesting than our talks in Moscow. I was struck by the scale of the effort undertaken in industry, agriculture and education. I could not but admire the results achieved and was moved by the pride of those who had helped to produce them. However, the great progress which had undeniably been achieved could not hide the poverty of the life in these regions. What one might call collective institutions were impressive, but the facilities available to the public as individuals were poor. There were vast stadiums, houses of culture, gigantic factories and huge public works schemes, while the housing was miserable and there were scarcely any consumer goods to be seen. In general, the people's life was hard and joyless, though not without its impressive side.

Such results as we did achieve during my visit were brought to nought immediately. I was still in Central Asia when the Hungarian rising broke out. News reached us only in driblets, but it was clear from the worried look on the faces of the Soviet officials escorting us that something important was afoot. I believe Khrushchev put off the Soviet armed intervention in Budapest as long as he could. He realized that this action would give rise to tremendous ill-feeling in the West and that he would instantly forfeit the achievements of his policy of moderation. However, in the circumstances he had no alternative but to act. To allow Hungary to secede from the Communist bloc established after the war would have been to accept its collapse, to tolerate a precedent which might well have repercussions in Poland and Eastern Germany. Khrushchev thus had no choice, but he took the steps he did reluctantly.

The emotional reaction in the free world was sincere and deep-felt. Everyone's sympathies went out to the rebels in Budapest. Not only was their rising profoundly moving, it also held a highly instructive lesson. The young people of Hungary, who had never lived under any regime other than authoritarian Communism and had never known the real meaning of liberty, were fighting and ready to die for it. Clearly, man has certain needs; he has certain feelings which are so deeply embedded in his nature that even prolonged exposure to a pitiless tyranny cannot extinguish them. This should give us hope for the future.

Reactions abroad to the events in Hungary were in line with Khrushchev's predictions and fears. In the United Nations, the USSR was condemned by a crushing majority. Once again, Russia appeared on the world stage in her most hateful guise, combining brutality with cynicism. To justify themselves, the Russians put forward the most far-fetched arguments, at variance with well established facts. Although they failed to convince anybody, the Russians refused to comply with the General Assembly's resolutions. We were back to the worst days of the cold war and Stalinism.

I have found among my papers the minutes, dated 7 January 1957, of a meeting I had that day with the Soviet Ambassador. I think there is an interesting lesson to be learned from this document.

'This morning, for the first time since my visit to the USSR, I had a visit from Ambassador Avilov. Our meeting, which lasted more than an hour, was frank, which is to say it was stormy. The Ambassador maintains that the events in Hungary were deliberately brought about by the United States, which, he says, wanted to use that country as a testing ground to find out just how far it could go in presuming on Soviet good will.

'He denied categorically that the USSR had inter-

411

vened in Hungary's internal affairs and declared that the Russian troops had been called in by a lawful Hungarian Government asking for help. He went on to claim that in the end the revolution had turned fascist.

'When I demurred, he maintained that evidence of his statements was available and that he would have it sent to me. I doubt very much that the Ambassador will be able to make good his promise since he also remarked that the evidence he had in mind had already been made public by Mr Shepilov, speaking in the United Nations in New York. What really scared me was that the Ambassador really seemed to believe what he was saying.

'Referring to events in Egypt, he declared that in actual fact the Americans approved of the French and British action there! I tried to make him understand that at any rate as far as the Middle East was concerned I was absolutely certain he was wrong and that Soviet policy was based on a misconception. Despite the emphasis with which I put my views, I failed to make any impression on him.

'The Ambassador stressed that all these developments must be seen as the result of a bid by the Americans to put an end to international relaxation: the Americans wanted to make their preparations for the third world war undisturbed. When I objected to these statements and remarked that I had met both Khrushchev and Eisenhower this very month and that, in my view, these two men were probably more strongly opposed to a third world war than anyone else because they knew what it would mean, he seemed taken aback. He asked me, after much beating about the bush and with some embarrassment, if I did not agree that it would be a good idea if I were to write a letter to either Bulganin or Khrushchev, setting out my views of the situation. I replied that I would think the matter over.

'In the course of our meeting, the Ambassador did not deny that the Russian action in Hungary had brought to nought all the efforts that had gone into earlier attempts to establish peaceful coexistence. He reiterated forcefully and even with some emotion that history would judge the USSR to have been right and that the reasons which had caused it to act as it did would in time come to be understood. It would appear from this meeting that, for the present at any rate, the Russians have not given up hope of being able one day to resume the policy they pursued prior to the events in Hungary.'

As Secretary-General of NATO from 1957 until the beginning of 1961, it was my task to defend and explain the decisions of that organization. As a result, it frequently fell to my lot to criticize Soviet policy. At first sight, therefore, there was every reason why my relations with the Soviet authorities should have failed to improve during that period. But, paradoxically, this was not the case. In fact, during that time I kept in close touch with an important Soviet official – Vinogradov, the Ambassador in Paris.

In February 1958, much to my surprise, Vinogradov requested a meeting with me. I decided to accept. I have always been in favour of maintaining the maximum personal contacts and have thought the attitude of those who are ready to condemn anyone out of hand who disagrees with their particular point of view without giving a hearing to the arguments of the other side petty and contemptible. I have always felt sufficiently sure of myself to meet my adversaries in debate. Usually, I have learned something from such confrontations. They helped me to understand both my opponents and their ideas better. More often than not these meetings strengthened me in my convictions.

I received Vinogradov at my private residence. He came, accompanied by an aide. In the months that followed, we met frequently; in fact between February 1958 and May 1960, at regular intervals. A small group of us would meet for dinner at the home of one or the other of us or, alternatively, at the Polish or Czechoslovak Ambassador's or at André de Staercks's. Vinogradov spoke perfect French, which made things a good deal easier. His manner was cordial. During our arguments his mood would vary from heated to tolerant. He was very frank but had no objection to the other side being equally outspoken. From the purely human point of view, our talks were fascinating.

Why had Vinogradov taken the initiative in suggesting these meetings? I can only surmise that he did so as part of his intelligence-gathering duties in Paris. At the same time, he undoubtedly regarded our talks as a means of conveying certain views to the NATO Powers by indirect and semi-official channels. At all events, these meetings left a very deep impression on me. This was partly due to the fact that I found the risks they entailed intriguing. I knew I had to be careful lest I commit an indiscretion and hoped that I would manage to pick up some useful bits of information myself.

Our talks were chiefly concerned with the preparations for the summit meeting to be held in Paris – the one which collapsed after the American U-2 aircraft had been shot down over Soviet territory.

Conditions favoured our meetings. Khrushchev had been to America and, on his return, had shown himself determined to pursue a policy of peaceful coexistence. He had adopted a completely new tone towards the USA and people were beginning to feel genuinely hopeful of an easing of tension. It was our duty to encourage this trend.

André de Staercke, whom I had asked to accompany me after our first meeting with the Soviet Ambassador because I thought it dangerous to be on my own face to face with four or five Communist diplomats, drafted minutes of these encounters which to this day make interesting reading. It would be wrong to publish these documents since they relate to statements made quite informally, and the minutes were therefore intended only for those actually present at the talks.

Vinogradov noted repeatedly that our meetings seemed to be worthwhile and that one or the other suggestion I had made had been taken up by the Soviet authorities. It was my impression that he was telling the truth. However, the hopes we cherished at the time were dashed by the U-2 incident. Khrushchev went out of his way to minimize its importance. I was told this at the time by Vinogradov, and Khrushchev confirmed the information to me later. The Soviet leader did his utmost to give

Eisenhower a chance to disclaim personal responsibility, and, had the President taken up the offer, the summit meeting would undoubtedly have taken place. However, the President thought it his duty to do otherwise. Amidst universal surprise, even in NATO circles, he backed the American intelligence services with his personal authority.

This was a heavy blow to Khrushchev's policy. From then on he could no longer speak of the good intentions of the United States and President Eisenhower, as he had just done in the USSR to the amazement of all and the indignation of some.

There were circles in Moscow which opposed the policy of *rapprochement*. The hard-liners were now ready to come out into the open again. Khrushchev did not have sufficient authority to stand up the wave of more or less artificial indignation which swept the USSR. Once again the policy of relaxation had suffered a setback.

Khrushchev was later to show how his attitude had changed by indulging in his well-remembered vulgar exhibition in the United Nations. More seriously, his position over Germany and Berlin also hardened.

Vinogradov assured me that between the time of Khrushchev's visit to the United States and 9 April 1960 no American aircraft had entered Soviet air space. He concluded from this that, by resuming these flights on the eve of the summit, the Americans wished to give a demonstration of what they meant by 'negotiating from strength'. He went on to say that if this were not the right explanation, the alternative was even worse, i.e. that there was a group of people in the United States out to thwart the policy of relaxation.

I had some difficulty in countering these arguments. So far as I am concerned the U-2 incident remains shrouded in mystery. No convincing explanation has been forthcoming. There can be no denying that this open flight over Soviet territory on the eve of the summit conference was a mistake.

In the summer of 1961, the situation in Europe was dominated by Soviet demands regarding Germany and Berlin. I thought it possible the Russians might at long last conclude the treaty with East Germany with which they had been threatening us for some time. It seemed probable that as a result the Russians would cede their rights in Berlin to the East Germans. I viewed this contingency with the utmost anxiety. There was a risk the West might be placed in a very awkward dilemma: either it would have to resign itself to losing face and accept the new situation or it would have to oppose it by force. While I was convinced of the need to prevent West Berlin from falling into Communist hands, I was equally certain that we would have the greatest difficulty in mobilizing public opinion in our various countries and persuading it to accept the risk of war if it were merely a matter of deciding whether control over the access routes to Berlin should be exercised by the Soviet authorities or the East Germans.

I thought the Western Powers' rigid attitude dangerous. While I was still Secretary-General of NATO I had made clear my regret at their lack of imagination in this context. Now that I was personally responsible for Belgium's foreign policy, I was even more disturbed.

Since I was convinced that there was no hope of successful negotiations on Germany's reunification, I was wondering whether it would not at least be advisable to work out a new statute governing the position in Berlin. I had felt for a long time that the West's position was weak. I thought it unreasonable that we should continue to justify the Western presence in the city by invoking the military victory of 1945. The years were rolling by and this line of argument seemed to me to be losing force with the passing of time. It seemed advisable to negotiate a new agreement with the Russians covering three essential points with regard to which compromise was out of the question:

1 The Berliners must be free – in the Western sense of that term – to choose their own institutions.

2 All communications by land and air between West Berlin and the West must be kept open.

3 This state of affairs must be guaranteed by the presence of Western troops in Berlin.

I thought it essential that the West should take the initiative and not allow the Russians to handle the issue their own way. However, I was alone in thinking this way. The Government in Bonn was utterly opposed to my views. It would not even think of negotiations unless they were comprehensive, and was not prepared to allow the Berlin issue to be dealt with separately from that of German reunification. The French backed Bonn unreservedly, while the United States, rather more hesitant, was disinclined to accept any responsibility in the matter.

At the end of August I was approached by the Soviet Chargé d'Affaires, who, on behalf of his Government, invited me to Moscow. The invitation was conveyed to me following my earlier talks with Ambassador Vinogradov. Clearly, Khrushchev knew that in regard to certain questions such as the advisability of a non-aggression pact between the NATO Powers on the one hand and the members of the Warsaw Pact on the other I tended to agree with him. In his eyes I was a negotiating partner who was not *a priori* hostile to all his ideas, who was convinced that new solutions must be sought.

I was inclined to accept the invitation without further ado but realized that the visit would not be welcomed by all NATO members. The Great Powers do not like it when the representatives of smaller states take too independent a line. I think they are wrong in this. In a situation such as the one we were facing in 1961, it was easier for Khrushchev to talk to me than to the Foreign Minister of the United States, Britain or France. It was easier for him to try out certain ideas on me than on one of my Great Power colleagues. Moreover, I had every reason to hope that I would glean some interesting new information during my talks with Khrushchev.

In a message to the Atlantic Council, I therefore informed Belgium's allies of my intention to visit Moscow. The Council's reaction was, as I had expected, polite but reserved. Only Mr Finletter, the US representative, backed my proposal. The following day I received a letter from von Brentano in which he expressed agreement in principle with the idea of my visit to Moscow. He asked me most emphatically, however, not to press Khrushchev for separate negotiations on Berlin. All the political parties in the Federal Republic, he declared, both those represented in the Government and the opposition, were opposed to such talks. I decided to comply with the German request.

Accompanied by Robert Rothschild, my principal private secretary, and André de Staercke, I was received by Khrushchev in the Kremlin on 19 September 1961. This meeting was one of the most interesting I have had with Khrushchev. He was in great form, fairly bubbling over, extremely well informed on current affairs, and he spiced his contributions to our discussions with anecdotes. His references to his fellow politicians were amazingly out-spoken; he would quote the views of some and make fun of others.

On my return to Brussels, I made a point of sending him a message of thanks for the welcome I had received, mentioning in particular the pleasant atmosphere during our talks.

At the same time I drew up a report for the members of the Atlantic Council. I had informed Khrushchev of my intention to do this and he had made no objection.

I think the reader may find this memorandum, which I subsequently expounded at a meeting of the Atlantic Council, interesting:

The German Problem

A. Mr Khrushchev reiterated his arguments about Germany in an attempt to justify, in the name of 'realism', acceptance of the existence of two German states and hence the need to sign peace treaties with each of them.

B. He declared that although, in his view, this would be the optimum solution, he had no wish to impose it and went on to say that he understood the West's position and was ready to help in the search for a compromise.

C. First compromise: a peace treaty might be signed with each of the two States, the socialist camp signing a treaty with East Germany and the West with West Germany. Certain countries, however, given certain conditions, might sign with both. The USSR, at all events, was prepared to do so.

D. The two treaties would include arrangements common to both of them. These would cover, for example:

1. The external frontiers of the two Germanies or of a future reunified Germany.
2. The search, at a later date, for a formula to govern the reunification of Germany. This must be done by the Germans themselves.
   Mr K. is not opposed to the idea of a confederation, although he does not consider it practicable for the present.
3. The inclusion in the treaties of an agreement on Berlin.

E. If the West were to find this formula unacceptable, Mr K. might be prepared for the 'socialist camp' alone to sign a treaty with East Germany. Although he thinks such a solution less satisfactory, he would be ready to concur if it were the only one that appeared feasible. At the same time, he is not prepared to modify his fundamental position over Berlin.

The Berlin Problem

I.   Mr K. felt that the Berlin problem was of no particular importance to him. What do two million Berliners matter when there are nearly a billion people in the Communist camp?

II.   Mr K. is prepared to see the Berliners choose their political institutions freely.

III.   Mr K. realizes the need for unimpeded communications between West Berlin and the Western world. However, since these lines of communication cross East German soil and air space, the issue must be settled by an agreement with that country.

IV.   Mr K. is ready to furnish guarantees for the implementation of an agreement on Berlin. He is not opposed to the presence of neutral troops or to any other formula guaranteed by the United Nations.

He is ready to accept the presence of American, British and French troops but demands that in that case Russian troops, too, should be present.

Finally, he would be prepared to see the seat of the UN moved to Berlin.

V.   Mr K. is not opposed to the idea of a four-Power agreement being concluded prior to the negotiations of a peace treaty or peace treaties with Germany.

Timing

Mr K. is in no particular hurry. He is not bound by any specific deadline, but, on the other hand, he does not want the solution of these problems postponed indefinitely.

Other Points

Mr K. would not object to other matters being discussed in the course of the negotiations, with a view to creating a better atmosphere.

a He is prepared to consider the idea of general disarmament as well as less ambitious schemes and is in favour of establishing a zone – not of disengagement – but one in which experiments for controlling the implementation of disarmament measures could be tested.

b He still thinks a non-aggression pact should be concluded between the NATO and the Warsaw Pact Powers.

The Council heard me out attentively, but I realized immediately that their reaction was one of mild scepticism. The permanent representatives had some difficulty in conceding that Khrushchev could possibly have spoken to me in such simple, straightforward terms. My account of our meeting did not in the least resemble the normal diplomatic encounters to which they were used, with the negotiating partners cautiously jockeying for position, veiling their thoughts in nebulous formulae and always keeping open a line of retreat. The proposals which I had brought back from Moscow were certainly open to objection in regard to various points of detail, but they added up to a coherent whole. They were logical and offered a chance of compromise. As I understood them, they clearly expressed a desire to lift our mutual relations out of the rut, and, as far as I was concerned, these proposals amounted to a viable basis for discussion.

My remarks gave rise to polite but reserved comment. I felt that several of the representatives thought that I had perhaps not properly understood what had been said to me. I was vexed by their attitude. I felt I had come back from Moscow with important information and had found there an atmosphere favourable to negotiation. I was amazed that so little value was being attached to my impressions.

After my return to Brussels, feeling somewhat irritated, I decided on an unusual – and possibly risky – move. I requested the Soviet Ambassador to pass on to Khrushchev a copy of my memorandum to the NATO Council. At the same time I asked Khrushchev to confirm that I had interpreted his thoughts correctly. To my great surprise, two days later I received a reply from Khrushchev. It was lengthy, to the point, and cordial. He said:

'Thank you for your message.

'I still remember with pleasure our meeting during the course of which we were able to undertake a frank exchange of ideas on the most important international issues and to achieve a better understanding of one another's viewpoints. I am happy to learn from your letter that our sincere talks in Moscow have been helpful to you in your efforts to promote an East-West *rapprochement*. For our part, we are ready to do our utmost to help reduce international tension and to maintain and consolidate peace. With this end in view, it is our aim, in particular, to resolve in the near future and on an agreed basis the problems arising in connection with the conclusion of a peace treaty with Germany and the normalization of the situation in West Berlin.

'I have noted with close attention the memorandum which you, Mr Vice-Premier, have circulated to the members of the NATO Permanent Council, summing up our conversations. The substance of the views I put to you is well set out in this document.'

There followed an analysis of my memorandum paragraph by paragraph. By and large, Khrushchev fully confirmed what I had said. He defined some of the points in greater detail, but on the whole his remarks accorded with the general sense of my own conclusions. Khrushchev only made one point worthy of special attention since, if he were to insist on it, it was liable to give rise to trouble. He declared: 'In my talks with you I spoke not only of the need to define the frontiers of the German states with their neighbours, but also of the frontier dividing the two German states themselves.'

It was obvious that the West would never agree to this demand if it were formulated in these terms.

Alas, I never had a chance of arguing my views in the Atlantic Council. On 27 September, the various governments having been consulted on my report, this document was subjected to merciless criticism. At that time, certain talks were in progress with the Russians. They were being conducted both by the Americans and by Lord Home, the British Foreign Secretary. Home had had a meeting with Gromyko which proved rather disappointing compared with the moderate optimism expressed in my memorandum. According to the British Foreign Office, Khrushchev's aim was merely to induce me to bring pressure to bear on the NATO Powers in favour of negotiations, and not to discuss with me the basis on which such talks could be held.

The British representative, Sir Paul Mason, proceeded to demolish all the arguments that had been put to me point by point, placing a restrictive or negative interpretation on every single one of them. He concluded by saying that the British Foreign Office did not think it advisable for the West to submit any counter-proposals, as seemed to be the Soviet Union's wish. The French and German representatives supported the British view.

My friend Boyesen, representing Norway, disagreed, stressing the positive and new elements in my report, and asked that it be given serious consideration. But what could the representative of a small country do against a coalition of all the Great Powers?

I regarded this episode then, as I do now, as a triumph of a certain type of diplomacy which considers rigidity of views to be the acme of wisdom. This attitude is due, chiefly, to fear of appearing naïve or of being taken in. Those who practise this form of diplomacy invariably feel that to do nothing is less dangerous than to act. They are sometimes right in the short run but are very often mistaken over the long term. This is the way chances are allowed to go to waste, never to return. This is how problems are allowed to drag on and to become more and more difficult to solve with the passing of time. This is how irremovable obstacles are allowed to accumulate and to hamper the cause of peace.

I cannot say if negotiations on Germany and Berlin in 1961 would have produced positive results, but I feel sure it would have been wise to have at least made the attempt.

What Khrushchev had said to me was more important than what Gromyko had said to Lord Home. Speaking to his British colleague, the Soviet Foreign Minister was bound to exercise caution, for Soviet policy depended on Khrushchev. It is the latter's statements that ought to have been weighed, examined and given the benefit of the doubt.

But all this is now so much water under the bridge. Everything I said was denied, nothing was tested and, eight years later, we are still where we were then. The champions of wait-and-see diplomacy are perhaps laughing to themselves now, for none of the dangers we then feared have in fact come to pass. Despite this, however, I maintain that our inability to tackle the problems arising out of the partition of Germany may, in the long run, have fateful consequences, if only for the state of opinion in Germany. Moreover, the situation in Berlin remains a trump card which the USSR can play whenever it so chooses. It may well be that the Soviet Union is in a better situation to do so now than it was in 1958, for the Atlantic Alliance no longer has the same cohesion or sense of purpose. I hope I am mistaken. Only the future will show if we are right in obstinately maintaining outdated attitudes.

While I was disappointed by my undoubted setback in NATO, this in no way diminished my resolve to do my best, within the limits of my now reduced possibilities, to seize the chances offered by the new atmosphere created by Khrushchev. It was my intention to pursue my policy of friendly contacts with the Soviet Union and the other Communist countries of Eastern Europe.

In May 1963 a correspondent of the Soviet paper

Izvestia requested an interview with me. I was aware of the dangers of such contacts but decided to go ahead with the interview all the same. My adversaries have often accused me of not showing sufficient independence *vis-à-vis* our allies and particularly the United States. Incidentally, the very people who made these allegations would often urge me – without realizing that they were contradicting themselves – to take advantage of my 'undeniable authority' in order to persuade the USA to make this concession or that.

I feel that I have always succeeded in preserving my freedom of action. A representative of a small country can only play a worthwhile part in international affairs if he shows himself discreet and refrains from trying to give lessons to others, above all those who represent countries more powerful than his own. One must not lose one's sense of proportion. It was only because my loyalty to the Atlantic Alliance and European unity was beyond question that I was able to take certain useful initiatives.

Between 1961 and 1966, the attempts I made to establish new contacts with the East were not welcomed everywhere. Some of Belgium's partners, including France, thought my moves inopportune and premature.

I refused to be impressed by the criticisms to which I was being subjected by people who now claim to have pioneered the policy of relaxation. I adapted my attitude to the USSR to the changes in its own policy, but in so doing I neither lost my sense of reality nor did I ever do anything liable to harm the cause of Atlantic unity or the integration of Europe.

In my *Izvestia* interview I advocated peaceful co-existence and the conclusion of a non-aggression pact between the NATO and the Warsaw Pact Powers. I spoke out against the dissemination of nuclear weapons and in favour of steps leading to disarmament in Europe. I also questioned the value of the Franco-German treaty of friendship and cooperation.

At that time all these views seemed rather novel and may have made me appear very independent. My statements were reproduced in full by *Izvestia*. The paper added a brief comment:

'Much of what M. Spaak has to say confirms the view that the Belgian ruling circles have given thought to the dangers of the nuclear arms race, to the threat inherent in the unity of the French and German militarists, as well as to the consequences of a new war in Europe.'

A few weeks later, Khrushchev invited me to pay him another visit. I left for Moscow on 7 July 1963 and arrived in Kiev on the 8th.

From the political point of view this meeting was less interesting than the one I had made in 1961, but from the human viewpoint it was fascinating. I was able to spend several hours with Khrushchev and other high-ranking Soviet officials in a completely relaxed atmosphere. Such a thing would have been unthinkable a few years earlier. It is of this aspect of our meeting that I wish to speak first.

When we arrived in the Soviet capital, I was told that it was in Kiev that I was to see Khrushchev. When we landed in the Ukraine the following day the weather was magnificent. The city seemed much gayer than Moscow, the people more relaxed, friendly and cordial.

We were taken to a village in the depths of the country where Khrushchev had his 'dacha'. It was a large, simple but comfortable house. Khrushchev received me cordially and suggested that we should talk in the garden. We sat down in a shady arbour round a simple table. On the Soviet side there were Khrushchev, Podgorny, Zorin and Gerasimov, the Soviet Ambassador in Brussels. On the Belgian side we had, in addition to myself, André de Staercke, Robert Rothschild and Cools, the Belgian Ambassador to the USSR. Khrushchev invited us to take off our jackets as it was very hot, and so we got down to our discussion in shirtsleeves.

Compared with 1961, Khrushchev seemed a changed man. Although he was just as talkative and ready to joke, friendly and severe in turn, he seemed more preoccupied with Soviet domestic issues than international affairs.

According to him, the latter did not, in any case, require urgent action.

After three hours of talks we sat down to a large lunch: two kinds of soup, hors d'oeuvres, fish, meat and dessert, with red and white wine and Crimean champagne. Such a meal, whatever the country, provided those present can stand up to it – and I could – is bound to create a relaxed atmosphere. Again we returned to the issues on our agenda, but this time we only alluded to them indirectly. A few jokes were exchanged about capitalism and socialism, about the West and the Communist world; they showed up our differences in outlook.

Khrushchev then invited us to take a rest on the banks of the Dnieper. We descended the side of a hill, crossing a small wood on the way, and sat down in a shady spot in a pleasant meadow. We then resumed our conversation. Khrushchev started telling anecdotes, some of which would not have been out of place in a barrack room. These highly spiced stories were not particularly funny. One had originally been told him by Tito and another by Premier van Acker of Belgium. What really amused me was the obvious embarrassment of my interpreter, Prince Guedroitz. To have to translate word by word a story which is rather close to the knuckle is hard on a man of distinction. Somewhat uncharitably, I was amused by the Prince's obvious discomfort.

The talk among the Russians present was rather more interesting. Here, in the Ukraine, they recalled their exploits in the Revolution. They had done much fighting, with great courage and in difficult circumstances, both against the Whites and foreign troops. It was quite evident that for them this was one of the most thrilling parts of their lives, the one of which they were proudest. It was enough to guide the conversation back into these channels by a stray remark or question and on they would go with their stories. These old warriors took tremendous pleasure in recounting their exploits. To hear about this side of the Russian Revolution, described by those directly involved, was a new and fascinating experience both for my companions and myself.

Among themselves, the Russians exchanged anecdotes

426

which seemed to point to certain worries. Khrushchev complained of the crushing burden of work with which he had to cope and the fact that he was often expected to take on the most serious responsibilities unaided. He added laughingly, referring to his colleagues: 'But that won't stop them throwing me out one of these days.' Everyone laughed. However, it was my impression that Khrushchev really meant what he said. Less than a year later his prediction came true.

The afternoon was drawing to a close. Khrushchev asked us if we would like to take a walk along the banks of the Dnieper. At the riverside we were joined by his grandchildren. One of his grandsons sat down in the fastest of the two boats, the one which had been reserved for us. He refused to get out when asked to rejoin his brothers and sisters. Khrushchev said to me, smiling: 'Now you'll never believe I am in control in this country; I can't even make my grandson do what I say.' Then, obviously for my benefit, he went about his duties as a grandfather in a most charming way.

After we had travelled a few miles down the river, we made fast at the bank by a large meadow. There, more food was waiting for us. There were two tables, one for the leaders, the other for the family. At the foot of a hay-stack someone had placed a camp bed. Khrushchev invited me to take a rest and sat down beside me. We chatted like a couple of old friends enjoying the last of the afternoon at the end of a day's work. The countryside, which always looks its best at this quiet hour of the day, was lit by the rays of the setting sun. It brought to mind Tolstoy's descriptions of the Russian landscape and it was as if Levine and Natasha were among us. Later, on the boat after a brief fishing trip down the river, Khrushchev began to sing, accompanied by the lusty and yet melodious and moving voices of the other Russians. The cold war seemed far away indeed, and there was an air of unreality about our discussions of the Berlin issue.

At last the time came to leave. Zorin was impatient: we must not miss our plane. The last peals of laughter rang out. Khrushchev, silhouetted against the setting sun, waved me a friendly farewell. I was never to see him again. A few months later he was an ordinary Soviet citizen living in obscurity.

On 11 July 1963, back in Brussels, I sent a summary of my talks in the USSR to President Kennedy:

'I returned from Kiev yesterday. On Friday next I shall report to NATO on my talks with Mr Khrushchev, but you might find it helpful if I were to give you without delay an outline of my main impressions, although I shall have some difficulty in giving an entirely clear account, for neither were the views expressed to us, and in my presence, always clear.

'Mr Khrushchev declared:

'I   That in his view an agreement could be reached on the cessation of nuclear tests in outer space, in the stratosphere and under water.

'II   That he could not accept the control measures the Americans have in mind for underground tests. However, he did not seem opposed to the idea of increasing the number of "black boxes" and appeared ready to accept some degree of international control.

'III   He was in favour – in order to prevent surprise attacks – of setting up fixed control posts on airfields and at principal railway and road junctions. He was ready to accept the establishment of such posts on Soviet territory and naturally demands that the same be done in the United States. However, he rejects the idea of roving control teams.

'IV   He said he favoured the conclusion of a non-aggression treaty between the NATO and the Warsaw Pact Powers. He did not indicate that such a pact must necessarily depend on an agreement on the points listed above.

'V   He again referred to the German problem as his chief concern – much to my surprise. He did not seem to me to have fully settled his ideas on this point, and I therefore prefer not to be too specific. However, it seemed to me that he did not believe there was any chance of agreement on disarmament unless the German question were cleared up first.

'Naturally, I reacted strongly to this and pointed out that such a demand would put everything else back in the melting pot and might endanger the recent improvement in the atmosphere. During the course of our ensuing exchanges, he relented somewhat, but did not abandon this view entirely.

'VI He referred in very positive terms to your speech of 10 June, adding, however, that it was too early to make a definitive pronouncement on it.

'VII Lastly, he seemed very worried about agricultural problems in his country. He explained to me at length how he hoped to tackle them. The emphasis with which he referred to these matters seemed to indicate that they are causing him deep concern.

'All in all, I formed the impression of a man who is entirely absorbed in the building of a Communist society in the USSR. This requires peace and also distracts his attention from the problems of world revolution. Though none of this information may be particularly new, it may prove helpful to those who are due to go to Moscow on 15 July next.'

This summary of what I had been told may well have put the results of our talks in terms which were too specific. Our meeting was quite helpful as regards the issues of disarmament and security; the outcome was much less favourable where German problems were concerned. Khrushchev's position on these issues had hardened.

Khrushchev was glad the West had rejected the proposals he had put to me in 1961: he believed he had gone much too far with his offers of concessions. Talking to me on this last occasion, he sang the praises of the Berlin wall – much to my embarrassment. What I found most worrying of all was his desire, expressed repeatedly, to make use of the German problem as a means of blackmailing the West. In Khrushchev's eyes Germany and Berlin were corns on the West's feet on which he proposed to tread from time to time. When I protested at this he relented a little and told me the story of a Russian fisherman who was in the habit of weighing down his nets with bolts stolen from a railway line. At his trial, he pleaded: 'I only stole every other bolt and there has never been an accident.' Khrushchev said he was going to be just as careful as that fisherman. He was going to make us wince every now and again but would stop short of provoking a disaster.

I remained unconvinced. In my letter of thanks for the welcome I had received, I stressed:

'Having just returned to Brussels, I should like to thank you once again most sincerely for your hospitality, which has moved me deeply. I shall always treasure the memory of the afternoon I spent with you.

'I have, of course, reflected deeply upon your arguments and shall now, if I may, put certain thoughts to you since I am none too sure that I have made myself entirely clear during our conversations.

'I   I am convinced that the idea of peaceful co-existence which you advocate is gaining ground. Most states in the Western world are now ready to accept this idea and to conduct their relations with the Communist world within such a framework.

'II   The number of governments in the Western world which favour an active policy in this sense is growing steadily. One of them is the Government of the United States, and Mr Kennedy's speech of 10 June last is of particular importance in this context.

'III   Nothing must therefore be done liable to hamper this trend or to strengthen the sceptics and those who prefer to wait and see.

'IV   It seems to me that major advances are possible in the sphere of disarmament, such as:

an agreement on the cessation of nuclear tests in the stratosphere, the atmosphere and under the sea;

perhaps even an agreement on the cessation of underground tests, provided the number of "black boxes" can be increased to more than three and agreement can be reached on the conditions to govern international control.

'V   If the question of fixed control posts in the Western and Communist world respectively – placed on airfields and at principal road and railway junctions with a view to forestalling the risk of a surprise attack – can be solved, this would make a tremendous impact.

'VI   If the ideas outlined in paragraphs IV and V above were carried out, a non-aggression pact between the NATO and the Warsaw Treaty Powers could, no doubt, be negotiated. I am certain that a legal formula can be devised – for the benefit of those who refuse to take this step – which would make it possible to avoid granting *de jure* recognition to Eastern Germany.

'VII   All this appears to me to be very positive, and if we take these measures we shall, beyond any doubt, have made a start. I am convinced this would open up fresh avenues of progress.

'VIII   I must admit, however, that there was one issue which cropped up in our talks which worried me somewhat. I refer to the German problem. As things stand, whatever view one may take of this issue, I do not believe that there is a solution which would command unanimous acceptance. If this problem were suddenly to be placed in the forefront again, the sceptics, and those who prefer to wait and see, would regain the ground they have lately lost, and this would be a great pity. If, on the other hand, the positive steps that I have outlined in this letter are taken, an entirely new atmosphere will have been created and goals which seem unrealistic today would be within our grasp. It might then be useful to return to the proposals on the German problem and on that of Berlin which you put to me in 1961.'

In general I found Khrushchev rather vague and distant in his comments on international issues, and he showed no sign of being in a hurry to see them resolved. While he stressed as forcefully as ever his anxiety to

431

pursue a policy of peaceful coexistence, he seemed readier than before to adopt a wait-and-see attitude and to hold on to all the trump cards he thought he held in his hand. This impression was confirmed by his emphasis on domestic issues. Not only did he speak to me at length and with pride of all the great projects under way in the USSR, but he also dealt in great detail with agricultural problems. The latter seemed to be his chief preoccupation. He proclaimed his conviction of being able to solve these difficulties, but I could sense that he was worried about the situation. Despite this show of optimism, there was no mistaking his concern. Agriculture rather than international affairs was the issue on which he would be judged, as he was well aware.

On 12 July I reported to NATO on my visit to Kiev. This time the atmosphere was much more relaxed than in 1961. This was due, above all, to the fact that during the two years which had elapsed several of the other foreign ministers had visited Moscow in their turn and I was consequently no longer in as dangerously an exposed a position as I had been then. Moreover, the information I had brought back with me was less momentous and called for no change of policy. This time my trip may well have seemed something of a routine operation.

The point which struck my audience most forcibly was the absence of any mention of the Chinese problem during my talks, although by that time Russo-Chinese relations had already begun to deteriorate. During my visit to Kiev an important Chinese delegation was in Moscow. When I hinted at this, Khrushchev evaded the issue. He preferred to say nothing, and this left the field wide open to speculation.

After an interesting discussion, the conclusion of the NATO meeting was that we had entered a phase when both the two great camps facing one another were quite happy to maintain the status quo, and this confirmed us in our decision to leave well alone.

The next year, in October, I visited Yugoslavia. I had been to that country several times before and had met Tito. The Yugoslav leader had received me in his lovely residence on the island of Brioni. Once the haunt of wealthy Austro-Hungarians, Brioni was now the residence of the Marshal and the upper crust of the Yugoslav regime.

Tito struck me as a man sure of himself, calm, biased in his opinions but able to keep his prejudices and feelings under control. He spoke clearly and with authority on a number of subjects which he evidently knew well.

It was Tito who first broached the subject of Khrushchev's personality. He stressed that it was very much in the West's interests to take Khrushchev's statements and the new Soviet policies he had initiated seriously. Subsequently, everything that Tito had said to me about the USSR proved correct, and I thought the information he gave me most instructive.

Tito is attractive as an individual. There may be a touch of exhibitionism about the man, the way he dresses and plays with the wild animals in his private zoo. However, behind these mannerisms, which to a critical observer might seem ridiculous, one could sense his courage and indomitable willpower. When I asked him what had been the most dangerous moment in his career, he replied without hesitation: 'The day I broke with Stalin.' Tito had fought in the Spanish civil war, he had fought in the Resistance and in some very tough battles, but none of these adventures was as perilous as his bid to shake off the Soviet yoke. He thought his country was about to be attacked, and all the necessary precautions had been taken. He was ready to resume his life as a fugitive in the mountains. His conduct set a fine example of human dignity and showed that patriotism and Communism are not necessarily incompatible. Happily for Tito, the attack never came. Stalin, certain that the Yugoslav regime, from which he had withdrawn his support, was bound to collapse, thought it best to await events and thus made the same miscalculation as Hitler in 1941.

My meetings with Tito in 1964 were less pleasant. Immediately on landing at Belgrade airport, I was whisked off into town in the company of my Yugoslav counterpart, Popovic. This time the Yugoslav leaders were not as relaxed and friendly as usual. On our way to town an evidently anxious Yugoslav Foreign Minister told me that Khrushchev had just been dismissed by his colleagues. This time the Yugoslavs had not foreseen the event and were unaware of the reasons for it. It was this uncertainty that worried them. During the three days I spent in Yugoslavia I had some difficulty in keeping the minds of my Yugoslav negotiating partners on the issues that I had come to discuss. They were thinking of other things, and I could hardly blame them.

Tito himself was not as sure of himself as usual. He was unwilling to comment on what had happened in Moscow. As regards the Congo, I found him hostile, poorly informed and utterly prejudiced. We parted on rather cool terms. I had completely failed to convince him. This I was later to see confirmed in the United Nations, where the Yugoslavs consistently opposed Belgium over the Congo issue. This somewhat diminished my admiration for Tito which I had conceived at our first meeting, and made me realize that there are limits to the extent to which we can expect to collaborate with his country.

For a long time, Tito showed great skill in playing off the USSR against the West. While he has done his best to extract the maximum advantage from this situation there can be no doubt that in the final analysis his heart is in the Communist camp. However, this does not detract from his qualities as a man of action and Head of State. Leaving aside his foreign policy, which I cannot approve, I believe the Socialist experiment which Tito is conducting in Yugoslavia is of the greatest interest and merits close attention.

In February 1965 I visited Warsaw. I met all the Polish leaders there, especially Rapacki, the Foreign Minister, whose disarmament plan had made him famous at home and abroad.

Of all the Communist leaders with whom I have ever had to deal, he is the one who is closest to the West in manner and temperament and the easiest to talk to. While he is a convinced Communist and a loyal supporter of the experiment which is being conducted in his country, he none the less tries to understand his negotiating partners' point of view. In talking to Rapacki, there is no need to scale the wall of prejudice, preconceived notions and slogans which make it difficult to do business with so many Communist leaders. In dealing with him, one has the feeling that the respective points of view are being brought closer together and that one is not wasting one's time. I am bound to say this is rare.

Rapacki later called on me in Brussels to return my visit to Warsaw. We thought that our loyalty to our respective powerful allies should not prevent us from attempting fresh initiatives of our own. The medium and small Powers have their part to play. We felt that we could, each in his own bloc, champion certain ideas we held in common.

Rapacki is sincerely devoted to peace and anxious to cooperate with the countries of Western Europe. I regret that events did not allow us to pursue the work which we had begun so promisingly.

When I left the Government in 1966, I was about to make my third trip to Moscow, where I was to meet the new Communist leaders. I had also accepted invitations to visit Prague and Budapest.

This policy of promoting peaceful coexistence through personal contacts must be pursued further. While it may not produce spectacular results immediately, it will in the long run – if it is applied with prudence and in good faith – open up fresh horizons. The peoples and governments of Europe, regardless of regime, are eager for peace. The many wars they have experienced have convinced them that resort to force is useless as a means of settling international disputes. Misunderstandings and doubts inherited from a recent past remain, but there is, on the other hand, the power of good will, born of our instinct of self-preservation, which must not be underestimated.

42

The Fouchet Plan

During the summer of 1960, General de Gaulle tried to put the idea of European political unity back on the agenda. Since I was not in the government at that time, I witnessed the beginning of these efforts as a private individual. I remember discussing the situation with Jean Monnet. We were both surprised at the General's move. We knew his ideas on Europe were very different from ours, but agreed that it would be wrong to oppose any attempt which held out any hope of progress in an area where virtually nothing had been achieved since the conclusion of the Treaty of Rome. What information we had about President de Gaulle's plans was not without interest and his ideas were certainly worth exploring.

Subsequently, after I had become Foreign Minister once more, I was able to study the papers at the Ministry and realized that the General's proposals had from the outset given rise to a good deal of suspicion among those to whom they had been put. His ideas were vague and the whole project was marked by a certain confusion. Those who were aware of French intentions feared that if it were realized the project might weaken the Atlantic Alliance and deprive the EEC Commission of some of its powers.

The negotiations on the French project made headway only slowly. Nevertheless, a conference was held in Bonn on 18 July 1961 under the chairmanship of Adenauer, with de Gaulle among those attending. It took us several hours to achieve the result we wanted, but finally we succeeded. The communiqué said: 'Those present agreed that only a united Europe allied to the United States and the other free peoples can face up to the dangers which threaten the free world....' It added: 'Desiring as they do the adhesion to the various European communities of the other European States ready to assume in all respects the same obligations and responsibilities as the present members, the Heads of State and Government present felt that action along these lines would facilitate the implementation of the Treaties of Paris and Rome.'

These statements reflected our success, a success that had not been achieved easily. Even then I was far from sharing the optimism of certain people. The day after this supposedly historic occasion, I drafted the following memorandum for my own files:

'We devoted the day in Bonn to an attempt to give fresh impetus to the policy of European unity. The final communiqué on our work does not sound too bad. It contains numerous references to the Treaty of Rome and affirms that we are determined to carry out in full the provisions of that document. It also mentions the wishes expressed by the European Assembly, and, above all, it charges the officials with the task of drafting specific proposals designed to crystallize European unity in the form of new institutions. All this sounds very grand, and the press seems disposed to attach great importance to what has been achieved. Personally, I am rather more sceptical. Our debate on the final communiqué showed up the very deep differences which exist, and I fear that the "constitutional" aspect of the various documents will soon be seen to be devoid of real practical importance.

'Apart from our discussion on the final document, everything else that happened during our conference left me with a somewhat unfortunate impression. It is quite obvious that General de Gaulle intends to be tough with the European commissions. We also had quite a set-to over Africa. After making a constructive contribution on the political and economic aspects of the African problem, the General said he would like the issue discussed in Paris, i.e. taken out of the Commission's hands.

'Supported only by the Dutch, I made my views on this point quite clear. The discussion ended on an ambiguous note. It seems to me that the French want to reduce the Commission's ability to act to the absolute minimum. They want its agenda to be purely technical and to strip it of all its political powers.

'The General's speech on defence was even more worrying. He maintained that the Six must be seen as a bloc apart from the other Powers and that the defence problems of the Six were not identical with those of the United States, the Scandinavian countries, or even those of Britain. His aim – which, incidentally, he did not define very clearly – is evidently to establish a European military entente. I believe none of the other delegations favoured these suggestions, but the Chancellor who supported the General strongly throughout the conference, went out of his way to discourage any discussion. It was my impression that – probably because of Berlin – Germany wants at all costs to avoid having to oppose France on any issue whatsoever. The Luxembourg Government also seems greatly impressed by General de Gaulle. The Italians, who were helpful during the debate on the final document – thanks to the influence of Ambassador Cattani – did not define their stand on the defence issue. Only the Dutch backed me vigorously, and Belgian-Dutch unity emerged strengthened from this conference.

'All in all, I am worried by the wide discrepancy between the published conference documents and the actual tenor of our discussions; the gulf between the documents and the facts as they really are is even wider.'

Events were to show that my concern was well-founded and my fears regarding certain aspects of French policy by no means exaggerated. However, we did not allow ourselves to be discouraged. A committee was set up, composed of senior officials of the Six, under the chairmanship of Christian Fouchet, who relinquished his post as French Ambassador to Denmark to take up this appointment. The story of the negotiations which took place in connection with the document known as the 'Fouchet Plan' has so far not been told in full. Moreover, much has been said in this context which does not stand up to scrutiny. I should like to put the true facts on record.

To understand what happened, one must compare the first version of the Plan, drafted at the beginning of 1961, with the one that was finally submitted to us by the French in April 1962. The amendments made to the original text, on which agreement had been reached in principle, concerned, in essence, four issues: the relations between the future united Europe and the Atlantic Alliance; those between the new organization and the Common Market; the prospects for the future; and British participation.

All these matters except the last had already been thrashed out in Bonn. In the first version the proposals on which agreement had been achieved were formulated very satisfactorily. The preamble declared that the parties involved were 'anxious to welcome in their midst any other European states ready to accept the same responsibilities and obligations'. Article 2 of this draft said that one of the aims of the new organization should be 'to devise a common policy designed to strengthen the Atlantic Alliance'. Article 16 provided that within three years of the treaty's coming into force it would be submitted to a full review to see what could be done to strengthen the union, having regard to the progress made in the meantime. The object of this review, it was stated, was to facilitate a gradual coordination of the foreign policies of the member states and to associate the European Assembly more closely with the formulation and execution of such joint policies.

Article 17 again referred to the suggestions previously mentioned in the preamble: 'Member states of the Council of Europe ready to accept the aims defined under Article 2 shall be free to join the Union. Such states will first be expected to join the European communities mentioned in the preamble to the Treaty.'

This document, drafted at a time when Britain had just made clear her intention of applying for membership of the Common Market, was excellent. The original version also suggested other worthwhile measures. For instance there was to be an executive committee and a secretary-general, who was to be an international civil servant. The new organization was not to be burdened with any economic duties. This meant that the Treaty of Rome would be respected and the powers of the European Commission would not be called into question.

I am convinced that all the ministers ought to have been able to agree on this text and, had this happened, a new impulse would have been given to the movement for European political unity. However, new negotiations were held between October 1961 and February 1962. The French suggested numerous amendments to the original draft. It was obvious that the French negotiators had been disavowed either by the Quai d'Orsay or, much more probably, by General de Gaulle himself.

During these few months, a protracted struggle took place between the French and their partners, who had agreed among themselves to submit joint drafts in accord with the spirit of the Bonn communiqué and the original version.

At the beginning of March, a further document was submitted to the ministers. There were two versions: one was supplied by the French and the other consisted almost entirely of passages drafted jointly by the other five. There had thus been no *rapprochement*. On the contrary, the longer the negotiations continued the wider the gulf between the two points of view. The changes made by the French delegation gave some indication of how far we were apart. The French version contained no reference at all to the Atlantic Alliance nor the possibility of new members joining the organization. The passage dealing with the review of the treaty after three years had been greatly watered down. Finally, according to the French text, the organization was to be given economic powers. In other words, everything we wanted had been left out and all those measures we most disliked had been included.

The two versions were submitted to a meeting of the Foreign Ministers of the Six held in Luxembourg on 20 March 1962. M. Schaus was in the chair. He was kindly and discreet but lacked the authority and experience of M. Bech, and was torn between his pro-French sentiments and the fact that his country was a member of Benelux.

Italy was represented by Signor Segni, well known for his devotion to the European cause. He was advised by Ambassador Cattani, who had played an important role in all the diplomatic battles which had preceded the establishment of the Common Market. He is a man on whom one can depend, a tower of strength, and he did not disappoint us. He proved himself a diplomat of the utmost courtesy, ready to consider any reasonable compromise, but adamant on issues of principle.

Germany's representative was Schroeder, whom I had met many times before but always found a very difficult person to sum up. He is undoubtedly a man of distinction, a skilful debater, and probably more Atlantic than European-minded. His personality is stronger than von Brentano's, whom he succeeded. At first a protégé of Adenauer's, he gradually drew away from his patron. He was one of the few German leaders who refused to be overawed by General de Gaulle, whose flatteries and un-friendly actions alike he resisted. And yet, I was not at all sure what his real aims were. He would often declare that he had made up his mind to take a tough line and then, all of a sudden, without any explanation, he would give way with an air of apparent indifference. I have always been puzzled as to his long-term aims and methods.

Luns represented the Netherlands. He has been his country's Foreign Minister for more than fifteen years now. In his own country he enjoys undeniable authority, although he seems to me to be the least Dutch of all the Dutchmen I have ever met. He is very tall – taller even than General de Gaulle – which enables him to claim that he is the only politician on whom the President of the French Republic cannot look down. He is amazingly industrious, ceaselessly travelling about the world on official business, and never misses a single international conference. He is gay, amusing and knows an incredible number of anecdotes, which he tells well. Luns is a pleasant *bon viveur* which whom I have shared many an excellent meal. He has the reputation of being the most determined opponent of French policy in the EEC, but this does not prevent him from visiting the Quai d'Orsay whenever he is in Paris nor from calling Couve de

Murville by his first name of Maurice. His country's policies have made him a very close partner of Belgium. I have always got on well with Luns. On important occasions, frank exchanges have nearly always enabled us to achieve a *rapprochement* between our respective points of view and to adopt common policies. We have both found that this has strengthened our ability to act. Within the EEC, Luns plays the game loyally, but I am not altogether convinced that the Community is all he would like it to be. Both for sentimental reasons and from conviction he bitterly regrets Britain's absence from the EEC.

He is too much of a realist to be anti-French, but has not altogether shed an old complex dating back to the seventeenth century, and instinctively distrusts the country of Louis XIV. Like Schroeder, he is occasionally very outspoken in discussion but does not always stand up for his point of view even when he might reasonably do so.

At the beginning of 1962, our views were in close accord and we helped one another loyally and constantly during the negotiations on the Fouchet Plan. Opposite us, we had Couve de Murville. He is an ideal minister to serve under de Gaulle, as much because of his faults as his virtues. He is profoundly sceptical and prepared to accept whatever directives are given him without insisting too strongly on his own views. Even when he disagrees as to the substance and, above all, the method, of whatever action he is ordered to take, he does not refuse to comply since he has no really strong convictions of his own. And yet he is extremely intelligent, highly cultivated and knowledgeable, having served both as a senior treasury official and a diplomat. He is always to the fore in any debate, precise, logical, imaginative. The weaker the cause he has to plead, the more arguments he manages to marshal. He is imperturbably cool, his manner one of distant courtesy which only barely allows one to glimpse the fact that he feels himself to be superior to his contemporaries. I have often had cause to admire the way he would face up, in isolation, to the combined pleas of his partners. Frequently I have felt sorry for him because he has had to champion so many doubtful causes and have regretted that a man of so many talents has not been able to harness them to the service of more deeply felt convictions. Rarely have I met anyone so different from myself whom, in my heart of hearts, I have yet liked so much.

We have had many a confrontation both in NATO and in the EEC Ministerial Council, and I have not always emerged victorious from these encounters. My own views could make no impression on this impassive man. If he had been fired by some profound conviction of his own he might have reached great heights. However, he was prepared to be one of those of whom General de Gaulle said in 1932: 'There are persons who are not devoid of the merit of self-abnegation and obedience and who take endless trouble to do as they are told.'

For a man like Couve de Murville, with gifts such as his, this is not enough. Foreign Minister of his country for longer than any of his predecessors, he would have been able to set the seal of his personality on his period of office had he not been content merely to carry out orders. What he lacked was the courage to be himself and the will to attempt the seemingly impossible.

Such were the men who met in Luxembourg on 20 March 1962 to attempt – unsuccessfully as it turned out – to give a fresh impulse to European unity. The following day I summed up my impressions in a circular addressed to Belgian Ambassadors abroad:

'I have the honour to append to this message a summary of the proceedings of the Council of Foreign Ministers of the Six, held in Luxembourg on 20 March last, to discuss the draft treaty for a Union of States.

'As you will see, the gulf between the views of France on the one hand and those of the five other Powers was not at all bridged in regard to the three essential issues over which the Powers have been at odds all along:

'The powers of the Union: the French would like to see economic problems included in its area of competence.

'Common defence: in this context France's partners

443

are asking for certain assurances with the aim of strengthening NATO.

'The general review: in this connection, adequate guarantees of future progress must be provided here and now.

'The meeting was certainly not a waste of time since it enabled us to make it clear to France why her partners are at present hesitant and doubtful about subscribing to a pact which appears to be virtually devoid of purpose, which does not look promising for the future and which, moreover, entails certain dangers to the activities of the various European communities already in existence.

'Personally, I made it my business to put specific questions to my French colleague on the various issues under discussion. I made no secret of the fact that my reservations regarding the attitude of the French Government are due, above all, to its treatment of various major issues of foreign and defence policy. France's stand on these matters is indicative of very serious differences between herself and her allies.

'The frank exchange of views which took place should allow all parties involved to take stock of the arguments put forward and get to grips with this problem with some promise of progress. However, it would be wrong to be too optimistic about our chances at the next ministerial meeting, due to take place in Paris on 17 April. In the meantime, new proposals may be submitted through diplomatic channels. At all events, the political planning commission will meet to revise the drafts and will, in so doing, look at various minor amendments which have been adopted.'

This account shows how heated had been the discussion. Contrary to what had been decided in Rome, Couve de Murville refused obstinately – one might almost say a little provocatively – to agree that a definite link should be established between the organization envisaged and the Atlantic Alliance. He also continued to insist that the organization should be given powers to deal with economic matters, a procedure which created a danger of duplication and thus threatened to weaken the EEC Commission.

The other ministers opposed these suggestions, some more, some less firmly, according to their temperament, the strength of their convictions and the policies of their respective governments. Luns and I were in the forefront of the battle. The others, though they agreed with us as to the substance of our case, were more restrained in putting their views. We parted discouraged, although it was agreed that we should meet again in Paris in a month's time.

As regards this latter meeting, held on 17 April, incomplete and biased accounts have been circulated. While it is true that my Dutch colleague and I resisted the French proposals, it is equally true that Couve de Murville, who was in the chair, did nothing to ensure the success of the meeting. Acceptable compromises were adopted – in response to Italian efforts under the guidance of Cattani – regarding the new organization's relations with the Atlantic Alliance and its economic powers: on the other hand, Couve de Murville did not even open the discussion on the organization's future. In my dispatch to the Ambassadors, I commented as follows:

'You will have noticed the officially inspired indignation of the French press, which blames Belgium and the Netherlands for the failure of our efforts to establish a political union. The summary of the proceedings will show you how inaccurate these accusations are and how hard I tried during our discussions to be flexible. The French press makes it quite clear that the chairman, M. Couve de Murville, was determined to cut the discussion short if the Belgians and Dutch did not submit to all the conditions laid down by the French Government.

'The crucial element in the Belgian position is this: In entering the proposed political union, the small countries can aspire to two possible safeguards – either the introduction of rules of procedure binding upon the members of the Community or the presence of Great Britain as a counterweight. The French plans

445

deny us both these safeguards. French commentators try to show that it is illogical to call at one and the same time for a supra-national Europe and for British participation. I agree that it would be too optimistic to hope for both these aims to be achieved simultaneously in present circumstances. However, Belgium believes it to be essential that either one or the other safeguard be provided. French policies are designed to deprive us of all hope of ever obtaining a supra-national political union. Consequently, Belgium would at least like to see Britain become a member. Since neither of these objectives proved attainable, we decided to play for time.'

The French press, obviously inspired by the Quai d'Orsay did its best to denounce the attitude of Luns and myself. It claimed we had been inconsistent in calling for both a supra-national Europe and British membership of the future organization. The fact is that we never asked that these demands be met at one and the same time. All we wanted was one or the other of these requests to be satisfied. Our position, far from being unreasonable, was in fact wholly logical.

I made my views on this subject clear at our meeting in Luxembourg in March. I said there that if Britain did enter the Common Market in the near future, I was 'prepared to pay a price for this'. This was the exact phrase I used. Regarding political integration, I made very modest demands, but pointed out at the same time that if Britain's entry were not forthcoming, I should have to review my position. In that event, I said, we would have to press for rapid progress towards European integration. At our meeting in Paris I took the same line. I recalled that Mr Heath had lately expressed the hope that Britain might be allowed to join in the consultations of the Six. I went on to say:

'The Belgian Government considers that the British request must be met.... If it should prove impossible to create a Europe along the lines set out in our document, Britain's presence would be a factor which would weigh with the Belgian Government. We would accept this somewhat unsatisfactory solution if that were the only way to secure British entry.'

The French position was altogether different. Not only did the French give no consideration at all to the possibility of establishing community institutions in Europe, but they were not prepared to give us a guarantee, or even a promise, that such institutions might be established at some time in the future. The treaty, according to the French, must be concluded immediately without any consideration being given to the problem of whether or not Britain should become a member of the future European political union.

Since agreement was clearly out of the question, the matter was left in abeyance and we began to discuss the draft treaty. Our exchanges proved difficult from the outset and soon became disagreeable. Couve de Murville, in his capacity as chairman, should have intervened and behaved impartially in order to facilitate a compromise. In actual fact, he showed himself intractable and brusque. To the surprise of all, at a time when there still seemed to be a chance of a *rapprochement,* he suddenly declared that there was no point in continuing the debate on the draft any further. Segni, Schroeder and Schaus tried to reconcile our differences and urged that a new effort be made. In reply, Couve agreed to a meeting which would be attended by the ministers, without their official aides, but, only after declaring that 'the fate of Europe's economic unity must be considered to be in the balance'. Belgium and the Netherlands were thus under maximum pressure. All that this restricted meeting produced was a set of minutes recording our disagreement.

We noted, however, that we had made some progress on two issues: (1) the Atlantic Alliance, and (2) the economic powers of the future European organization. This shows that Luns and myself were less uncompromising than we were subsequently alleged to have been. On the other hand, we had to admit that no agreement had been reached regarding the clause providing for a review of the functioning of the Treaty. In fact, this issue was not even broached during our discussions, since Couve refused to allow the matter to be dealt with. I consider this incident revealing. It is my opinion that in Paris on 17 April the French delegation in fact no longer wanted the negotiations to succeed, either because it thought its partners, particularly the Dutch and Belgians, too intractable or – and I believe this to be the truth of the matter – because it wanted to avoid the risk of having one day to accept British participation in one form or another.

I have attended many international conferences and none has ever been so deliberately manoeuvred into a blind alley by its chairman as this one. If Eden at our conference in London in 1954 or I myself at our meeting in Brussels at which we discussed the future Treaty of Rome had behaved with such impatience and intransigence as Couve, we should never have reached agreement. As Couve's competence cannot be in question, it is his good will one cannot help but doubt. Most likely, his brief was definite on this point: either the Belgians and the Dutch give way all along the line or the talks must be broken off.

I said as much during the debate: 'This is not how I envisaged a united Europe; this is not the language Adenauer, de Gasperi and Schuman used in addressing us.'

But times had changed and it was clear that every effort was being made to leave us in no doubt on this score. In view of what had happened, the ministers decided that there was no point in fixing a date for a further meeting. We made the best of things by consoling ourselves that we would be able to resume our talks either in Athens or in Brussels and would reach agreement then. But in fact, everyone had lost hope. Our bid to give a fresh impulse to the movement for European unity had failed.

I have often asked myself in a mood of self-criticism if I was not wrong in opposing acceptance of the Fouchet Plan. But even after all this time, having reflected on what had happened, I still believe that my reasons for behaving as I did were valid. The fact that France has withdrawn from NATO and that her continued membership in the Atlantic Alliance is doubtful; the various crises she has provoked in the EEC; her hostility to the

Commission; her attempts to reduce the latter's powers and her self-willed refusal to permit Britain's entry into the Common Market – all this is proof that our fears were justified and the guarantees we demanded essential. Germany's present policy of unconditional loyalty to France also highlights the risk facing small countries in an organization such as the one proposed under the terms of the Fouchet Plan. In such a body, small countries are bound to be at the mercy of the pressures which the Great Powers can bring to bear on them. Today, the inadequacies of the Fouchet Plan, as we saw them at the time, can be considered to have been amply demonstrated. It was during the negotiations on the Plan that, for the first time, I decided to be difficult and, up to a point, negative, at a European meeting, but to this day I remain convinced that I was right in acting as I did.

Nevertheless, I was saddened by the failure of the negotiations. I went on pondering the problems we had failed to solve and seeking ways of reopening the discussion. On 24 July 1962, I sent the following letter to de Gaulle:

'My dear General,

'I should like, if I may, to put to you some of my views on the subject of Europe's political unity.

'I have all along been unable to accept the Fouchet Plan as it now stands. Whether Britain joins the Common Market or not, I am convinced that it would be advisable to work for progress towards Europe's political unity. I have therefore tried to devise some intermediate scheme, halfway between the Fouchet Plan and the ideal European political union – something that could be accepted as a compromise between the various concepts which have been put forward of late. It seems to me that, for the time being at least, it should be possible to renounce the ideas of both a Federal Europe and a supra-national structure provided we are prepared to learn from our recent experience in the Common Market.

'I believe that all who have taken part in the work of the EEC in Brussels would agree that the progress that has been made – and our advance has been faster than originally expected – is largely due to the work of the

Commission. The clash of ideas between the national governments on the one hand and the Community authorities on the other has undoubtedly been fruitful. It would, I think, be true to say that the common agricultural policy would never have been established without the efforts of the Community. This justifies the assumption that it is not by the conventional approach that the Europe of the future will be created but by means of joint authorities which will gradually assert themselves in the face of purely national influences. Could we not draw our inspiration from this concept and apply on the political plane the approach we have used so successfully in the economic sphere?

'You yourself, my dear General, at your press conference on 15 May, indicated that other commissions, each concerned with a specific field and working to its own rules, could be established side by side with the Economic Commission in Brussels. I should like to satisfy myself that I am right in thinking that this proposal of yours can be reconciled with the ideas I have tried to outline in this letter. Briefly, would it not be possible, within the framework of the Fouchet Plan, to establish a European Political Commission which would draw its members, not from civil servants answerable to their own governments, but from persons jointly appointed by all the partners? The members of this commission would be independent and their main task would be to represent the common interests of all *vis-à-vis* the various national governments.

'In the first stage, at any rate, the rule of unanimity would apply in the commission, which would confine itself to such duties as preparing the ground for future discussions, promoting the interests of the community and possibly executing any decisions taken by the Ministerial Council or Councils. I should like to emphasize that such an approach must be regarded as a compromise for, on the one hand, it implies a renunciation of the supra-national concept while, on the other, it recognizes the need to establish forthwith a joint authority which would exist side by side with the various national Governments. Naturally, a great many details would have to be settled, but this work can only be usefully attempted if you agree with the basic concept.

'Before closing, I should like to draw your attention to one aspect of this issue which seems very important to me. Whenever you have spoken of the Fouchet Plan, you have stressed that you regard it as merely a realistic beginning, as a first step. I do not, of course, doubt your assurances on this score and am therefore convinced that you have further developments in mind for the future.

'However, if in a few months from now the Europe we are building is no longer the Europe of the Six we know now but a Europe of seven or even nine or ten Powers, the developments which you now consider to be but a beginning may well be regarded by others as the final goal. We have seen this sort of thing happen before in connection with the establishment of the Council of Europe. I therefore consider it essential – even though it may mean that we have to proceed with great caution during the initial stages of such an enterprise – that we create here and now the foundations of an organization which would be able to develop normally without being frustrated by the veto of the most timid among the partners involved.

'I should be most grateful if you would be good enough to consider this suggestion. If you have no objection in principle, it would become necessary to elaborate the scheme in greater detail. We should thus be able to resume our study of various problems which we have had to abandon in a half-finished state, and might also make some progress towards a politically more united Europe. I have long believed in the need for this, and do so now more than ever.

'I hope you will forgive me, my dear General, for having addressed this message to you personally, thus disregarding certain rules of diplomatic etiquette. It was my belief, however, that the kindness you have been good enough to show me on many occasions in the past gave me the right to act as I did. I decided to proceed in this way because I am well aware that in the last resort all depends on you.

'Please allow me to assure you of my respect and devotion.'

Before commenting on my proposals, I feel bound to confess that in acting in this way I committed an error or, to put it more bluntly, a *gaffe*. I should not have written to the President of the French Republic in person, using informal language. What I could do in my contacts with men like Adenauer, Kennedy, Eden and even Khrushchev would never do in my dealings with de Gaulle, and I should have known better. I should have maintained a respectful distance and gone through the proper channels. It goes without saying that, regardless of the approach employed, I would in any case have failed in my attempt, but at least I would have been spared a reply beginning with the words 'M. le Président' and ending with 'Yours truly'. To know those one has to deal with is one of the prerequisites of success, and this I had forgotten.

Nevertheless, my proposal reflected a genuine desire for an understanding and contained a good many concessions. It suggested an approach to our problems which, in view of our recent experience in the EEC, seemed worth following up. By 1962, we knew full well that the Europe of the future could not be based on a federal pact. We had also by then come to realize the inadequacy and slowness of purely economic solutions. On the other hand, we had learned to appreciate the benefits to be derived from a dialogue between international organizations on the one hand and national governments on the other. It thus seemed to us that this new method looked promising.

In his reply, General de Gaulle rejected all my suggestions. It seemed unthinkable to him that political responsibilities – even minor ones on the lines I had indicated – should be entrusted to a commission in whose independence he had no faith. The General rejected the idea of the dialogue I had suggested. It was the tone of his reply even more than its substance which made me realize that there was no point in continuing my efforts. His letter was icy, couched in terms of so stiff a courtesy that I concluded that it was out of the question that I should continue this correspondence.

I also failed in an attempt to enlist Chancellor Adenauer's interest in my efforts. At a meeting with him in Bonn on 22 July, I handed him a copy of my letter to the General. Although Adenauer seemed inclined to agree with my ideas, in fact by then his mind was made up: he had made his choice between de Gaulle on the one hand and his erstwhile partners in the struggle for a united Europe on the other. He had forgotten his former suspicions, his oft-declared hostility to the Gaullist view of Europe. He was by now beguiled and conquered and had decided to submit to the French. A few months later he set all doubts at rest when he signed the Franco-German Treaty of Friendship. This document was to lead to an exchange of letters between von Brentano, who at that time was no longer German Foreign Minister, and myself.

As I have already noted, I had criticized this Treaty in my *Izvestia* interview. On 22 May 1963, von Brentano wrote to me:

> 'I feel entitled, in view of our friendly cooperation over many years, to inform you that your comments have amazed me and that many of my friends have intimated to me that they share my views.'

While recognizing that the Franco-German Treaty had given rise to certain misconceptions, von Brentano believed that these had been dissipated by the preamble to the deed of ratification adopted by the Bundestag. He went on to proclaim his opposition to the idea of a non-aggression pact between the NATO and Warsaw Pact Powers on the grounds that this might entail recognition of Eastern Germany. In somewhat austere tones, he made it clear that he thought statements advocating such a pact 'incompatible with both the letter and the spirit of our treaties of alliance'. However, since von Brentano followed up his criticisms with a phrase recalling our long-standing friendship, I could hardly say in my reply that I was shocked by his letter.

I answered him forthwith:

'You raise three objections in your letter: the first relates to my views on the Franco-German Treaty; the second to the suggested non-aggression pact between the NATO and the Warsaw Pact Powers, and the third to the tenor of my letter.

'I must admit that I am surprised you should say my statements are incompatible with the letter and the spirit of our treaties of alliance. I believe I can prove to you that my statements do not carry the meaning that you impute to them. Moreover, if such statements as you allege I have made are in fact uttered by anybody, it is because treaties such as the one between France and Germany have been concluded without any consultation by these two Powers with their allies. I might even go so far as to say that this was done as a revenge for certain attitudes which emerged during the debate on the so-called Fouchet Plan. It seems to me, if I may be allowed to say so, that it is far more serious to have concluded such a treaty than to pronounce judgement on it. What, in fact, did I say about the Franco-German Treaty? With a great deal of moderation, I declared that it was popular neither in Brussels, nor in Rome nor in The Hague – and you know full well that this is the case.

'The question of whether or not the Franco-German Treaty complies with the letter, or at least the spirit, of the Treaty of Rome, is open to discussion. Personally, I do not think it does, and when I see that nowadays certain decisions have to be postponed because the Chancellor and General de Gaulle must be allowed to consult first, I am convinced I am right. The Franco-German Treaty has introduced a new and unforeseen element into the EEC and I doubt whether that element will prove helpful.

'However, neither in Parliament nor anywhere else did I speak out against the treaty in vehement terms. Quite candidly, the reason I have not opposed the treaty openly is because I do not believe that it will in fact stand the test of time. It seems to me that it is based on an ambiguity. You mention the preamble that has been adopted by the Bundestag. I am absolutely certain this preamble will not be accepted by the French Government. This alone shows on how fragile a foundation the treaty rests. I greatly fear that this document, instead of improving Franco-German relations – and this has always been our aim – will in fact render them more difficult and that the quarterly bilateral consultations which are to be held will very soon highlight the differences between the respective policies of the two Governments. You only have to look at what has happened in connection with Britain's approaches to the EEC, the planning of the Community's policy and, above all, the planning of Europe's defence. I should hope that, in view of these facts, you will concede that my opposition to the Treaty is not wholly unfounded.

'While it would not be accurate to say that I have at any time come out strongly in favour of the conclusion of a non-aggression treaty between the member countries of NATO and the Warsaw Pact, you may remember that even while I was still Secretary-General of NATO I was not averse to the idea of such a treaty. Though I do not believe that the treaty should be allowed to stand on its own, I think it could form a useful complement to an agreement either on disarmament or the Berlin problem.

'I am, of course, quite aware that there are legal difficulties and that we must avoid giving recognition to Eastern Germany by virtue of such a treaty. On the other hand, I am absolutely certain that formulae can be devised to avoid this difficulty.

'It is my firm belief that we must make the best of the present breathing space in international affairs to take some sort of action. I do not think an excessively passive policy would be helpful and feel, on the contrary, that if we do take this latter course, our inaction may well one day be held against us.'

I consider that the arguments I advanced then, in 1963, remain valid to this day. While Erhard was Chancellor, the bilateral Franco-German meetings failed to narrow the gulf between the two countries. The fact that, as I write this, this state of affairs has now apparently changed is entirely due to Chancellor Kiesinger's toal surrender to France. I do not think this can continue indefinitely.

In September 1964 I made a further attempt to give fresh impetus to the plans for a united Europe. Addressing the Parliamentary Commission of the Western European Union, I proposed – worried as I was by the resurgence of certain nationalistic moods and the total absence of any progress towards political integration – that a treaty be concluded which would remain in force for a maximum of three years. The arrangements envisaged under the terms of the Fouchet Plan were to be applied as an experiment. At the same time, the idea of a political commission, which I had earlier put to General de Gaulle, would be put into effect. After this trial period, each of the participating countries would be free either to continue these arrangements, to improve them or to withdraw.

While this plan was very favourably received by the majority of the Members of Parliament present, including the Gaullists, it was not followed up in practice since the Governments were not really prepared to undertake the experiment. I made vain approaches to Bonn and Paris. In the former capital, I was received courteously. Agreement was given in principle, but no action followed. The French attitude was one of extreme scepticism. All eyes were on the economic difficulties of the moment, and it was felt that the time was not yet ripe for a new political initiative – a situation which was accepted without undue distress. I thus had no choice but to bow to the facts: the time was not right for a new advance towards political unity.

43

The Crisis of the Atlantic Alliance

By 1961 the aspirations which in 1956 had led to the adoption of the report of the 'Three Wise Men' had been abandoned. There was no sequel to the progress which had been accomplished during the first two years of my tenure of office in NATO.

General de Gaulle must be considered the chief culprit. As soon as his plan for a triumvirate had been rejected by the Americans and British, he began to pursue a policy which gradually opened up a gulf between France and her allies. He claimed he was making good his bid for independence by refusing to take part in the projected integration of military forces, by creating his own nuclear strike force and adopting an approach to international affairs which in fact isolated him more and more.

Among the developments which occurred between 1961 and 1966 there are two with which I propose to deal in detail: France's consistent refusal to agree with her partners in what area of international relations the concept of peaceful coexistence between the West and the Communist camp should be applied, and his no less obstinate refusal to define the reforms which, in his view, should be introduced within the Western alliance. He kept up a stream of criticism of the alliance while at the same time justifying his refusal to make known his wishes on the grounds that his partners in any case had made up their minds not to listen to him no matter what he had to say.

Within the alliance, I advocated a policy of *rapprochement* with the European Communist countries, a policy which I had myself applied in practice during my two visits to the USSR and also when I established contact with Poland.

There was not a single meeting of the Atlantic Council between 1962 and 1966 at which I did not put forward my ideas in order to rid the Alliance of its inertia, which I personally found worrying. My aim was to try to get the alliance to explore and exploit the possibilities I could see emerging as a result of the USSR's new policies. It was Couve de Murville who opposed my arguments most strongly. In recalling this phase, I cannot help smiling when I now see General de Gaulle courting public acclaim in Moscow, Warsaw and Bucharest as if he were the first statesman to have advocated an East-West *rapprochement*. The truth of the matter is very different. For a number of years it was in fact de Gaulle who prevented the Atlantic Alliance from taking this particular course. True, he was not alone in being sceptical of the chances of a *rapprochement*, but if, instead of throwing cold water on our enthusiasm and rejecting all initiatives, he had helped those who wanted to strike out along fresh paths, there would have been some progress, for neither the Americans nor the British were opposed to these efforts. In fact, Macmillan pursued such a policy *vis-à-vis* the Soviet Union, independently and outside the Alliance; and Kennedy solemnly declared that the West's relations with the Communist world would have to be put on a new footing.

I pleaded tirelessly that, in view of the changes which had occurred, it was the Alliance as a whole which should take a fresh look at its position and that such a joint initiative was bound to have a much more telling effect than separate action by individual members of the Alliance. I also pointed out that by acting in concert we would avoid being forced to bid against one another.

Couve de Murville did not deny that certain changes had in fact taken place in the USSR, but he considered that they had not gone far enough to justify either a fresh initiative or a modification of our existing policies. I must admit I was exasperated by his sceptical attitude. At the time I summed up Couve's views in a single brief sentence: 'When things go badly, one must not negotiate under duress; when they go well, there is no point in negotiating.' I refused to believe that such inaction was a sign of wisdom.

Our confrontation was to be repeated at all the meetings of the Atlantic Council: in Ottawa in the spring of 1963, in Paris in December of the same year, and, above all, at The Hague in May 1964.

One day – probably some time in the distant future – when the minutes of the Atlantic Council are made public, my views will be seen to have been correct. The closing passage of my speech in Ottawa summed up both my own feelings and the views of the two camps:

'I believe we must choose between two foreign policies. One is to cling to our old arguments and to maintain our positions intransigently; the other is a dynamic policy which would take into account the changes and the progress that have been made, a policy based on the new situation – which may turn out to be more than just a passing phase. This policy would enable us to go over from the defensive to the offensive in our diplomacy.'

These discussions were interesting but, unfortunately, they failed to produce any noteworthy result owing to the paralysing effect of the rule of unanimity. The ministers made their speeches one by one and explained their points of view, and that was the end of it. No action followed and we went our several ways. The boldest among us were hamstrung by the most timid.

In December 1963, the discussions were resumed on a wider basis. In Couve de Murville's view, the chances of an East-West *détente* depended exclusively on the USSR. He said it would be an illusion to believe that we could exert any influence on Soviet policy. There must be no change until the Soviet Union had recognized the German people's right to self-determination. I could not agree either with his assessment of the situation or with his conclusions. It seemed to me both wrong and indolent to expect the Russians alone to modify their policies and to make fresh proposals if the West were not prepared to do likewise. I also thought it wrong to assume that nothing we might say or do could possibly influence events. I believed it to be a mistake to expect the Russians to settle the German problem in accordance with our views in advance of any progress towards an understanding. It was this latter view, in particular, that I opposed. I thought it unwise to regard a solution of the German problem as a precondition. In my opinion, a settlement of that issue must, on the contrary, be seen as the crowning achievement of a future *rapprochement.* Recalling what I had earlier said in Ottawa, I declared that international politics was not an exact science but rather an art which called for a great deal of intuition on the part of its practitioners. I said the Atlantic Alliance must take stock of the transformation which had occurred in the Communist world, that it must explore the situation and refuse to be content with a policy of inaction. I added that if we were to explore the situation we must not just sit back and wait for the USSR to come forward with fresh proposals; we, too, must produce new ideas.

But the text of the final communiqué put before us once again reiterated the conventional policies of the Atlantic Alliance in the same old terms which had been employed by us for years. There was a protracted discussion on the wording; since it became apparent that no compromise was in sight on matters of substance, we finally agreed on a colourless formula.

The Council's meeting at The Hague in May 1964 proved both more difficult and more important. This time it was not only the policy of the Alliance which was at stake but its very existence.

On the eve of the session, I received Dean Rusk in Brussels. Ever since our first meeting I had felt a very real liking for the American Secretary of State, a feeling which grew stronger as the years went by. I have always found Rusk a wonderful ally, understanding and loyal. I admire him all the more because of the difficulties he has had to face in recent years, the responsibilities he has had to bear and the painful decisions he has had to take. I find his constancy in battle deeply moving and I sympathise with him in his dilemma in having to overcome his instinctive feelings for the sake of what he believes to be the common good. No one who has ever met him can have failed to realize that here is a man who hates war. His moderation, his courtesy and goodness are reflected in the kindly look in his eyes and his gentle smile. Kennedy chose Dean Rusk to be his Secretary of State despite the fact that he did not know him personally. Rusk had been recommended to the President by two or three individuals whose judgement he trusted and he was persuaded to give up the humanitarian work he was doing at the head of a great foundation. Rusk's aim in accepting the unexpected offer of this high office – despite the dangers and the heavy responsibilities involved – was to promote the cause of international friendship in a more important sphere. His has been a strange destiny. This quiet, peaceable and tolerant man was called upon to deal, as Secretary of State, with the Cuban and Vietnam crises. I have heard him tell of the hours he lived through during the crucial week before Kennedy finally decided to ask the Russians to dismantle their missile bases on the island. Even some months after that event, Rusk could not hide his feelings at the memory of what had gone before: he had to live with the thought that war was a distinct possibility.

I was to meet him again in 1968 after a lapse of several years and was impressed by the strength of his convictions. He has been through some trying experiences. In the United States, he has to contend with fierce opposition and is not always understood outside his own country either. He is forced to pursue a policy which cannot possibly be to his own liking and which he knows to be unpopular. Despite this, he will never fail to do his duty as he sees it. Without in any way resembling Foster Dulles, he is, like his predecessor, able to see world problems as a whole. Though less abrupt in manner, he is, for all that, just as determined as Dulles. Rusk is a man who will stand his ground, and whatever he has to do he will see through to the end, without fuss and without fear.

In this month of May 1964, the situation was not yet as grave as it was to become later but it was already giving us cause for concern. Those responsible for the conduct of NATO affairs were asking themselves what attitude to adopt towards France, whose policies were making the life of her allies increasingly difficult.

In reviewing the situation for Dean Rusk's benefit, I stressed that the question to be decided during our meeting at The Hague was whether we were to make a genuine attempt to tackle our problems or to pretend that they did not exist. My own view was that we must adopt the first of these alternatives. Referring to Stikker's report, I said I was struck by the fact that it obviously reflected the Secretary-General's secret dilemma. In his capacity as in international civil servant, Stikker, I said, was doing his best to appear optimistic, but as a statesman he could not but show his anxiety at the many, and growing, difficulties facing the Alliance.

By recognizing Communist China, by her attitude to the Vietnam issue and her latest decisions on military policy, France was making it increasingly clear that she was determined to take an independent line. In his most recent speech, Couve de Murville had himself put the fundamental question, i.e. whether the Alliance should be maintained. My own view, I said, was very clear: something must be done to stop this process of deterioration. What we must do was to avoid polemics with our French partners and at the same time ask them to explain their intentions. If they thought the Alliance had weaknesses, that it was poorly organized, let them tell us what changes were necessary. It was our duty to look at any ideas the French might care to submit, but we must not allow the present equivocal situation to continue.

I said I was aware that since the signing of the Treaty of Washington the international situation had changed but that, in my opinion, the continued existence of the Alliance was essential if we were to deal with the new problems that had arisen. In conclusion, I stressed that Couve de Murville had many times referred to the developments which had occurred in the world during the last year and a half, but that he had never made it clear what consequences, in his view, these changes implied for the Alliance. The time had come to ask him to tell us what was in his mind. To do nothing, to remain silent, I said, would merely land us in an impasse. There must be a frank discussion at the meeting at The Hague.

There were no major differences between Rusk and myself. The Secretary of State, too, was worried by the situation. He felt that Couve was difficult to pin down, that he refused to enter into a genuine discussion and merely kept repeating that there was no point in his making any proposals since everybody was determined in advance to reject them. This attitude, rather like that of a sulky child, was no doubt the outward expression of France's resolve to 'go it alone'.

The future was to show that Rusk was right. On 12 May, at The Hague, during our discussion of the Secretary-General's report, Couve made an astonishingly banal speech. He made no mention whatever of the situation in the Alliance, did not repeat the criticisms he had made earlier in the French National Assembly and did not ask for any changes. It was quite clear that he wished to avoid any debate on contentious issues. To further her own policies, France was determined to surround herself with an aura of mystery.

On the morning of 12 May, I received Butler, the British Foreign Secretary. Butler was familiar with my intentions and knew that I wanted to put specific questions to Couve in order to force him to clarify his intentions. The Foreign Secretary asked me to do nothing of the sort. Although he shared my own and Dean Rusk's views, he was anxious to avoid a clash. I have never been able to understand why the British Foreign Office has invariably shown itself so hesitant in facing up to certain issues nor what it hoped to achieve by this timid attitude. I think that in the absence of any real expectation that de Gaulle might yet change his policy – and no one was so naïve as to believe *that* – the British view was that one of these days de Gaulle would be out of office and that the French Government which would take over from him would resume its country's traditional policies. I felt that such hopes were misplaced. There was no reason, in 1964, to believe that the de Gaulle era was nearing its end. No one could tell how many years he would have to keep silent and remain passive if we acted on this hypothesis. Above all, no one could foresee what unpleasant – and potentially fateful – surprises might be in store for us in the meantime.

I refused to comply with Butler's request and merely promised to exercise restraint in putting my views. On 13 May I made a long speech based both on the Secretary-General's report and on a statement by Maurice Schumann, the Chairman of the French National Assembly's Foreign Affairs Committee.

The Secretary-General had declared that the Alliance was 'in an unhealthy condition', and coming from so moderate a man as Stikker such a statement was all the more noteworthy. M. Schumann had said:

'If it is true that the Atlantic Alliance must both be maintained and reformed, should we wait until the eve of the day the NATO agreements are due to expire? I should like to ask the governments whether we should not, on the contrary, reform NATO while we can still do so free from undue pressures and while the Treaty still has several more years to run. Would this not be preferable – in fact is this not the only way – of avoiding a break up? France, it is true, has had to take certain unilateral actions in order to get the arrangement revised. She has acted in this way in view of the refusal with which she has met to discuss these matters and, above all, the refusal to acknowledge the fact that since the end of the war in Algeria the French Navy has been bearing an increased burden of responsibility in the Atlantic. But, for all this, the fact remains that such a reform is the best way to ensure the continued existence of this essential alliance.'

This statement was particularly interesting since it came from a Gaullist holding an important position and had not been disavowed by Couve de Murville. It could therefore be legitimately considered an expression of official French thinking. However, it contained an inaccuracy which called for a rebuttal. It was wrong to say that France's allies were unwilling to discuss the position. It was in fact France herself who remained obstinately silent. My aim at The Hague was to persuade the French to break this silence.

I therefore tried in my speech – after recalling the origins of the Alliance and its objects as defined in 1949 –

to set out the principal changes which had taken place since that time and which might justify a change in our policies. I noted that the United States had lost its nuclear monopoly and remarked on the emancipation of the former colonial territories, the reconversion of Europe's economy from a wartime to a peacetime footing, the changes which had occurred in Soviet policy, and, finally, on the fact that the Communist danger had shifted from Europe to Asia. In conclusion, I declared that these events did not mean that there was now any less need for the Alliance but merely that it must be adapted to fit the changed circumstances. I said I realized that these views were not necessarily shared by all those present but that I felt they should at least be discussed, and stressed that the present atmosphere of misunderstanding must not be allowed to persist.

Commenting on the French attitude, I declared:

'If it is true that the Alliance needs changing, surely the least we have a right to expect from those who take this view is that they should tell us what exactly it is they want. It is unthinkable that we should have an ally in our midst – and one of the most important ones at that – who says: "Our basic principles are now out of date and should be replaced. We should like something new to be done, but since you refuse to discuss matters with us, we prefer to keep our own counsel." But in fact it is not we who are refusing to discuss matters; on the contrary, this is precisely what we want.'

I am convinced to this day that I was right in making this appeal, unsuccessful though it was. Not only was it treated by Couve de Murville with the silence of contempt, but those who shared my views gave me no support whatever. In private conversation everyone spoke his mind freely, criticized and decried the French attitude, but the moment we met on an official footing no one was prepared to strike the first blow. At all costs, there must be no incident, no objective examination of the situation – that was the order of the day. The majority seemed to think that to say nothing, to pretend that nothing was wrong and to hope that things would come right of their own accord was the best way to deal with the situation.

Protected by this fear, which he had succeeded in inspiring in his allies, General de Gaulle continued his systematic destruction of NATO. Two years later this policy was to culminate in the French withdrawal from the Organization, a step which was taken without de Gaulle ever having explained to his allies the changes he considered essential. In fact, he was afraid that any proposals he might make might be accepted. His aim was not to convince but to destroy.

At the meeting in December 1964, the Canadians made yet another effort to persuade the French to clarify their views. Paul Martin, the Canadian Minister of External Affairs, called for an appraisal of the problems which had arisen in connection with the state of the Atlantic Alliance as well as of those we might yet have to face in the future. This task was entrusted to the permanent representatives.

In June 1965, Secretary-General Brosio convened a meeting at which a preliminary report on the situation was discussed. Pierre de Leusse, the French representative, announced that he was in no position to make any concrete proposals since the French Government had not yet made up its mind on the problems under examination. This was two years after General de Gaulle, Pompidou and Couve de Murville had spoken of the need to modify the NATO agreements, but when France's partners wanted to discuss the matter, her representative declared that the time was not yet ripe! General de Gaulle was moulding his policy in solitude and was not prepared to spare much thought for his allies. He was not even willing to unbend so far as to explain to them what precisely it was he wanted, and in fact he rejected the very idea of discussion.

This comedy was to continue for the best part of another year, during which the French President did his utmost to keep up this state of confusion. In his meetings with the Secretary-General he hinted at his desire to quit the Alliance and to replace the existing multilateral agreements with bilateral ones. In his usual skilful way, he first made people fear the worst. Then, when he had refrained

from going to extremes, those who had allowed themselves to be taken in by these tactics would heave a
sigh of relief. Thinking that all was not yet lost, they
would delude themselves that they had made a good
bargain.

On 7 May 1966, ignoring the Atlantic Council, General
de Gaulle put his cards on the table. He wrote to President
Johnson to say that while France intended to renew her
signature of the Treaty of Washington when the latter
expired (i.e., in 1969) – provided, always, that no changes
had occurred in East-West relations in the meantime – she
was cancelling the military arrangements which had been
put into effect since the conclusion of the Alliance by
virtue of either multilateral or bilateral agreements. This,
he said, implied an end to military integration and the
departure from France of all allied troops stationed there.
General de Gaulle declared that he was ready to discuss
the detailed implementation of these *decisions*, which
were, however, irrevocable and not to be treated as mere
proposals.

President Johnson acknowledged receipt of the letter
the same day. He made it clear that he had reservations
regarding the implications of the French action and indicated that he would be in touch with his allies to review
the situation. On 10 May, three days later, France officially
informed her other allies of her decision. One passage from
the French memorandum is worth quoting:

'No doubt, negotiations could have been held with a
view to an agreed modification of existing arrangements, and if it had had the slightest reason to suppose
that such contacts would produce the desired results,
the French Government would have been only too
happy to suggest such talks. Unfortunately, there was
every indication that such an attempt was doomed to
fail since France's partners all appeared to be – some
even proclaimed themselves to be – protagonists of the
status quo. Some actually wanted to take the existing
state of affairs to even greater lengths, regardless of the
fact that present arrangements are unacceptable to
France.'

Rarely had an ally pursued so contemptuous and brusque a policy towards faithful friends, a policy so contrary to certain self-evident truths! How much trust can one still place in France, who, without warning, has unilaterally broken her engagements, thus creating havoc in an organization established at the cost of enormous financial sacrifice by all concerned? Some Frenchmen may derive pleasure from such conduct and regard it as proof of their country's greatness and independence. But such Frenchmen do not realize the tremendous resentment of those who have been treated in so cavalier a manner. The day will come when the French will realize that their country, which is loved and admired by so many, stands to gain nothing from the use of such methods.

On 22 May, President Johnson replied to the French note on behalf of the United States. In his letter, he expressed his bitter disappointment. He recalled the aims of the architects of the Treaty of Washington and the achievements of the Alliance. In this context he stressed that NATO had given peace to Europe and rightly spoke of the advantages of its military organization over similar arrangements in the past. He went on to note the gains in terms of efficiency which had resulted from the modest measure of integration accomplished.

What is surprising about General de Gaulle's theories is that by no stretch of the imagination can they be regarded as an innovation. He wants us to return to military concepts which have been seen to have failed in the past. He pays lip service to the Treaty of Washington but refuses to accept the discipline which must go hand in hand with the Treaty, i.e. he denies it the chance to function effectively.

Two wars have shown that alliances invariably have to face problems of integration and coordination of command. Thanks to NATO, these problems are being attended to in times of peace, in orderly conditions. But General de Gaulle says that before looking at these problems we should wait until hostilities have broken out, regardless of the fact that we should then have to improvise and work in haste. It is only too obvious that such an approach is unwise. To follow France along this path would be to repeat the errors of the past instead of preparing for the future.

Fortunately, the reaction of France's fourteen allies was all that one could have wished. They replied to the French memorandum in a joint declaration of loyalty to the Atlantic Alliance and of confidence in its military organization. Without making any complaint – as they would have been entitled to do – they moved the Atlantic Council to Brussels and their military staff headquarters to Mons. They have since continued discussing the organization of their joint defence and have made further progress. They have made only one mistake: they have been much too generous in conceding some of the French demands. The French Government is bold, if nothing else. It rejects all obligations which flow from its membership of NATO but is quite ready to take part in any joint projects from which it stands to gain. Thus, the French have announced that they wish to continue their participation in the construction of the major radar network on which NATO is at present engaged. That is quite understandable: without these radar installations, France's small nuclear strike force would be reduced to utter impotence. Without it, it would be deaf and blind. Strangely enough, France's partners have consented to this odd bargain.

What would become of the Alliance if all its members accepted its advantages but rejected any obligations that might benefit their partners? It is mistaken decisions such as this that encouraged General de Gaulle to think he could afford to indulge his every whim.

Perhaps we may find some consolation in the closing paragraph of President Johnson's letter:

'In fact, we find it difficult to believe that France – a Power which has made a decisive contribution to the development of Western security – will for long hold aloof from our common efforts and her NATO responsibilities. As an old friend and ally, her seat will remain vacant until such time as she decides to play once more the important part which is rightly hers.'

This indeed is what we all hope.

469

44

The Crisis of the
European Community

General de Gaulle has never liked the Treaty of Rome. When I arrived in Paris in 1957, I requested an audience with him. Having repeatedly met him in London, as well as later, when he was in power after France's liberation, I thought it polite to call on him. I must admit I was also curious to meet him again.

He received me in the suite of the mansion where, each week, emerging from his retreat at Colombey, he would welcome his visitors. As soon as I had crossed the threshold, before I could so much as open my mouth he declared: 'I expect you have come to ask me to do something for your Common Market!' I was somewhat taken aback by this welcome. After I had recovered my composure, I said my only object in coming to see him was to present my respects to the General, adding that I had no intention of discussing the merits of the European Community with him. At this, he relented and proceeded to speak to me in a more conciliatory tone. He criticized at length the Treaty of Rome, which had just been signed but was still awaiting ratification by the French Parliament. He was opposed to the supra-national tendency reflected in that document and declared that our work had not been done well. He then proceeded to give me an account of his own views on Europe, which were the same as those Michel Debré and General Koenig had argued in the Strasbourg Assembly. However, having done this, he did his best to pacify me, assuring me that despite his opposition to the Treaty he had no intention of repeating his action over the ratification of the European Defence Community Treaty. He would not ask, he said, for the

Treaty to be rejected as he could see no point in another confrontation. He was – or at least he seemed to be – discouraged. It was at this last meeting of ours that he told me there was nothing more that could be done in the next ten years to restore France to her former greatness and give her back her rightful place in the world. A new generation would have to take over first.

I remember the visit well. Later, during the years that followed, it was always with some surprise that I heard him insist that the European Community as established under the Treaty of Rome must be maintained. De Gaulle tends to adopt this rigid stance to prevent Britain's entry into the Common Market; on the other hand, he is apt to disregard the Treaty altogether when it is a matter of respecting the powers of the EEC Commission or of submitting to a majority vote.

I remain convinced that it was in 1957 that General de Gaulle gave me a true account of his thinking about the Treaty of Rome. All we know about his views goes to show that there is in fact a wide gulf between his ideas and that document, which derives from the concepts of Jean Monnet and Robert Schuman and must be seen as a landmark along the road to supra-national integration.

Within the framework of the European Community, France has, nevertheless played an important part. The devaluation of the franc, skilfully executed by Antoine Pinay, enabled France to cope with the problems of her adaptation to the EEC more smoothly than would otherwise have been the case. To meet her legitimate wishes, an agricultural policy was adopted of which she was the main beneficiary. This, together with the work done in other fields, gave the Community the necessary balance. France has also benefited from the undoubted qualities of the men who have represented her on the EEC Ministerial Council – men such as Couve de Murville, Giscard d'Estaing, Michel Debré and Pisani. In the various organizations of the Community she has been represented by Jean Monnet, René Mayer, Louis Armand, Hirsch and Marjolin. The lucidity, the ability to sum up an argument and the imaginative thinking of these men – all this has enabled France to play a considerable part in the

471

Community, and she could in fact have become its leader but for the General's uncertain temper and his policy, which has all too often been arbitrary and abrupt.

In July 1961 Macmillan indicated that Britain wished to join the European Community and made a statement to this effect in the House of Commons on the 31st. Earlier, on the 28th, he had informed the Belgian Premier of his intentions. In his letter to the Premier he made no secret of the difficulties: agriculture and Britain's relations with the Commonwealth and the EFTA countries were the chief obstacles. However, Macmillan was confident and expressed the hope that the Belgian Government would support his efforts.

It was at this time that I first met Edward Heath, the Lord Privy Seal, who was to be his country's principal negotiator. Since then, Heath's political career clearly marked him out as a future Prime Minister. I have never been able to understand the difficulties with which he has met and the criticisms to which he has been subjected, for he seems to me to have all the qualities required for the highest political office. He is said to be a poor television performer. Is this to be the decisive criterion of statesmanship? If this is so, it is one more count to add to the indictment of this awful mass media. Having frequently met and negotiated with Edward Heath, I knew him to have many gifts both as an individual and a politician: he is courteous, moderate, natural and devoid of all conceit. He likes to laugh, which I consider an essential quality. He is knowledgeable in a variety of fields and his experience is wide. He puts his views clearly and knows both how to listen and to argue. In Brussels, during many months of discussions, everyone thought highly of him. He enjoyed undeniable authority and inspired confidence in his fellow negotiators. I am convinced that his many gifts will carry him to the top eventually.

We tried to coordinate our efforts. I was far too happy to see Britain finally adopt a policy which I had myself advocated to deny her my assistance now. In acting thus I was loyal both to myself and to the letter and spirit of the Treaty of Rome. I have always believed in the need for Britain's entry into Europe and deplored the refusal of both Labour and Conservative governments to join in our enterprise. Now that an opportunity to make good this omission seemed to be within our grasp, I was determined to take advantage of it and to press for the adoption of any reasonable compromise.

After Macmillan's statement in the Commons, the Six discussed the venue of any future negotiations and the procedure to be adopted. The French made an extraordinary demand: they insisted that the first meeting – the one at which Heath would officially submit his country's candidature for membership – should be held in Paris. There was no reason whatever to justify such a choice. Brussels was the seat of the Community and it was there the meeting should have been held.

For once, Couve de Murville's debating skill deserted him. He did not succeed in justifying his demand. It was simply a question of French prestige and *amour propre*. However, anxious to be conciliatory, France's partners, as so often, bowed to her wish.

The discussion on the procedure was far more important. I suggested we should follow the methods which had enabled us to draw up the Treaty of Rome. I said a politician should be appointed to preside over the negotiations, a statesman who, while impartial, was anxious to promote the success of the negotiations.

I must confess that I hoped I might be entrusted with the task. I thought I might be able to help Britain without betraying the spirit of the Treaty of Rome. However, my hopes were not to be fulfilled: France categorically opposed the procedure suggested by me. Couve de Murville maintained that the Six must agree among themselves as a group on every issue before confronting the British. According to him, they must present a united front. These were not to be negotiations between seven governments but between the Community on the one hand and Great Britain on the other. Couve de Murville adopted a very subtle line of argument. It was difficult to reject a procedure which appeared to be based on the need to maintain European unity. However, I could see the danger implicit in Couve's proposal. My own recent experience had convinced me that the presence of an impartial chairman was essential: his task was to bring the various points of view together and to act as mediator. I realized that to accept the thesis that the Six must agree among themselves prior to any confrontation with the British meant that we would have to comply with the wishes of the most reluctant and most obstinate among us. Negotiations held in such conditions were bound to start under the most unhappy auguries. However, I had to give way for, on this occasion, I had no support.

As we were at that time beginning to consider various ways of establishing Europe's political unity, we decided that any new Powers about to join the European Community should also take part in fashioning the political organization we were planning to set up. This was a logical and reasonable proposal, but it begged one important question: was Great Britain to join in our negotiations? The Belgians, Dutch and Luxembourgers said yes; the Italians, too, were largely in favour; the Germans were rather more reserved and the French were definitely against.

It must be remembered that at that time – October 1961 – the French Government had not yet openly advanced any of the objections to Britain's entry into the Common Market that it was to raise later. And yet, all the obstacles to Britain's entry mentioned by de Gaulle at his press conference in January 1963, as well as those which he put forward subsequently, in 1968, on the occasion of Britain's second attempt, already existed. However, in October 1961 General de Gaulle had, to all appearances, resigned himself to Britain's entry into the European Community.

It was on 10 October 1961 at the Quai d'Orsay that Edward Heath officially submitted to the Six his country's application to join the Common Market. He made an excellent speech from which it was clear that not only was Britain ready to accept the Treaty of Rome and the decisions taken by the Community since 1957, but also the political union of Europe implied in the Treaty. Britain's only request was that certain special problems should be examined: agricultural policy and the position of the Commonwealth and EFTA countries, and in this context she asked for certain temporary relaxations. Those present when Heath made his speech realized that there would be numerous technical problems to solve, but of these none seemed any more difficult than those encountered during the drafting of the Treaty of Rome. Provided we were still inspired by the same sense of purpose, there was no reason why these difficulties should not be overcome. However, the fact was that this determination was now lacking; one of the partners, General de Gaulle, shared neither our enthusiasm nor our hopes. Our failure was thus a foregone conclusion.

The negotiations were held in Brussels and took up the whole of 1962. They were made difficult by the method we had decided to apply: the Six were to hold separate meetings to examine the issues under discussion. We were expected to present unanimous conclusions, and this proved difficult. When, after long hours of debate, such conclusions were eventually reached, the Six would meet the British to acquaint them with the results of their consultations. The British would thereupon withdraw to determine their own position and announce their conclusions upon returning to the conference chamber. No real discussion got under way since none of the Six was entitled to speak as an individual Power. This procedure made speedy progress impossible. With each side merely restating its arguments, our discussions dragged on painfully and all my worst fears seemed to be coming true. And yet, for all this, every now and again we seemed to be making a little headway and many people in fact thought they could already glimpse success over the horizon.

An important meeting was due to be held some time in mid-January 1963. It was the turn of the Belgian representative to take the chair, and the task fell to Henri Fayat, the Deputy Foreign Minister. During the week preceding this meeting, he went to Paris to discuss procedure with Couve de Murville. As always, Couve was ready to listen and, though a hard bargainer, he was not intransigent. None of us had any inkling that a sensation was in the offing. As for Couve, either he knew what was coming and was aware of the coup General de Gaulle was about to spring upon the world – in which case he was a consummate actor – or he knew nothing of the General's plans, and in that case the fact that he was merely a subordinate official without any responsibilities of his own was made even more glaringly obvious than it was already. I believe it is the second of these alternatives that applied. It is out of the question that Couve should have deliberately concealed his intentions and deceived the man due to take charge of the coming meeting of the Six. If I am wrong in this, then the less said the better, for if I have to choose between ignorance and duplicity, I would much rather have ignorance.

The meeting began as planned on 13 January. The French delegates were there and took part in the discussions. During the afternoon of the 14th, while we were in session, the official messengers brought us news flashes of the press conference General de Gaulle was just holding in Paris. Once we had seen these dispatches we could no longer keep our minds on the technical issues before us. A new political event of extreme importance was in the making: General de Gaulle had torpedoed our negotiations without having warned either his partners or the British. He had acted with a lack of consideration unexampled in the history of the EEC, showing utter contempt for his negotiating partners, allies and opponents alike. He had brought to a halt negotiations which he had himself put in train in full agreement with his partners, and had done so on the flimsiest of pretexts.

What had happened? There is every reason to believe that it was the attitude adopted by Macmillan at his meeting with Kennedy in Bermuda which so upset the President of the French Republic. Macmillan's crime was to have reached agreement with the President of the United States on Britain's nuclear weaponry. He had in fact arranged for the purchase of Polaris missiles from the United States. In General de Gaulle's eyes this cooperation with the Americans was tantamount to treason of Europe's interests and justified his refusal to allow Britain into the Common Market. The General's resentment was all the greater because a few days before the Bermuda meeting he had received Macmillan at Rambouillet. The British Prime Minister, he claimed, had told him nothing of his nuclear plans. On the other hand, de Gaulle gave Macmillan no warning that he was about to torpedo the negotiations in Brussels. I think the full truth about these events still remains to be told. The French and British versions which have been circulating in the chancelleries differ, but what is certain is that France, without consulting her partners, unilaterally withdrew from negotiations to which she had earlier agreed and that she did so, moreover, after first insisting that the Six must present a united front.

We were faced with a complete *volte-face*. Stunned and angry, our first reaction was to ignore what had been said in Paris and to continue the negotiation as if nothing had happened. The British showed extraordinary sang-froid. Although, deep down, they were greatly shocked, they gave no outward sign of this and continued to present their arguments at the negotiating table with imperturbable calm. This comedy continued for the best part of another forty-eight hours. At the end of a long day's work, Couve de Murville had a meeting with Henri Fayat. Puzzled, Couve asked Fayat if he had failed to grasp the meaning of General de Gaulle's statements at his press conference, adding – just in case there was any doubt – that the negotiations with Great Britain were at an end. We had one last meeting to put the facts on record. The British behaved with great dignity, while France's partners expressed their disapproval of, and disappointment at, her conduct. We were deeply hurt. Erhard and Piccioni, who were normally very calm and by no means extreme partisans of European unity, were among the most outspoken in their condemnations. They knew the meaning of dictatorship and could not but point to certain similarities. Their deep dismay was evident.

Had the British wished to take advantage of our anger, the five of us could have caused a commotion in the Common Market. However, the British were surprisingly restrained in the circumstances and went out of their way to calm our feelings.

On 24 January 1963, I was asked in the Senate by spokesmen of the three main political parties to explain what had happened and what conclusions I proposed to draw from the latest events. In my reply I gave free rein to my concern and dismay. So far as I was concerned, General de Gaulle's policy was inadmissible as to its form and his arguments to sustain it were childish and in part even ludicrous. I said the General had not disclosed to us what was really in his mind and added that for the first time in Belgium's history the three main parties were at one in condemning French policy. I then went on to give an account of the background of these events.

I stressed that not only was I appalled by the methods used but that the ideas that had been put forward seemed to me to be contrary to the spirit and the letter of the Treaty of Rome. I declared:

> 'This press conference reflects a concept of the Community which cannot but give rise to the most profound misgivings. I have never held the view that the European Community should be a grouping of six Powers – closed, autarchical, inward-looking, selfish, concerned mainly with the comfort and wealth of its own population and heedless of the problems we have created for others by signing the Treaty of Rome. If we retreat within our own group, if we give up all thought of higher ambitions, if we – rich and powerful nations that we are – do not act in a spirit of cooperation and generosity, it will not be very long before the ideals which have guided our steps have been destroyed. If that should happen, instead of creating a Europe capable of illuminating the world with its message – the aim we have so often proclaimed with passion and emotion – we shall very quickly become the object of hate and envy both in Europe and in the world at large.'

I put the chief blame for what had just happened on General de Gaulle – on his personality, his character and psychology. I went on to read to the Senate a long passage from de Gaulle's *The Edge of the Sword* – the book which, though published as far back as 1932, seemed to me to presage all the main features of French policy twenty-five years later.

I then set out to prove that Britain was part of Europe, that we must not forget that her resistance in 1940–41 had saved us, that without her sacrifices we should never have been able to undertake our great enterprise.

Having read the very good speech Macmillan had just made in Liverpool, I quoted certain passages from it. These I contrasted with General de Gaulle's arbitrary attitude. Macmillan had said:

'Relations between friends and allies must be based on equality and understanding, with none of the partners seeking to dominate the others. . . . It is in this way that a powerful Europe will in the long run be able to play its rightful part in cooperating with the American people, not only in the economic field and in the area of trade relations, but also in all the other aspects of our complex modern way of life, whether it be in defence, in the formulation of political ideas or in aid to the underdeveloped countries. . . . It is only thus that we shall be able to persuade the entire world, the non-aligned countries, the new nations, that this European movement which we wish to join is a movement that is not coloured by memories of the past or the ambitions and rivalries which have brought so much misery upon the world. It must be inspired by new ideas and nobler visions.

'Only if we pursue these visions, which inspired the founders of the European movement, shall we have the right to call upon the world not to allow this great opportunity to be wasted.'

I concluded from these words that we were in duty bound not to refuse Britain's request to join Europe, our common ideals having been so forcibly expressed by her Prime Minister. I went on to declare that it would be wrong to say that our negotiations had failed. On the contrary, I declared, not only the representatives of five of the governments but also the members of the Commission believed that we could bring our efforts to a successful conclusion.

Finally, I said:

'No doubt, a victory of sorts can be won by force, by a *diktat* or an ultimatum. In this way you may succeed once or twice, but sooner or later you are bound to provoke a revolt and disaster will follow.

'If the other five members of the Community, conscious of the justice of their cause, give way in the face

479

of what they consider to be a diplomatic *coup de force* based on false assumptions, the last hour of our solidarity as a community will have struck.'

My speech was well received and a resolution submitted to the House following the debate was adopted unanimously. Presented by the leaders of the three main parties, this document recalled that it had been hoped ever since its establishment that one day the European Community would be enlarged. The resolution went on to welcome the fact that Britain was ready to subscribe to the Treaty of Rome and expressed the hope that the efforts to bring Britain into the Common Market would continue.

Alas, these efforts had no tangible result since they were resisted with icy determination by General de Gaulle. Fear lest the European organization be destroyed and all our past efforts brought to nought paralysed the will to resist of France's five partners.

At the beginning of March, accompanied by Luns, I went to London to discuss the situation with our British friends and to devise a common strategy. The outcome of these talks was disappointing. We arrived at the conclusion that for the moment there was no point in resuming negotiations and no hope of the solution suggested by Belgium on 13 February – which called for the creation of a customs union applicable to industrial products only – being adopted. Having re-signed ourselves to this position, we concluded that the only thing to do now was to strengthen the links between the United Kingdom and Western Europe and to make sure that the economic policies pursued by Britain on the one hand and the Six on the other did not diverge too far. We decided to call a meeting of the Western European Union with a view to the establishment of an economic consultative committee which would maintain as wide a measure of coordination as possible and facilitate Britain's eventual entry into the Common Market. Another object of the meeting was to revitalize the Ministerial Council of the Union by increasing the number of its meetings on political, cultural and defence issues. This was a meagre achievement and in fact we could not even be said to have succeeded in devising a satisfactory face-saving formula.

General de Gaulle's press conference of 14 January 1963 must be seen as a turning point in the life of the European Community. Thereafter, the confidence and spirit of co-operation which had been such a feature of the first years of the Community's existence were never to regain their former vigour. The undeserved humiliation which General de Gaulle had inflicted on his partners was never to be forgotten and a certain thirst for revenge resulted. It was to show itself in 1965.

In 1963, when he was wrong both as to the substance and form of his policies, General de Gaulle emerged victorious from the troubles he had created. In 1965, when he was at least partly right, he was forced to accept a compromise because this time he was faced with five partners determined not to give way.

The 1965 crisis is difficult to explain because there were several problems at issue at one and the same time and also because the responsibility was shared by several parties: (1) The Commission, which was guilty of a tactical error; (2) Italy, Germany and the Netherlands, whose governments seemed to be looking for a pretext which would enable them to avoid having to honour their commitments; and (3) France, who, having failed to obtain satisfaction of her legitimate demands, adopted a position which ran counter to the provisions of the Treaty.

Only the Belgian and Luxembourg delegations tried to facilitate a compromise between the various points of view and this was not enough to ensure success.

To understand what had happened, one must remember that the Council of Ministers had decided that by 30 June 1965 at the latest a decision must be agreed on ways to finance the common agricultural policy. The Council had also instructed the Commission to submit a comprehensive set of proposals on the Community's future policy.

In the spring of 1965 the Commission drafted a report which covered the following three main issues: (1) provision of funds for the common agricultural policy; (2) establishment of the Community's own financial resources; and (3) stronger powers for the European Assembly.

Hallstein, the Chairman of the Strasbourg Assembly, made the mistake of putting these proposals before the Assembly without first submitting them to the Council of Ministers. Understandably, the Assembly eagerly agreed to the proposals, which were calculated to increase its own importance. The Assembly's endorsement of the proposals placed the various governments involved in a delicate position. Their freedom of action was impaired. The Commission was in even greater difficulty. Its hands were tied and it was no longer able to carry out its normal task of mediation.

When the ministers met in Brussels from 28 to 30 June 1965, they had to consider the following two conflicting points of view: the French were asking for the immediate implementation of the resolution which promised that agreement on ways to finance the common agricultural policy would be reached before the end of the month; the German, Italian and Dutch delegations, on the other hand, invoking the Commission's report, called for all the various problems to be tackled as a whole. Acceptance of this latter suggestion would be tantamount to postponing a solution of the financial issue since it was physically impossible to find, in the short space of seventy-two hours, an answer to all the questions posed by the need to create the EEC's own resources and by the demand that the powers of the Assembly should be strengthened.

The French were angry at what they considered to be a breach of a definite commitment. I must admit that, in justifying their point of view, the Germans, Italians and Dutch did not appear to be acting in complete good faith. It looked as if they had seized on the Commission's report as a pretext for refusing to honour their commitments, or at least as a means of extorting concessions in return for the sacrifices they were being asked to make.

The French delegation was strong. In addition to Couve de Murville, whose qualities as a debator I have already mentioned, it consisted of Pisani, the Minister of Agriculture, who knew the problems under discussion well and whose contributions were remarkable for their clarity and accuracy, and of Valéry Giscard d'Estaing, whose technical expertise and impassioned oratory were bound to impress any impartial observer.

The French, who insisted implacably that agricultural finance should be the only issue discussed, showed themselves subtle, inventive and generous in regard to the practical solutions which they suggested should be adopted. All their proposals were met with the intransigent – and not always justified – refusal of their adversaries, who, heedless of all reminders of past promises, demanded that the discussion should cover all the points mentioned in the Commission's report. The members of this latter body, contrary both to their usual practice and their duty, remained strangely inactive.

I felt ill at ease. In the main, I approved the Commission's proposals. Had they been adopted, this would have marked the beginning of a new era in the building of a united Europe. However, I could not help feeling that the Commission had been wrong in making its proposals public without first trying to ascertain whether the various governments involved were likely to agree. Moreover, I thought it wrong to use the proposals as a means of delaying the implementation of a firm commitment. These were the points I tried to make. I said the problem of agricultural finance should be settled without further delay as promised and the other issues examined and solved thereafter in accordance with a definite timetable.

Like my colleagues, I still remembered the way the French Government had treated us over the talks with Britain, but I was determined not to allow my resentment to get the better of me. I was not to be side-tracked by thirst for revenge. I felt that the creation of a united Europe called for complete impartiality in assessing the problems before us and that any failure in this respect was bound to jeopardize our future efforts. However, there was nothing to be done. None of the delegations would budge. The German, Italian and Dutch delegates completely rejected all the French proposals, some of which were ingenious. Their refusal to look at the French suggestions was all the more ominous as it took the form of a contemptuous silence.

At midnight on 30 June, no agreement having been

reached, Couve de Murville declared the discussion closed after noting the failure of our efforts. Though France may not have been wrong in these exchanges, her subsequent reaction was once again intolerable. Contrary to her obligations, she refused to send her representatives to the Ministerial Council and the Council of Deputy Chief Delegates, thus paralysing the efforts of the Community. France's attitude ran counter to her Treaty obligations, for under the terms of that document members are obliged to facilitate the smooth functioning of the Community. By thus 'going on strike', General de Gaulle was violating one of the most important provisions of the Treaty.

The crisis which resulted went on for six months and deteriorated rapidly. Thanks to the technical work and proposals of the Commission, which had fortunately resumed its activity, it soon became apparent that agreement on agricultural finance was, in fact, possible. However, this was not enough to bring France's delegates back to the council table. Making the most of its grievances, the French Government was pressing for a revision of the Treaty and notably for the abolition of the provision relating to the majority vote. At the same time, the French presented a whole series of demands which, if accepted, would have diminished the prestige and authority of the Commission. It was at this time that the attacks began on Hallstein, the Commission's chairman.

There was no reason for this campaign. As a statesman, Hallstein had valuable qualities, as well as some minor faults. There was no denying his services to the cause of European unity. Thanks to his drive, the Community's organizational structure was rapidly being perfected and Hallstein played an essential part in these efforts to build a united Europe. As a result of the work of the Commission over which he presided we were able to implement the complex provisions of the Treaty of Rome. It was the Commission which was in fact responsible for producing the main proposals which made it possible for the aims of the Treaty to be attained.

As chairman of the Commission, Hallstein was impartial, and, above all, independent. This latter quality is the most important attribute required of the holder of that post. His devotion to the European ideal was complete. Quite legitimately, he sought to use the Treaty to enhance his own standing and that of his colleagues; on the other hand, he did not shrink from responsibility. He considered himself the chief representative of an authority enjoying government status. In taking this view he interpreted the intentions of the architects of the Treaty of Rome correctly.

However, this independence was not to General de Gaulle's liking, and the General made this quite clear when he demanded the dismissal of Hirsch, the French chairman of Euratom. In the General's eyes, Hirsch was guilty of not having at all times and on every occasion defended the views of the French Government and of having obeyed his own convictions rather than the orders Paris thought itself entitled to give him.

Compared with the services he had rendered, the complaints that could be levelled against Hallstein were trivial. True, during a visit to Washington he had asked to be lodged at Blair House, the residence set aside for foreign Heads of State. He also established somewhat too ostentatious a ceremonial for the reception of ambassadors accredited to the Common Market. These foibles may call for a wry smile but they cannot obscure Hallstein's sterling qualities. On no account can they be said to justify the injustice to which he was subjected in 1967 when he was asked to accept intolerable conditions while remaining in office in a 'caretaker' capacity.

But, as I have already said, it cannot be denied that Hallstein was at fault in submitting the Commission's report to the Assembly without first making sure that the various governments agreed with its suggestions, at least in principle. By his failure, he risked coming into conflict with some of the governments. But even if this particular aspect of Hallstein's conduct was open to criticism, this was no reason to inflict a humiliation on the Commission as a whole, a humiliation which, in fact, reflected on the Community as such.

Since France refused to be represented on the Council of Ministers, her five partners were compelled to meet without her, and in so doing they raised certain delicate legal problems. At the time, the Council was presided over by Emilio

Colombo of Italy. This was fortunate, for he was one of the best statesman we had, a clever diplomat, whose subtle and constructive mind were to prove of great value to us. It was he who acted as our go-between with the French.

He accomplished this task with superb skill. His courtesy and firmness allowed him to convey the most difficult messages without arousing extreme reactions. He knew how to take his stand on essentials while at the same time enabling his adversary to save face. He already plays a major role in Italian politics, the importance of which will undoubtedly grow in the days to come. He is one of the most valuable and respected of European statesmen.

Under Colombo's direction we succeeded in planning our political strategy and tactics. Basing ourselves on the Commission's new proposals for financing Europe's agriculture, we made real progress towards a solution. This, however, had no chance of ever coming into effect without French support. We also decided that there was no question of our revising the provision of the Treaty regarding the majority vote. Finally, we agreed that a special private session of the Ministerial Council should be held, with the representatives of the Commission excluded, to examine the general situation in the Community. This latter proposal had a difficult passage since the Commission was strongly opposed to it. However our rules did contain a provision for such a procedure. After a meeting with Colombo, Couve de Murville agreed to our proposal.

The foreign ministers met in Luxembourg first on 17 and 18 January and again on 28 and 29 January and, after a protracted discussion, agreed on a compromise. Throughout this whole time, I acted as mediator between France on the one hand and Germany and the Netherlands on the other. The two latter Powers were the most adamant among the Five. The French attitude did not seem to me entirely unjustified, though there was no question of a compromise on the matter of the majority vote. Our aim was merely to affirm our common desire to continue to strive in good faith for unanimous agreement. However, we felt that if we failed in this effort the provisions of the Treaty must be applied. Couve de Murville was not satisfied with this.

As regards the relations between the Ministerial Council

and the Commission – though our difficulties in this respect were much less important and some of them were in fact rather trivial – it took a great deal of patience before a compromise was reached. Late during the night of 29–30 January, we finally succeeded in drafting an agreed communiqué. Referring to the issue of the majority vote, we noted that a divergence of views persisted, with France maintaining her position. Her five partners had refused to give way. The communiqué went on to say that the Five, after proclaiming their desire to reach unanimously agreed solutions as rapidly as possible, had emphasized that in the event of this proving impossible despite all their efforts, decisions would have to be taken by a majority vote. The communiqué noted that the French delegation had placed its objections to this on record, but this difference, the document declared, was not such as to prevent a resumption of the Community's normal activities.

In a reference to the relationship between the Council and the Commission, a number of very sound rules were proclaimed. If they are complied with, better cooperation between these two crucially important authorities of the EEC should be the result. The powers of the Commission were left undiminished. The grave crisis which began on 30 June with France's refusal to be represented on the Community authorities had thus been overcome and the Community was again free to function normally.

This, however, was not to be our last crisis. In 1967, the British Government made another attempt to join the Community. It was brusquely rejected by General de Gaulle, whose obstinacy proved too strong for his five partners. But, as for myself, I no longer played any part in these events, for, in August 1966, I had decided to quit politics.

Epilogue

45

My Last Speech

My party was defeated in the elections in the spring of 1965. The language problem, especially in my own Brussels constituency, proved our undoing.

Pierre Harmel, Deputy for Liege, became Premier of the new Government, and my friend Spinoy Vice Premier, while I kept my post as Foreign Minister. The Government proved short-lived: less than one year after taking office it was overthrown in grotesque circumstances, for which the leaders of the Socialist Party were largely responsible. I was opposed to the policy which had been adopted but no longer had the necessary energy to go through with the fight. For years I had devoted myself to international affairs, and domestic politics tended to seem rather petty to me. The struggle which had fascinated me for so long now interested me less and less. The length of time I had been in office – I had been a minister for more than twenty out of the previous thirty years – made it increasingly difficult for me to submit to party discipline; moreover, I no longer had any stomach for opposition politics. Being in opposition all too often means that one is expected to criticize the very policies one would pursue if one were in office. My mind was made up: I would not stand as a candidate in the next elections. I hoped that in this way I would avoid becoming involved in the decline I could see coming. I thought that I had thus given myself three years' grace, but events were to decide otherwise.

Pierre Harmel took over from me at the Foreign Ministry. Our temperaments were so different that, despite the fact that we had been acquainted for years, it took an exceptional set of circumstances for us to come to know one another really well. As Premier, Harmel was completely loyal to his colleagues, and, aware of his good will and high principles,

I did my best to help him. After I had left the Government we remained the best of friends.

At the beginning of 1966, after the outbreak of the NATO crisis due to France's withdrawal, Harmel warned me that Allied headquarters might have to be moved to Belgium and asked me to help him in obtaining the Socialist Party's approval. When I immediately consulted the Party chairman, Léo Collard, he seemed to listen to me with only half an ear. I was concerned at his apparent indifference, for I knew there was an anti-NATO faction in the Party and that these elements might try to make the most of this opportunity to give vent to their hostility.

I mention my differences with Léo Collard only because they were in part responsible for my decision to go into retirement. Collard once said about himself: 'I am slow to make up my mind but once I have done so I stick to my guns.' Because of this slowness, he took no interest in the problem I had put to him. I should like to believe that his attitude was due to his temperament and was not part of a political plot. Whatever the facts of the matter, when the issue of the transfer to Belgium of the Supreme Headquarters Allied Powers in Europe (SHAPE) became urgent and a decision had to be taken in Parliament, Collard called a meeting of the General Council of the Socialist Party. No effort had been made to inform the members of the issues involved, and the various branches had been left entirely to their own devices. Collard did not seem to understand the importance of the issue. Despite my warnings, he let things slide. His only worry was to avoid a clash with the so-called 'Left', whose help he needed in the dispute between Walloons and Flemings. On no account was he willing to put his authority in the party at risk. Collard was ready to go along with any decision the General Council, which was more interested in electoral advantage – real or apparent – than in formulating a correct foreign policy, might care to take.

It was in this atmosphere that the debate began in the General Council on 15 June 1966. Henri Rolin had been appointed to act as spokesman for the faction opposed to SHAPE's transfer to Belgium while I was to expound the policy of a coalition of which my party was no longer a

492

member. An event occurred unparalleled in all the foreign policy discussions of the preceding thirty years: I was defeated by a crushing majority. This was a verdict I could not accept. I thought it wrong to submit blindly to whatever orders might be given me by opponents I felt knew less of the issues at stake than myself. A policy I had spent a life-time in championing was in jeopardy, and I refused to be deterred – merely for the sake of party discipline – from speaking and acting as I thought right.

I need hardly say that to this day I find the memory of that meeting painful. I was alone among a group of men whom I had so often in the past succeeded in convincing – even those among them who at first doubted or opposed my opinions. I realized I had come to the end of a chapter in my life. The fact that not all those who voted against me were genuinely opposed to my views only made the situation more distasteful. My adversaries were not actuated by deep convictions or generous passion. The whole thing was a political manoeuvre. Some of them might have been eager to get their own back on me who, to their way of thinking, had been in authority for too long. Regarding this all too human reaction, I have no complaint to make.

All but four members of the General Council voted in favour of a resolution which to this day fills me with shame, so full was it of contradictions. After declaring that there could be no doubt about NATO's general policy being correct, just because of the difficulties due to the conduct of one of the member-states, it went on to say that the Socialist group of Parliament could nevertheless not accept any share of the political responsibility the Government had taken upon itself in consenting to the transfer of SHAPE to Belgium. Collard tried to justify this absurdity by saying: 'The government has taken a political decision. I fail to see why we should associate ourselves with the actions of an administration to which we deny our confidence.'

I do not wish to be too severe on my Party colleagues. I, too, have probably occasionally sacrificed principle to electoral advantage during one time or another in my politi-cal career. But having reached mature years and become more aware of my responsibilities, and after spending many years in government office, I could accept no share in their conduct. I could not deny what I knew to be right and proper merely in order to make life difficult for the government in office.

When the General Council had taken its vote, I was deeply hurt – I admit it quite frankly. It does not matter how clearly you may have seen certain situations coming and how well you may have prepared yourself for them, once they are upon you, you are still shaken. I recall without much pride that at one time during the proceedings I tried to enlist Collard's interest in my personal fate. I pointed out that the vote placed me in a very difficult position, that I could not deny my convictions and would have no choice but to take a grave decision. However, as so often, Collard remained impassive and replied coldly that, in view of the attitude of the meeting, there was nothing to be done. He was not interested in my personal problems.

The Chamber met the following day, 16 June, and I made the last speech of my career. It was not a good speech. Reading it again, I can still feel the emotion which gripped me and prevented me from speaking as clearly as I should have done. Though I managed to set out the arguments I was trying to develop, they were not presented in the right sequence. I tried to say too much. Above all, I sought to defend the Atlantic Alliance and to show that there was no acceptable alternative to it regardless of what new factors might have emerged on the international scene. I went on to say that those who shared my views were in honour bound, following France's decision, to do whatever was in their power to help NATO overcome its crisis, and if it was felt that the transfer of SHAPE to Belgium was the best available solution to the difficulties of the Alliance, we must do our duty, a duty, moreover, which entailed neither additional dangers nor particular sacrifices for Belgium.

After my speech there was prolonged applause on the majority benches, which was understandable, and – as the parliamentary record shows – there was even some support for it on the Socialist benches. My political colleagues were in fact applauding views against which they were about to vote. As Gladstone has put it – a speech may cause a person to change his mind but never his vote.

The vote in the Chamber was due to be taken the following day and, had I wished to do so, I could have abstained or even absented myself. However, I refused to take the easy way out. I was determined to vote with the Government against my own Party, if need be alone. In actual fact, I was not entirely alone: one Socialist Deputy followed my lead – one only, but the best, my friend Spinoy, the hope of Belgian Socialism. Thus, in the ballot on 17 June 1966, ours were the only two Socialist names among the serried ranks of Christian Socialist and Liberals. Spinoy did not let me down, and this was some consolation to me in my distress.

After the vote, I left the House discreetly without saying goodbye to anyone. I knew I would never be back. My wife was waiting for me at the bottom of the great staircase. She took me by the arm. My life was about to take a new turn.

My parliamentary career was thus ended by my resolve to keep faith with one of the great causes I had espoused. Where I made my mistake was to have shown that those who in the past had reproached me with being inconstant were wrong. I made it clear that in my old age at least I simply did not have it in me to make certain compromises.

Am I entitled to claim that after forty years I have become a better man, that my many successes and failures, the many events in which I have taken part, have neither turned me into a cynic nor even robbed me of my illusions? Am I entitled to claim that I have remained loyal to the last to my convictions and am ready to make sacrifices for them? I should like to believe that I am.

There is no denying that I was sad on this final day, but I consoled myself by recalling the battles which I had fought and the successes I had helped to win. By playing my part in forging the Atlantic Alliance, I had promoted the cause of peace in Europe and European unity. I had made two of my dreams come true and thus my efforts had been rewarded.

I have no complaints, but neither can I feel entirely happy at the present situation. I realize I have left many battles unfinished.

Index

Index

Index

Turkey, 141, 279, 281, 283, 287, 292, 299, 300, 303, 304

U-2 flight incident (May 1960), 277, 415
Ukraine, The, 107
Union Minière Company, 374–5
United Nations Organization; First Assembly, 86, 95, 105–13; San Francisco (April 1945), 101–4; Spaak elected chairman of, 108; Preparatory Committee, 105; General Committee, 109, 110; Russia and the veto at, 110–11, 136; and disarmament, 112, 113; Second Session of General Assembly of (Sept. 1947), 114; Señor Aranha elected chairman of (1947), 114; and debate on Greek affairs (1947), 114–16; and meeting in Paris (1948), 117–24; and attack by Vyshinsky (1948), 117–8; and Spaak's reply to Vyshinsky (Sept. 1948), 118–24; and Suez crisis, 133–5; General-Secretaries of, 135–7; and defence of South Korea (1950), 154; and question of re-arming Germany (1950), 154–5; and Cyprus problem, 281, 304; and the Congo, 359, 360–1, 363, 364; offensive at Elizabethville (Sept. 1961), 364; and second military operation against Katanga (Sept. 1961), 368; and victory in Katanga (Dec. 1961), 369; and offensive at Elizabethville (Dec. 1961), 375–6; and modernization programme in the Congo, 381; and Soviet intervention in Hungary, 411
United States of America; State Department, 10, 373–4; and Vichy, 88; at Dumbarton Oaks, 95; and UN (April 1945), 101; and First Assembly (Jan. 1946), 106–13; and the Suez crisis,

128–35; and the Washington Treaty, 149–53; and EDC, 156; and London Conference (1954), 179, 183–4; and the Marshall Plan, 191; and the Four Power Summit meeting (May 1959), 271–7; Air Force and nuclear arms, 320; plan for IRBM in Europe, 324–5; and MLF, 331; and arms to Algeria, 332–3; opposition to nuclear forces (1960), 345; and the Congo, 359, 370, 379; mentioned, 83, 117, 125, 147, 217
Uri, Uierre, 231, 239

Vandenbroek, Herman, 78
Venice; and conference on Spaak report, 240, 243–6; mentioned, 232
Vichy, 53, 57, 58, 88
Vinogradov, Ambassador, 413–5
Vyshinsky, Andrei; and criticism of UN (1948), 117–8; mentioned, 86–7, 110, 111, 113, 115, 406

Walle, Colonel van de, 376
Walston, Lord, 397
War, commencement of Second World, 34
Ward, Irene, 76
Warsaw; and Spaak's visit (Feb. 1965), 434–5
Warsaw Treaty Powers, 409
Washington, 83, 99
Washington, The, 150–3, 266, 467
Western Europe Union; Organisation of, 82; support by Russia; mentioned, 82, 87, 456
Weygand, General; and account of Ypres meeting (May 1940), 40–2; mentioned, 37, 39, 48
White House, The, 98
Wijnendaele Castle, 45, 48, 49
Wilgress, Mr, 256
Williams, Mennen, 371
World Bank, The, 105